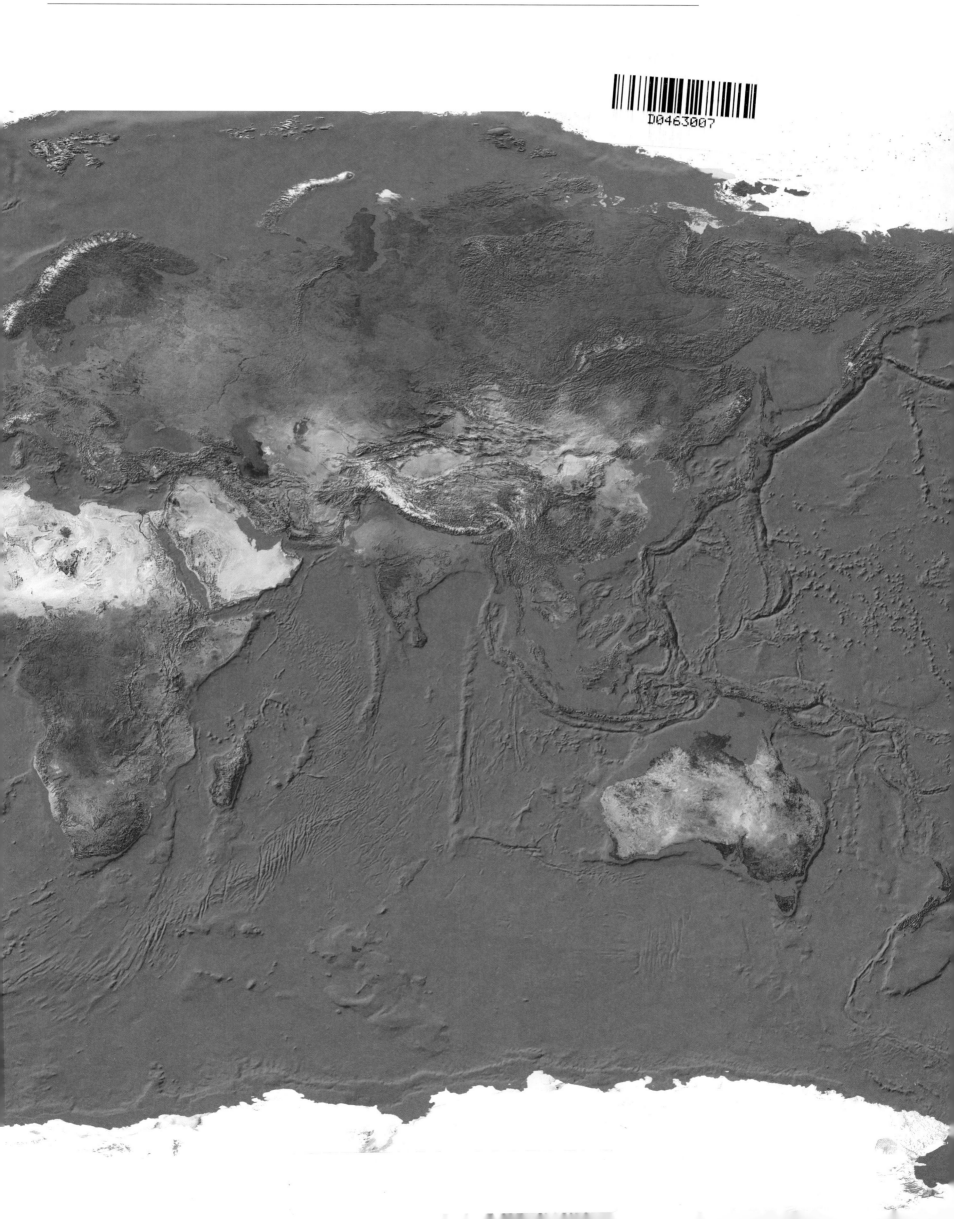

THE CARTOGRAPHIC
SATELLITE ATLAS
OF THE
WORLD

Credits

© 1997 Warwick Publishing Inc.
© 1997 WorldSat International Inc.
© 1997 ROBAS BV, Weesp, The Netherlands
© 1997 European Map Graphics Ltd., Finchampstead, UK
© 1997 SPOT Image, Toulouse, France
© 1997 SSC/Satellitbild, Kiruna, Sweden

Published by:
Warwick Publishing Inc.
388 King Street West, Toronto, Ontario M5V 1K2
1424 N. Highland Avenue, Los Angeles, CA 90028

Production of Satellite Imagery: Robert Stacey, WorldSat International Inc.,
Mississauga, Ontario, Canada.
1km Resolution Images produced from source data © WorldSat International Inc./Jim Knighton

Satellite Data: National Oceanic and Atmospheric Administration, Washington D.C.
Ocean Floor Bathymetry: NOAA courtesy of United States Geologic Survey
Satellite Imagery for pages 56, 57, 68, 69, 70 & 71 based on Resurs Imagery: SSC/Satellithild,
Kiruna, Sweden
Digital Imaging Equipment: Silicon Graphics workstation with PCI EASI/PACE software

Cartographic Design and Layout: European Map Graphics Ltd., Finchampstead, U.K.
Production Director: Alan Horsfield
Cartographers: Tom Carlin, Ian Dewsbery, Chris Hilford, Mark Lewis, Adam Meara
Editorial: Jon Watkins, Peter Butler
Reprographics: Jon Pattingale
Consultants: Simon Butler, Menno-Jan Draak, Emery Miller, Edith Stacey, Robert Stacey

Cover and Preliminary Section
Research: Professor Menno-Jan Kraak, TU; Delft, The Netherlands, Emery Miller
Design: Mercer Digital Design Inc., Toronto, Ontario

Film Production: Global Film Services, Markham, Ontario
Pre-Press and Assembly: John Willis, WorldSat International, Mississauga, Ontario
Printing: Friesens

ISBN 1-895629-99-3

Bookstore and Library Distribution:
Firefly Books Ltd.
3680 Victoria Park Avenue
Willowdale, Ontario M2H 3K1
(416) 499-8412
1-800 387-6192 (Canada)

U.S. Offices
230 Fifth Avenue #1607
New York, NY 10001
1-800 803-8488 (United States)

Printed and bound in Canada

THE CARTOGRAPHIC
SATELLITE ATLAS
OF THE
WORLD

WorldSat

W

Warwick Publishing
Toronto Los Angeles

Foreword

The advancing world of technology has done wonders for the armchair traveler, as mankind's perspective on the world has brought about an ever more exciting outlook on our surroundings. We have advanced from climbing the nearest hill to see what was on the other side of the mountain, to the first tentative ventures in hot air balloons, to aircraft and cameras, and finally on into space through the eyes of the astronauts and surveillance satellites that constantly monitor our Earth today.

Central Scotland

The Changing Perspective

It is important to recognize the very significant advances that both aerial photography and satellite imagery have brought to the process of mapping. Aerial photography enabled man to see the reality of vast areas of land, not as interpreted by random sampling or a particular individual's perspective, but as it actually was. In addition to this "perfect" view, aerial photography was also able, using two photographs taken from different angles, to calculate the changing elevations of the rolling hills, mountains and valleys of the world. It brought the flat Earth into the third dimension.

Not only did satellites add a new viewpoint from which to observe the world they also added a new point of view from which to assess our geography and vegetation or lack thereof. The viewpoint of Earth from space allowed mankind to see vast geological and biological features of the earth that were not visible in the relative close-up views from aircraft. Such views

resulted in the discovery of the "overthrust" belt in North America from which followed the strike of vast oil reserves buried thousands of meters below existing wells. It lead to views of depletion of the Amazon and other tropical rain forests that were not previously suspected and it allowed us economic access to regions of the world such as the Arctic and Antarctic that were not viable using traditional methodologies.

Equally important, the satellite added a new perspective from which to look at the world — one which used highly accurate color information collected by the satellite in both the visible and infra-red regions of the electromagnetic spectrum, revealing things that would normally be invisible to the naked eye. It could detect stress in vegetation before it became visible, it could distinguish different species of trees and vegetation from each other from space and it could detect anomalies in vegetation, water and bare earth. Best of all, the data, or imagery, existed as digital data — not as film. This meant that images could be compared to each other electronically and added to or subtracted from one another. Detecting and mapping change was now easier, and the prospect of "looking at" and mapping continuous and subtle changes in vegetation over large areas became a reality.

The New Perspective

While it is true that public sector surveillance satellites have been around since the early '70s it is only recently that space-based composite images of the entire earth have been available. The first of these were based on the NOAA (National Oceanic and Atmospheric Administration) series of satellites designed specifically to monitor and forecast weather around the world. Of all of the satellites launched, the weather satellites have done more to benefit mankind than any other, having saved thousands of lives through their ability to predict major catastrophes, forever changing man's approach to the weather. It seems somehow fitting that the first cloud-free, composite images of the

Earth should be based on this data. The result is a view of Earth as it would appear from 800 kilometers in space and devoid of any cloud cover. For the first time man can now gaze down at a realistic miniature of his home in the confidence that this is reality. The distribution of continents are not presumed or calculated; they are actual photographs.

The Atlas

The production of this atlas brings a new era in map reproduction, where we can not only look at the boundaries that are delineated by the cartographer but also the underlying reality. In the process of creating these images it was necessary to further enhance the imagery that went into the construction of the atlas.

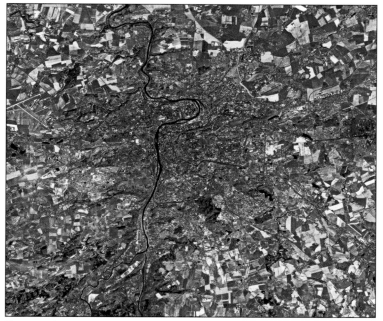
Prague

We matched elevation data for the entire earth to the space imagery and generated shaded relief which imparts a third dimension to the final maps. In deference to the other two-thirds of our world, we incorporated relief data on the ocean floor so that you could peer through the water and study the variations in terrain (or elevation) that exist under our vast oceans. Finally, we incorporated traditional cartography, delineating the non-visible components of our

world, such as political boundaries and place names for towns and regions, to provide an all-encompassing perspective of our new Earth.

Finally

This "space-based" atlas reveals the Earth with all of its flaws and in all of its beauty. The scars of the rain forests of South America, and the Pacific Rim can no longer hide under a surface of clouds or in inaccessibility any more than the scars of logging in western Canada or the dumping of pollutants in our vast and heretofore remote oceans, can hide from the prying eyes of the ever-vigilant satellites.

Many would say that we have not treated our home very well. From the dawning of the industrial revolution through the technological revolution and on into the information age we have treated mother earth with disdain and indifference. Would we be so callus and unconcerned if this same book had been published in 1896? Would the comparative differences shock and dismay us? Will the 2096 edition give us pause to reflect? Will we congratulate ourselves on a job well done or will we just wonder where the time went? The publishers of this book hope that this will be the first step in opening our eyes, to presenting an image of the world that will stand as reference to future generations and as a guide to the new mappers of our world. As we approach the frontiers of a new millennium it would seem an appropriate time to adjust our view of the world, to embrace the technologies that will improve our understanding of our home and provide a 21st century perspective and outlook to our world. We hope that you enjoy this atlas as much in the reading as we did in its compilation.

Start the fire, curl up in your chair, journey and enjoy.

Emery Miller
WorldSat International Inc.

Contents

Key to Symbols and Images

This section helps you to find your way around this atlas quickly, to check the page location and scale of each of the maps and to familiarize yourself with the symbols, abbreviations and typography used throughout.

Satellite Mapping

In order that you can fully understand the complex process by which the satellite maps featured in this atlas are created, this section provides both a simple introduction to satellite mapping and some additional facts for the technically minded.

Satellite Images of the World

A seven page selection of stunning satellite images featuring major cities and contrasting geographical habitats from around the world. These "zoomed in" images of earth are breathtakingly detailed and provide another perspective of our natural and man-made world.

Maps of the World

This major section of brand-new mapping boasts three unique features:

The first ever satellite cartography at a 1 kilometer resolution, making this the most realistic view of earth ever made and so instantly outdating every other world atlas produced.

The most up-to-date ground elevation data ever produced, copyrighted by the producers of this atlas and exactly matching the satellite imagery thus creating an enhanced three dimensional effect that gives this atlas its so-realistic view from space.

An unprecedented clarity of both legend and image achieved, for the first time, by reversing the map lettering out of the colorful map relief backgrounds.

The maps are presented by continent, beginning with North America. Each section starts with a double page spread featuring the continent in question, followed by larger scale maps of individual countries.

North America

South America

Key to Symbols and Images

Whether you are searching specifically for a geographic location or for statistical information or just browsing idly through this atlas, an understanding of the symbols and images employed will help you get the most enjoyment and use from *The Cartographic Satellite Atlas of the World*.

Time spent studying the pointer labels and tables alongside will be time well spent.

The map shown here depicts different aspects of the information presented in this atlas, allowing you to get a feel for the symbols, abbreviations and type styles used throughout.

Finally, a comprehensive table appears under the map that covers every symbol, abbreviation and type style used in this atlas.

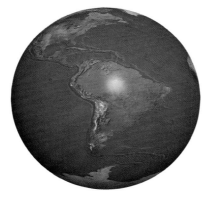

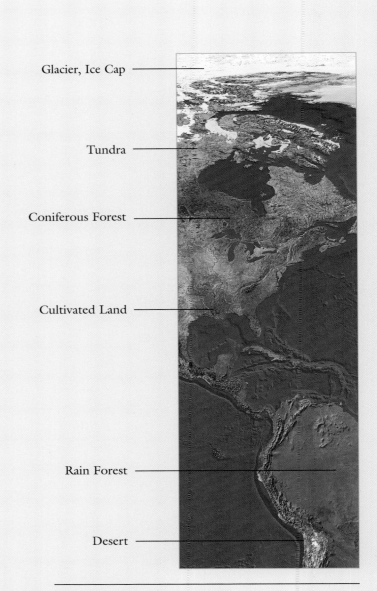

Glacier, Ice Cap

Tundra

Coniferous Forest

Cultivated Land

Rain Forest

Desert

Scale

A scale of 1:12 000 000 means that the distance on the map is 12 Million times smaller than the actual distance measured at the Earth's surface; e.g. 1 centimeter on the map represents 12 Million centimeters or 120 kilometers in reality.

Graticule

Lines of Longitude and Latitude provide a co-ordinate system that allows the user to pin-point the exact location of any feature on the Earth's surface. Latitudes are measured in terms of degrees(°), minutes(') and seconds("), North and South of the Equator, while Longitudes are measured West and East of Greenwich. This would be typically expressed in the following manner;
e.g. 35° 20' 30"N 20° 35' 20"W

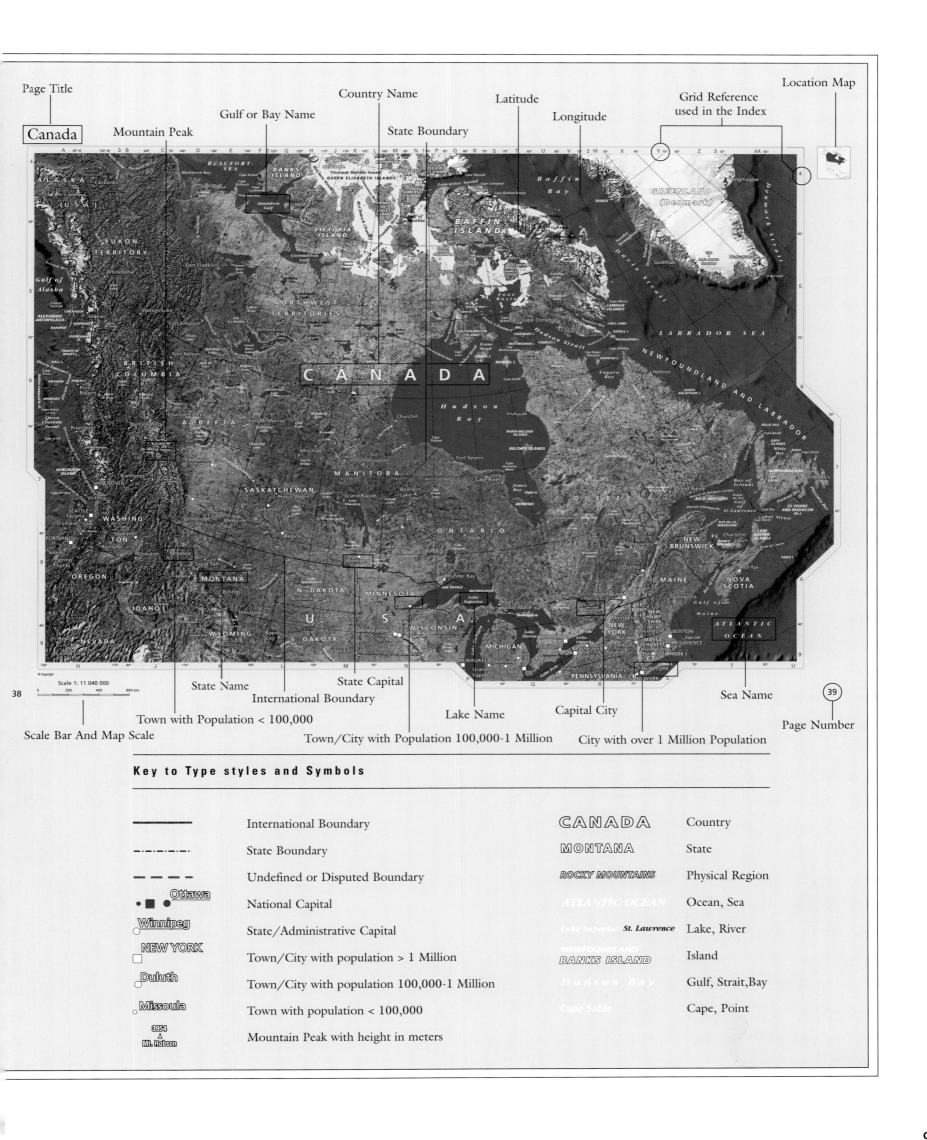

Page Title

Canada

Mountain Peak

Gulf or Bay Name

Country Name

State Boundary

Latitude

Longitude

Grid Reference used in the Index

Location Map

State Name

International Boundary

State Capital

Lake Name

Capital City

Sea Name

Town with Population < 100,000

Scale Bar And Map Scale

Town/City with Population 100,000-1 Million

City with over 1 Million Population

Page Number

Scale 1: 11 040 000

38

39

Key to Type styles and Symbols

	International Boundary	CANADA	Country
	State Boundary	MONTANA	State
	Undefined or Disputed Boundary	ROCKY MOUNTAINS	Physical Region
● ■ ● Ottawa	National Capital	ATLANTIC OCEAN	Ocean, Sea
Winnipeg	State/Administrative Capital	Lake Superior St. Lawrence	Lake, River
NEW YORK	Town/City with population > 1 Million	NEWFOUNDLAND BANKS ISLAND	Island
Duluth	Town/City with population 100,000-1 Million	Hudson Bay	Gulf, Strait, Bay
Missoula	Town with population < 100,000	Cape Sable	Cape, Point
3954 △ Mt. Robson	Mountain Peak with height in meters		

Index to Map Pages

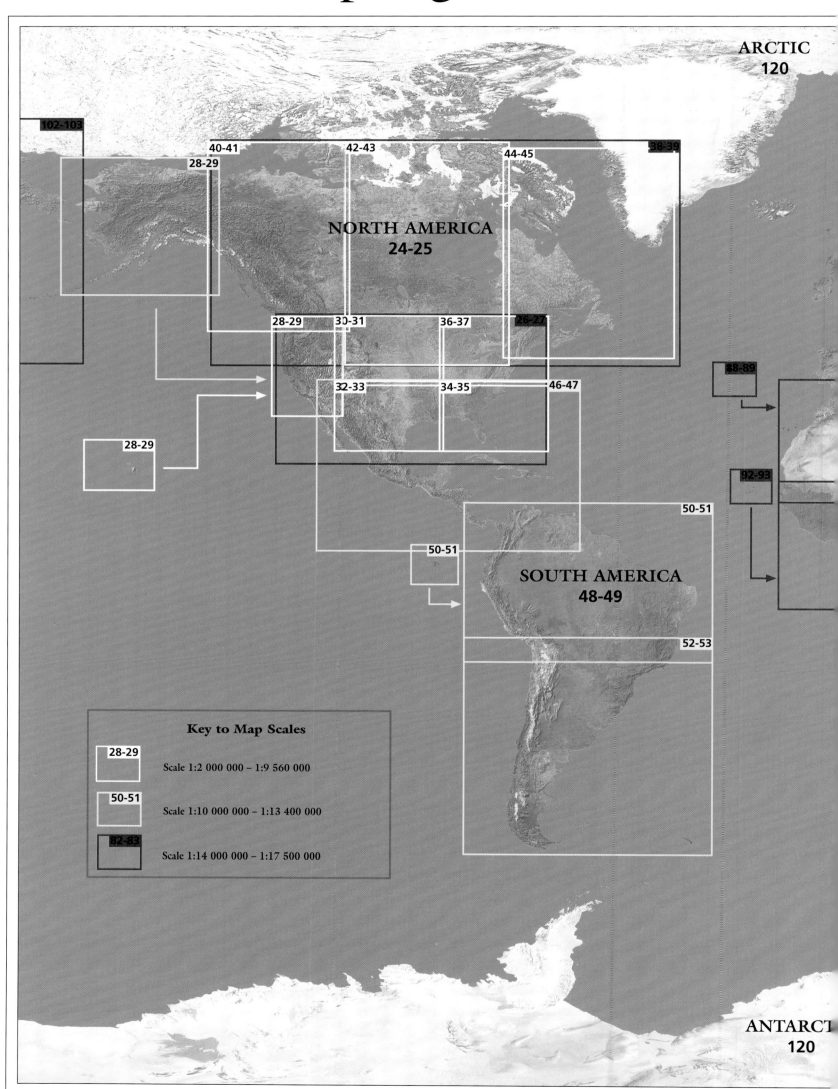

ARCTIC
120

102-103

40-41

28-29

42-43

44-45

38-39

**NORTH AMERICA
24-25**

28-29

30-31

36-37

26-27

88-89

32-33

34-35

46-47

28-29

92-93

50-51

28-29

50-51

**SOUTH AMERICA
48-49**

52-53

Key to Map Scales

28-29   Scale 1:2 000 000 – 1:9 560 000

50-51   Scale 1:10 000 000 – 1:13 400 000

82-83   Scale 1:14 000 000 – 1:17 500 000

ANTARCT
120

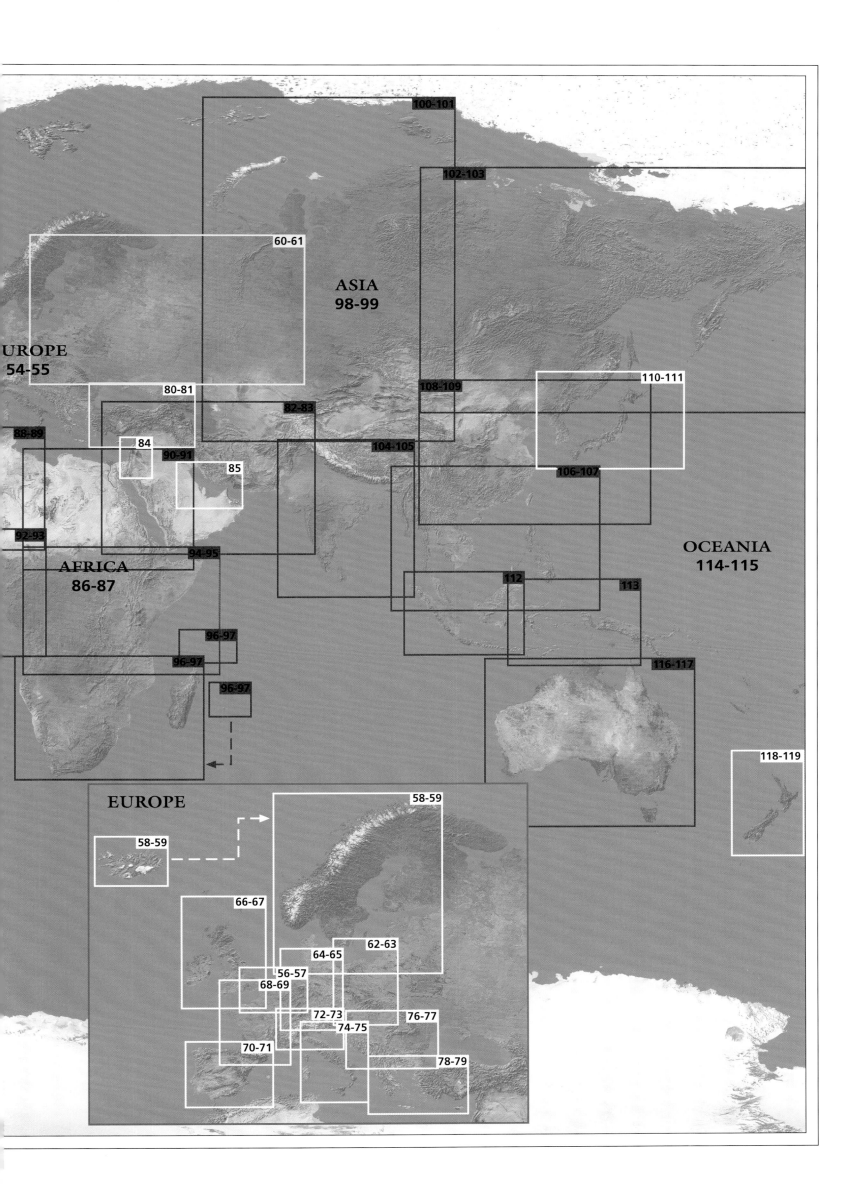

ASIA
98-99

UROPE
54-55

EUROPE
86-87

AFRICA
86-87

OCEANIA
114-115

100-101

102-103

60-61

80-81

82-83

108-109

110-111

104-105

88-89

84

90-91

85

106-107

92-93

94-95

112

113

96-97

96-97

116-117

96-97

118-119

EUROPE

58-59

58-59

66-67

62-63

64-65

56-57

68-69

72-73

76-77

74-75

70-71

78-79

Satellite Mapping

The images in this Atlas have been created by processing signals gathered in space by satellites circling the Earth in near polar orbits.

Sensors on the satellite register different kinds of electromagnetic energy emitted or reflected from the Earth's surface. This data is collected digitally and transmitted to ground stations where it is compiled into digital images. These images can then be used to create products such as the pictorial images in this Atlas, or to produce digital data sets used in Geographic Information Systems (GIS), or the data may be analyzed using special computer software to extract information such as environmental conditions on the Earth's surface or to detect stress and/or vigor in vegetation, to mention but a few of the possible applications of this technology.

Image Processing and Analysis:

The raw data received from the satellite includes a number of serious distortions induced by perturbations in the satellite's platform and orbit, the Earth's atmosphere, irregularities in the sensor and many other factors. Image processing removes these distortions and provides an output that is spectrally and geographically accurate.

Image analysis is the process of looking into the spectral content of the data to extract information that is not otherwise obvious. Some of the areas where these techniques are used is in the detection of stress in vegetation before it is otherwise visible, in automatically discriminating and mapping different classes of ground cover and in the detection of pollutants in surface water and underground creep.

Maps as Interpreted Images of Earth:
Satellite imagery and image analysis provides the ability to extract many different data sets from a single source. Not only can it be used in the generation of maps as seen in traditional atlases or as combined imagery and cartography, as seen in this atlas, but it can also be used to extract vegetation and land cover information. Such information would include discrimination of forests, pastures, agriculture lands, swamps, deserts, stress in the vegetation, pollutants in the ground and water, used in creating land use and "thematic" maps (thematic maps being maps that present geographic information of a specific "theme", such as land use, mapping vegetation stress or geological structures).

The Final Touches:
The ultimate differences in maps derived from the same source can be found in the "artistic license" that is applied by the cartographer. This encompass such issues as whether or not to apply shaded relief, highlighting terrain variations and imparting a sense of 3-D to the image - as was done in the case of this atlas -, selecting the size and orientation of the text used on the map, selecting background colors, which can range anywhere from none to actual satellite images as seen in this atlas, and the representation of the water regions which, again, can cover a broad spectrum of choices. In the case of this atlas we chose to apply ocean floor relief (derived from NOAA's ETOPO-5 files) allowing us to view through the water and visualize the continuous geological structures of our Earth. The artistic license applied in this atlas is "reality", bringing the reader closer to a true view of our planet.

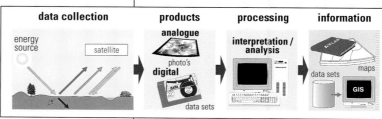

Landsat Satellite:

The American Landsat satellites (left) were the first satellites to make space imagery available to the general public. These satellites are based on one of two specific instruments, respectively referred to as the "MSS" (Multi-Spectral Scanner) and "TM" (Thematic Mapper) imagers. The MSS scanner collects data in 4 bands (or regions) of the electromagnetic spectrum and the TM imager expands this capability by acquiring data in 7 bands.

Interpreting Satellite Images:

The ability to interpret satellite imagery falls into three basic categories: 1) visual interpretation, as in photography; 2) analysis of the spectral content of the imagery as noted under "image analysis" and 3) texture and pattern analysis. Texture and pattern analysis is relatively new and promises to significantly enhance the capabilities of the whole "image analysis" process.

The ability to extract specific information is dependent on the particular characteristics of the satellite. Each type of satellite is configured differently and each configuration has strengths that will determine the specific application for which the satellite is best suited.

The Orbit and Sensor Characteristics of NOAA's AVHRR:

The Advanced Very High Resolution Radiometer (AVHRR) refers to the specific sensor aboard the National Oceanographic and Atmospheric Administration's (NOAA) polar orbiting environmental satellites (as different from the GOES - Geostationary Orbiting Environmental Satellites). The AVHRR based satellites are primarily designed for monitoring and forecasting weather, following a sun-synchronous orbit at a height of 833 kilometers and circling the Earth 14 times a day (102 minutes/orbit). During each passage the imager picks up a ground track that is 2399 km wide (see diagram) and registers pixels that are 1.1 km x 1.1 km.

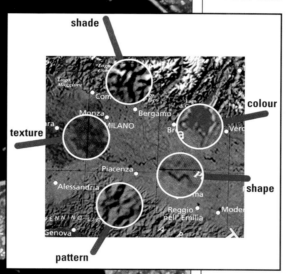

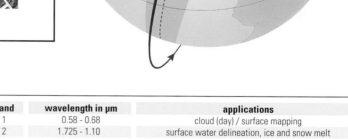

altitude 833 km
orbit period 102 minutes

SATELLITE ORBIT

GROUND TRACK

band	wavelength in µm	applications
1	0.58 - 0.68	cloud (day) / surface mapping
2	1.725 - 1.10	surface water delineation, ice and snow melt
3	3.55 - 3.93	sea surface temperature, night-time cloud mapping
4	10.30 - 11.30	sea surface temperature, cloud mapping (day and night)
5	11.50 - 12.50	sea surface temperature, cloud mapping (day and night)

The AVHRR imager collects data in 5 electromagnetic bands as indicated in the above diagram.

Satellite Imagery for the Technically Minded

The Electromagnetic Spectrum:

The Electromagnetic Spectrum encompasses that set of energy that we define as radio, light, x-rays and gamma rays. The surveillance type satellites, used in the collection of the type of imagery seen in this atlas, sense energy that exists in and near the "visible light" portion of the electromagnetic spectrum (visible light, infra-red and thermal energy - see diagram).

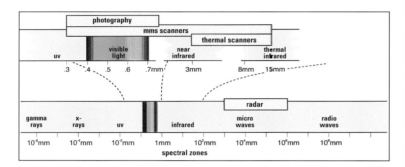

There are two basic types of sensors - passive and active. Passive sensors like the AVHRR detect naturally emitted or reflected energy (such as the emitted temperature of vegetation or reflected light of the sun). Active sensors create and emit signals, measuring the changes to, or timing of, the return signals. Radar is an example of an active sensor.

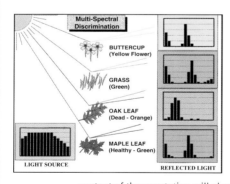

The Nature of Analysis:

While there are many approaches to analyzing satellite imagery, the fundamental process underlying satellite image discrimination is based on the different way in which light reflects off of all objects. For example: when sunlight reflects off vegetation it reflects light that is representative of the colors we see. In addition, the water content of the vegetation will absorb light in the infrared region reducing reflectance in this portion of the electromagnetic spectrum. If the light were reflecting off of a painted picture of the same vegetation the visible colors would look the same, however, there would be much greater reflectance of infrared due to the lack of water absorption. In simple terms, it is the analysis and assessment of this type of difference in the reflected electromagnetic spectrum that forms the basis for analysis of satellite imagery (see diagram). In recent years differences in patterns and texture of the imagery have also been applied in refining the analytical process.

The specific process of discrimination is somewhat more complex as atmospheric absorption of portions of the electromagnetic spectrum (see diagram) have to be dealt with and the actual spectral differences between different species of vegetation or land cover can be very minute. In order to improve the discrimination capability of the satellite, the satellites "sight" is limited to very specific portions of the electromagnetic spectrum that optimize this process of discrimination. If the satellite were to view the entire spectrum the "noise" of the rest of the spectrum would hide or confuse the signal that is so critical in the discrimination process.

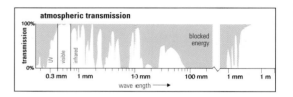

The Landsat Satellite Scanner

Two principle imaging systems are the scanning and the pushbroom imager. The American Landsat satellites use an across-track scanning system which consists of a rotating mirror which moves along a line perpendicular to the satellite's path of movement constantly registering a strip (scan-line) of the earth.

The electromagnetic energy that enters the sensor is spilt into several spectral components. The visible light and the reflective infra red are separated from the thermal infra red. The first component is further split into bands or channels which represent their different wavelength zones.

Measuring Resolution in "Pixels"

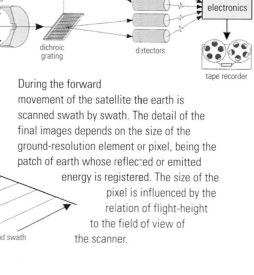

During the forward movement of the satellite the earth is scanned swath by swath. The detail of the final images depends on the size of the ground-resolution element or pixel, being the patch of earth whose reflected or emitted energy is registered. The size of the pixel is influenced by the relation of flight-height to the field of view of the scanner.

SATELLITE IMAGES
OF THE
WORLD

A seven page selection of stunning satellite images featuring major cities and contrasting geographical habitats. These "zoomed in" images of Earth are breathtakingly detailed and provide another perspective of our natural and manmade world.

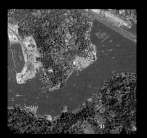

Source Data: SPOT ® © CNES 1997 provided by © SSC/Satellitbild

This satellite image of Hong Kong is a composite of 20 meter and 10 meter Spot imagery, providing a true color image at 10 meter resolution. The images were acquired in January of 1997 and clearly show the new airport under construction as well as the new bridge from the airport into Kowloon (lower left of the image).

© WorldSat International Inc.

Source Data: Spot data © CNES 1993 provided by SPOT Image Corporation

This satellite image combines 30 meter Landsat colour imagery with 10 meter black and white Spot data generating a 10 meter resolution image of the greater Chicago area. At this resolution stadiums, individual streets and even the shadows from the downtown skyscrapers can be seen.

This is another example of combining satellite imagery from two different sources and resolutions (Landsat 30 meter and Spot 10 meter) to obtain optimum results. In this case, the extreme terrain effects caused the process to be uniquely difficult. Observe the shadows to appreciate the very severe differences in elevation in this image.

More than 40 Landsat MSS images were needed to produce this mosaic of Lake Ontario. The imagery was reproduced at a 60 meter pixel resolution, allowing coverage of a large area and still maintaining enough detail to distinguish cities, towns and all of the waterways and small lakes in the region.

A spectacular view of Istanbul and the Bosporus created from a mosaic of 4 French Spot II images which are simulated in Natural Colour. This highly detailed image shows the spectacular growth of the city either side of the Isthmus.

This brilliantly clear natural colour image of glaciers in Antarctica highlights the importance of satellite images. It enables scientists to monitor accurately the depleting ice flows and the movement of sheet ice.

A very detailed infra red image of the metropolis of New York, taken by the French Spot 1 satellite. The resolution of the data is so good that roads, residential blocks and features in the harbor area may be seen. This Spot image has a resolution of 20 meters.

SATELLITE MAPS
OF THE
WORLD

Fifty-one full color satellite maps covering
the entire world from pole to pole, each
interpreted and enhanced with elevation
data and overlaid with cartographic detail.
These comprehensive maps provide a
unique perspective of our world, seen for
the very first time as it truly is.

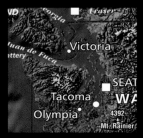

North America

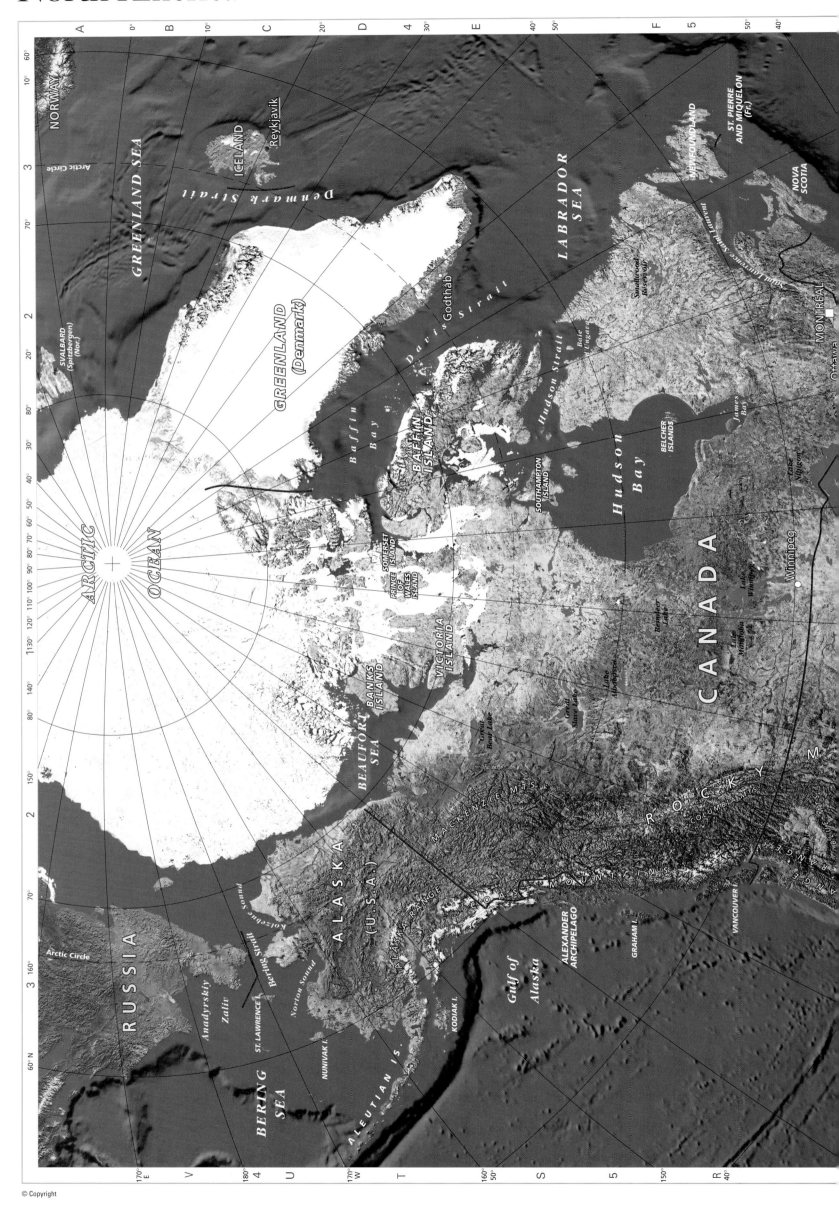

Scale 1 : 27 600 000

0   500   1000   1500   2000 km

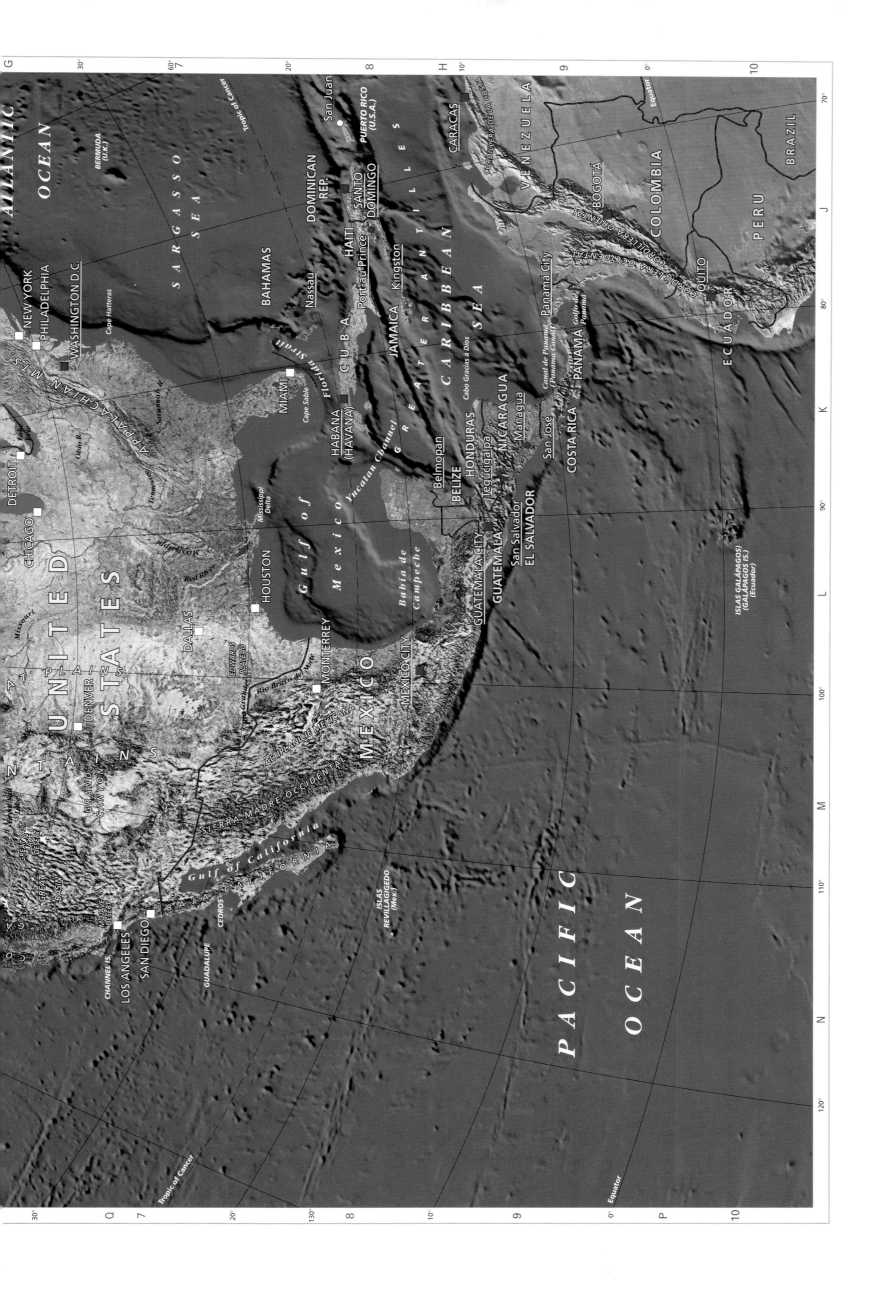

United States of America

Scale 1 : 12 328 000

0   200   400   600   800 km

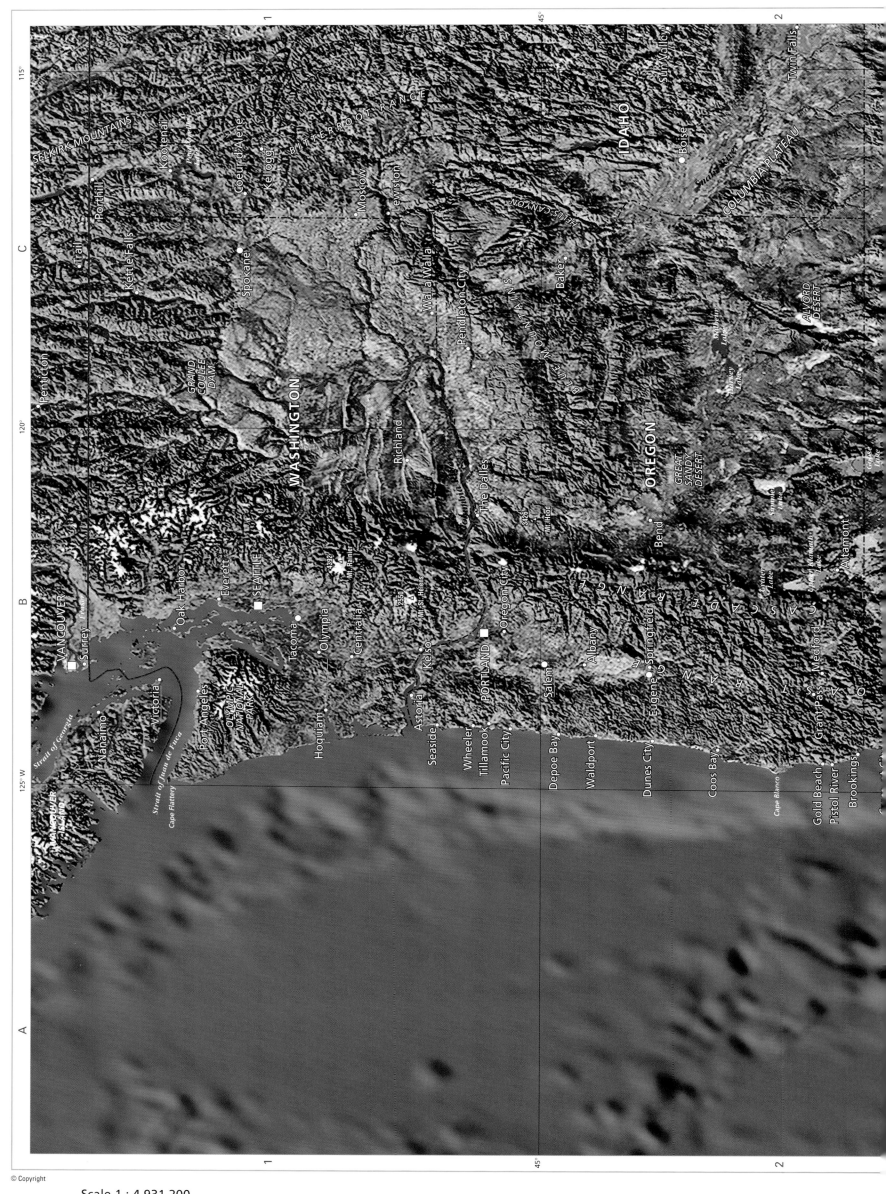

Scale 1 : 4 931 200

0   200   400   600   800 km

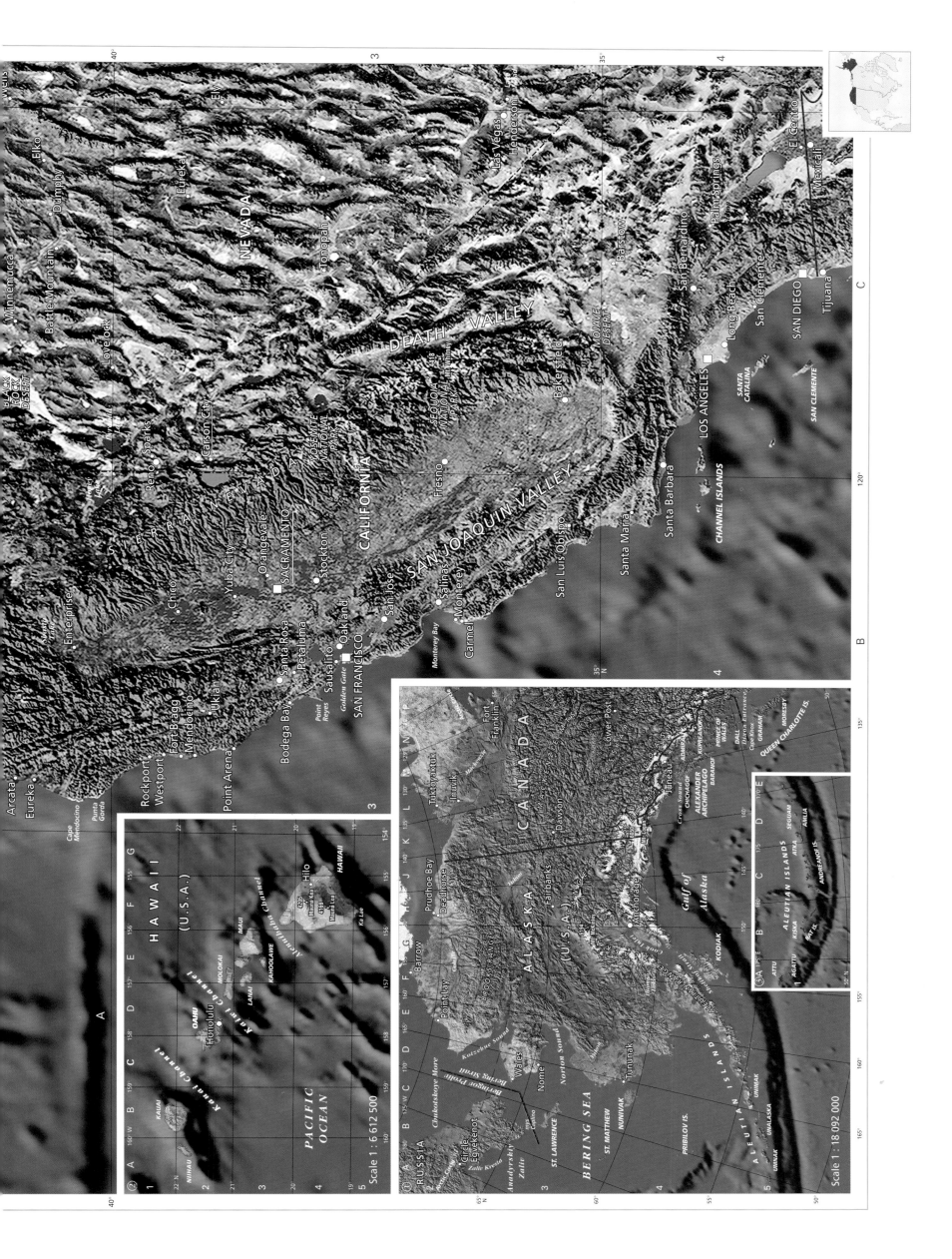

United States, North Central

SASKATCHEWAN

ALBERTA
Lethbridge
CYPRESS HILLS

GLACIER NATIONAL PARK

R O C K Y

SELKIRK MOUNTAINS

Porthill

Kootenai

Kalispell

Flathead Lake

Shelby

Havre

Glasgow

Wolf P

Fort Peck Lake

Spokane

Coeur d'Alene

Osborn

BITTERROOT RANGE

Great Falls

MONTANA

Pullman

Missoula

Helena

Wolf Creek

Miles C

Lewiston

M O U N T A I N S

Bighorn
Custer

Kooskia

Butte

Billings

Bozeman

Big Horn Lake

45°

IDAHO

3859
Borah Peak

YELLOWSTONE NATIONAL PARK

Cody

BIG HORN MOUNTAINS

Sheridan

OREGON

Caldwell

Sun Valley

4013
Cloude Peak

Boise

Idaho Falls

Teton Village

Mountain Home

Alpine

4207
Gannett Peak

WYOMING

Pocatello

Riverton

Casper

LARA MOUN

Twin Falls

3

2966
Granite Peak

Logan

Brigham City

Rock Springs

Rawlins

Wells

Ogden

Evanston

FLAMING GORGE NATIONAL PARK

Lara

Elko

Great Salt Lake

SALT LAKE CITY

Battle Mountain

Wendover

GREAT SALT LAKE DESERT

Park City

DINOSAUR NATIONAL MONUMENT

Naples

Provo

WASATCH RANGE

40°

Austin

Eureka

Grand Junction

4399
Mt. Elbert

Ely

UTAH

ARCHES NATIONAL PARK

4

NEVADA

COLORADO

Moab

3710
Delano Peak

Hanksville

Beaver

Tonopah

Cedar City

C   115°   D   110°   E

© Copyright

Scale 1 : 5 360 000

0   100   200   300 km

30

A N A D A

MANITOBA

Brandon

Winnipeg

Pembina

Lake of the Woods

Minot

Williston

Churchs Ferry

NORTH DAKOTA

Red River of the North

East Grand Forks

Grand Forks

Upper Red Lake

Lower Red Lake

MINNESOTA

Bemidji

Grand Rapids

Leach Lake

Sidney

Lake Sakakawea

Washburn

Medora Dickinson Mandan

Bismarck

Jamestown

Fargo Moorhead

Mille Lac Lake

Fort Yates

Missouri R.

Little Eagle

Meadow

Aberdeen

Peever

Browns Valley

Minnesota

Watertown

Willmar

ST. PAUL

MINNEAPOLIS

2

45°

Lake Oahe

SOUTH DAKOTA

Pierre

BIG BEND DAM

Huron

Brookings

New Ulm

Mankato

Owatonna

BLACK HILLS

Rapid City

MOUNT RUSHMORE NAT-MON

Okaton

Oacoma

Mitchell

Sioux Falls

Fairmont

Albert Lea

BADLANDS NATIONAL PARK

Lake Francis Case

Wewela

Spencer

Mason City

Yankton

Sioux City

IOWA

3

Fort Dodge

Sunrise

Torrington Scottsbluff

Chugwater

North Platte R.

Broadwater

NEBRASKA

Norfolk

Boone

Newton

Columbus

Fremont

Des Moines

yenne

Pine Bluffs

Brule

North Platte

Omaha

Council Bluffs

Sterling

South Platte R.

Grand Island

Kearney

Platte River

Lincoln

reeley

Weldona

Hastings

Beatrice

Maryville

Loveland

McCook

Alma

40°

DENVER

Goodland

Atchison

St. Joseph

Missouri R.

Colorado Springs

Oakley

KANSAS

Hays

Manhattan

Salina

Junction City

Topeka

KANSAS CITY

Independence

Marshall

Ottawa

Warrensburg

eblo

La Junta

Arkansas River

Caddoa

Garden City

Great Bend

McPherson

Emporia

MISSOURI

4

GREAT PLAINS

United States, South Central

Scale 1 : 5 360 000

0   100   200   300 km

United States, Southeast

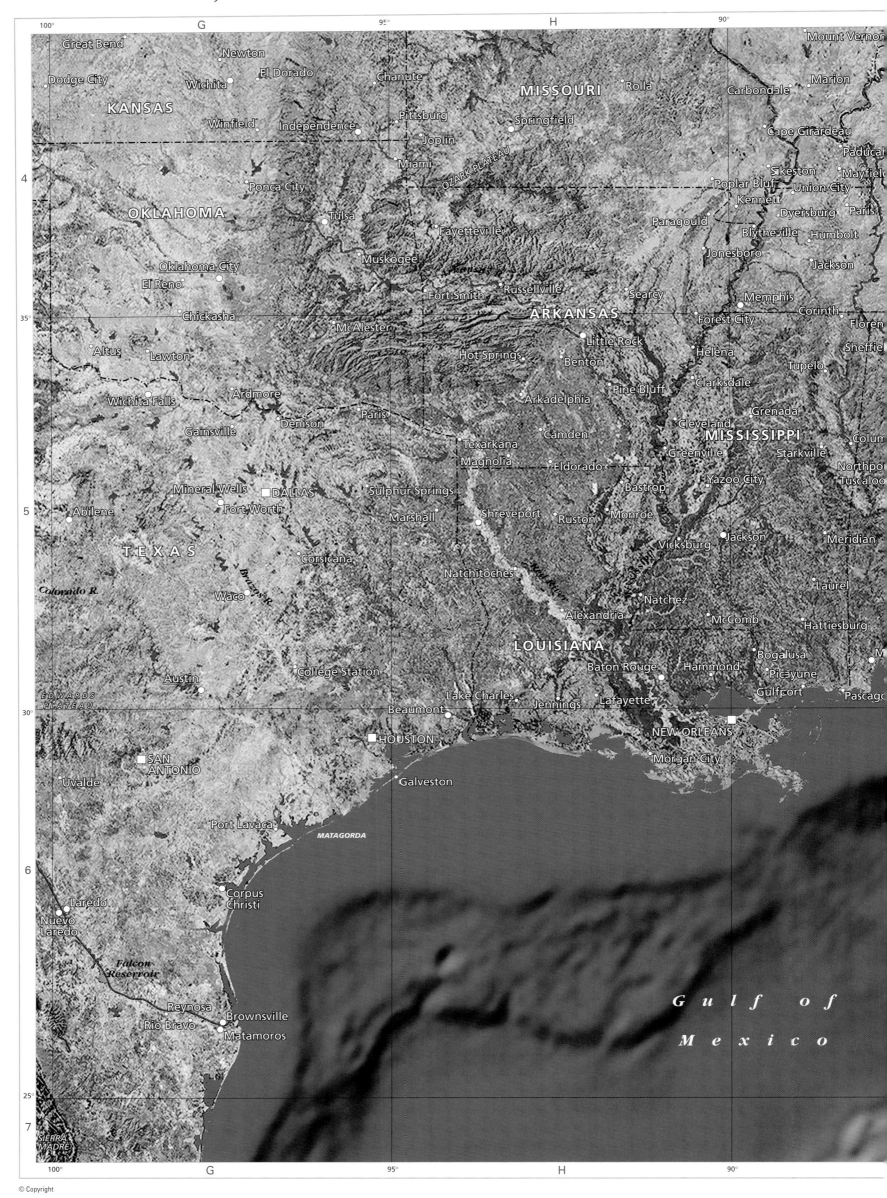

Scale 1 : 5 826 000

0   200   400   600   800 km

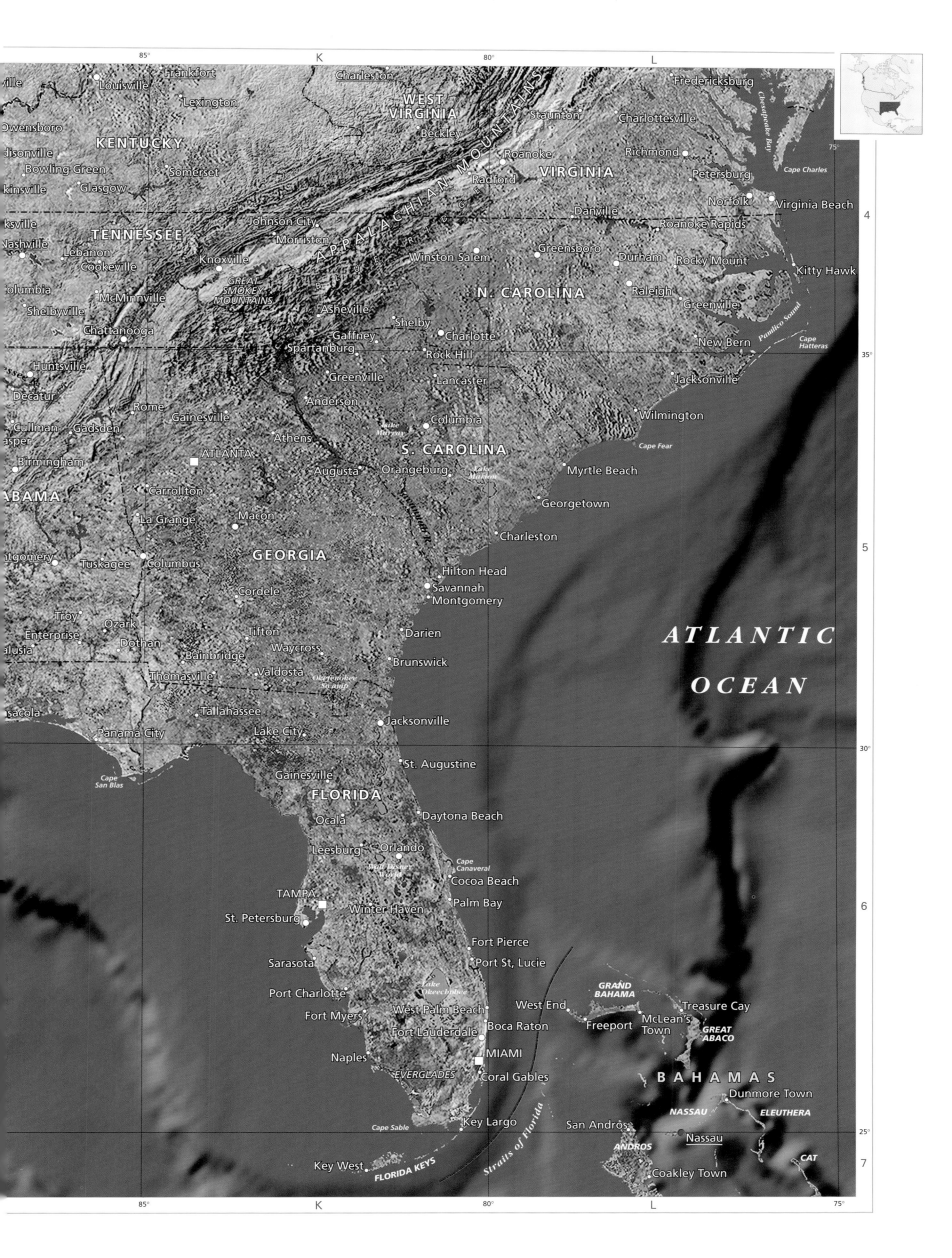

85° K Charleston 80° L Fredericksburg 75°

ville Louisville Frankfort WEST Charleston Fredericksburg Chesapeake Bay
  Lexington VIRGINIA Staunton Charlottesville Cape Charles
OWensboro KENTUCKY Beckley Richmond Petersburg
disonville Bowling Green Somerset Roanoke VIRGINIA Norfolk Virginia Beach 75°
kinsville Glasgow Radford Danville Roanoke Rapids 4
  TENNESSEE Johnson City Morriston Greensboro Durham Rocky Mount Kitty Hawk
Nashville Lebanon Knoxville Winston-Salem N. CAROLINA Raleigh Greenville
Columbia Cookeville GREAT SMOKEY MOUNTAINS Asheville Shelby Charlotte New Bern Cape Hatteras 35°
Shelbyville McMinnville Gaffney Rock Hill Lancaster Pamlico Sound
Huntsville Chattanooga Spartanburg Greenville Columbia Jacksonville
Decatur Rome Gainesville Anderson Lake Murray S. CAROLINA Wilmington
Cullman Gadsden Athens Columbia Cape Fear
asper Birmingham ATLANTA Augusta Orangeburg Lake Marion Myrtle Beach 5
BAMA Carrollton Macon Georgetown
tgomery La Grange GEORGIA Charleston
  Tuskagee Columbus Hilton Head
Troy Cordele Savannah ATLANTIC
Enterprise Ozark Tifton Montgomery
alusia Dothan Waycross Darien OCEAN
  Bainbridge Brunswick
  Thomasville Valdosta Okefenokee Swamp
saicola Tallahassee Lake City Jacksonville 30°
Panama City Cape San Blas St. Augustine
  Gainesville FLORIDA
  Ocala Daytona Beach
  Leesburg Orlando Walt Disney World Cape Canaveral
  TAMPA Cocoa Beach
  Winter Haven Palm Bay 6
St. Petersburg
  Sarasota Fort Pierce
  Port St, Lucie GRAND BAHAMA Treasure Cay
Port Charlotte Lake Okeechobee West End McLean's Town GREAT ABACO
  Fort Myers West Palm Beach Freeport
  Fort Lauderdale Boca Raton
  Naples MIAMI BAHAMAS
  EVERGLADES Coral Gables Dunmore Town
  Cape Sable Key Largo San Andros NASSAU ELEUTHERA 25°
  San Andros Nassau
  ANDROS CAT
Key West FLORIDA KEYS Straits of Florida Coakley Town 7

85° K 80° L 75°

35

Thunder Bay

ONTARIO

Lake Superior

Timi

Duluth

Superior

APOSTLE
ISLANDS

Sault
Sainte Marie

Sudbury

Espanola

Escanaba

GARDEN
PENINSULA

BEAVER
ISLAND

Mackinaw City

MANITOULIN
ISLAND

Georgi
Bay

ST. PAUL

MINNEAPOLIS

Chippewa Falls

Wausau

Marinette

DOOR PENINSULA

Traverse City

*Lake
Huron*

BRUCE PENINSULA

Owen
Sound

Eau Claire

WISCONSIN

Stephens Point

Appleton

Green Bay

MICHIGAN

Oshkosh

*Lake
Winnebago*

Manitowoc

Ludington

La Crosse

Sheboygan

Big Rapids

Mt. Pleasant

Bay City

Kitch

Mason City

Madison

*Lake
Michigan*

Muskegon

Grand
Rapids

Flint

Port Huron

Sarnia

Lon

MILWAUKEE

Lansing

DETROIT

*Lake
St. Clair*

Chatham

Waterloo

Dubuque

Janesville

Kenosha

Kalamazoo

Battle Creek

Ann Arbor

Windsor

Lake Erie

IOWA

Cedar Rapids

Rockford

Benton Harbor

Jackson

Ashtab

Iowa City

Clinton

Rock Falls

CHICAGO

Joliet

Gary

South
Bend

Goshen

Toledo

CLEVELAN

Davenport

Moline

La Salle

Defiance

Bowling
Green

Fremont

Youngst

Muscatine

Ottawa

Kankakee

Fort Wayne

Akron

Ottumwa

Galesburg

Streator

Logansport

Lima

Mansfield

Cant

Burlington

Peoria

Bloomington

Lafayette

OHIO

Fort Madison

Macomb

ILLINOIS

INDIANA

Sidney

Delaware

Quincy

Champaign

INDIANAPOLIS

Dayton

Columbus

Cambridge

Whe

Hannibal

Springfield

Decatur

Richmond

Mexico

Mattoon

Terre Haute

CINCINNATI

Chillicothe

Mari

Parkers

Effingham

Seymour

Madison

Portsmouth

V

Jefferson City

Wood River

Washington

Frankfort

Huntington

Charles

ST. LOUIS

East St. Louis

Vincennes

New Albany

Missouri R.

Mount Vernon

Evansville

Louisville

Lexington

Beckley

MISSOURI

Marion

Owensboro

Elizabethtown

Richmond

Cape Girardeau

KENTUCKY

Scale 1 : 5 826 000

0   200   400   600   800 km

Kirkland
Lake

Rouyan-
Noranda

Val-d'Or

QUÉBEC

Lac Saint-
Jean

Alma

Jonquière

Chicoutimi

Rimouski

Tadoussac

Rivière-du-Loup

La Tuque

Edmundston

Caribou

Aroostook

Montmagny

Presque Isle

th Bay

Lake
Nipissing

Québec

Shawinigan Falls

Trois Rivières

Saint Laurence River

Sorel

Thetford Mines

MAINE

Vanceboro

St. Stephen

Chalk River

Pembroke

MONTRÉAL

St. Hyacinthe

Granby

Sherbrooke

Moosehead
Lake

Huntsville

Ottawa

Valleyfield

St. Jean
Sur Richelieu

Magog

Canaan

Midland

Orillia

Smith Falls

Massena

Rouses Point

Plattsburgh

St.
Albans

Montgomery
Center

Dixville Notch

Newport

Bangor

Ogdensburg

Burlington

1917
Washington

Augusta

rrie

Lake
Simcoe

Peterborough

Belleville

Kingston

THOUSAND
ISLANDS

Watertown

Montpelier

Stowe

1483

Whiteface

Lake
Champlain

VERMONT

St.
Johnsbury

Berlin

Auburn

Bath

Brunswick

MOUNT DESERT
ISLAND

CRANBERRY
ISLES

Cobourg

Lake Ontario

Oswego

White River

Rutland

Lake
Winnipesaukee

South Portland

ONTO

St. Catharines

Rochester

Rome

Glens Falls

Claremont

NEW HAMPSHIRE

Concord

Portsmouth

gara Falls

Niagara Falls

Batavia

Geneva

Syracuse

Utica

Saratoga
Springs

Brattleboro

Keene

Manchester

Welland

BUFFALO

NEW YORK

Albany

North Adams

Newburyport

Fredonia

Ithaca

Northampton

MASSACHUSETTS

BOSTON

Jamestown

Olean

Corning

Endicott

CATSKILL
MOUNTAINS

Springfield

Worcester

Cape Cod

Warren

Bradford

Kingston

Windsor Locks

Woonsocket

Plymouth

Oil City

PENNSYLVANIA

Poughkeepsie

CONNECTICUT

Hartford

PROVIDENCE

RHODE I.

Waterbury

Norwich

Westerly

Scranton

Beacon

Danbury

New
Haven

New
London

MARTHA'S
VINEYARD

NANTUCKET
ISLAND

Wilkes-Barre

Bridgeport

Long Island Sound

Lock Haven

Sunbury

Allentown

Jersey City

Stamford

Hudson R.

Lewistown

NEWARK

NEW YORK

PITTSBURGH

Altoona

Harrisburg

New Brunswick

Trenton

Cumberland

PHILADELPHIA

Morgantown

Hagerstown

Wilmington

NEW JERSEY

ksburg

Martinsburg

MARYLAND

BALTIMORE

Atlantic City

Ocean City

Dover

WASHINGTON D.C.

DELAWARE

Harrisonburg

SHENANDOAH
NATIONAL
PARK

Fredericksburg

Salisbury

Staunton

Lexington Park

Charlottesville

VIRGINIA

Richmond

Chesapeake Bay

Cape Charles

Canada

Scale 1 : 11 040 000

0   200   400   600 km

© Copyright

Cape Sherard · Lancaster Sound · Cape Liverpool · BYLOT I. · Cape Graham Moore · Cape Adair · *Baffin Bay* · DISKO · Godhavn · **GREENLAND (Denmark)** · Angmagssa · *Denmark Strait*

BAFFIN ISLAND · Clyde · Cape Christian · Cape Raper · **Home Bay** · *Penny Highlands*

CROWN PRINCE FREDERIK I. · Igloolik · KOCH I. · ROWLEY I. · BRAY I. · FOLEY I. · AIR FORCE I. · PRINCE CHARLES ISLAND · *Nettilling Lake* · *Nordre Strømfjord* · *Søndre Strømfjord* · Godthåb · 1890 △ J.A.D. Jensens Nunatakker · Narsarsuaq

WALES I. · *Davis Strait* · Kap Farvel

Foxe Basin · VANSITTART I. · WHITE I. · Cape Wilson · *Amadjuak Lake* · *Cumberland Sound* · Cape Mercy · LEMIEUX ISLANDS

Foxe Channel · Cape Queen · Cape Dorset · MILL · Iqaluit · *Frobisher Bay* · LOKS LAND · *LABRADOR SEA*

Roes Welcome Sound · SOUTHAMPTON ISLAND · SALISBURY I. · *Hudson Strait* · EDGELL I. · RESOLUTION I. · 55°

Field Inlet · Cape Low · *Fisher Strait* · *Evans Strait* · COATS I. · NOTTINGHAM I. · Cap Wolstenholme · CHARLES I. · *Gabriel Strait* · Cape Chidley · *NEWFOUNDLAND AND LABRADOR*

D · **A** · MANSEL I. · Ivujivik · Cape Smith · Cap Hopes Advance · AKPATOK I.

Hudson Bay · Inukjuak · Kangirsuk · *Ungava Bay* · *Rivière aux Feuilles* · Hebron · SOUTH AULATSIVIK I. · 60°

Lac Nantais · *Koksoak R.* · *George R.* · Rigolet · *Lake Melville* · BELLE ISLE · Cape Bauld · 50°

Fort Severn · NORTH BELCHER ISLANDS · *Lac Minto* · Schefferville · *Smallwood Réservoir* · *Churchill R.* · *Strait of Belle Isle* · GREY ISLANDS · White Bay · FOGO · Cape Freels

Cape Henrietta Maria · BELCHER ISLANDS · Kuujjuarapik · *Lac Caniapiscau* · Gander · NEWFOUNDLAND · 70°

Lake River · *James Bay* · TWIN IS. · Deer Lake · Corner Brook · *Trinity Bay* · St. John's

AKIMISKI · **QUÉBEC** · *Manicouagan Réservoir* · Havre-Saint-Pierre · *Bay of Islands*

ONTARIO · Vaskaganish · *Lac Mistassini* · *Lac Albanel* · Sept-Îles · *Détroit de Jacques-Cartier* · ÎLE D'ANTICOSTI · Pointe de l'Est · Gulf of St. Lawrence · Fortune Bay · ST.-PIERRE AND MIQUELON (Fr.) · *Placentia Bay* · 45°

Ogoki · *Lac Evans* · *Réservoir Pipmuacan* · *Détroit d'Honguedo* · Cape Ray · *Cabot Strait* · Cape North

Lake Nipigon · Jonquière · *Lac Saint-Jean* · *St. Lawrence* · *MONTS NOTRE-DAME* · *Baie des Chaleurs* · ÎLES DE LA MADELEINE · P.E.I. · PRINCE EDWARD · Charlotte-town · CAPE BRETON ISLANDS · *Strait of Canso* · SABLE I.

Thunder Bay · Timmins · *Réservoir Gouin* · Val-d'Or · Québec · **NEW BRUNSWICK** · Fredericton · Halifax

ISLE ROYALE · MICHIPICOTEN · *Lake Superior* · North Bay · MAINE · **NOVA SCOTIA** · 80°

A. · Sault Sainte Marie · *Lake Nipissing* · Ottawa · *Ottawa R.* · MONTRÉAL · Augusta · *Gulf of Maine* · Cape Sable · *Bay of Fundy*

MANITOULIN · Montpelier · VER-MONT · NEW HAMP-SHIRE · *ATLANTIC OCEAN*

NSIN · Appleton · *Lake Michigan* · *Lake Huron* · TORONTO · *Lake Ontario* · NEW YORK · Concord · BOSTON · Cape Cod · 40°

MICHIGAN · *Lake Winnebago* · Hamilton · Rochester · Albany · MASSA-CHUSETS · Hartford · PROVIDENCE · RHODE I.

Flint · *Niagara Falls* · BUFFALO · Syracuse · CT. · LONG I.

MILWAUKEE · Lansing · DETROIT · *Lake Erie* · Erie · Jersey City · NEW YORK · 65°

Grand Rapids · **PENNSYLVANIA** · NEWARK

39

Canada, West

BANKS ISLAND

Sachs Harbour

Cape Kellett

Cape Lambton

Cape Bathurst

Amundsen Gulf

Franklin Bay

BEAUFORT-SEA

MELVILLE HILLS

Echo Bay

Great Bear Lake

Faber Lake

Yellowknife

Paulatuk

Tuktoyaktuk

Eskimo Lake

Fort Good Hope

Norman Wells

Fort Franklin

Lac La Martre

Mackenzie R.

FRANKLIN MOUNTAINS

Inuvik

Fort MacPherson

Mackenzie R.

Mackenzie Bay

Fort Simpson

RICHARDSON MTS.

MACKENZIE MOUNTAINS

Old Crow

Arctic Circle

Porcupine R.

MACKENZIE MOUNTAINS

SELWYN MOUNTAINS

Watson Lake

YUKON

TERRITORY

Dawson

Faro

Ross River

PELLY MOUNTAINS

Yukon R.

Yukon R.

Fairbanks

WHITE MOUNTAINS

ALASKA

(U.S.A.)

Mount Hayes 4216

Mt. Blackburn 4996

Mt. Logan 5551

Whitehorse

CASSIAR MOUNTAINS

O

R

Teslin

CHICHAGOF

ADMIRALTY

Yakutat Bay

Cross Sound

Gulf of Alaska

ALEXANDER ARCHIPELAGO

BARANOF

Scale 1 : 4 416 000

0   200   400   600 km

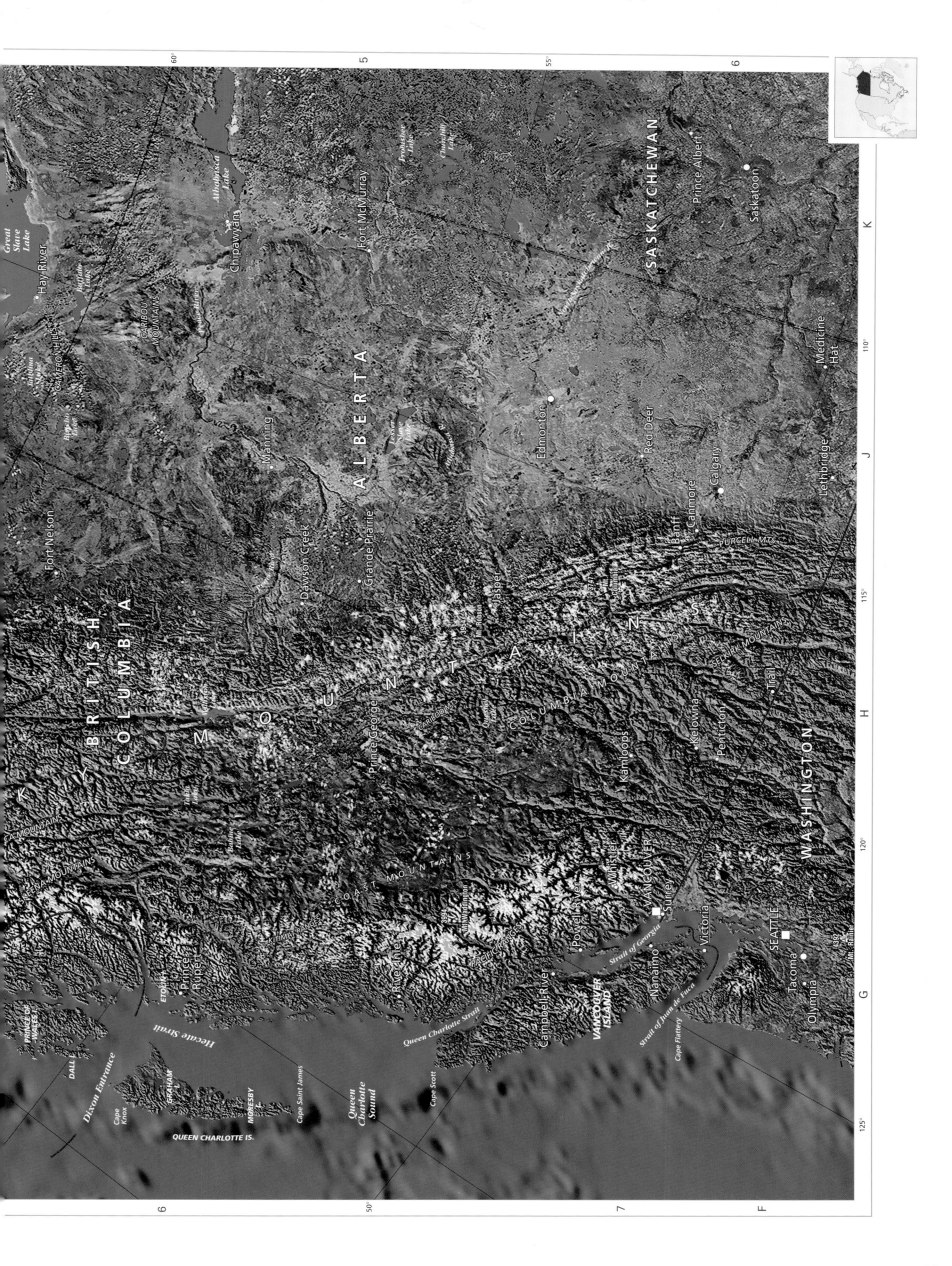

Canada, Central

Scale 1 : 6 732 000

0   200   400   600 km

Canada, East

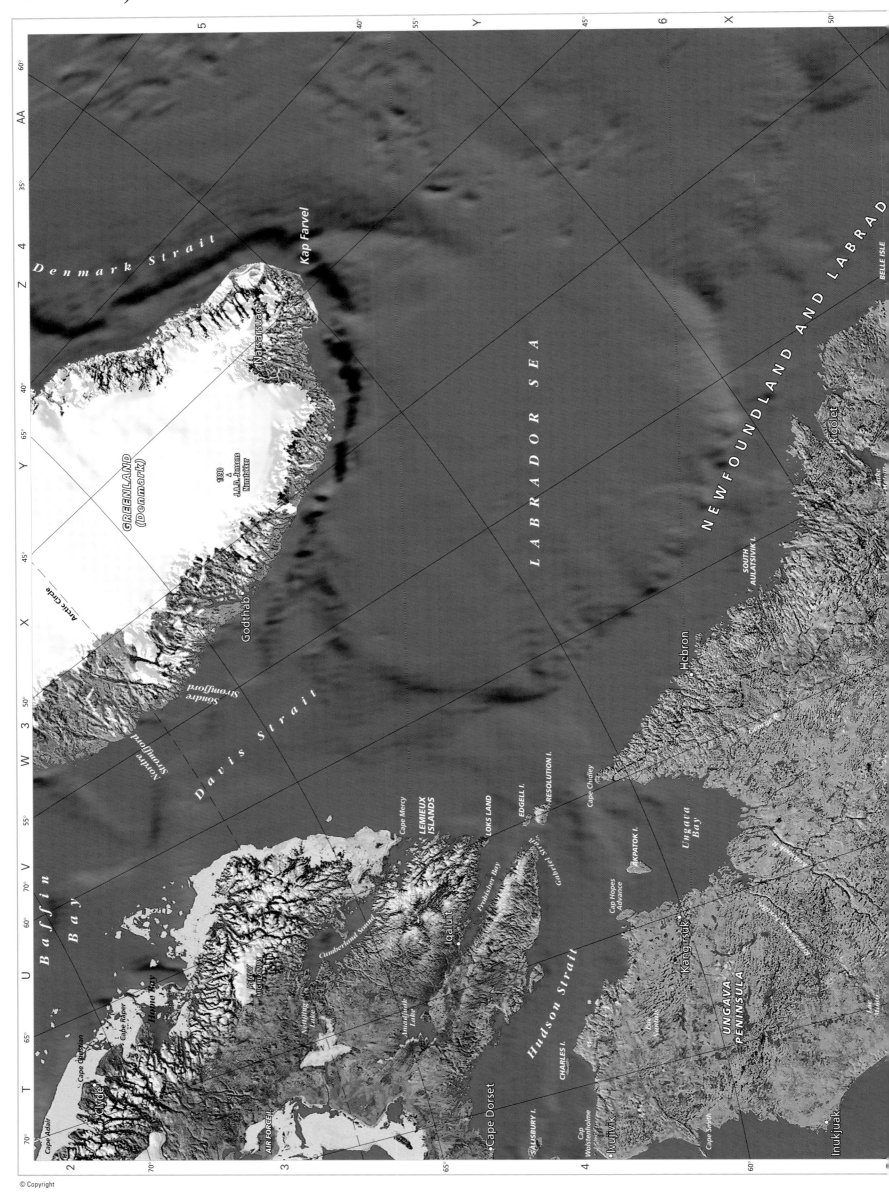

Denmark Strait

Kap Farvel

Narsarsuaq

GREENLAND
(Denmark)

1830
△
J.A.D. Jensens
Nunatakker

Godthåb

Søndre Strømfjord

Nordre Strømfjord

LABRADOR SEA

NEWFOUNDLAND AND LABRAD

BELLE ISLE

Rigolet

Hebron

SOUTH
AULATSIVIK I.

Davis Strait

Arctic Circle

Cape Mercy

LEMIEUX
ISLANDS

LOKS LAND

EDGELL I.

RESOLUTION I.

Cape Chidley

AKPATOK I.

Ungava
Bay

Baffin

Bay

Frobisher Bay

Cumberland Sound

PENNY
HIGHLANDS

Nettilling
Lake

Amadjuak
Lake

Gabriel Strait

Cap Hopes
Advance

Kangirsuk

Cape Raper

Home Bay

Cape Dyer

Hudson Strait

CHARLES I.

Cap
Wolstenholme

UNGAVA
PENINSULA

Cape Adair

Clyde

AIR FORCE I.

SALISBURY I.

Cape Dorset

Ivujivik

Cape Smith

Inukjuak

© Copyright

Scale 1 : 6 611 000

0   200   400   600 km

45

Central America and the Caribbean

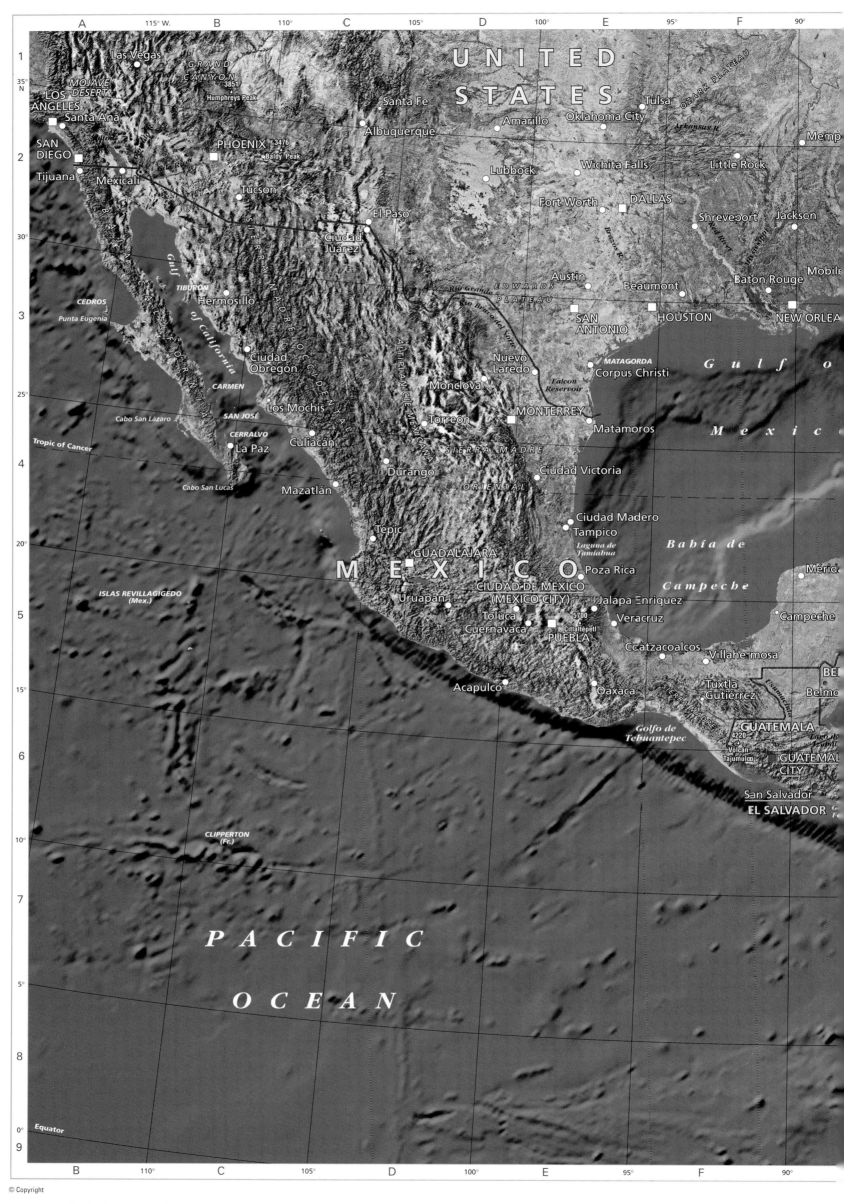

Scale 1 : 12 880 000

0   200   400   600   800 km

© Copyright

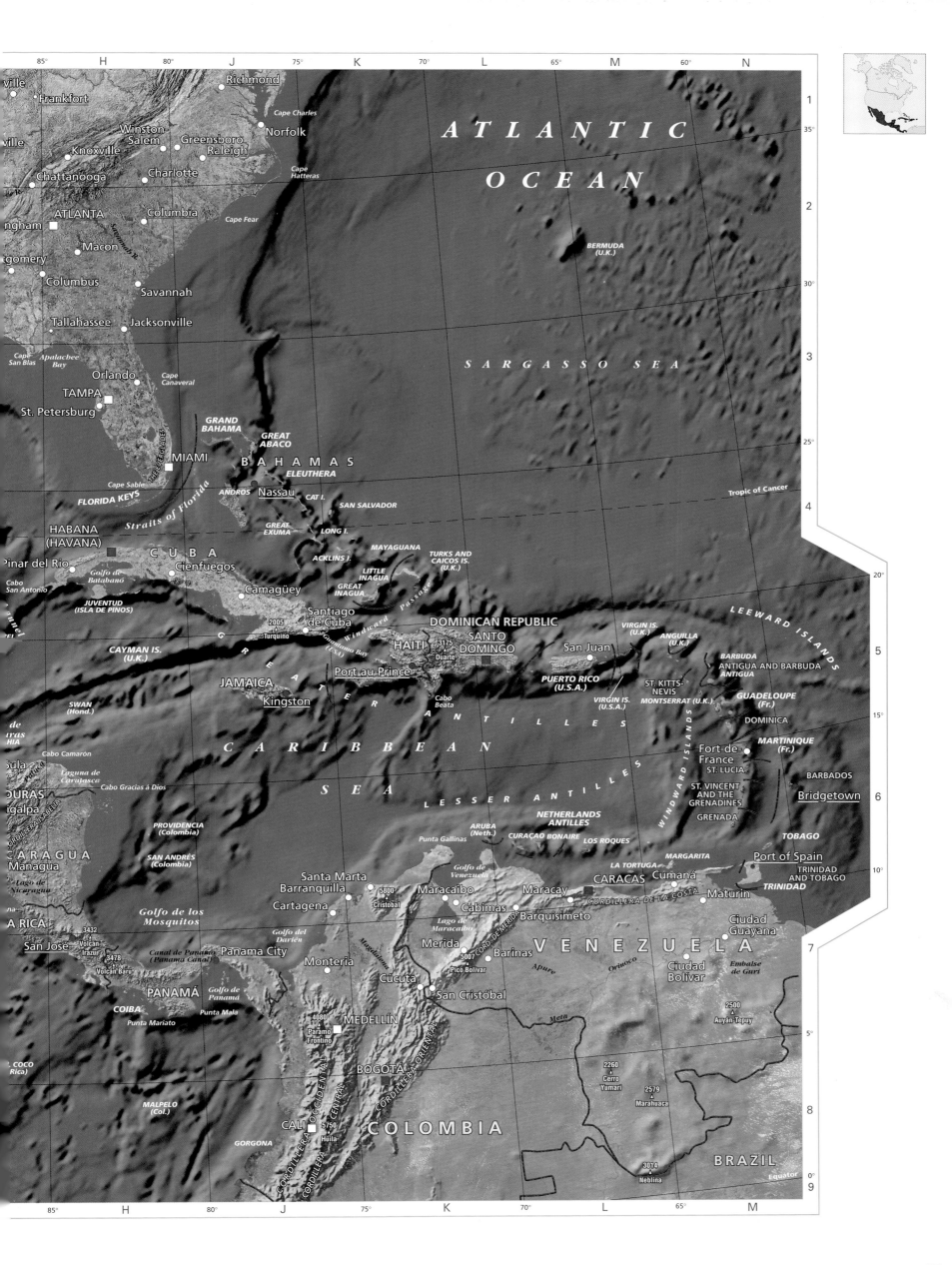

South America

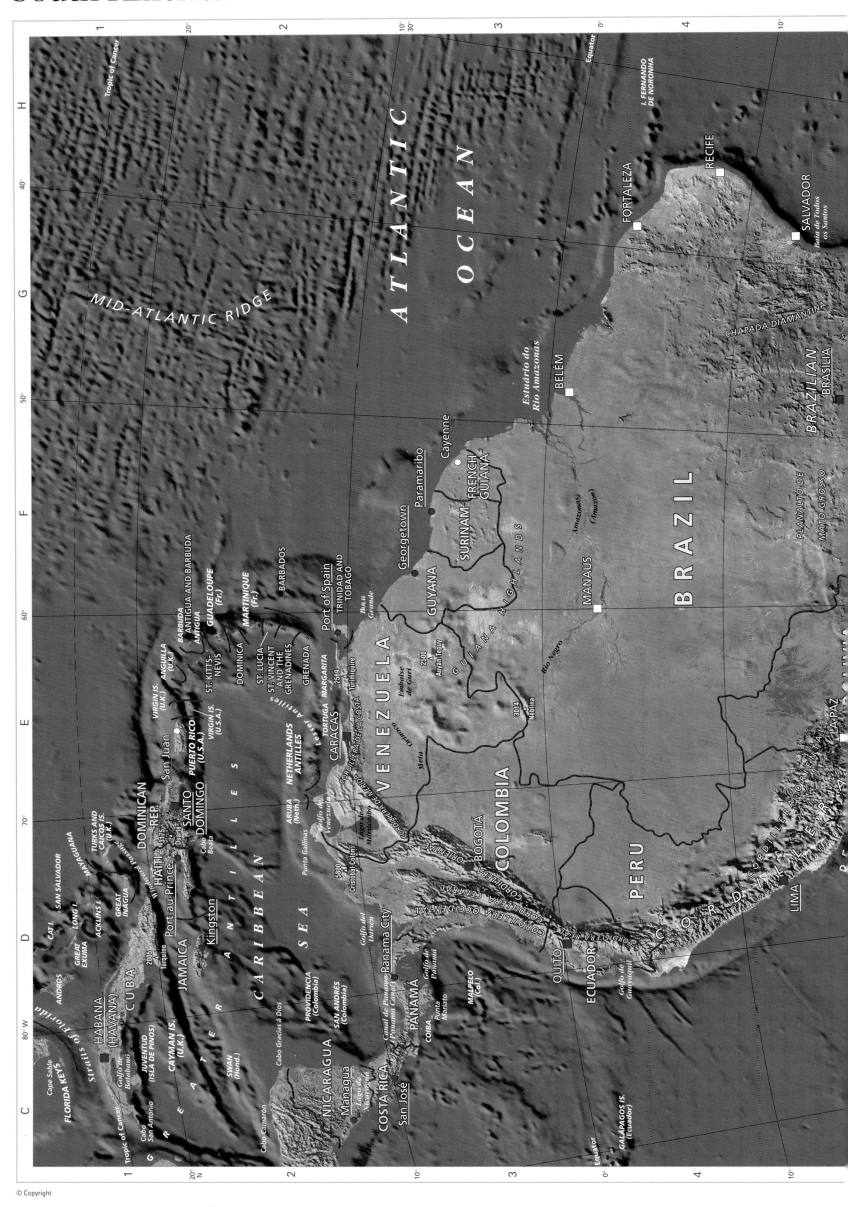

Scale 1 : 22 356 000

0   200   400   600   800   1000 km

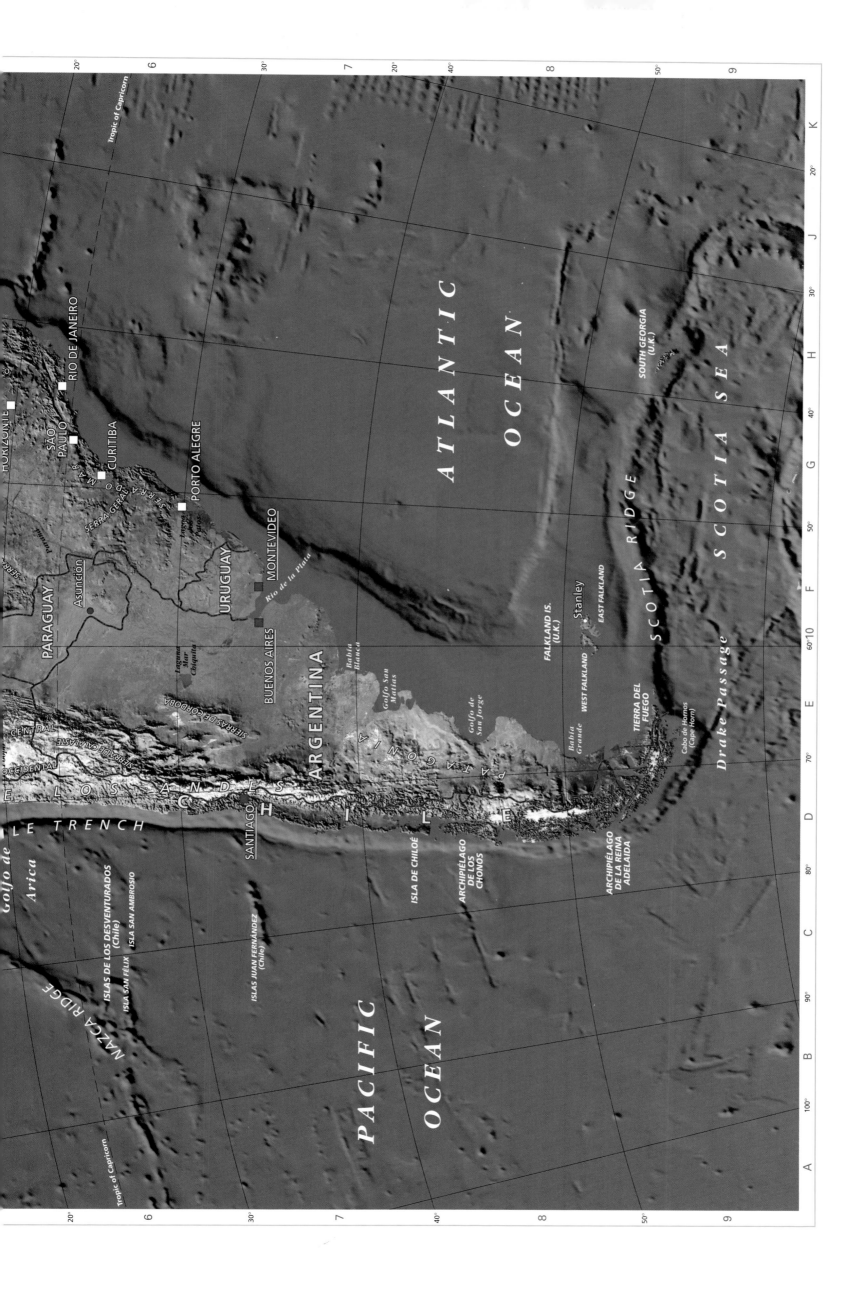

PACIFIC

OCEAN

ATLANTIC

OCEAN

SCOTIA SEA

NAZCA RIDGE

Tropic of Capricorn

Arica

Golfo de

CHILE TRENCH

ISLAS DE LOS DESVENTURADOS
(Chile)
ISLA SAN FÉLIX
ISLA SAN AMBROSIO

ISLAS JUAN FERNÁNDEZ
(Chile)

ISLA DE CHILOÉ

ARCHIPIÉLAGO
DE LOS
CHONOS

ARCHIPIÉLAGO
DE LA REINA
ADELAIDA

SANTIAGO

C H I L E

D E   L O S   A N D E S

OCCIDENTAL

CENTRAL

SIERRA DE CATAMARCA

SIERRAS DE CÓRDOBA

Laguna
Mar
Chiquita

ARGENTINA

P A T A G O N I A

Bahía
Blanca

Golfo San
Matías

Golfo de
San Jorge

Bahía
Grande

TIERRA DEL
FUEGO

Cabo de Hornos
(Cape Horn)

WEST FALKLAND

EAST FALKLAND

FALKLAND IS.
(U.K.)

Stanley

Drake Passage

SCOTIA   RIDGE

SOUTH GEORGIA
(U.K.)

Asunción

PARAGUAY

SERRA

SERRA GERAL

SERRA DO MAR

URUGUAY

MONTEVIDEO

BUENOS AIRES

Río de la Plata

PORTO ALEGRE

CURITIBA

SÃO
PAULO

RIO DE JANEIRO

HORIZONTE

Tropic of Capricorn

Tropic of Capricorn

South America, North

© Copyright

Scale 1 : 12 880 000

0   200   400   600 km

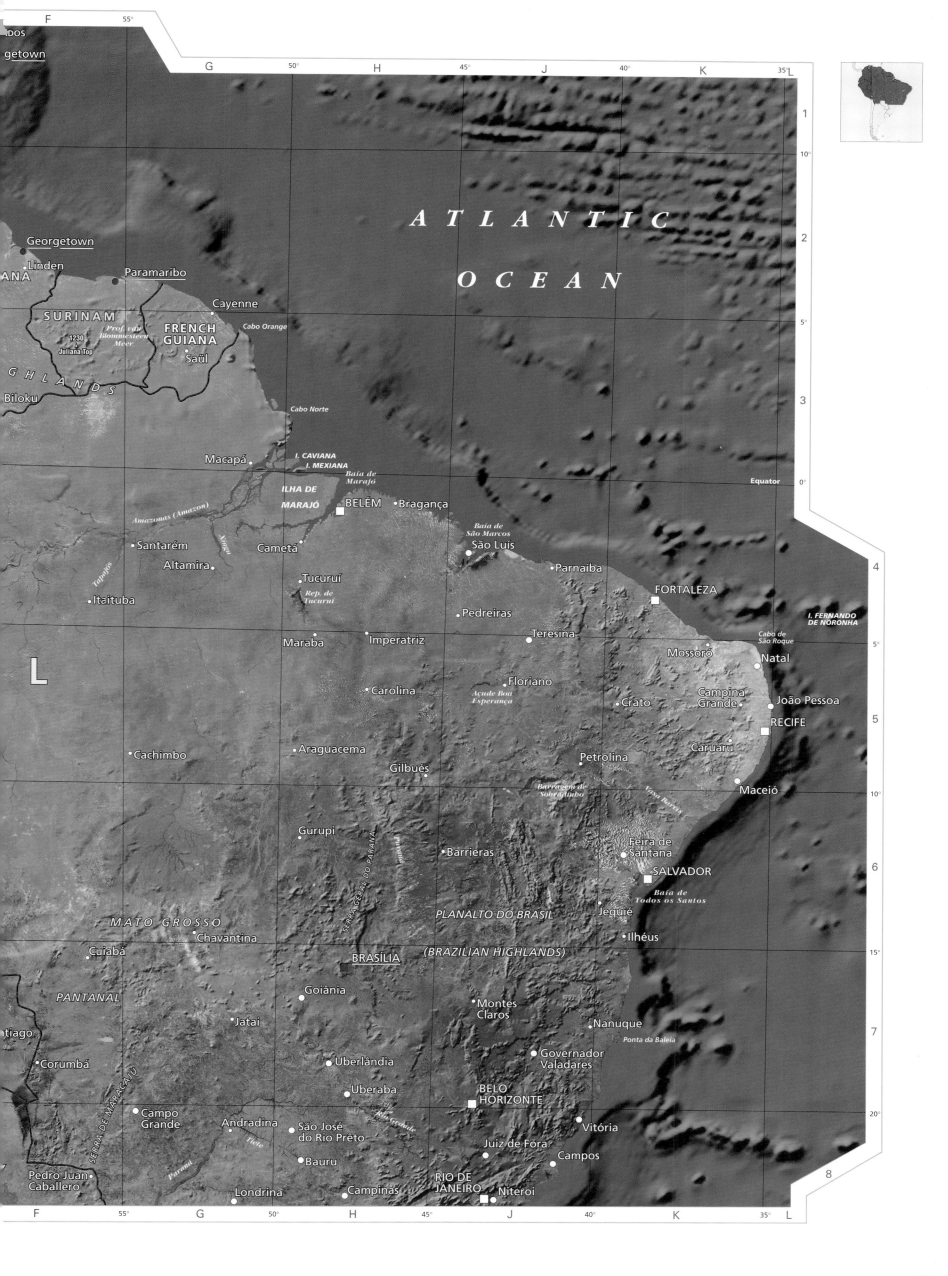

F | 55° | G | 50° | H | 45° | J | 40° | K | 35° | L

DOS

getown

Georgetown

Linden

ANA

Paramaribo

SURINAM

FRENCH
GUIANA

Cayenne

Prof. van
Biommesteen
Meer

1230
Juliana Top

Saül

Cabo Orange

GHLANDS

Biloku

Cabo Norte

Macapá

I. CAVIANA
I. MEXIANA

Baía de
Marajó

ILHA DE
MARAJÓ

BELÉM

Bragança

Amazonas (Amazon)

Baía de
São Marcos

São Luís

Santarém

Cametá

Parnaíba

Xingu

Altamira

Tapajós

Tucuruí

FORTALEZA

I. FERNANDO
DE NORONHA

Itaituba

Rep. de
Tucuruí

Pedreiras

Teresina

Cabo de
São Roque

Maraba

Imperatriz

Mossoró

Natal

L

Carolina

Floriano

Açude Boa
Esperança

Crato

Campina
Grande

João Pessoa

RECIFE

Cachimbo

Araguacema

Gilbués

Petrolina

Caruaru

Barragem de
Sobradinho

Maceió

Gurupi

Barrieras

Feira de
Santana

SALVADOR

Baía de
Todos os Santos

MATO GROSSO

Chavantina

PLANALTO DO BRASIL

Jequié

Ilhéus

Cuiabá

BRASÍLIA

(BRAZILIAN HIGHLANDS)

PANTANAL

Goiânia

Montes
Claros

tiago

Jatai

Nanuque

Ponta da Baleia

Corumbá

Uberlândia

Governador
Valadares

SERRA DE MARACAJU

Uberaba

BELO
HORIZONTE

Campo
Grande

Andradina

São José
do Rio Prêto

Vitória

Tietê

Juiz de Fora

Campos

Pedro Juan
Caballero

Bauru

Paraná

RIO DE
JANEIRO

Niteroi

Londrina

Campinas

A T L A N T I C

O C E A N

Equator

1

10°

2

5°

3

0°

4

5°

5

10°

6

15°

7

20°

8

F | 55° | G | 50° | H | 45° | J | 40° | K | 35° | L

51

South America, South

Arequipa
Lago Titicaca
LA PAZ
Cochabamba
Santa Cruz
CORDILLERA
BOLIVIA
Tanca
6542
Nevado de Sajama
Oruro
CORDILLERA ORIENTAL
CHACO BOREAL
Arica
Potosí
Sucre
15° S
Salar de Uyuni
Golfo de Arica
Tarija
PARA
Iquique
E020
Cerro Nuevo Mundo
Calama
Tartagal
2
PERU
CORDILLERA DE PARAGUAI
CORDILLERA DEL OCCIDENTAL
LOS ANDES
Punta Angamos
Salar de Atacama
Salta
Las Lomitas
GRAN CH
NAZCA RIDGE
Antofagasta
CHACO AUSTRAL
Resiste
20°
CHILE TRENCH
San Miguel de Tucumán
Santiago del Estero
Reconqu
3
Tropic of Capricorn
Copiapó
Flambala
ARGENTINA
ISLAS DE LOS DESVENTURADOS (Chile)
ISLA SAN FÉLIX
La Serena
La Rioja
Laguna Mar Chiquita
ISLA SAN AMBROSIO
25°
Punta Lengua de Vaca
288C
CÓRDOBA
SIERRAS DE CÓRDOBA
Santa Fé
Champaqui
Paraná
San Juan
Rosario
4
6960
Cerro Aconcagua
Mendoza
Río Cuarto
Valparaíso
Junin
SANTIAGO
San Rafael
Chivi
Rancagua
30°
3810
El Navado
P A M P A S
Talca
Santa Rosa
Olava
ISLAS JUAN FERNÁNDEZ (Chile)
4800
Volcán Domuyo
Chillán
Bah
Blan
Talcahuano
5
Punta Lavapié
Concepción
Neuquén
General Roca
Be
Bl
P A C I F I C
Temuco
3740
Negro
Viedm
Volcán Lanin
Valdivia
35°
O C E A N
San Carlos de Bariloche
Golfo San Matias
Puerto Montt
PATAGONIA
Esquel
Trelew
6
ISLA DE CHILOÉ
2300
Volcán Corcovado
Chubut
Cabo Dos Bahías
Lago Colhué Huapi
Golfo de San Jorge
Lago Musters
Comodoro Rivadavia
40°
ARCHIPIÉLAGO DE LOS CHONOS
Lago Buenos Aires
Cabo Tres Puntas
4058
Cerro San Valentín
Chile Chico
7
San Julián
Lago Viedma
Lago Argentino
Bahía Grande
2360
Cerro Paine
45°
Río Gallegos
Estrecho de Magallanes
ARCHIPIÉLAGO DE LA REINA ADELAIDA
Punta Arenas
ISLA GRANDE DE TIERRA DEL FUEGO
ISLA
ESTA
8
ISLA SANTA INÉS
Ushuaia
Cabo
(Cape
Drake Passage

Scale 1 : 12 880 000

0   200   400   600 km

NTANAL

Uberlândia

Campo
Grande

Uberaba

BELO
HORIZONTE

Governador
Valadares

Ponta de Baleia

mbá

Vitória

2

São José
do Rio Prêto

Andradina

Juiz de Fora

20°

BRAZIL

Bauru

Campos

Y

Pedro Juan
Caballero

Campinas

Niteroi

Londrina

SÃO PAULO

RIO DE
JANEIRO

3

oncepción

Santos

Represa
de
Itaipu

Cascavel

CURITIBA

Tropic of Capricorn

Caaguazú

suncíón

nosa

Encarnación

Erechim

Florianópolis

25°

entes

Posadas

4

Uruguaiana

Santa
Maria

PORTO ALEGRE

Lagoa dos
Patos

Rivera

Pelotas

30°

URUGUAY

Lagoa
Mirim

Rio Grande

Negro

Embalse
del Río
Negro

Mercedes

MONTEVIDEO

5

OS
ES

Rio de la Plata

35°

Mar del Plata

6

$A\ T\ L\ A\ N\ T\ I\ C$

$O\ C\ E\ A\ N$

40°

7

45°

8

FALKLAND IS.
(U.K.)

D

Stanley

50°

EAST FALKLAND

$S\ C\ O\ T\ I\ A\ \ \ R\ I\ D\ G\ E$

SOUTH GEORGIA
(U.K.)

9

$S\ C\ O\ T\ I\ A\ \ \ \ S\ E\ A$

10

Europe

© Copyright

Scale 1 : 16 100 000

0   250   500   750   1000 km

BARENTS SEA

WHITE
SEA

2

80'

Ozero
Onezbskoye
(Lake Onega)

ngfors
lsinki)

Ladozbskoye
Ozero
(Lake Ladoga)

50'

R U S S I A

U R A L' S K I Y K H R E B E T
(U R A L M O U N T A I N S)

Ob

Pskovskoye Ozero
(Lake Peipus)

Rybinskoye
Vdkbr.

ius

MOSKVA
(MOSCOW)

3

70'

MINSK
LARUS

Volga

KAZAKHSTAN

KYYIV
(KIEV)

Volga

Aral'skoye
More
(Aral Sea)

UZBEKISTAN

40'

U K R A I N E

MOLDOVA

Chişinău

Sea of
Azov

C a s p i a n   S e a

Kara-
Bogaz-
Gol

TURKMENISTAN

Ashgabat
(Ashkhabad)

BUCURESTI
(BUCHAREST)

BLACK   SEA

Elbrus
5642

C A U C A S U S

GEORGIA

TBILISI
(TIFLIS)

ARMENIA

AZERBAIJAN

BAKI
(BAKU)

4

IA

YEREVAN

AZER.

ANKARA

T U R K E Y

TEHERAN
(TEHRAN)

60'

TOROS DAGLARI

30'

I R A N

CYPRUS

Levkósia
(Nicosia)

SYRIA

LEBANON

DIMASHQ
(DAMASCUS)

BAGDAD
(BAGHDAD)

BEYROUTH
(BEIRUT)

ISRAEL

I R A Q

Jerusalem

AMMAN

KUWAIT

Kuwait

OMAN

5

P e r s i a n   G u l f

ELQAHIRA
(CAIRO)

JORDAN

S A U D I   A R A B I A

BAHRAIN

UNITED
ARAB
EMIRATES

GYPT

QATAR

Belgium and the Netherlands

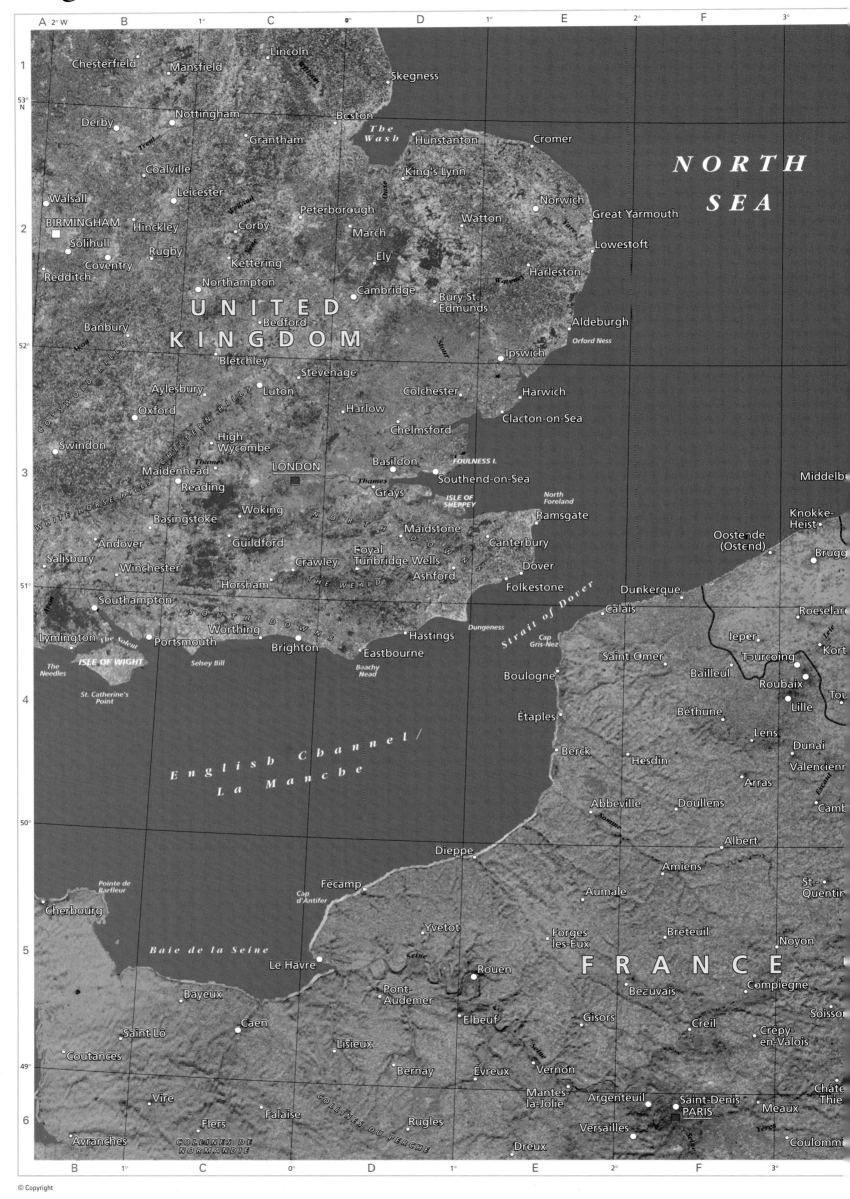

NORTH SEA

UNITED KINGDOM

FRANCE

NORTH DOWNS

THE WEALD

SOUTH DOWNS

English Channel / La Manche

Baie de la Seine

COLLINES DE NORMANDIE

COLLINES DU PERCHE

Strait of Dover

A 2° W   B   1°   C   0°   D   1°   E   2°   F   3°

Chesterfield   Mansfield   Lincoln   Skegness

53° N

Derby   Nottingham   Boston   The Wash   Hunstanton   Cromer

Grantham   King's Lynn   Norwich   Great Yarmouth

Coalville   Leicester   Watton   Lowestoft

Walsall   Peterborough   March   Harleston

BIRMINGHAM   Hinckley   Corby   Ely

Solihull   Rugby   Kettering   Cambridge   Bury St. Edmunds

Coventry   Northampton

Redditch   Aldeburgh   Orford Ness

Banbury   Bedford   Ipswich

52°   COTSWOLD HILLS   Bletchley   Stevenage   Colchester   Harwich

Aylesbury   Luton   Clacton-on-Sea

Oxford   CHILTERN HILLS   Harlow   Chelmsford

Swindon   High Wycombe   Basildon   FOULNESS I.

Maidenhead   LONDON   Southend-on-Sea   Middelb

WHITE HORSE HILLS   Reading   Thames   Grays   ISLE OF SHEPPEY   North Foreland   Knokke-Heist

Basingstoke   Woking   Maidstone   Ramsgate   Oostende (Ostend)

Andover   Guildford   Canterbury   Brugg

Salisbury   Royal Tunbridge Wells   Dover

51°   Winchester   Crawley   Ashford   Folkestone   Dunkerque   Roeselar

Horsham   Dungeness   Calais   Ieper   Kort

Southampton   Hastings   Cap Gris-Nez   Saint-Omer   Tourcoing

Lymington   The Solent   Worthing   Brighton   Eastbourne   Beachy Head   Boulogne   Bailleul   Roubaix

ISLE OF WIGHT   Portsmouth   Selsey Bill   Béthune   Lille

The Needles   St. Catherine's Point   Étaples   Lens   Dunai

4   Berck   Hesdin   Arras   Valencienr

Abbeville   Doullens   Camb

50°   Somme

Pointe de Barfleur   Dieppe   Albert

Cap d'Antifer   Fécamp   Amiens

Cherbourg   Aumale   St.-Quentin

Yvetot   Forges-les-Eux   Breteuil   Noyon

5   Le Havre   Seine   Rouen   FRANCE   Compiègne

Bayeux   Pont-Audemer   Beauvais   Soisso

Saint Lô   Caen   Elbeuf   Gisors   Creil   Crépy-en-Valois

Lisieux   Seine

49°   Coutances   Bernay   Évreux   Vernon   Mantes-la-Jolie   Argenteuil   Saint-Denis   Meaux   Châte Thie

Vire   Rugles   PARIS

6   Flers   Falaise   Versailles   Coulomm

Avranches   Dreux

B   1°   C   0°   D   1°   E   2°   F   3°

© Copyright

Scale 1 : 1 840 000

0   50   100 km

56

WADDENEILANDEN
JUIST
BORKUM MEMMERT
ROTTUMERPLAAT
SCHIERMONNIKOOG
AMELAND

H 4° 5° K L 8° M

Emden 1
Delfzijl Leer
Groningen Oldenburg Bremen
Leeuwarden Papenburg
Smallingerland Bassum 53°
Stadskanaal
Sneek Assen Cloppenburg
Heerenveen Meppen Diepholz 2
Emmen Quakenbrück Dümmer-
Den Helder Hoogeveen see
Noordoostpolder Hardenberg Lingen Minden
Heerhugowaard Hoorn Nordhorn Hase
Alkmaar Kampen Mittellandkanal
Lelystad Zwolle Almelo Rheine Osnabrück
Zaandam Raalte Enschede Herford
Haarlem Amsterdam Harderwijk Ahaus Teutoburger Wald Bielefeld 52°
Hilversum Apeldoorn Ems
Leiden Utrecht Münster Gütersloh
's-Gravenhage Gouda Ede Doetinchem Dülmen Paderborn
(Den Haag) Arnhem Bocholt
(The Hague) Nijmegen Hamm Lippstadt
Rotterdam Tiel Waal GERMANY
Gorinchem Maas Kleve Wesel Dortmund Möhne Marsberg 3
Dordrecht Goch Bochum
's-Hertogenbosch/ Oberhausen Essen Witten Meschede
Breda Den Bosch Duisburg Mülheim Hagen
Bergen Tilburg Venraij Krefeld Wuppertal Lüdenscheid Kahler Asten
op Zoom Deurne Düsseldorf Lennestadt
Goes Eindhoven Venlo Mönchen- Solingen 51°
Turnhout Weert gladbach Leverkusen Gummersbach Siegen
Lokeren Antwerpen Geel Peer Hückelhoven Marburg
Aalst Mechelen Hasselt Jülich KÖLN
Maastricht (COLOGNE)
BRUXELLES Aachen Düren Gießen 4
BRÜSSEL Tienen Liège Bonn
(BRUSSELS) Verviers Euskirchen
BELGIUM Halle Schleiden Neuwied Limburg
Mons Namur Huy Malmédy Hohe Acht Andernach Koblenz
Charleroi Prüm Daun Frankfurt
Rochefort Cochem Wiesbaden 50°
Couvin Bastogne Bitburg Simmern Mainz
Diekirch Darmstadt
Bertrix LUXEMBOURG Bad Kreuznach Bensheim
Charleville- Arlon Trier Erbeskopf Idar- Worms
Mézières Virton Luxembourg Oberstein Mannheim
Sedan Esch-sur-Alzett Sankt Ludwigshafen 5
Rethel Longuyon Wendel Kaiserslautern Landau
Buzancy Charleville- Saarbrücken
Mézières Thionville Pirmasens
Reims Metz Forbach Karlsruhe 49°
Suippes Verdun Sarreguemines
Châlons- Morhange Pforzheim
sur-Marne Vaubecourt Haguenau 6
Beaumont Baden-Baden
Nancy Sarrebourg

H 5° J 6° K 7° L 8° M

© Copyright

Scale 1 : 4 600 000

300 km

200

100

0

59

European Russia

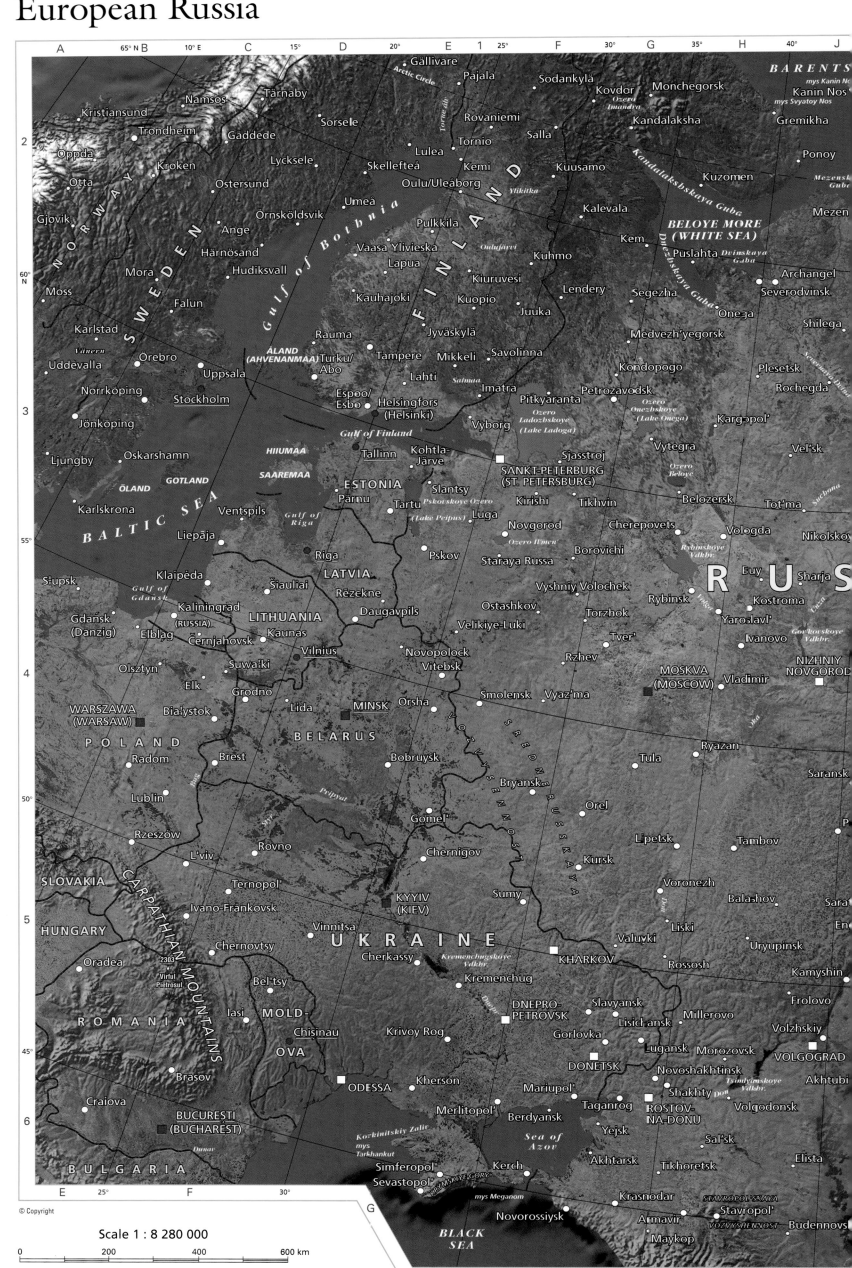

Scale 1 : 8 280 000

0   200   400   600 km

© Copyright

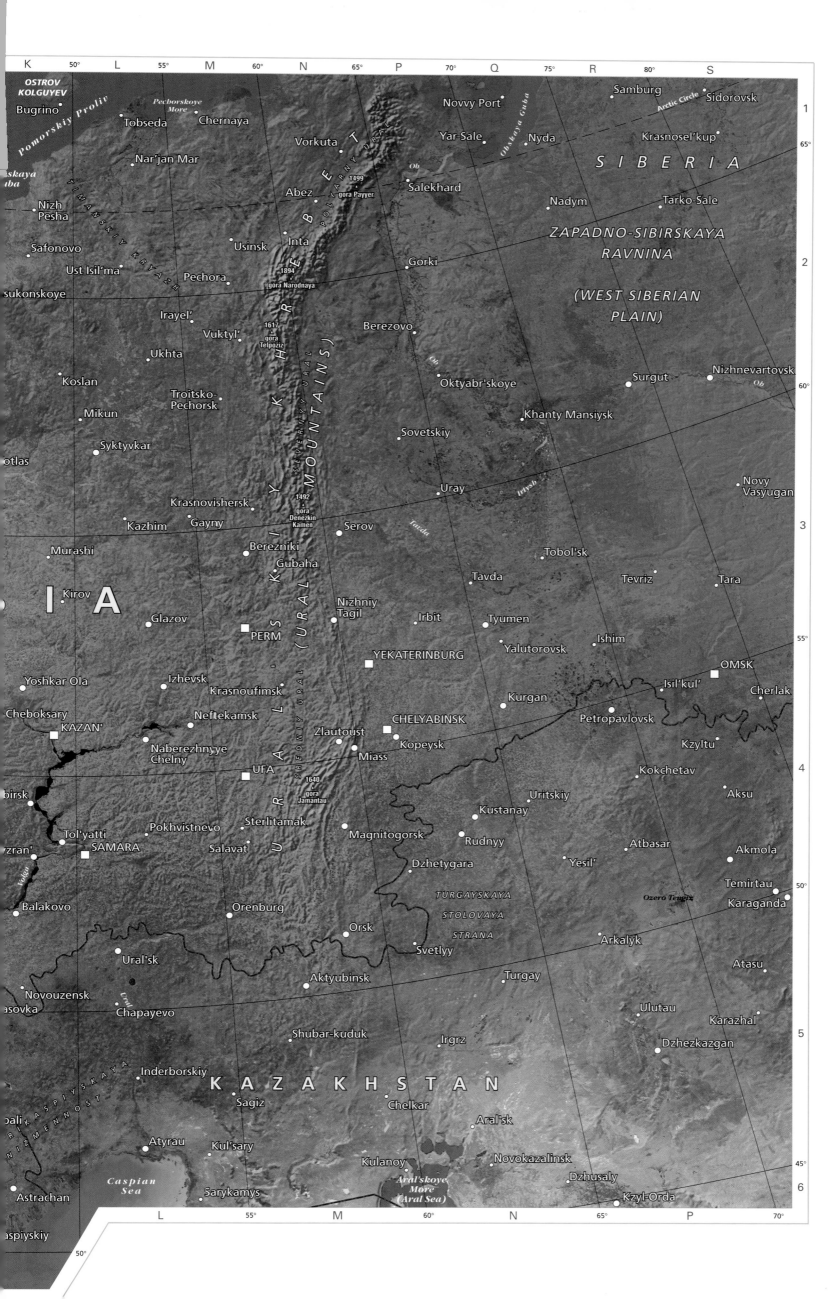

OSTROV
KOLGUYEV

Bugrino

Pomorskiy Proliv

Tobseda

Pechorskoye
More

Chernaya

Samburg

Arctic Circle

Sidorovsk

Nar'jan Mar

Vorkuta

Novvy Port

Obskaya Guba

Yar-Sale

Nyda

Krasnosel'kup

S I B E R I A

skaya
uba

Nizh
Pesha

Abez

gora Payyer
1499

Salekhard

Ob

Nadym

Tarko-Sale

65°

Safonovo

Usinsk

Inta

ZAPADNO-SIBIRSKAYA
RAVNINA

Ust Isil'ma

Pechora

gora Narodnaya
1894

Gorki

2

sukonskoye

Irayel'

Vuktyl'

gora
Telpoziz
1617

Berezovo

(WEST SIBERIAN
PLAIN)

Ukhta

Koslan

Troitsko-
Pechorsk

Ob

Oktyabr'skoye

Surgut

Nizhnevartovsk

60°

Mikun

Khanty Mansiysk

Ob

Syktyvkar

Sovetskiy

Novy
Vasyugan

otlas

Krasnovishersk

gora Denezkin
Kamen
1492

Uray

Irtysh

Kazhim

Gayny

Serov

Tavda

3

Murashi

Berezniki

Tobol'sk

Tevriz

Tara

Kirov

A

Gubaha

Tavda

Glazov

PERM

Nizhniy
Tagil

Irbit

Tyumen

Ishim

OMSK

55°

Yoshkar Ola

YEKATERINBURG

Yalutorovsk

Isil'kul'

Cherlak

Izhevsk

Krasnoufimsk

Kurgan

Petropavlovsk

Cheboksary

Neftekamsk

Zlautoust

CHELYABINSK

Kzyltu

KAZAN'

Kopeysk

Kokchetav

Naberezhnyye
Chelny

Miass

Aksu

birsk

UFA

gora
Jamantau
1640

Uritskiy

Kokchetav

4

Tol'yatti

Pokhvistnevo

Sterlitamak

Kustanay

Atbasar

Akmola

zran'

SAMARA

Salavat

Magnitogorsk

Rudnyy

Ozero Tengiz

Temirtau

50°

Balakovo

Orenburg

Dzhetygara

'Yesil'

Karaganda

Orsk

TURGAYSKAYA
STOLOVAYA
STRANA

Arkalyk

Atasu

Ural'sk

Svetlyy

Novouzensk

Aktyubinsk

Turgay

Ulutau

Karazhal

asovka

Chapayevo

Ural

Dzhezkazgan

5

Shubar-kuduk

Irgrz

KAZAKHSTAN

Inderborskiy

ali

Sagiz

Chelkar

Aral'sk

Novokazalinsk

Atyrau

Kul'sary

Kulanoy

Dzhusaly

45°

aspiyskiy

Caspian
Sea

Sarykamys

Aral'skoye
More
(Aral Sea)

Kzyl-Orda

6

Astrachan

61

Poland, Czech Republic, Slovakia and Hungary

© Copyright

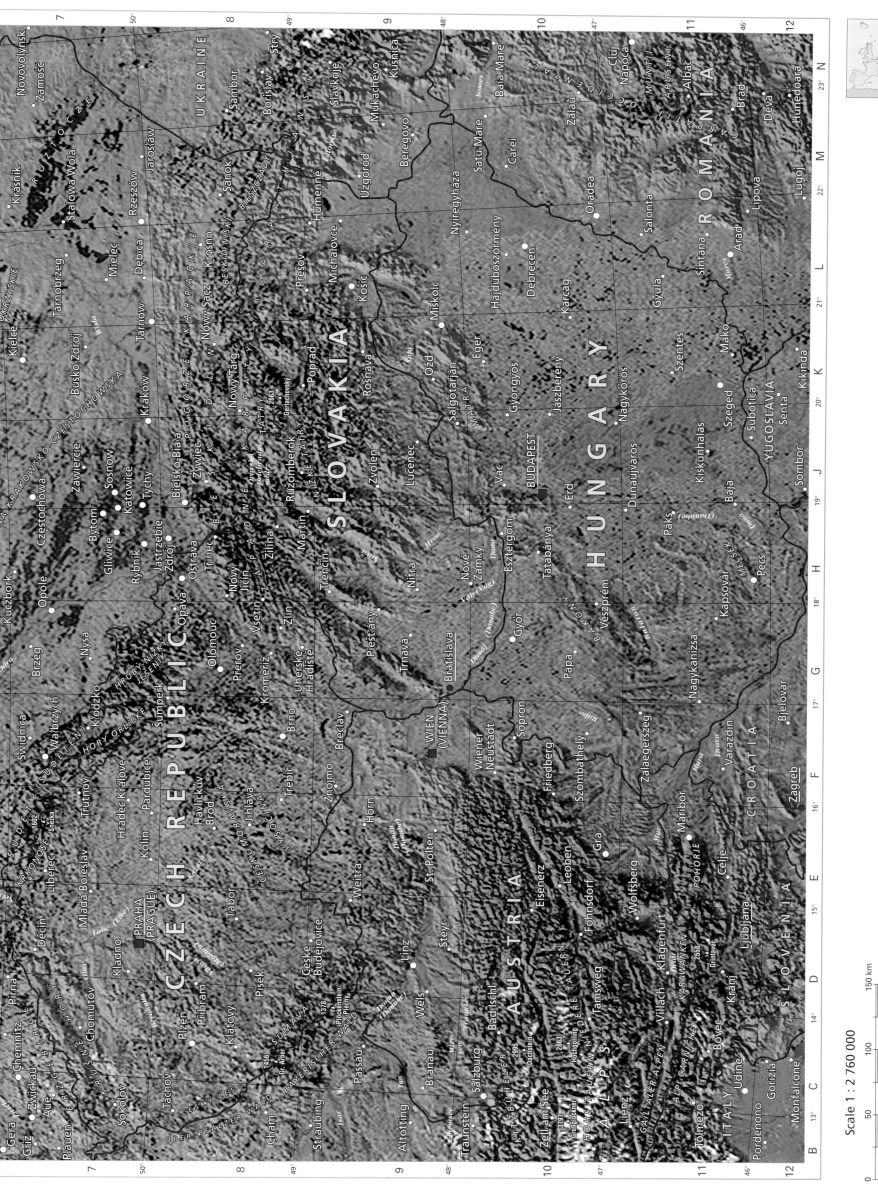

Scale 1 : 2 760 000

150 km

50   100

0   50

63

Germany

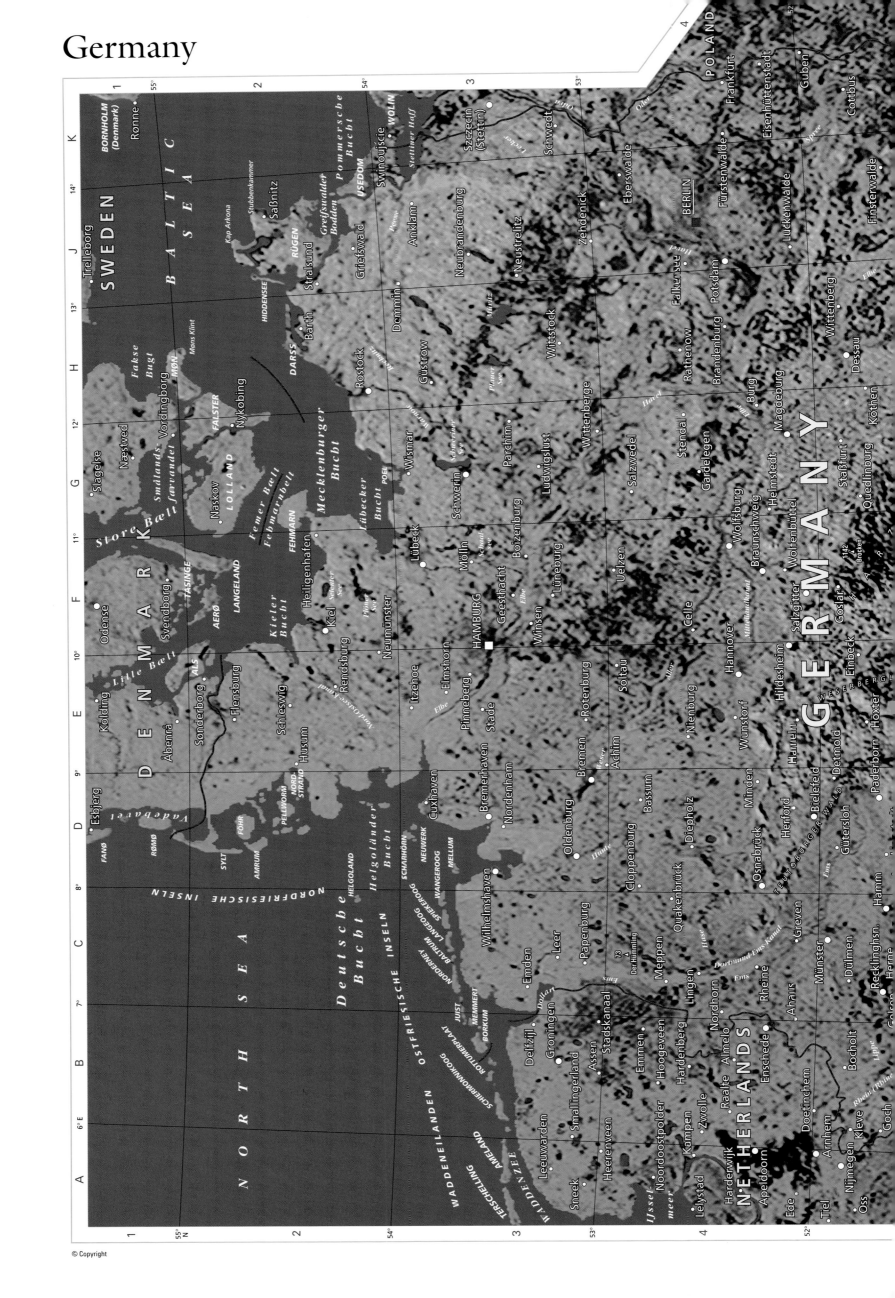

Scale 1 : 2 070 000

65

United Kingdom and Ireland

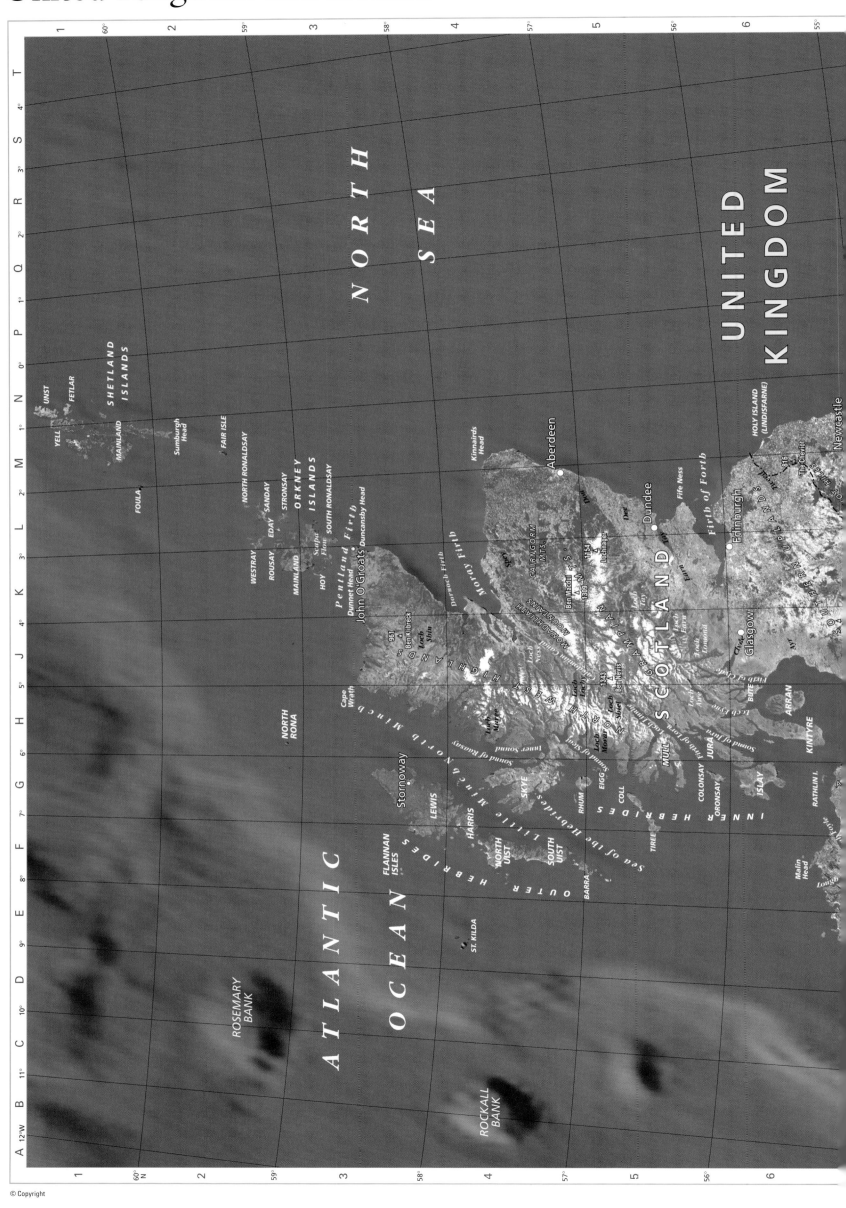

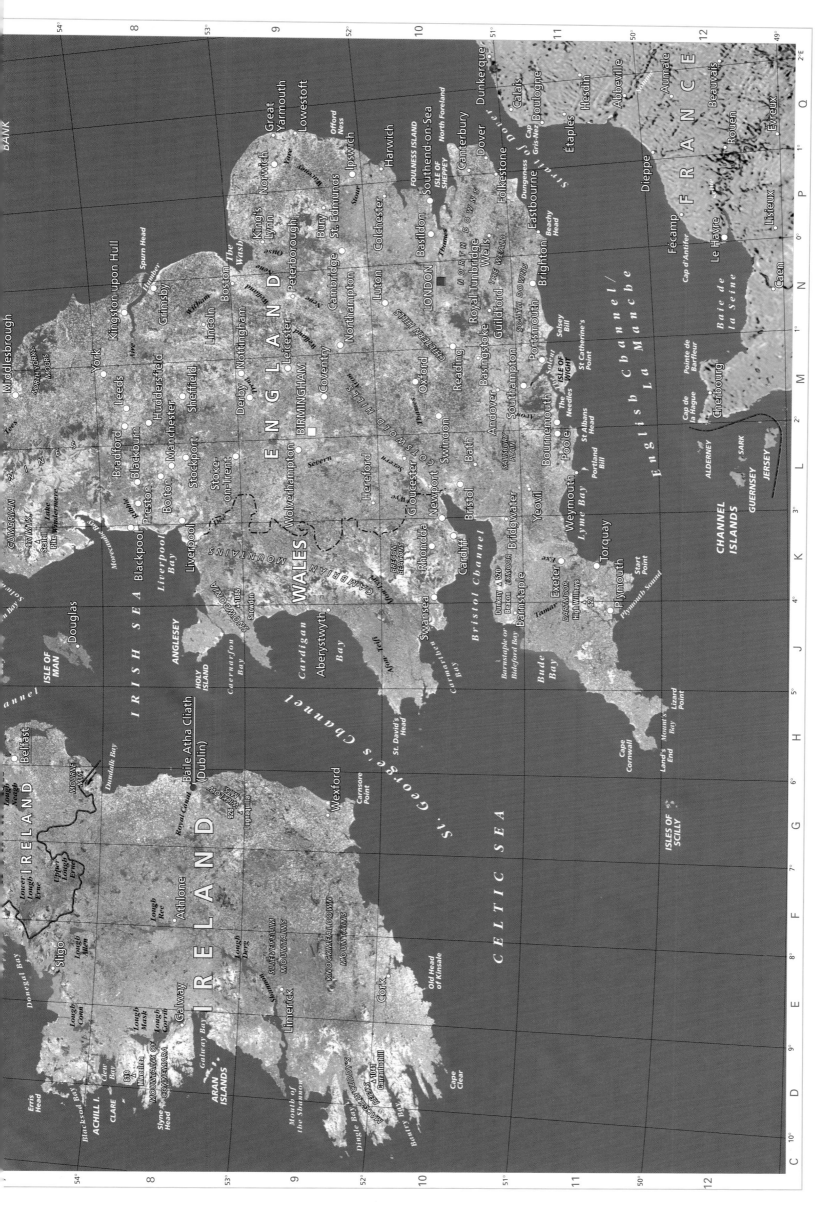

Scale 1 : 2 760 000

0   50   100   150 km

France

© Copyright

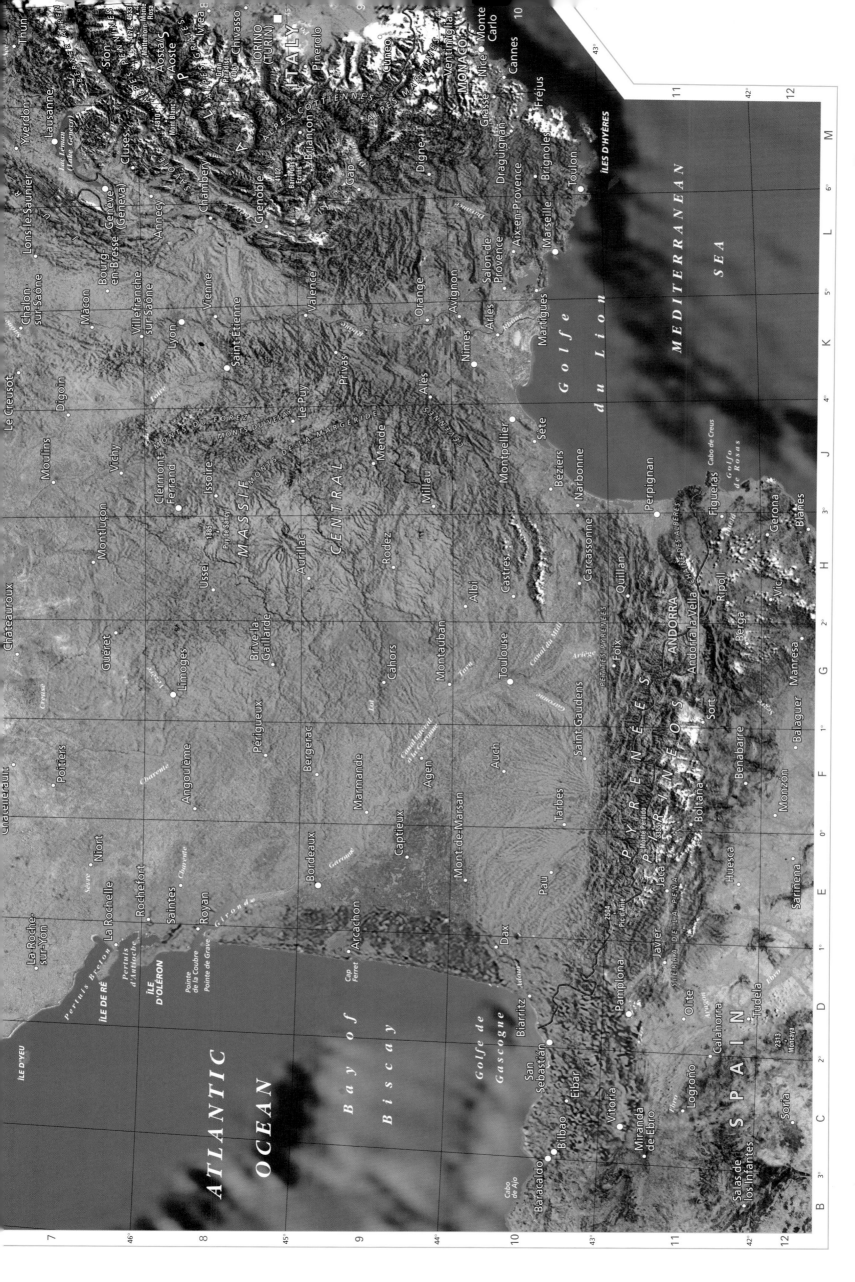

Scale 1 : 2 760 000

© Copyright

Spain and Portugal

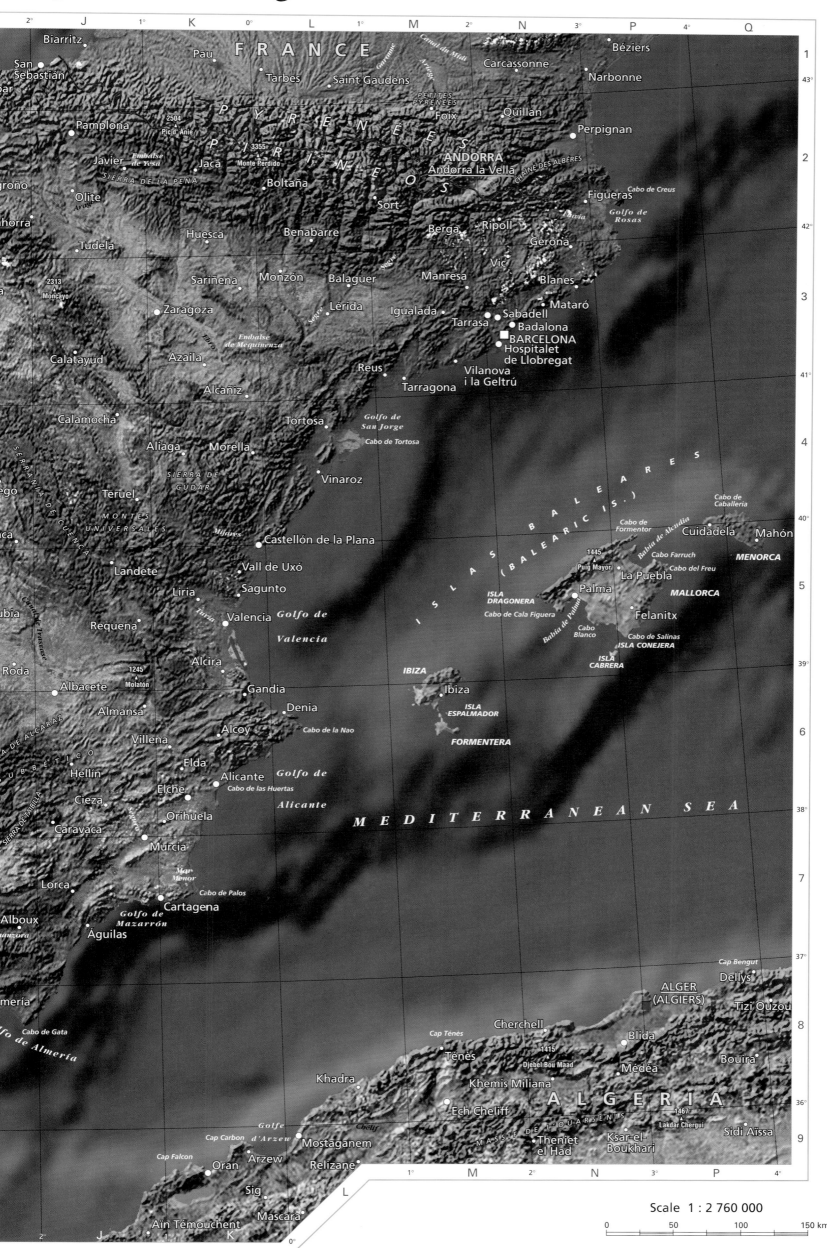

Scale 1 : 2 760 000

0   50   100   150 km

The Alpine States

Scale 1 : 2 070 000

0   50   100   150 km

© Copyright

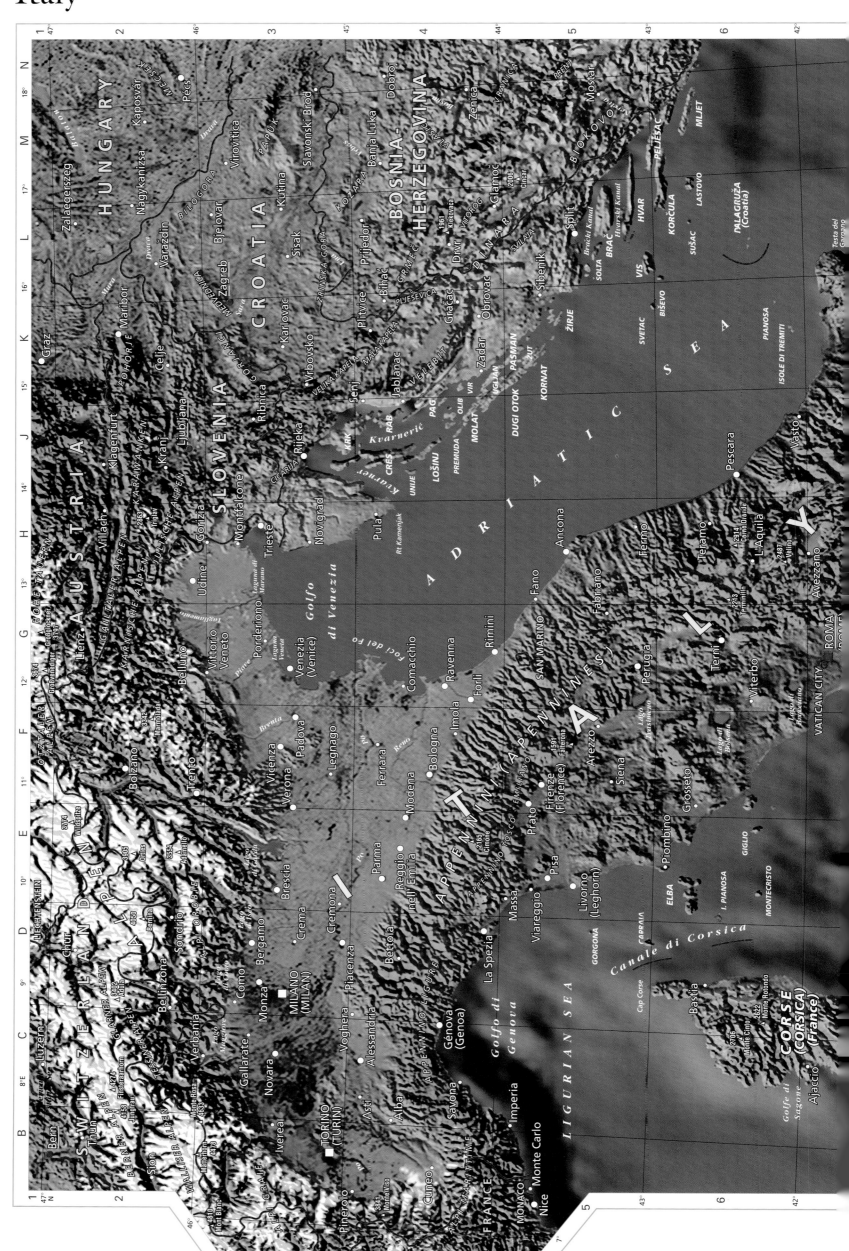

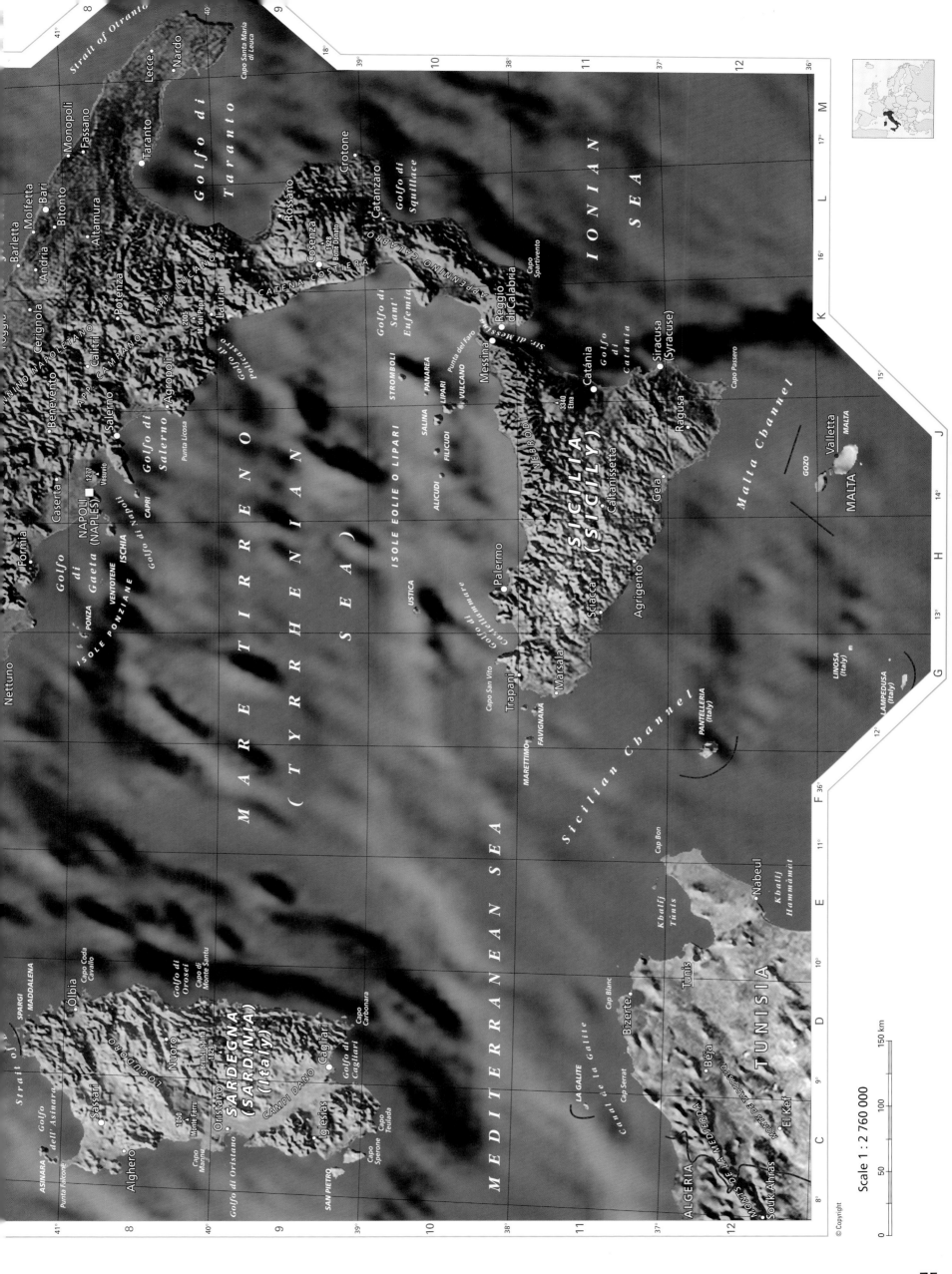

Scale 1 : 2 760 000

0   50   100   150 km

© Copyright

75

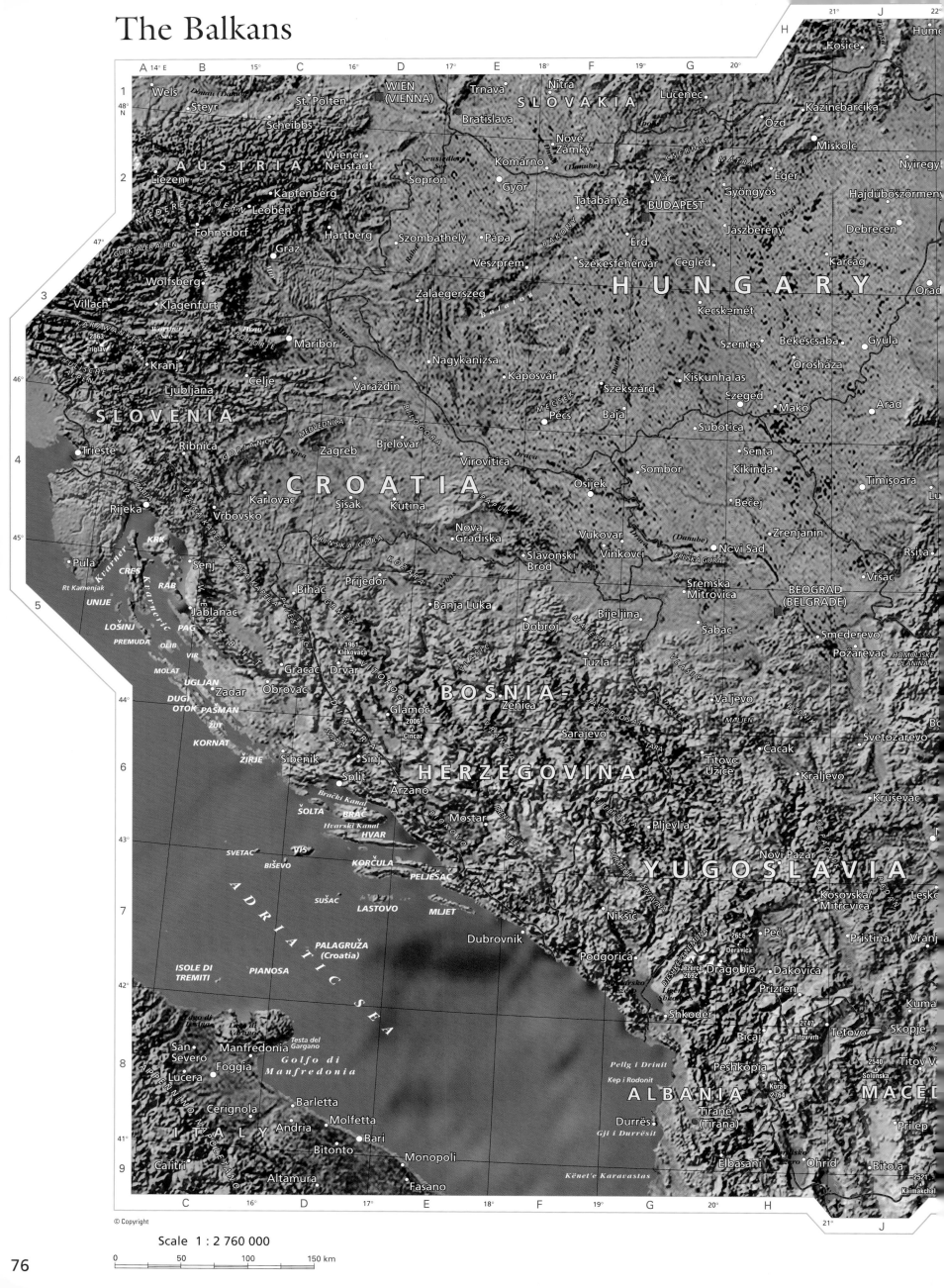

The Balkans

Scale 1 : 2 760 000

© Copyright

0   50   100   150 km

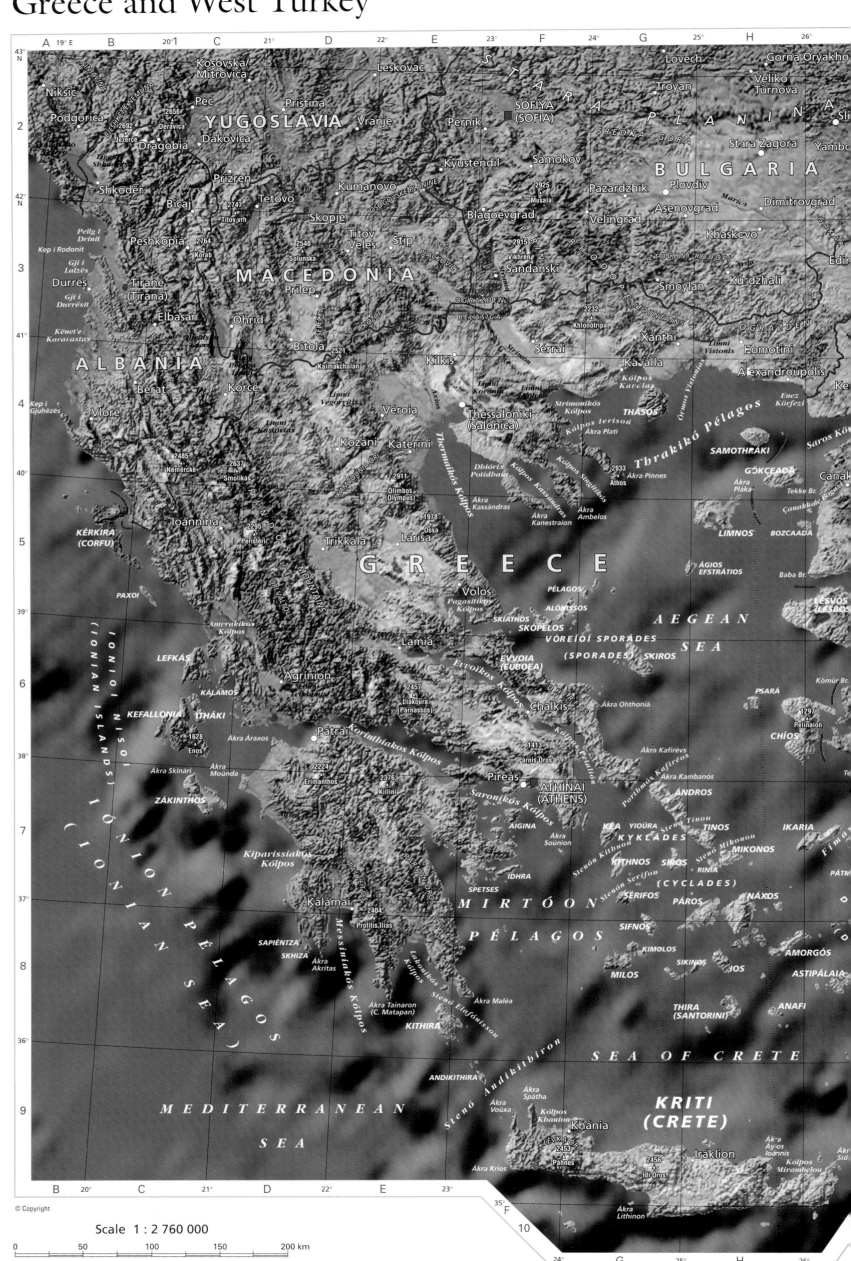

Scale 1 : 2 760 000

0   50   100   150   200 km

© Copyright

Turkey

Scale 1 : 4 600 000

| 0 | 100 | 200 | 300 km |

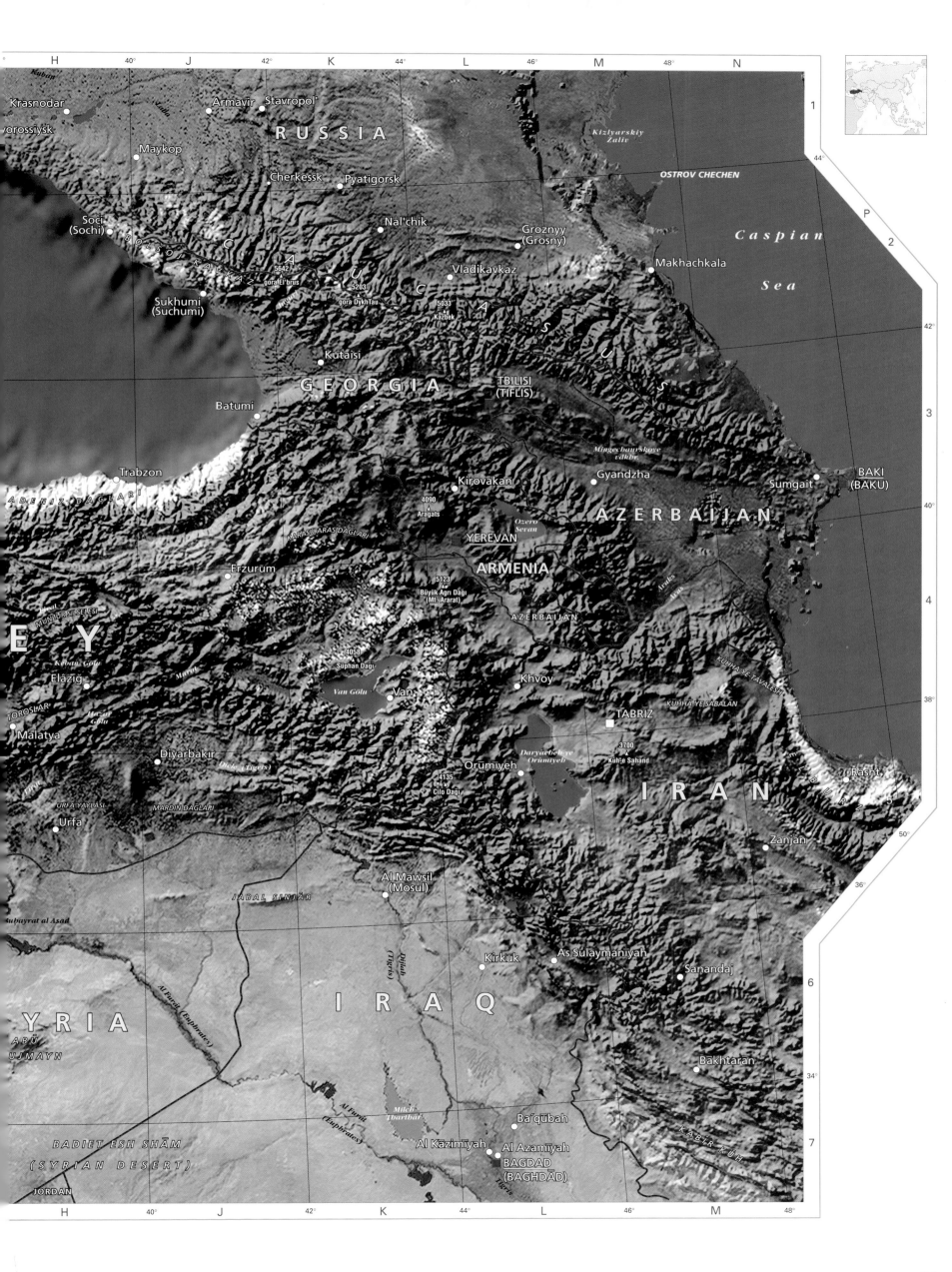

Krasnodar
orossiysk
Maykop
Armavir Stavropol'
RUSSIA
Cherkessk Pyatigorsk
Soči
(Sochi)
BOLŠO
KAVKAZ
Nal'chik
5642
goraEl'brus
Vladikavkaz
Groznyy
(Grosny)
OSTROV CHECHEN
Makhachkala
Sukhumi
(Suchumi)
5203
gora DykhTau
C
A
U
C
A
S
U
S
Caspian
Sea
5033
Kazbek
Kutaisi
GEORGIA
TBILISI
(TIFLIS)
Mingechaurskoye
vdkhr.
Batumi
Gyandzha
Sumgait
BAKI
(BAKU)
Trabzon
ADENIZ DAĞLARI
Kirovakan
AZERBAIJAN
4090
Aragats
Ozero
Sevan
KARASU ARAS DAĞLARI
YEREVAN
ARMENIA
Erzurum
5123
Büyük Ağrı Dağı
(Mt. Ararat)
AZERBAIJAN
Aras
Aras
EY
Frat
MUNZUR SILSELESI
Keban Gölü
4058
Süphan Dağı
KÜHHA-YE TAVALESH
Elâziğ
Murat
Van Gölü
Van
Khvoy
KÜHHA-YE SABALAN
TOROSLAR
Hazar Gölü
Malatya
Diyarbakır
Dicle (Tigris)
4135
Cilo Dağı
TABRIZ
3700
Kuh-e Sahand
IRAN
Rasht
Orūmīyeh
Daryaebeh-ye
Orūmīyeh
Urfa
URFA YAYLASI
MARDIN DAĞLARI
Zanjān
Firat
Al Mawsil
(Mosul)
JABAL SINJĀR
uhayrat al Asad
Kirkuk
As Sulaymānīyah
Sanandaj
YRIA
ABŪ
UJMAYN
Dijlah (Tigris)
IRAQ
Bākhtarān
KABIR KUH
Al Furāt
(Euphrates)
Milch
Tharthār
Ba'qūbah
BADIET ESH SHĀM
(SYRIAN DESERT)
Al Furāt
(Euphrates)
Al Kazimīyah
Al Azamīyah
BAGDAD
(BAGHDAD)
JORDAN
Tigris

Middle East

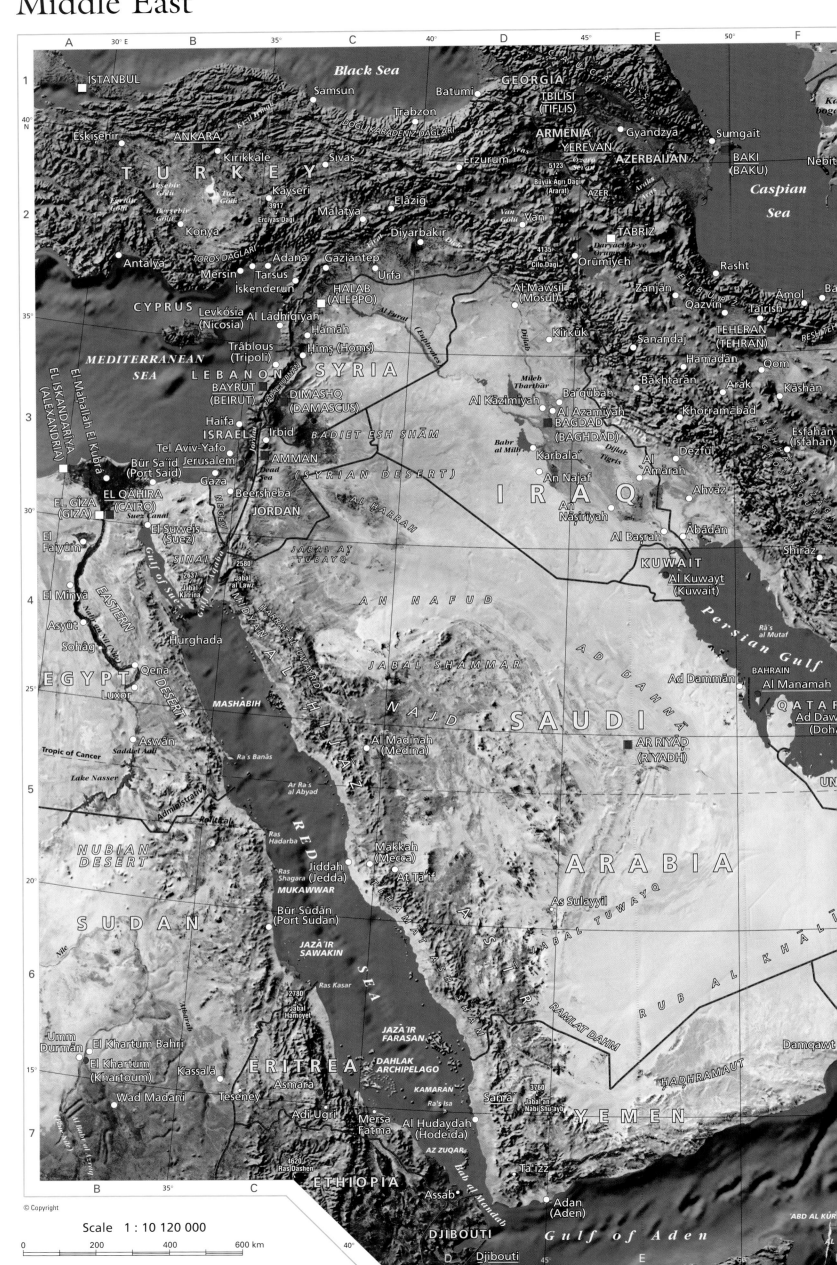

Black Sea

GEORGIA
TBILISI
(TIFLIS)

İSTANBUL
Samsun
Batumi
Trabzon
ARMENIA
YEREVAN
Gyandzya
Sumgait

Eskişehir
ANKARA
Kırıkkale
Sivas
Erzurum
5123
Büyük Ağrı Dağı
(Ararat)
AZERBAIJAN
BAKI
(BAKU)
Nebit

T U R K E Y
Konya
Kayseri
3917
Erciyas Dağı
Malatya
Elâzığ
Diyarbakır
Van Gölü
Van
4135
Cilo Dağı
Orūmīyeh
Daryācheh-ye
Orūmīyeh
TABRIZ
Rasht

Antalya
Mersin
Tarsus
Adana
Gaziantep
Urfa
Al Mawşil
(Mosul)
Zanjān
Āmol

CYPRUS
İskenderun
ḤALAB
(ALEPPO)
Al Ladhiqiyah
Ḥamāh
Kirkūk
Sanandaj
Qazvīn
Tajrīsh
TEHERAN
(TEHRAN)

MEDITERRANEAN
SEA
LEBANON
S Y R I A
Al Furat
(Euphrates)
Dijlah
Hamadān
Qom

Trâblous
(Tripoli)
Ḥimş (Homs)
Bā'qūbah
Bākhtarān
Arāk
Kāshān

BAYRŪT
(BEIRUT)
DIMASHQ
(DAMASCUS)
BĀDIET ESH SHĀM
Mileh Tharthâr
Al Kāzimīyah
Al Azamīyah
BAGDAD
(BAGHDĀD)
Khorramābād
Eşfahān
(Isfahan)

Haifa
Irbid
Bahr al Milh
Karbalā'
Dezfūl

ISRAEL
Tel Aviv-Yafo
AMMAN
(SYRIAN DESERT)
I R A Q
Al 'Amārah
Ahvāz

Jerusalem
Dead Sea
An Najaf
An Nāşirīyah

Būr Sa'īd
(Port Said)
Gaza
Beersheba
JORDAN
AL HARRAH
Al Başrah
Ābādān
Shirāz

EL ISKANDARÎYA
(ALEXANDRIA)
EL QĀHIRA
(CAIRO)
EL GÎZA
(GIZA)
Suez Canal
El Suweis
(Suez)
KUWAIT
Al Kuwayt
(Kuwait)

El Faiyûm
SINAI
JABAL AŢ TUBAYQ
Rā's al Mutaf

El Minyâ
2637
Jabal Katrina
2580
Jabal al Lawz
A N   N A F U D
Persian Gulf

Asyût
EASTERN
GULF OF AQABA
AD DAHNĀ
BAHRAIN
QATAR

Sohâg
DESERT
JABAL SHAMMAR
Ad Dammān
Al Manamah
Ad Daw
(Doh

Qena
Hurghada
N A J D
S A U D I

E G Y P T
Luxor
MASHĀBIH
HIJAZ

Aswân
Saddel Aali
Tropic of Cancer
Ra's Banâs
Al Madīnah
(Medina)
AR RIYĀḌ
(RIYADH)

Lake Nasser
Ar Ra's al Abyad
A R A B I A

Administrative
Political
RED
Ras Hadarba
As Sulayyil

NUBIAN DESERT
Ras Shagara
MUKAWWAR
Makkah
(Mecca)
Jiddah
(Jedda)
At Ţā'if
JABAL ŢUWAYQ

Būr Sūdān
(Port Sudan)
SEA

S U D A N
JAZĀ'IR SAWAKIN
RUB AL KHĀLI

2780
Jabal Hamoyet
JAZĀ'IR FARASAN
RAMLAT DAHM

Umm Durmân
El Khartum Bahri
Ras Kasar
DAHLAK ARCHIPELAGO
Damqawt

El Khartum
(Khartoum)
Kassalâ
ERITREA
KAMARAN
Ra's Isa
3760
Jabal an Nabi Shu'ayb
San'ā
ḤAḌHRAMAUT

Wad Madani
Teseney
Asmara
AZ ZUQAR
Y E M E N

Adi Ugri
Mersa Fatma
Al Hudaydah
(Hodeida)
Ta'izz

4620
Ras Dashen
ETHIOPIA
Assab
Bab al Mandab
Adan
(Aden)
'ABD AL KŪR

DJIBOUTI
Djibouti
Gulf of Aden

© Copyright

Scale   1 : 10 120 000

0   200   400   600 km

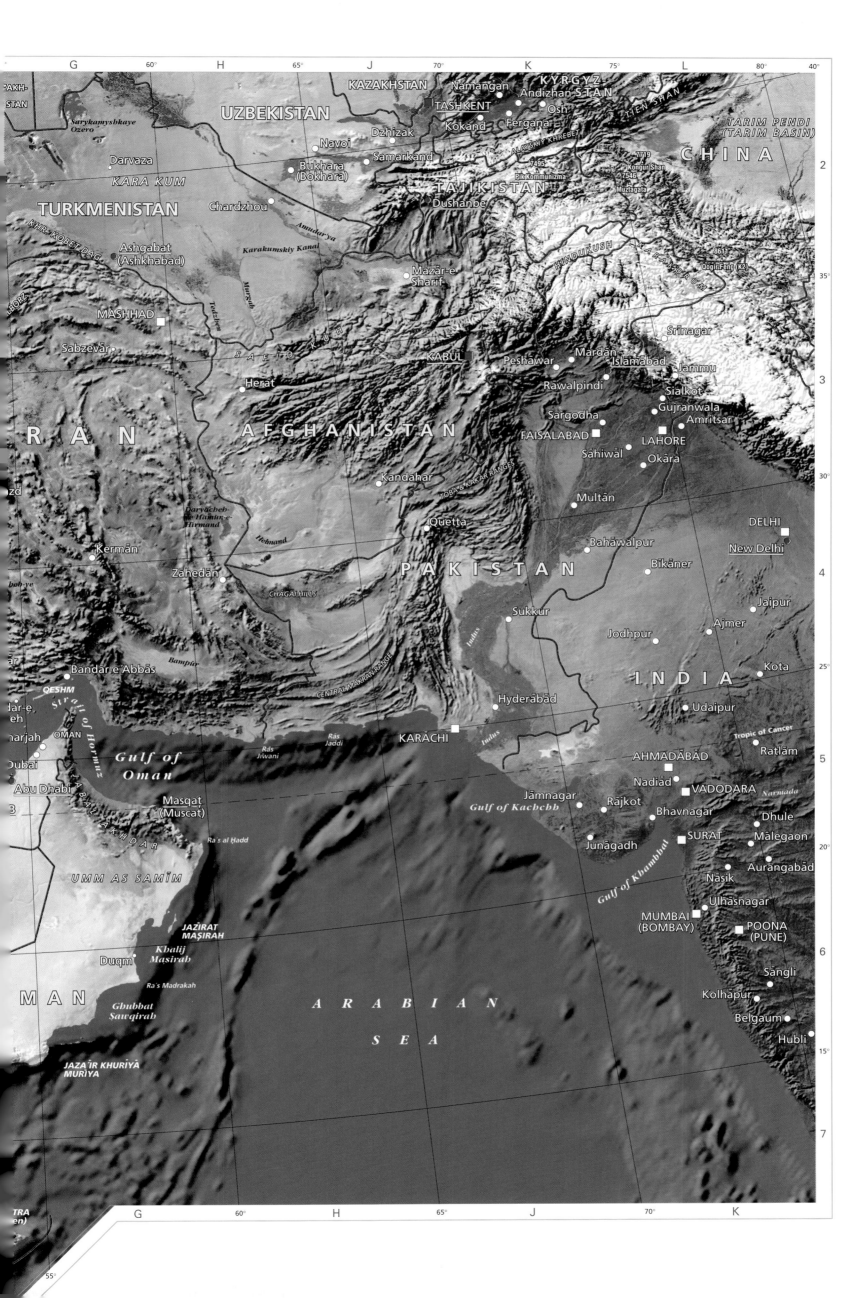

KAZAKHSTAN

UZBEKISTAN

KYRGYZ-
Namangan STAN
TASHKENT   Andizhan
Osh

Dzhizak   Kokand   Fergana

Navoi

Sarykamyshkaye
Ozero

Darvaza

Samarkand

TIEN SHAN

CHINA

TARIM PENDI
(TARIM BASIN)

KARA KUM

TURKMENISTAN

Chardzhou

Amudarya

Karakumskiy Kanal

TAJIKISTAN

7495
Pik Kommunizma

7719
Kongur Shan
7546
Muztagata

2

Ashgabat
(Ashkhabad)

KHR. KOPET DAG

Murgab

Tedzhen

Mazār-e
Sharif

HINDU KUSH

KARAKORUM

8611
Qogir Feng (K2)

35°

MASHHAD

Sabzevār

HERAT

Herāt

KABUL

Peshawar
Rāwalpindi

Srinagar

Mardān
Islāmābād
Jammu

Sialkot
Gujranwala
Amritsar

3

I R A N

A F G H A N I S T A N

Sargodha

FAISALĀBĀD

LAHORE

Sāhiwāl
Okāra

yd

Kermān

Zāhedān

Kandahar

TOBA & KAKAR RANGES

Quetta

Helmand

Daryācheh-
ye Hāmūn-e
Hirmand

CHAGAI HILLS

P A K I S T A N

Multān

Bahāwalpur

DELHI

New Delhi

Bīkāner

Jaipur

30°

4

bah-ye

Bampūr

Sukkur

Indus

Jodhpur

Ajmer

Kota

25°

Bandar-e Abbās

QESHM

Strait of Hormuz

Central Makran Range

Hyderābād

I N D I A

Udaipur

harjah
OMAN

eh

Dubai

Ras
Jaddi

Ras
Jiwani

KARĀCHI

Indus

Tropic of Cancer

AHMADĀBĀD

Ratlām

5

Abu Dhabi

JABAL AKHDAR

Masqat
(Muscat)

Ras
Jiwani

Jāmnagar

Gulf of Kachchh

Rajkot

Nadiād
VADODARA

Bhavnagar

Narmada

Dhule

3

Gulf of
Oman

Ra's al Ḥadd

Junāgadh

Gulf of Khambhat

SURAT

Mālegaon

Aurangābād

20°

UMM AS SAMĪM

Nāsik

Ulhāsnagar

JAZĪRAT
MAṢĪRAH

MUMBAI
(BOMBAY)

POONA
(PUNE)

6

M A N

Duqm

Khalīj
Maṣīrah

Sāngli

Ra's Madrakah

Kolhapur

Ghubbat
Ṣawqirah

A R A B I A N

S E A

Belgaum

Hubli

15°

JAZĀ'IR KHURĪYĀ
MURĪYA

7

TRA
en)

55°

Israel, Jordan and Lebanon

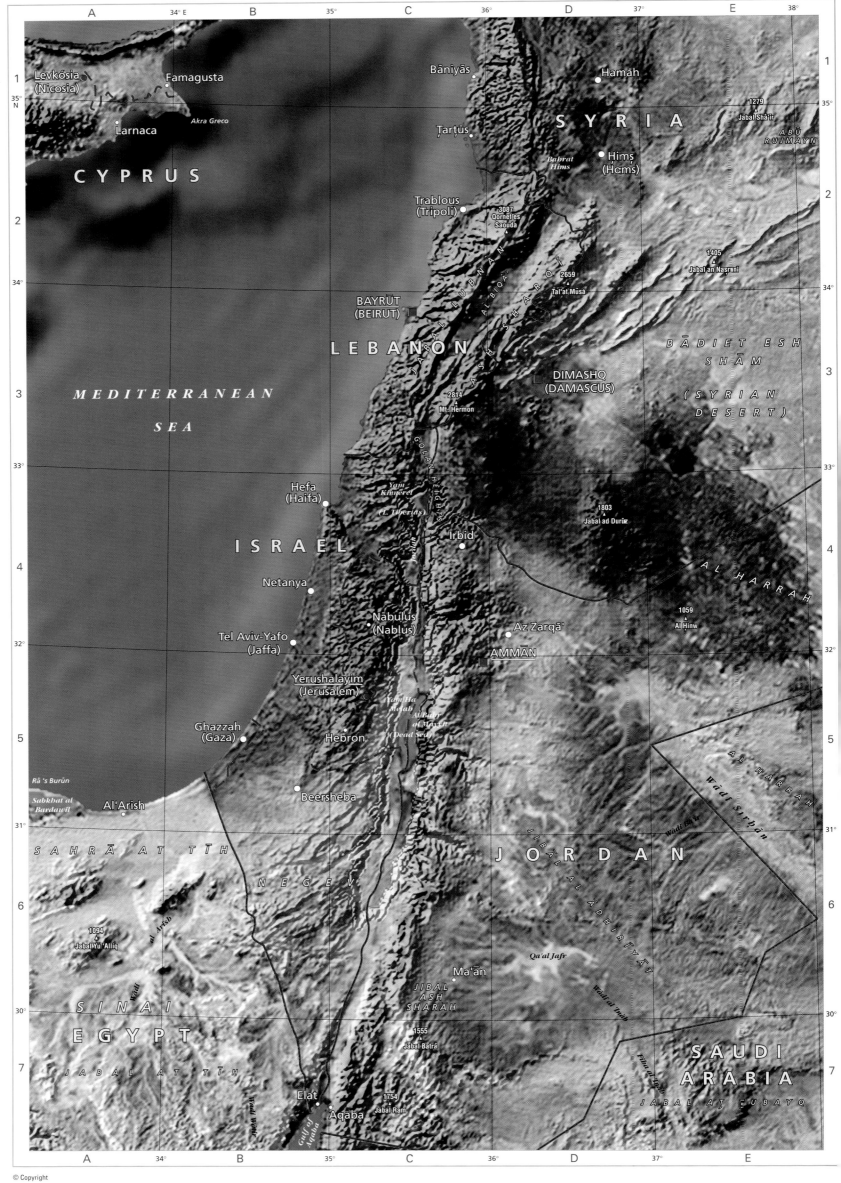

Levkósia (Nicosia)

Famagusta

Larnaca

Akra Greco

CYPRUS

Bāniyās

Ṭarṭūs

Hamāh

SYRIA

Jabal Shā'ir 1279

ABŪ RUJMAYN

Hims (Hcms)

Baḥrat Hims

Trablous (Tripoli)

3087 *Qornet es Saouda*

2659 *Tal'at Mūsá*

1405 *Jabal an Nasrāni*

BAYRŪT (BEIRUT)

JABAL LUBNĀN

ASH SHARQĪ

AL BIQĀ'

DIMASHQ (DAMASCUS)

BĀDIET ESH SHĀM

(SYRIAN DESERT)

LEBANON

MEDITERRANEAN SEA

2814 Mt. Hermon

GOLAN HEIGHTS

Hefa (Haifa)

Yam Kinneret (L. Tiberias)

1803 *Jabal ad Durūz*

AL ḤARRAH

ISRAEL

Irbid

Netanya

1059 *Al Hinw*

Nābulus (Nablus)

Az Zarqā'

AL ḤARRAH

Tel Aviv-Yafo (Jaffa)

AMMĀN

Yerushaláyim (Jerusalem)

Yam Ha Melaḥ

Al Baḥr al Mayyit (Dead Sea)

Ghazzah (Gaza)

Hebron

Wādī Sirḥān

Beersheba

Rā 's Burūn

Sabkhat al Bardawil

Al'Arish

JORDAN

SAHRĀ AT TĪH

Wādī Ghīr

NEGEV

JIBĀL AL 'ADHIRĪYĀT

al 'Arīsh

1094 *Jabal Yu'Alliq*

Qa'al Jafr

Ma'ān

SINAI

JIBAL ASH SHARAH

Wādī al Tmah

EGYPT

1555 *Jabal Bātrā*

SAUDI ARABIA

JABAL AT ṬUBAYQ

JABAL AT TĪH

Elat

1754 *Jabal Ram*

Āqaba

Gulf of Aqaba

© Copyright

Scale 1 : 2 300 000

0   50   100   150 km

The Gulf States

Scale 1 : 4 600 000

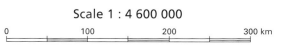

0   100   200   300 km

Africa

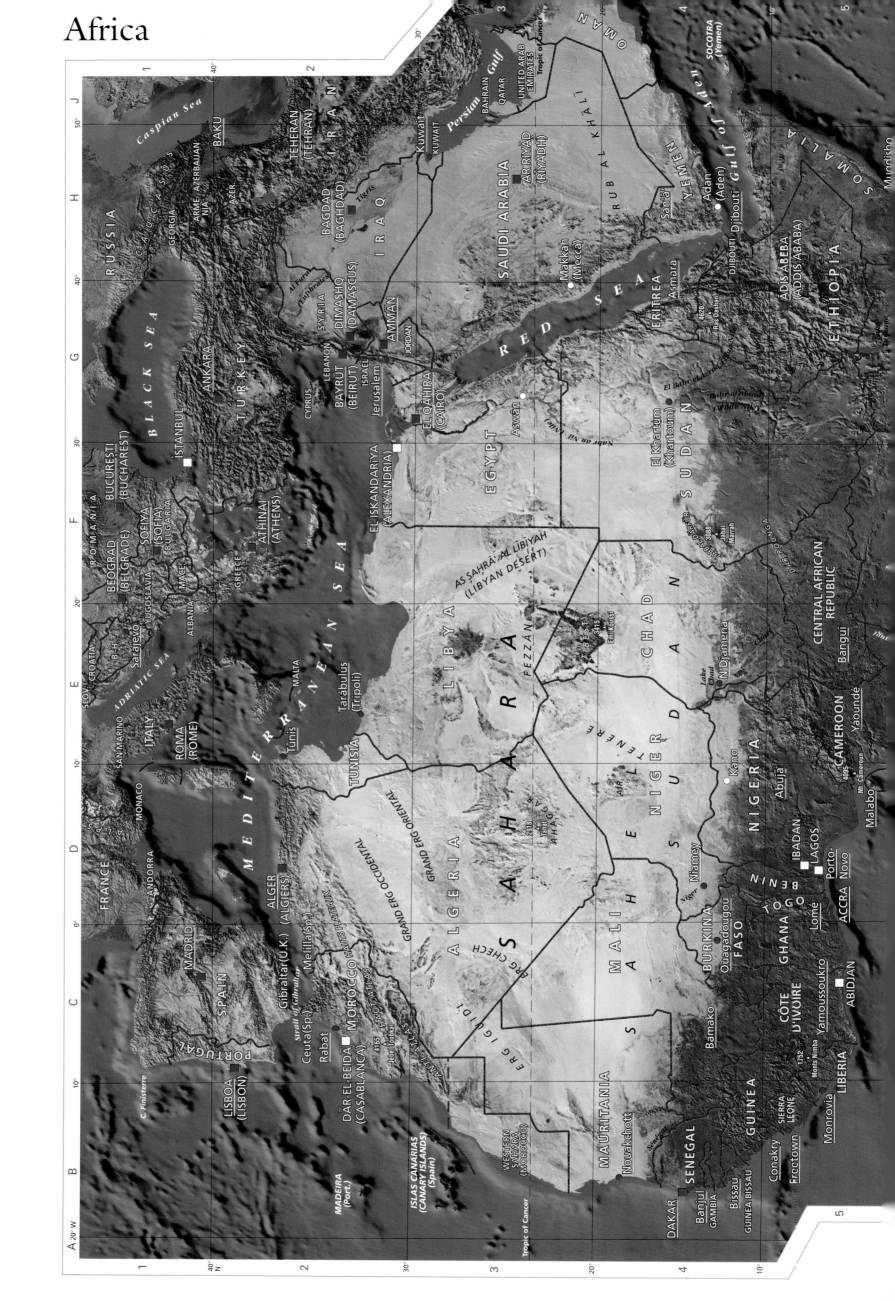

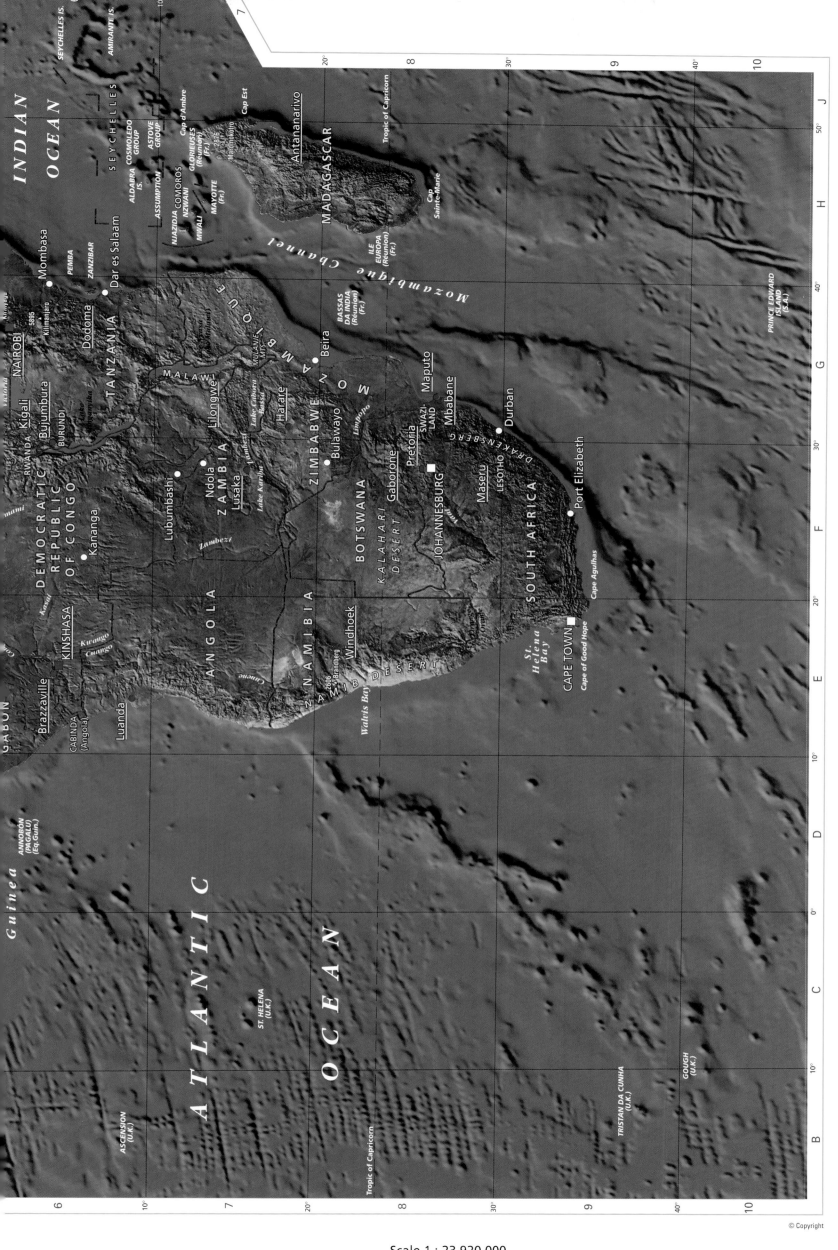

INDIAN OCEAN

SEYCHELLES IS.

AMIRANTE IS.

SEYCHELLES

COSMOLEDO GROUP
ALDABRA IS.
ASSUMPTION
ASTOVE GROUP

Cap d'Ambre

Cap Est

NJAZIDJA COMOROS
NZWANI
MWALI
MAYOTTE (Fr.)

GLORIEUSES (Réunion)
2876 Marotrokotra

Antananarivo

MADAGASCAR

Cap Sainte-Marie

Mombasa
PEMBA
ZANZIBAR
Dar es Salaam

Dodoma

NAIROBI
5895 Kilimanjaro

Kigali
Bujumbura
RWANDA
BURUNDI

TANZANIA

MALAWI

Lilongwe

Harare

ZIMBABWE

Bulawayo

Beira

ILE EUROPA (Réunion) (Fr.)

BASSAS DA INDIA (Réunion) (Fr.)

MOZAMBIQUE

Mozambique Channel

PRINCE EDWARD ISLAND (S.A.)

Lake Tanganyika
MULANJE MTS.
Lake Cabora Bassa

Limpopo

Maputo

Mbabane
SWAZI-LAND

Durban

DRAKENSBERG

DEMOCRATIC REPUBLIC OF CONGO

Lubumbashi

Kananga

KINSHASA

Ndola
ZAMBIA
Lusaka

Lake Kariba

Zambezi

Pretoria

Gaborone

BOTSWANA

JOHANNESBURG

KALAHARI DESERT

Maseru
LESOTHO

SOUTH AFRICA

Port Elizabeth

Cape Agulhas

Brazzaville

GABON

CABINDA (Angola)

Luanda

ANGOLA

NAMIBIA

Windhoek
2606 Brandberg

Cunene

Kwango
Cuango

Kasai

Okavango

Orange

NAMIB DESERT

Walvis Bay

St. Helena Bay

CAPE TOWN
Cape of Good Hope

ATLANTIC

OCEAN

Guinea

ANNOBÓN (PAGALU) (Eq.Guin.)

ASCENSION (U.K.)

ST. HELENA (U.K.)

TRISTAN DA CUNHA (U.K.)

GOUGH (U.K.)

Tropic of Capricorn

Tropic of Capricorn

Scale 1 : 23 920 000

0   500   1000   1500 km

Northwest Africa

Açores (Azores) (Port.)

CORVO
FLORES
GRACIOSA
SÃO JORGE
FAIAL
PICO
TERCEIRA
SÃO MIGUEL
FORMIGAS
SANTA MARIA

Funchal
MADEIRA (Port.)
PORTO SANTO

ILHAS SELVAGENS (Port.)

LA PALMA
GOMERA
TENERIFE
Santa Cruz
3710
Pico de Teide
GRAN CANARIA
HIERRO
Las Palmas
ISLAS CANARIAS (CANARY ISLANDS) (Spain)
LANZAROTE
FUERTEVENTURA
Cap Juby

Cádiz   Malag
Gibra
Strait of Gibraltar (U
Tanger   Ceuta (
(Tangier)   Tétou
Kéritra   Fès   Ta
Salé   Meknès   3340
Rabat   Jbel Bou
DĀR-EL-BEIDĀ   Naceur (
(CASABLANCA)   MOROCC
Ras
Beddouza   Beni Mellal   ATLAS
Safi   Marrakech   Er Rac
Cap   4165   407
Sim   HIGH
Jebel Toubkal   Irhil M'Goun
Cap   Agadir   Ouarzazate
Rhir   Taroudannt
ANTI-ATLAS
Guelmine   JEBEL OUARKZIZ
Tan-Tan   Sebkha de
Tindouf
Saguia el-Hamra   Tindouf   M'CHERRAH
Laâyoune   Es Semara   ERG IGUIDI   EL EGLAB
Cabo Bojador   Aïn Ben Tili   ERG CHEC
Tropic of Cancer   Bir Mogreïn
Ad Dakhla   Sebkhet Oumm   MDENNAH
Punta Sarga   WESTERN SAHARA   ed Droûs Telli
(MOROCCO)   Sebkhet Oumm   Oued el Ma
Bahia de Río de Oro   ed Droûs-Guebli
Zouérat   S   A
Rás   EL DJOUF
Nouâdhibou   Nouâdhibou   Taoudenni
Dakhlet Nouâdhibou   Atâr
ILE TIDRA   Chinguetti
Cap Timiris   Akjoujt
Nouakchott   HODH   EL MREYYÉ
Sebkra du   MAURITANIA   M
Ndaghamcha   Tidjikja   A
ATLANTIC   AOUKÂR   AZAOUÂD
OCEAN   St Louis   Dagana   Lac
Kaédi   Kiffa   'Ayoûn el Atroûs   Faguibine   Tombouctou
Cap Vert   Thiès   'Ayoûn el Atroûs   Niger
DAKAR   SENEGAL   Lac
Kaolack   MONTS MANDINGUES   Niangay   GOURMA
Banjul   GAMBIA   KAARTA   Lac
Tambacounda   Kayes   Débo   Ga
Cap Roxo   Mopti   S
Medina   SASSA
Gounas   U
Bissau   GUINEA-   MASSIF DU TAMGUE   Bamako   Ségou
BISSAU   FOUTA   Djibo   Dori
ORANGO   DJALLON   Labé   Tougan   BURKINA
GUINEA   Ouagadougou
Cap Verga   Kindia   Bobo   FASO
Conakry   LOMA   Dioulasso
MOUNTAINS   Kankan

Scale 1 : 9 200 000

0   200   400   600 km

© Copyright

SPAIN
Almeria
Cabo de Gata
Melilla (Sp.)
Oran
Mostaganem
Oujda
ALGER (ALGIERS)
Cap Bengut
Blida
Ech Chélif
Tizi Ouzou
Skikda
Cap de Fer
Annaba
Sétif
Constantine
Batna
HAUTS PLATEAUX
Chott Ech Chergui
Chott el Hodna
MONTS DES KSOUR
Djelfa
2236
Djebel Aissa
Biskra
Oued Djedi
Béchar
Ghardaïa
El Oued
Tozeur
Chott el Jerid
Gabes
Khâlij Qâbis
TUNISIA
Kairouan
Sfax
JUZUR QARQANNAH
Sousse
Khâlij Hammâmât
TÜNIS
Cap Bon
PANTELLERIA
ITALY
Palermo
SICILIA (SICILY)
Catania
LAMPEDUSA (Italy)
MALTA
MEDITERRANEAN SEA

GRAND ERG OCCIDENTAL
El Goléa
Ouargla
DUNES DE DOKHARA
Zuwarah
Tarâbulus (Tripoli)
Al Khums
Misrâtah
Khâlij Surt (Gulf of Sirte)
i-Abbès
Ghadamis
Bani Walid
Gharyan
JABAL NAFUSAH
Sabkhat Täwurgha
Zamzam
Bays al Kabir
AS SIDRAH
Surt (Sirte)
Sebkha de Timimoun
Timimoun
Adrar
PLATEAU DU TADEMAÏT
GRAND ERG ORIENTAL
AL HAMMADAH AL HAMRA
ALGERIA
In Salah
eggane
HAMMADAT TINGHARAT
JABAL AS SAWDA
Hun
LIBYA
Zarzaïtine
Sebkha Mekkerrhane
AWBÂRÎ SAHRÂ
Wadi ash Shati
Amguid
IDHÂN AWBÂRI
AL HARUJ AL ASWAD
Sebkha Azzel Matti
Amguid
Illizi
Sabhâ
ZEGROUFT
SAHARA
Arak
TASSILI N'AJJER
2254
Tehi-n-Isser
Ghat
FEZZAN
JABAL BIN GHANIMAH
TANEZROUFT-TAN-AHENET
2918
Tahat
Djanet
IDHÂN MURZUQ
SAHRÂ MARZÛQ
Tamanrasset
Tropic of Cancer
SARÎR TIBESTI
Bordj Mokhtar
HAMADA MANGUENI
TÉNÉRÉ DU TAFASSASSET
Madama
MISSI
ADRAR DES IFORAS
PLATEAU DU DJADO
3265
Pic Toussidé
MASSIF D'AFAFI
TIBESTI
3150
Tarso-Emissi
In-Guezzam
MASSIF D'ABO
Kidal
TALAK
VALLÉE DE L'AZAOUAK
AÏR (AZBINE)
3415
Emi Koussi
BORKOU
Arlit
2022
Monts Bagzane
Bilma
GRAND ERG DE BILMA
MEUZENTI
Faya
NIGER
Agadez
TÉNÉRÉ
ERG DU TÉNÉRÉ
BODÉLÉ
FALAISE DE TIGUIDIT
MASSIF DE TERMIT
TI-N-TOUMMA
CHAD
Tahoua
Dallol Bosso
KANEM
MANGA
Niger
Niamey
Maradi
Zinder
Komadugu Gana
Bahr el Ghazal
Diapaga
Sokoto
NIGERIA
Katsina

Northeast Africa

MEDITERRANEAN

TUNISIA

Zuwārah · Tarābulus (Tripoli)
Al Khums
Gharyān · Misrātah
Banī Walīd
JABAL NAFŪSAH
Sabkhat Tawurghā
Zamzam
Bayy al Kabīr
Ghadamis
Surt (Sirte)
Banghāzī (Benghazi)
AL JABAL AL AKHDAR
Tubruq
Ra's al Milḥ
BARQAH AL BAHRĪYAH
MEDITERRANEAN
Khalij Surt (Gulf of Sirte)
AS SIDRAH
Ajdābiyā
Sabkhat Shunayn
Sabkhat Ghuzayyil

AL HAMMADĀH AL HAMRĀ
JABAL AS SAWDA
Hun
HAMMĀDAT TINGHARAT
Zarzaïtine
AWBĀRĪ ŞAḤRĀ
Wādī ash Shāṭi
IDHĀN AWBARI
Sabhā
WAḤĀT JĀLŪ
AS ŞAḤRĀ AL LĪBĪYAH (LIBYAN DESERT)
KATTĀ
SENK
Illizi

ALGERIA

2254 Tehi-n-Isser
Ghāt
FEZZĀN
LIBYA
SARĪR KALANSHIYŪ
SAHARA
TASSILI N'AJJER
IDHĀN MURZUQ
JABAL BIN GHANĪMAH
ŞAḤRĀ RABYĀNAH
AL KHUFRAH
Al Khufrah

Djanet
SAHRĀ MARZŪQ
Tropic of Cancer

AŞ ŞAḤ

SARĪR TIBASTĪ
AS ŞAḤ

HAMADA MANGUENI
SARĪR TIBASTĪ
TÉNÉRÉ DU TAFASSASSET
Madama
MASSIF D'AFAFI
MASSIF D'ABO
PLATEAU DU DJADO
3265 Pic Tousside
TIBESTI
MASSIF D'ABO
3150 Tarso Emissi
ERDI
ERDI MA

NIGER
TÉNÉRÉ
Bilma
ERG DU TÉNÉRÉ
GRAND ERG DE BILMA
3415 Emi Koussi
MEUZENTI BORKOU
DÉPRESSION DE MOURDI
Faya
ENNEDI
MASSIF DE TERMIT
BODÉLÉ
TI-N-TOUMMA

CHAD
Howa
MANGA
KANEM
Bahr el Ghazal
MASSIF DU KAPKA
SU
Hadejia
Lac Tchad (Lake Chad)
Abéche
El Geneina
3088 Jabal Marrah
El Fasher
Komadugu Gana
Maiduguri
N'Djamena
Ati
OUADDAI
DARSILA
JABAL DARFŪR
Nyala
Gongola
Massenya
Mongo
DARSILA
Maroua
MONTS MANDARA
Bongor
Chari
Aouakale
Birao
Benue
Laï
Bahr Salamat
DAR ROUNGA
AS Ş
Lol

NIGERIA
Sarh
Bahr Aouk

CAMEROON
Moundou
CENTRAL AFRICAN REPUBLIC
MASSIF DES BONGOS

Scale 1 : 9 200 000

0   200   400   600 km

SEA

Haifa
ISRAEL
Tel Aviv-Jafo
Irbid
Jerusalem
Gaza
AMMAN
EL
NDARÎYA
XANDRIA)
Bûr Sa'îd
(Port Said)
Beersheba
JORDAN
nhur
Țanțā
Ismâ'îliya
EL GIZA
(GIZA)
El Suweis
(Suez)
EL QÂHIRA
(CAIRO)
SINAI
NEGEV
Gulf of Aqaba
JABAL
AT TUBAYQ
AN NAFUD
iyûm
iinyâ
2580
Jabal
al Lawz
2637
Jabal
Kātrīna
JABAL SHAMMAR
Asyûṭ
Hurghada
Sohâg
Qena
Luxor
El Khârga
MASHÂBIH
EL WÂHÂT
EL KHÂRGA
Aswân
RED
ANUBÎYAH
Sadd el Aali
Lake
Nasser
Ras Bânâs
HARRAT AL 'UWAYRID
AL
HIJAZ
Al Madînah
(Medina)
Tropic of Cancer
SAUDI
ARABIA
AR RIYÂD
(RIYADH)
JABAL TUWAYQ
Asb Shallâl
atb Thâni
Wadi
Halfa
AS SAHRA' AN NUBÎYAH
Ras Hadarba
(NUBIAN DESERT)
Makkah
(Mecca)
Jiddah
(Jedda)
Aṭ Ṭā'if
Ras Shagara
MUKAWWAR
Asb Shallâl
atb Thâlith
Bûr Sûdân
(Port Sudan)
JAZÂ'IR
SAWAKIN
RUB AL KHÂLÎ
Dongola
Asb Shallâl
ar Rabi'
Asb Shallâl
al Khâmis
Ras Kasar
RAMLAT DAHM
SAHRA'
BAYYUDAH
2780
Jabal
Hamoyet
JAZÂ'IR
FARASAN
El Milk
Asb Shallâl
os Sablûkah
Nile
DAHLAK
ARCHIPELAGO
San'â'
3760
Jabal an
Nabi Shu'ayb
Umm Durmân
(Omdurman)
El Khartum Bahrî
Kassalâ
ERITREA
KAMARÂN
Ra's Îsa
YEMEN
Asmara
El Khartum
(Khartoum)
Teseney
Adi Ugri
Mersa
Fatma
Al Ḥudaydah
(Hodeida)
AZ ZUQAR
Wad Medani
Serit
Ta'izz
EL GEZIRA
Bab al Mandab
Assab
Adan
(Aden)
Gulf of
Aden
4620
Ras Dashen
DJIBOUTI
El Obeid
Gonder
Djibouti
Lake
Tana
Berbera
Desē
4231
Guna
Terara
Roseries
Reservoir
JIBÂL AN
NUBAH
4152
Biharn
4000
Abuyemeda
Dirē Dawa
SOMALIA
Hargeysa
Burao
HAUD
ÂDIS ÂBEBA
(ADDIS ABABA)
ETHIOPIA
OGADEN
Dembî Dolo
AUDO
Lake Zway
Jima

IRAQ
Babr al
Milh
Karbala'
An Najaf
Al Furat
(Euphrates)
Djilah
(Tigris)
Al Amârah
Ahvâz
Al Baṣrah
(Basra)
Âbâdân
An Nâṣirîyah
A' HARRAH
KUWAIT
The
Persian
Al Kuwayt
(Kuwait)
Gulf
Munifah
AD DAHNÂ

91

West Africa

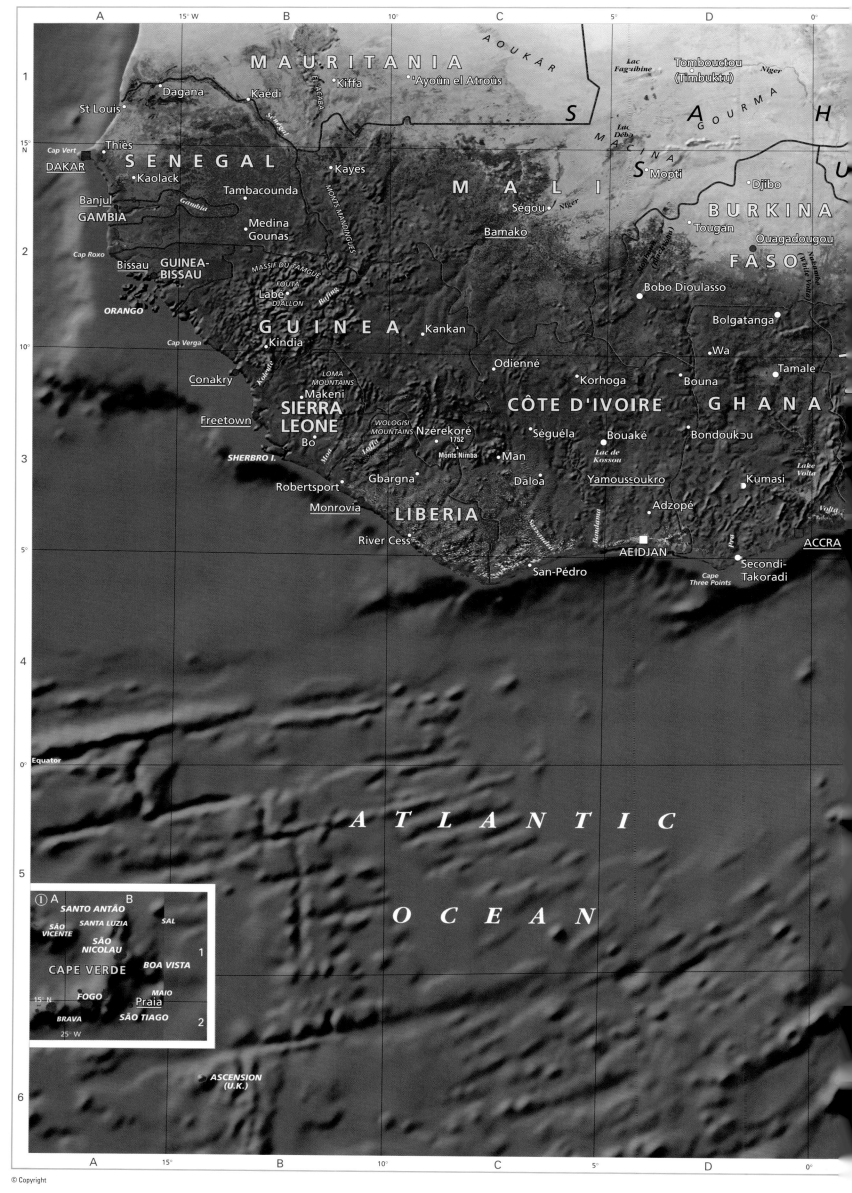

MAURITANIA

Aoukâr

Lac Faguibine

Tombouctou (Timbuktu)

Niger

Kiffa

'Ayoûn el Atroûs

S

A

GOURMA

H

Dagana

Kaédi

El Acaba

Sénégal

St Louis

Thiès

Lac Débo

MACINA

S Mopti

Djibo

Cap Vert

DAKAR

SENEGAL

Kayes

MALI

BURKINA

Kaolack

Ségou

Niger

Tougan

Ouagadougou

Banjul

Gambia

Tambacounda

Bamako

FASO

GAMBIA

MONTS MANDINGUES

Bobo Dioulasso

Cap Roxo

Bissau

Medina Gounas

GUINEA-BISSAU

MASSIF DU TAMGUE

FOUTA

Labé

DJALLON

Bafing

Bolgatanga

ORANGO

Buffing

GUINEA

Kankan

Wa

Tamale

Cap Verga

Kindia

Odienné

Korhoga

Bouna

Kolente

LOMA MOUNTAINS

CÔTE D'IVOIRE

GHANA

Conakry

SIERRA LEONE

WOLOGISI MOUNTAINS

Nzérékoré

Séguéla

Bouaké

Bondoukɔu

Freetown

Bo

1752

Monts Nimba

Man

Lac de Kossou

Kumasi

Lake Volta

SHERBRO I.

Moa

Loffa

Gbargna

Daloa

Yamoussoukro

Volta

Robertsport

Monrovia

LIBERIA

Adzopé

ACCRA

Bandama

River Cess

Sassandra

Bandama

AƐIDJAN

Secondi-Takoradi

San-Pédro

Pra

Cape Three Points

A T L A N T I C

Equator

O C E A N

A

SANTO ANTÃO

B

SÃO VICENTE

SANTA LUZIA

SAL

SÃO NICOLAU

1

CAPE VERDE

BOA VISTA

FOGO

MAIO

Praia

BRAVA

SÃO TIAGO

2

25° W

ASCENSION (U.K.)

Scale 1 : 9 200 000

0   200   400   600 km

E · · · · · 5° · · · · · F · · · · · 10° · · · · · G · · · · · 15° · · · · · H · · · · · 20° · · · · · J

ERG DU TÉNÉRÉ

BODELÉ

ERG DU DJOURAB

•Agadez

FALAISE DE
TIGUIDIT

MASSIF DE
TERMIT

TI-N-TOUMMA

1

E
L

N I G E R

MANGA

C H A D

15°

•Tahoua

KANEM

15°

D

A

N

iamey

•Maradi

•Zinder

•Ati

•Abéché

2

•Sokoto

•Katsina

Hadejia

Lac Tchad
(Lake Chad)

Lac Fitri

•Birnin-Kebb

•Gusau

•Kano

•Maiduguri

N'Djamena

1613 •Mongo

•Mont du Guéra

•Zaria

•Massenya

NIN

•Kaduna

•Bongor

10°

gou

•Kumo

Maroua

MONTS
MANDARA

10°

•Kandi

•Jos

•Laï

•Sarh

•Parakou

•Minna

Abuja

JOS PLATEAU

•Yola

•Garoua

•Moundou

Bahr Aouk

•Saki

•Ilorin

N I G E R I A

Niger

•Bida

2049 •Hoséré Vokré

Lac de
Logdo

3

gbomosho

•Oshogbo

Benue

•Makurdi

GOTEL
MOUNTAINS

•Ngaoundéré

C E N T R A L

okuta •IBADAN

•Akure

A F R I C A N

•Bozoum •Bossangoa

•Enugu

•Bamenda

•Bouar

R E P U B L I C

•Sibut

o- •Ikeja

•Benin-City

2740

•Ijebu

Monts Bambouto

•Otonou LAGOS

•Uyo

•Calabar

•Nkongsamba

Sanaga

•Bertoua

Ubangi

5°

ght of Benin

•Port Harcourt

C A M E R O O N

•Berbérati

Bangui

4

4095

•Mbaïki

Mouths of the Niger

Mont Cameroun

Gulf of

Malabo

•Douala

•Yaoundé

BIOKO
(FERNANDO
PÓO)

Guinea

PRÍNCIPE

EQUATORIAL
GUINEA

Zaïre

SÃO TOMÉ AND PRÍNCIPE

Cabo San Juan

Ubangi •Impfondo

SÃO TOMÉ

Libreville

•Ouésso

Lulonga

•São Tomé

C O N G O

•Mbandaka

Equator

Baie du Cap Lopez

G A B O N

•Owando

D E M O C R A T I C

0°

Cap
Lopez

MASSIF DU CHAILLU

R E P U B L I C   O F

•Port Gentil

C O N G O

ANNOBÓN
(PAGALU)
(Eq. Guinea)

Lac
Mai-Ndombe

•Kuto

5

Kwa

•Bandunda

Lukenie

PLATEAUX BATÉKÉ

Kasai

Zaïre

•Brazzaville

KINSHASA

•Kikwit

5°

•Pointe Noire

Livingstone Falls

CABINDA
(Angola)

•Matadi

Ponta da Narca

•M'banza
Congo

Kwango

6

Baía do Bengo

•Uige

A N G O L A

Luanda

•Malanje

E · · · · · 5° · · · · · F · · · · · 10° · · · · · G · · · · · 15° · · · · · H · · · · · 20° · · · · · J

Central Africa

NIGERIA

CHAD

Maroua
MONTS MANDARA
Bongor
Laï
Moundou
Sarh
Chari
Bahr Salamat
Bahr Aouk

DAR SILA

Aoukalé

Birao

JIBAL AN NUBAH

DAR ROUNGA

MASSIF DES BONGOS

SUDAN

Lol

AS SUDD

UBANGI-CHARI

CENTRAL AFRICAN REPUBLIC

Bouar
Bozoum
Bossangoa
Sibut
Bria
Yalinga

Rumbek

ADAMAOUA

CAMEROON

Berbérati
Bangui
Mbaïki
Ubangi
Gemena

Bangassou

Obo
Mbomou
Bomu

Dungu

(White Nile)

Bondo

Buta

Lisala
Bumba

Impfonda
Zaïre
Lutonga

Kisangani
Boyoma Falls

Albert Nile

Lac Mobutu Sese Seko
(Lake Albert)

Ouésso
GABON

Mbandaka

Boende
Tshuapa

Zaïre
Lomami

5110
Mt. Stanley
Lac Rutanzige
(Lake Edward)

Equator

Owando

CONGO

Lac Mai-Ndombe

DEMOCRATIC

SALONGA NATIONAL PARK

450?
Karisimbi
RWANDA
Kigali

Kwa
Kuto
Lukenie

REPUBLIC

Zaïre
Lake Kivu
Bukavu

MITGMB

Bandundu
Kasai

OF

Kindu
Uvira
BURUNDI
Bujumbura

Brazzaville
PLATEAUX BATÉKÉ
Zaïre

KINSHASA

Kikwit

CONGO

Lusambo
Sankuru

Kongolo

MONTS MUGILA

Lake Tanganyika

Matadi
Livingstone Falls

Kananga
Kabinda
Kalemie

MONTS MITUMBA

Ponta da Narca
M'banza Congo

Kwango
Mbuji-Mayi
Gandajika

MONTS MALIMBA

Uíge

Chitato
Mwene-Ditu
Kamina

MONTS MARUNGU
Sumbaw

Baía do Bengo

Lulua
Cassai

Luanda

Malanje
Cuanza

Saurimo

K A T A N G A

Lake Mweru

MONTS KUNDELUNGU

Lulua

ATLANTIC OCEAN

Waku-Kungo

ANGOLA

Luena

Likasi
Mansa
Lake Bangweulu

Lobito
Benguela
Huambo
Kuito
Cuanza

Zambezi

Solwezi
Chingola
Mufulira

Kitwe-Nkana
Ndola
Luanshya
Kasan

PLANALTO DO BIÉ

ZAMBIA

© Copyright

Scale 1 : 9 200 000

0   200   400   600 km

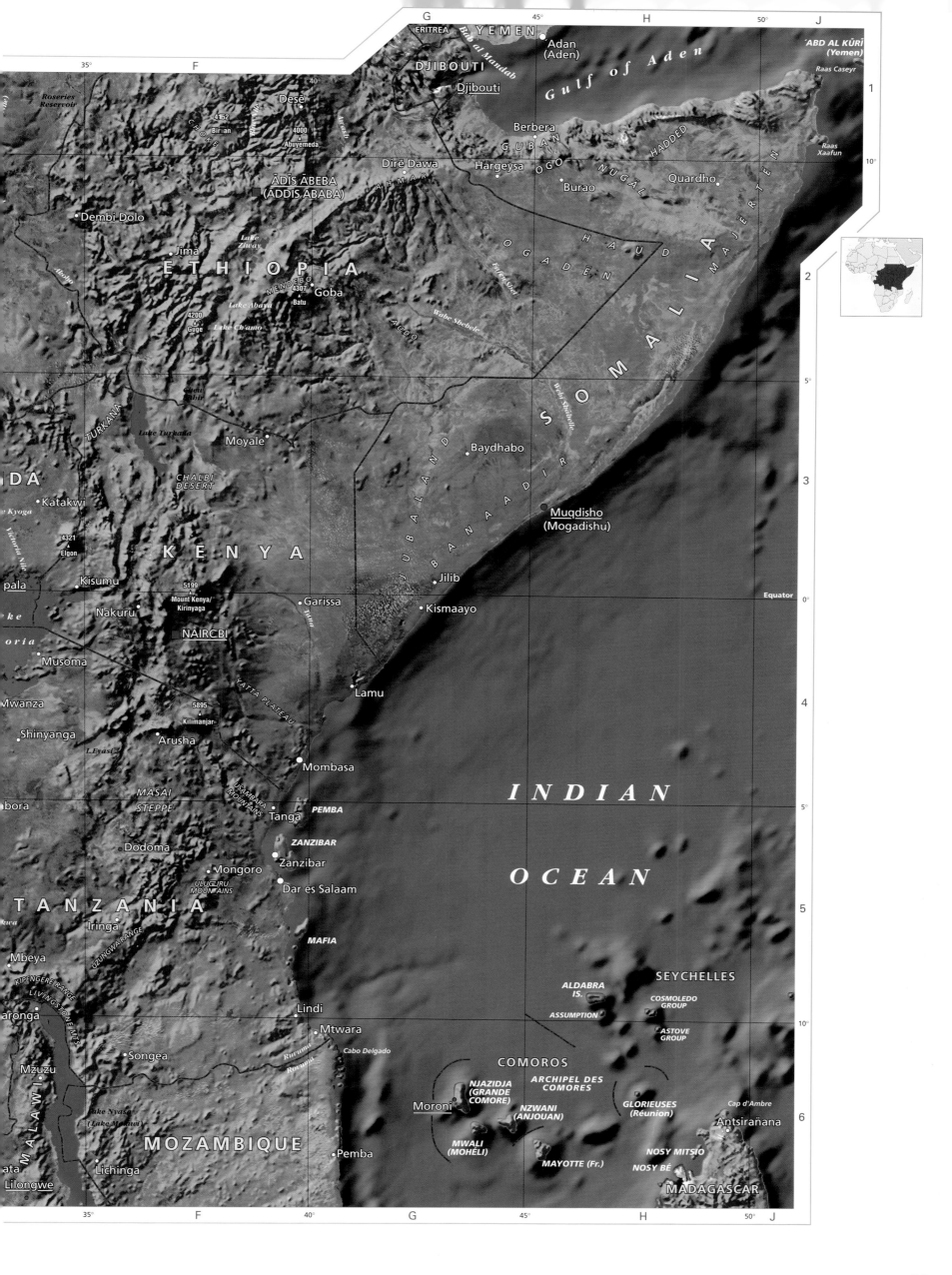

ERITREA
YEMEN
Bab el Mandeb
G
45°
H
50°
J

Adan
(Aden)
Gulf of Aden
'ABD AL KŪRĪ
(Yemen)
Raas Caseyr

DJIBOUTI
Djibouti

1

Berbera
G U B A N
HADDED
Raas
Xaafun

10°

Desē
Birḥan
4152
4000
Abuyemeda
Micssa

Dirē Dawa
Hārgeysa
O G O
N U G A L
Quardho

ĀDIS ĀBEBA
(ADDIS ABABA)
Burao

Dembi Dolo

Jima
Lake
Ziway

E T H I O P I A
A H M A R
O G A D E N
H A U D

Mendebo
4307
Goba
Batu

M A J E R T E N

2

4200
Guge
Lake Abaya
Lake Ch'amo
Wabe Shebele
A U D O

Fafen Shet'
Wabi Shebelle

S O M A L I A

Chew
Bahir

Lake Turkana
Moyale

5°

T U R K A N A

CHALBI
DESERT

K E N Y A

J U B A L A N D

Baydhabo

3

DA

Katakwi

Lake Kyoga

4321
Elgon

B A N A A D I R

Muqdisho
(Mogadishu)

pala

Kisumu

5199
Mount Kenya/
Kirinyaga

Jilib

Equator
0°

Nakuru

NAIRObI

Garissa

Kismaayo

oria

Musoma

Yatta
Tana

I N D I A N

4

Mwanza

Y A T T A   P L A T E A U

Lamu

Shinyanga

5895
Kilimanjar.

Arusha

L. Eyasi

Mombasa

O C E A N

5°

bora

MASAI
STEPPE

USAMBARA
MOUNTAINS

Dodoma

Tanga
PEMBA

ZANZIBAR

Mongoro

Zanzibar

ULUGURU
MOUNTAINS

Dar es Salaam

5

T A N Z A N I A

Iringa

MAFIA

UZUNGWA RANGE

Mbeya

KIPENGERE RANGE

Lindi

SEYCHELLES

LIVINGSTONE MTS.

ALDABRA
IS.

COSMOLEDO
GROUP

10°

aronga

Mtwara

ASSUMPTION

ASTOVE
GROUP

Mzuzu

Songea

Cabo Delgado
Ruvuma
Rovuma

COMOROS

ARCHIPEL DES
COMORES

Lake Nyasa
(Lake Malawi)

NJAZIDJA
(GRANDE
COMORE)

NZWANI
(ANJOUAN)

GLORIEUSES
(Réunion)

Cap d'Ambre

6

MALAWI

Moroni

Antsiraňana

ata

MOZAMBIQUE

Pemba

MWALI
(MOHÉLI)

MAYOTTE (Fr.)

NOSY MITSIO

NOSY BÉ

MADAGASCAR

Lilongwe

35°
F
40°
G
45°
H
50°
J

Southern Africa

© Copyright

Scale 1 : 9 200 000

0   200   400   600 km

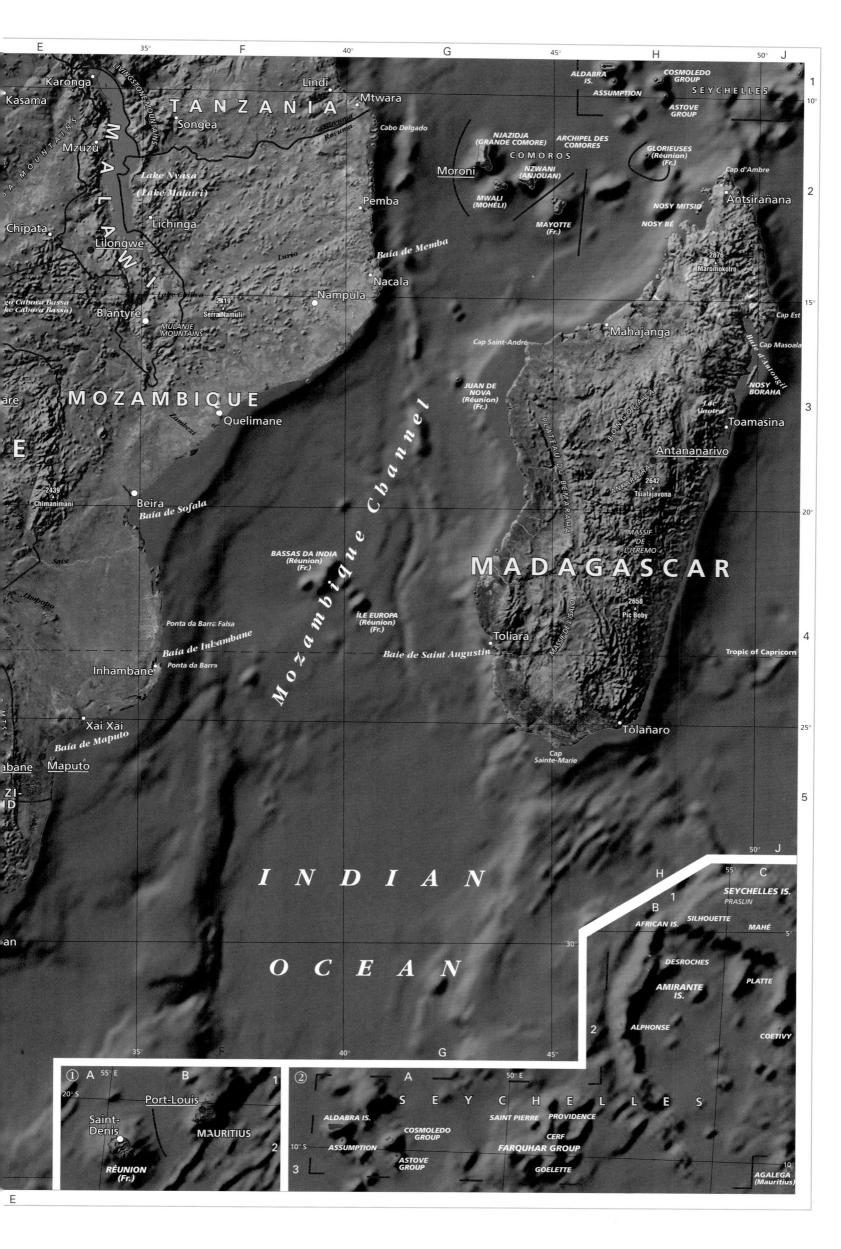

E · 35° · F · 40° · G · 45° · H · 50° · J

Karonga
Kasama
Mzuzu
LIVINGSTONE MOUNTAINS
Chipata
Lichinga
Lilongwe
Blantyre
Cabora Bassa (Lago Cabora Bassa)
Serra Namuli 2419
MULANJE MOUNTAINS
Lake Chilwa

TANZANIA
Songea
Lindi
Mtwara
Ruvuma
Cabo Delgado
Pemba
Lake Nyasa (Lake Malawi)
Lurio
Baía de Memba
Nacala
Nampula

MALAWI
MOZAMBIQUE
Zambezi
Quelimane

COMOROS
NJAZIDJA (GRANDE COMORE)
ARCHIPEL DES COMORES
Moroni
NZWANI (ANJOUAN)
MWALI (MOHÉLI)
MAYOTTE (Fr.)

ALDABRA IS.
ASSUMPTION
COSMOLEDO GROUP
SEYCHELLES
ASTOVE GROUP
GLORIEUSES (Réunion) (Fr.)
Cap d'Ambre
NOSY MITSIO
Antsirañana
NOSY BÉ
2876 Maromokotro
Cap Est
Mahajanga
Baie d'Antongil
Cap Masoala
NOSY BORAHA
Cap Saint-André
JUAN DE NOVA (Réunion) (Fr.)
Lac Alaotra
Toamasina
PLATEAU DU BEMARAHA
BONGOLAVA
Antananarivo
ANKARATRA
2642 Tsiafajavona

Chimanimani 2439
Beira
Baía de Sofala
Save

MASSIF DE L'ITREMO
MADAGASCAR
2658 Pic Boby
MASSIF DE L'ISALO

BASSAS DA INDIA (Réunion) (Fr.)
ÍLE EUROPA (Réunion) (Fr.)
Baie de Saint Augustin
Toliara

Ponta da Barra Falsa
Baía de Inhambane
Ponta da Barra
Inhambane
Limpopo
Mozambique Channel

Tropic of Capricorn
Tôlañaro
Cap Sainte-Marie

Xai Xai
Baía de Maputo
Maputo
abane
ZI-D
an

INDIAN

OCEAN

10°
2
15°
3
20°
4
25°
5

J
50°
H · 55° · C
SEYCHELLES IS.
B · 1 · PRASLIN
AFRICAN IS.
SILHOUETTE
MAHÉ · 5°
DESROCHES
PLATTE
AMIRANTE IS.
2
ALPHONSE
COETIVY
35° · F · 40° · G · 45°

① A 55° E · B · 1
20° S
Port-Louis
Saint-Denis
MAURITIUS
2
RÉUNION (Fr.)
E

② · A · 50° E
SEYCHELLES
ALDABRA IS.
SAINT PIERRE
PROVIDENCE
COSMOLEDO GROUP
CERF
10° S
ASSUMPTION
FARQUHAR GROUP
ASTOVE GROUP
GOELETTE
AGALEGA (Mauritius)
3 · 10°

97

Asia

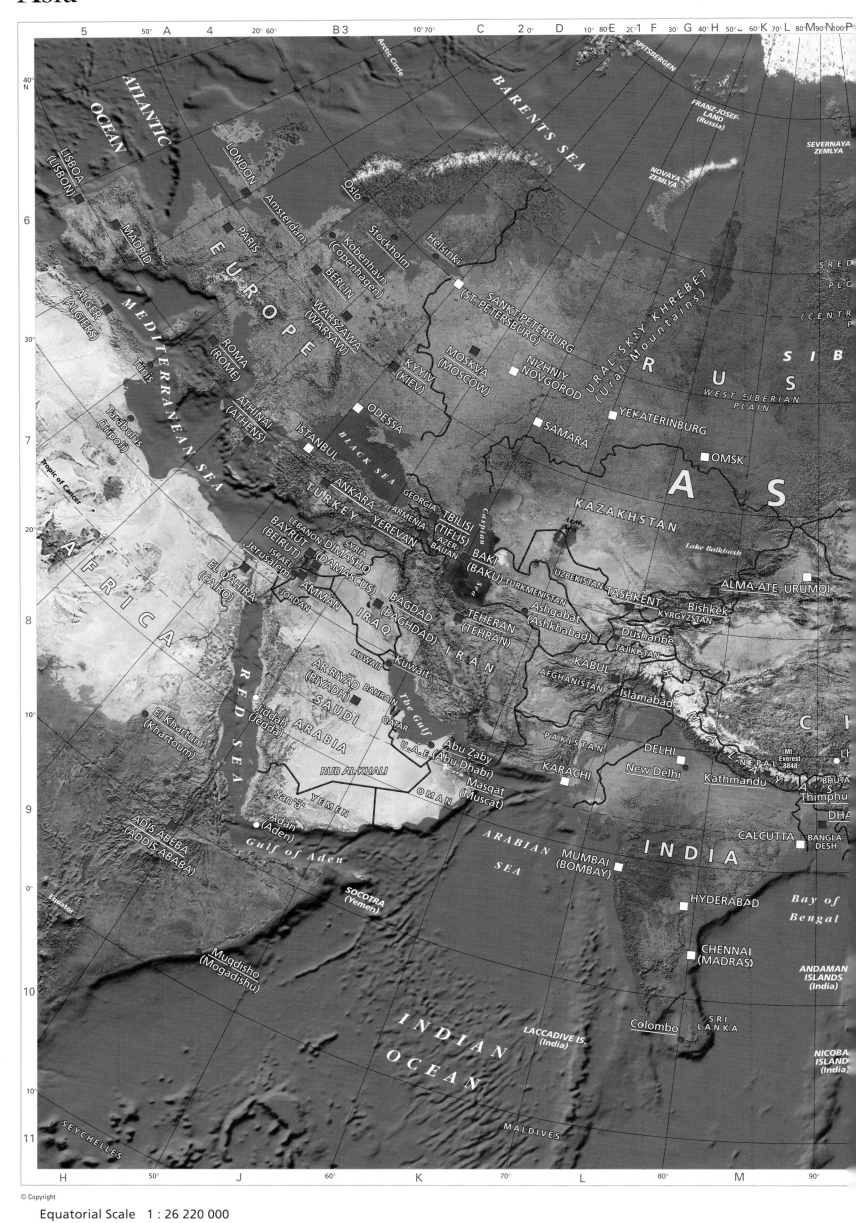

Equatorial Scale   1 : 26 220 000

| 0 | 400 | 800 | 1200 | 1600 km |

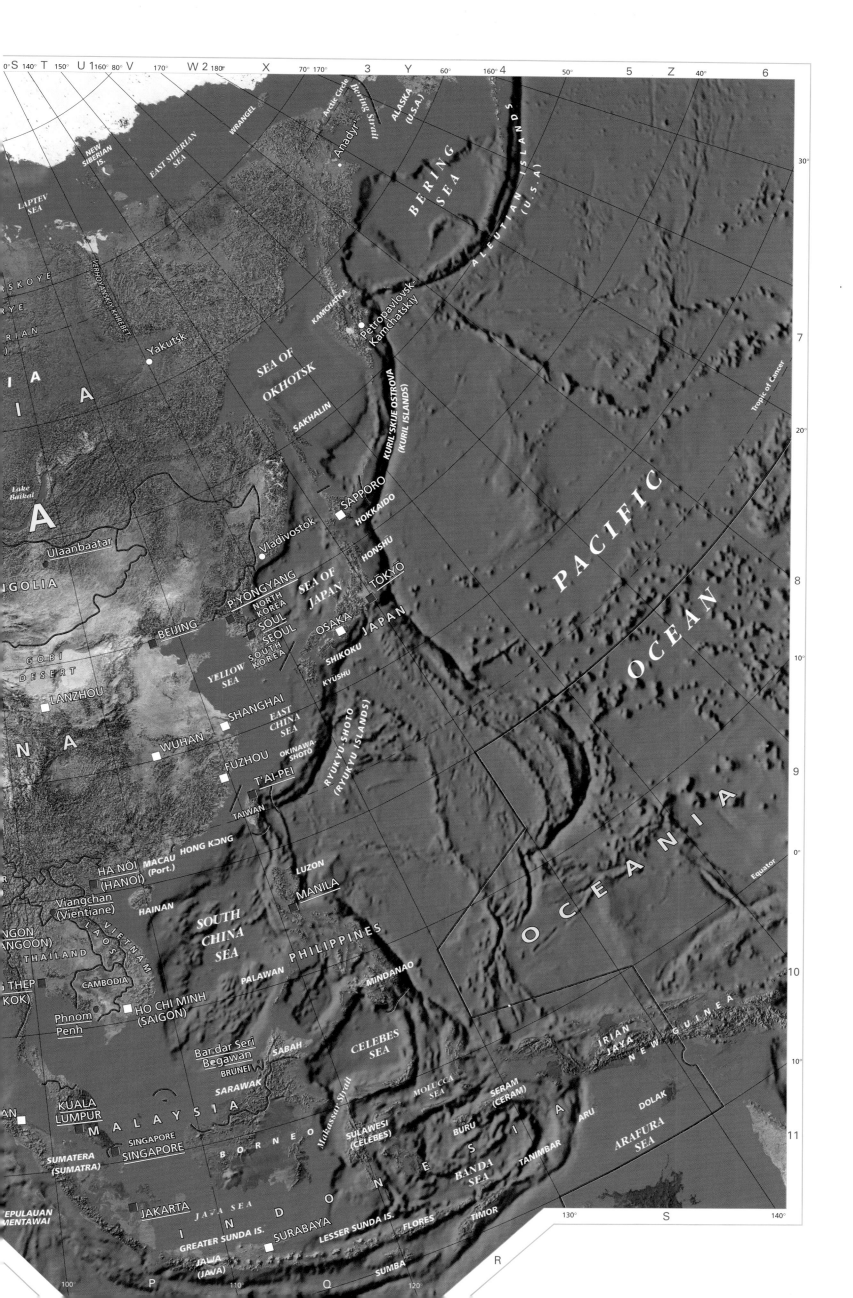

140° 150° 160° 80° 170° 2 180° 70° 170° 3 60° 160° 4 50° 5 40°

LAPTEV
SEA

NEW
SIBERIAN
IS.

EAST SIBERIAN
SEA

WRANGEL

Arctic Circle

Bering Strait

ALASKA
(U.S.A.)

Anadyr

BERING
SEA

ALEUTIAN ISLANDS
(U.S.A.)

30°

VERHOYANSKIY KHREBET

Yakutsk

KAMCHATKA

Petropavlovsk-
Kamchatskiy

7

Tropic of Cancer

20°

SEA OF
OKHOTSK

SAKHALIN

KURIL'SKIJE OSTROVA
(KURIL ISLANDS)

PACIFIC

Lake
Baikal

SAPPORO

HOKKAIDO

Ulaanbaatar

Vladivostok

HONSHU

TOKYO

8

IGOLIA

P'YONGYANG

NORTH
KOREA

SEA OF
JAPAN

OCEAN

BEIJING

SOUL
SEOUL

OSAKA

JAPAN

GOBI
DESERT

SOUTH
KOREA

SHIKOKU

10°

YELLOW
SEA

KYUSHU

LANZHOU

SHANGHAI

EAST
CHINA
SEA

RYUKYU-SHOTO

9

WUHAN

FUZHOU

OKINAWA-
SHOTO

RYUKYU ISLANDS
(RYUKYU ISLANDS)

T'AI-PEI

TAIWAN

0°

HA NOI
(HANOI)

MACAU
(Port.)

HONG KONG

Equator

LUZON

Viangchan
(Vientiane)

HAINAN

MANILA

NGON
NGOON)

LAOS

VIETNAM

SOUTH
CHINA
SEA

PHILIPPINES

THAILAND

10°

S THEP
KOK)

CAMBODIA

PALAWAN

MINDANAO

Phnom
Penh

HO CHI MINH
(SAIGON)

CELEBES
SEA

IRIAN
JAYA

NEW GUINEA

Bandar Seri
Begawan

SABAH

10°

BRUNEI

MOLUCCA
SEA

SERAM
(CERAM)

SARAWAK

DOLAK

KUALA
LUMPUR

M A L A Y S I A

BURU

ARU

ARAFURA
SEA

11

SUMATERA
(SUMATRA)

SINGAPORE

SINGAPORE

B O R N E O

Makassar Strait

SULAWESI
(CELEBES)

I N D O N E S I A

BANDA
SEA

TANIMBAR

EPULAUAN
ENTAWAI

JAKARTA

JAVA SEA

GREATER SUNDA IS.

SURABAYA

LESSER SUNDA IS.

FLORES

TIMOR

130°

140°

JAWA
(JAVA)

SUMBA

R

100° P 110° Q 120°

S

Northwest Asia

Scale 1 : 11 040 000

0   200   400   600 km

© Copyright

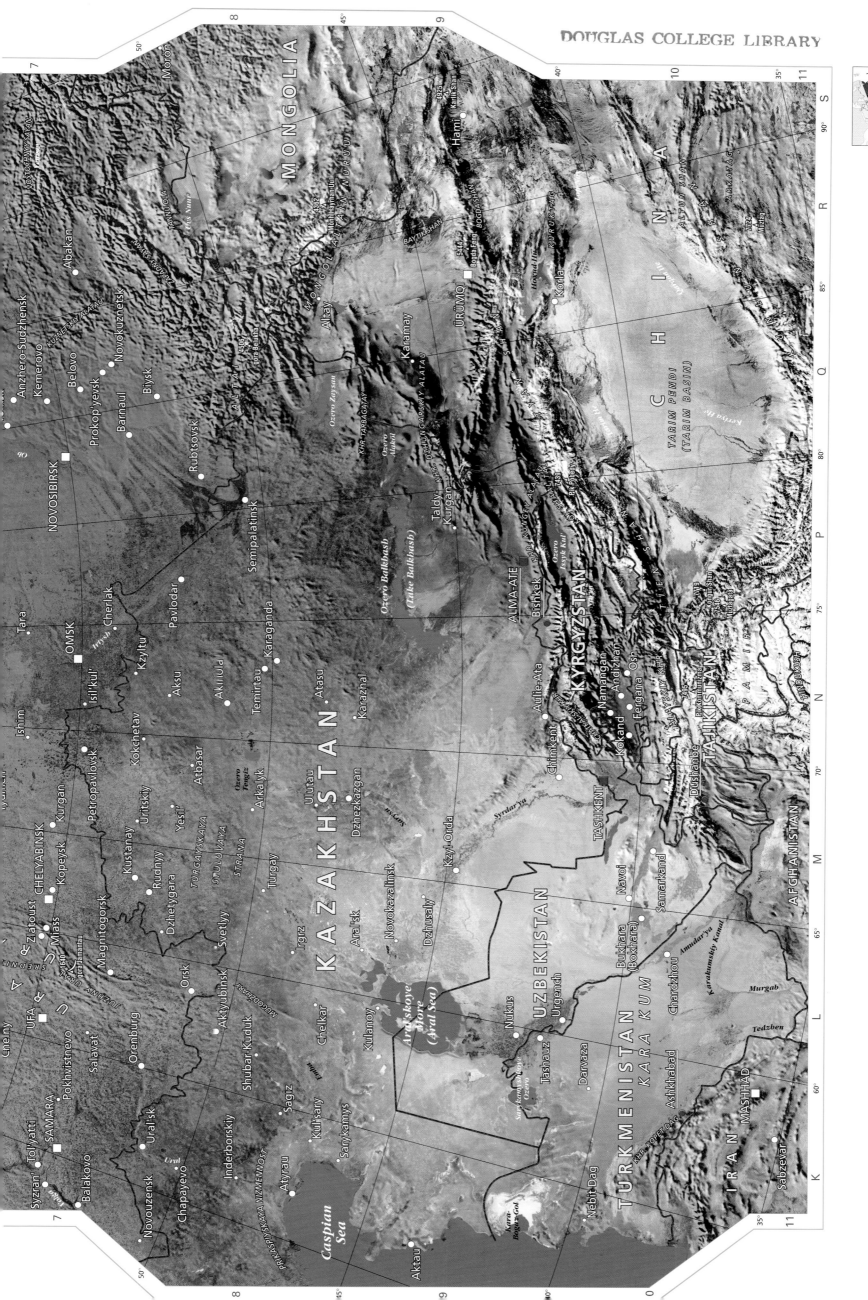

Northeast Asia

A 75° E 65° N B 80° C 3 85° D 70° 90° E 95° 2 F 100° G 105°

MORE LAPTEVYKH

OSTROV
BOL'SHOY
BEGICHEV

(LAPTEV SEA)

Tarko-Sale

Krasnosel'kup

Sidorovsk

Noril'sk

Igarka

Kheta

Novorybnoye

Khatanga

ANABARSKOYE
PLOSKOGORYE

OSTROV
STOLBO

4

GORY
PUTORANA

Kulyu

Anabar

Olenëkskiy
Zaliv

Tiksi

Guba
Buorkhaya

Surgutikha

Chirinda

60°
N

Olenëk

Komsa

Yenisey

Lena

SREDNESIBIRSKOYE
PLOSKOGORYE

Tura

Muna

VERKHOYANSKIY KHREBET

Bajkit

Udachnyy

Zhigansk

(CENTRAL SIBERIAN PLATEAU)

Lesosibirsk

RUSSIA

55°

Krasnoyarsk

Yenisey

Angara

Podkamennaya Tunguska

Nizh. Tunguska

Yerbogachen

Vilyuyskoye
Vdkhr.

Vilyuy

Aldan

Yakutsk

Ust-Ilimsk

Lensk

Lena

Zena

Anga

Bratsk

Bratskoye
Vdkhr.

PATOMSKOYE
NAGORYE

6

Nizhneudinsk

LENO-ANGARSKOYE
PLATO

BAIKALSKIY KHREBET

Nizhneangarsk

STANOVOYE
NAGORYE

Aldan

ALDANSKOYE
NAGORYE

3492
Gora
Munku Sardyk

Angarsk

Irkutsk

Ozero Baykal
(Lake Baikal)

BARGUZINSKIY KHREBET

2467
Gora
Golets-Skalistyy

50°

Hövsgöl
Nuur

Möron

Ulan-Ude

STANOVOY KHREBET

Zeya

Zeyskoye
Vdkhr.

KHREBET DZAGDY

YABLONOVYY KHREBET

Chita

7

Orhon

Khilok

Selenga

Argun

Zeya

2519
Gora
Burun-Sabartuj

Ergun He

Heilong Jiang

Bureya

Ergun Zuoqi

Ideriyn Gol

Ulaanbaatar

CHENTIYN NURUU

Onon

Kerulen

Hulun
Nur

Blagoveshchensk

KHREBET TURANA

45°

Choybalsan

Buyr
Nuur

Nen Jiang

Khabaro

Bulgan

MONGOLIA

QIQIHAR

Hegang

Amur
(Heilong Jiang)

8

Saynshand

CHINA

Baicheng

Jiamusi

**GOBI
DESERT**

Erenhot

Bairin Zuoqi

HARBIN

Jixi

Songhua Jiang

Mudan Jiang

Ozero
Khanka
(L. Khanka)

40°

BAOTOU

Hohhot

CHANGCHUN

JILIN

Mudanjiang

Ussuriysk

9

ZHANGJIAKOU

DA HINGGAN LING

Datong

Vladivostok

Nakho

H 110° J 115° K 120° L 125° N

© Copyright

Scale 1 : 11 040 000

0   200   400   600 km

**NORTH
KOREA**

M

130°

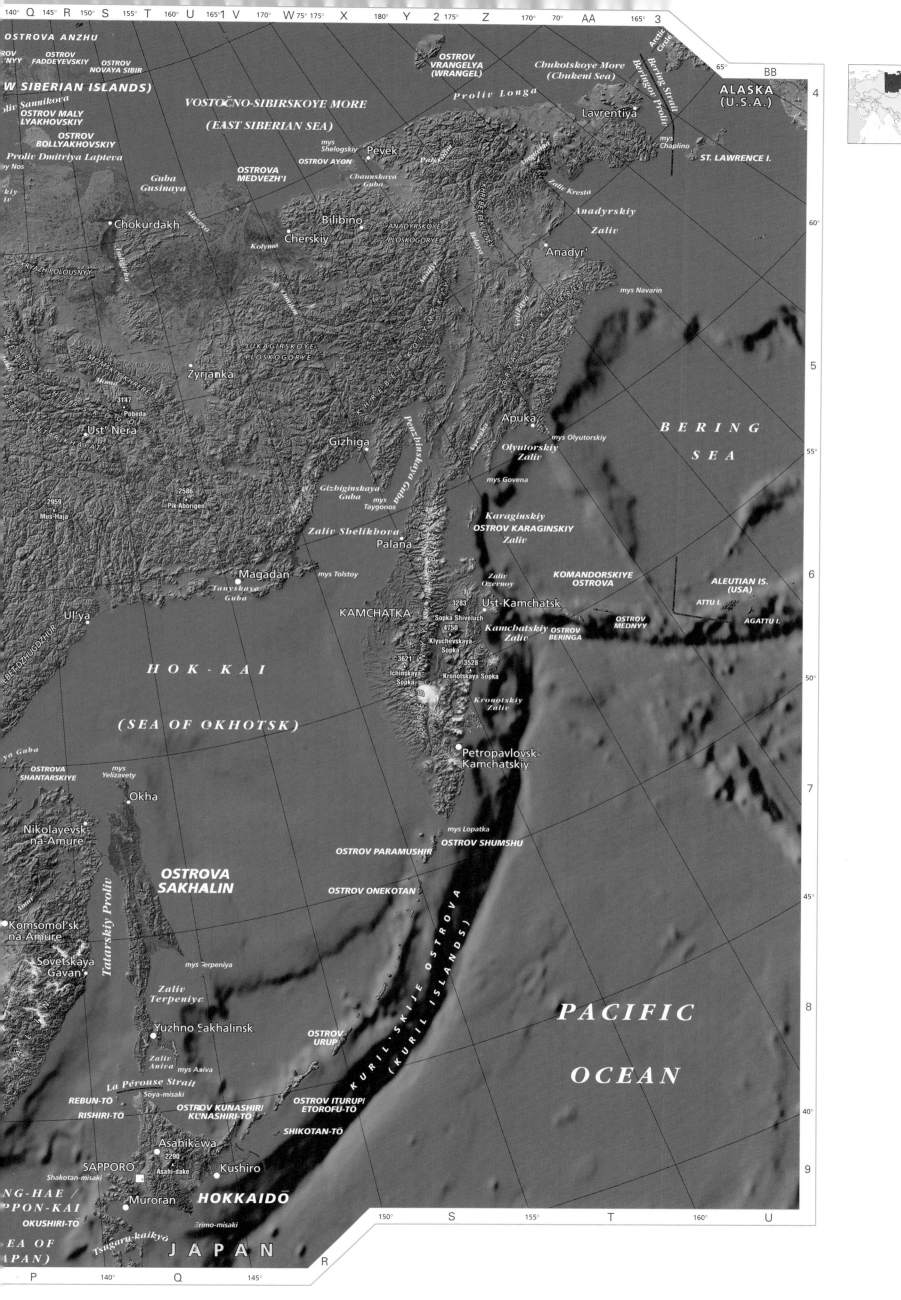

OSTROVA ANZHU

'NYY
OSTROV
FADDEYEVSKIY
OSTROV
NOVAYA SIBIR

W SIBERIAN ISLANDS)

OSTROV
VRANGELYA
(WRANGEL)

Chukotskoye More
(Chukchi Sea)

ALASKA
(U.S.A.)

BB

oliv
Sannikova
OSTROV MALY
LYAKHOVSKIY

OSTROV
BOLLYAKHOVSKIY

Proliv Dmitriya Lapteva
y Nos

kiy
iv

VOSTOČNO-SIBIRSKOYE MORE

(EAST SIBERIAN SEA)

Proliv Longa

Lavrentiya

65°

Guba
Gusinaya

mys
Shelogskiy

OSTROVA
MEDVEZH'I

OSTROV AYON

Chaunskaya
Guba

Pevek

mys
Chaplino

ST. LAWRENCE I.

4

Zaliv Kresta

Chokurdakh

Alazeya

Bilibino

ANADYRSKOYE
PLOSKOGORYE

Anadyrskiy
Zaliv

60°

KRYAZH POLOUSNYY

Cherskiy

Kolyma

Anadyr'

Žyrjanka

JUKAGIRSKOYE
PLOSKOGORYE

mys Navarin

5

3147
Pobeda

Ust'-Nera

Moma

Gizhiga

Apuka

mys Olyutorskiy

BERING

SEA

55°

2959
Mus-Haja

2586
Pik Aborigen

Gizhiginskaya
Guba

mys
Taygonos

mys Govena

Olyutorskiy
Zaliv

Zaliv Shelikhova

Palana

Karaginskiy
OSTROV KARAGINSKIY
Zaliv

Magadan

mys Tolstoy

Zaliv
Ozernoy

KOMANDORSKIYE
OSTROVA

6

Tauyskaya
Guba

Ul'ya

KAMCHATKA

3283
Sopka Shiveluch
4750
Klyuchevskaya
Sopka

Ust-Kamchatsk

Kamchatskiy
Zaliv

OSTROV
BERINGA

OSTROV
MEDNYY

ALEUTIAN IS.
(USA)
ATTU I.

AGATTU I.

H O K - K A I

3621
Ichinskaya
Sopka

3528
Kronotskaya Sopka

Kronotskiy
Zaliv

50°

(SEA OF OKHOTSK)

ya Guba

OSTROVA
SHANTARSKIYE

mys
Yelizavety

Okha

Petropavlovsk-
Kamchatskiy

7

Nikolayevsk-
na-Amure

OSTROVA
SAKHALIN

mys Lopatka
OSTROV SHUMSHU

OSTROV PARAMUSHIR

Komsomol'sk-
na-Amure

OSTROV ONEKOTAN

45°

Sovetskaya
Gavan

mys Terpeniya

PACIFIC

8

Zaliv
Terpeniye

Yuzhno-Sakhalinsk

OSTROV
URUP

OCEAN

Zaliv
Aniva
mys Aniva

La Pérouse Strait

REBUN-TŌ
RISHIRI-TŌ

Soya-misaki

OSTROV KUNASHIRI
KUNASHIRI-TŌ

OSTROV ITURUPI
ETOROFU-TO

40°

SHIKOTAN-TŌ

Asahikawa

9

SAPPORO
Shakotan-misaki

2290
Asahi-dake

Kushiro

NG-HAE /
PPON-KAI

Muroran

HOKKAIDŌ

OKUSHIRI-TŌ

Erimo-misaki

EA OF
APAN)

Tsugaru-kaikyo

J A P A N

Southern Asia

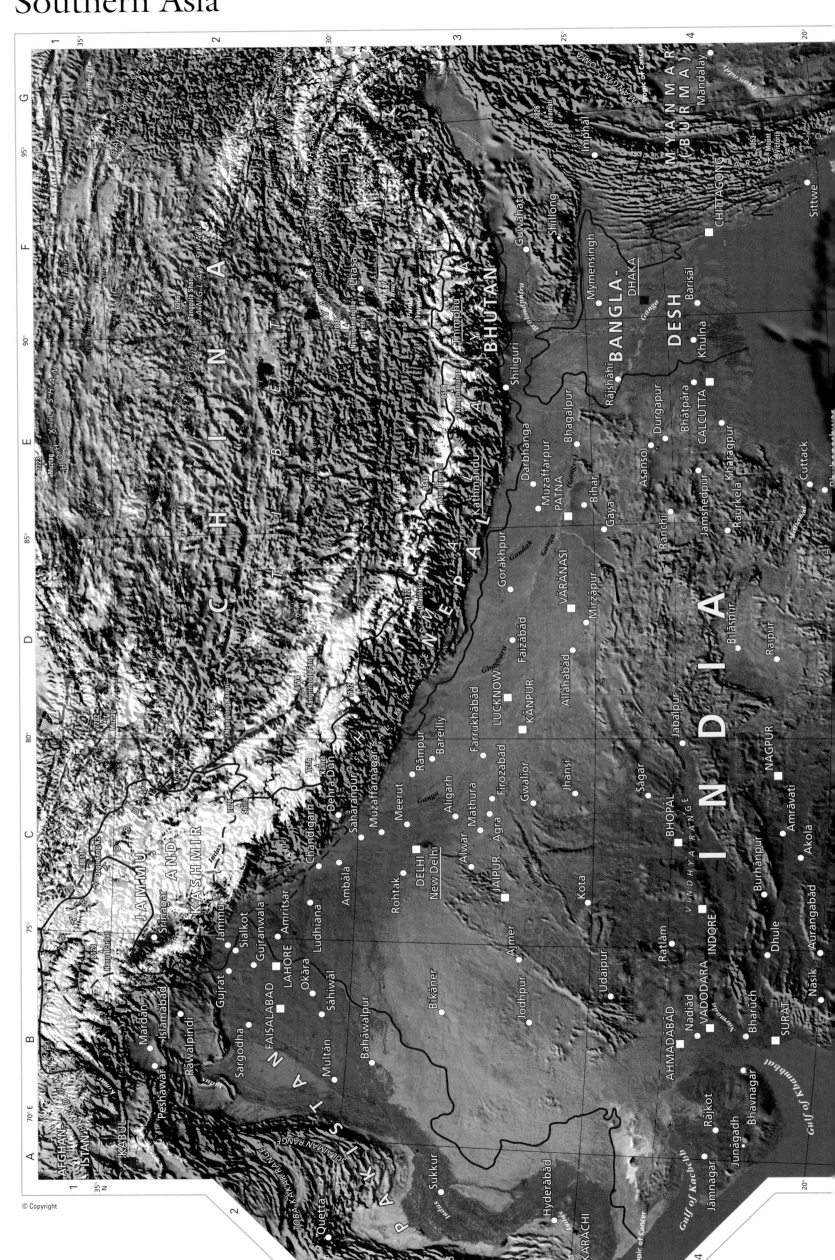

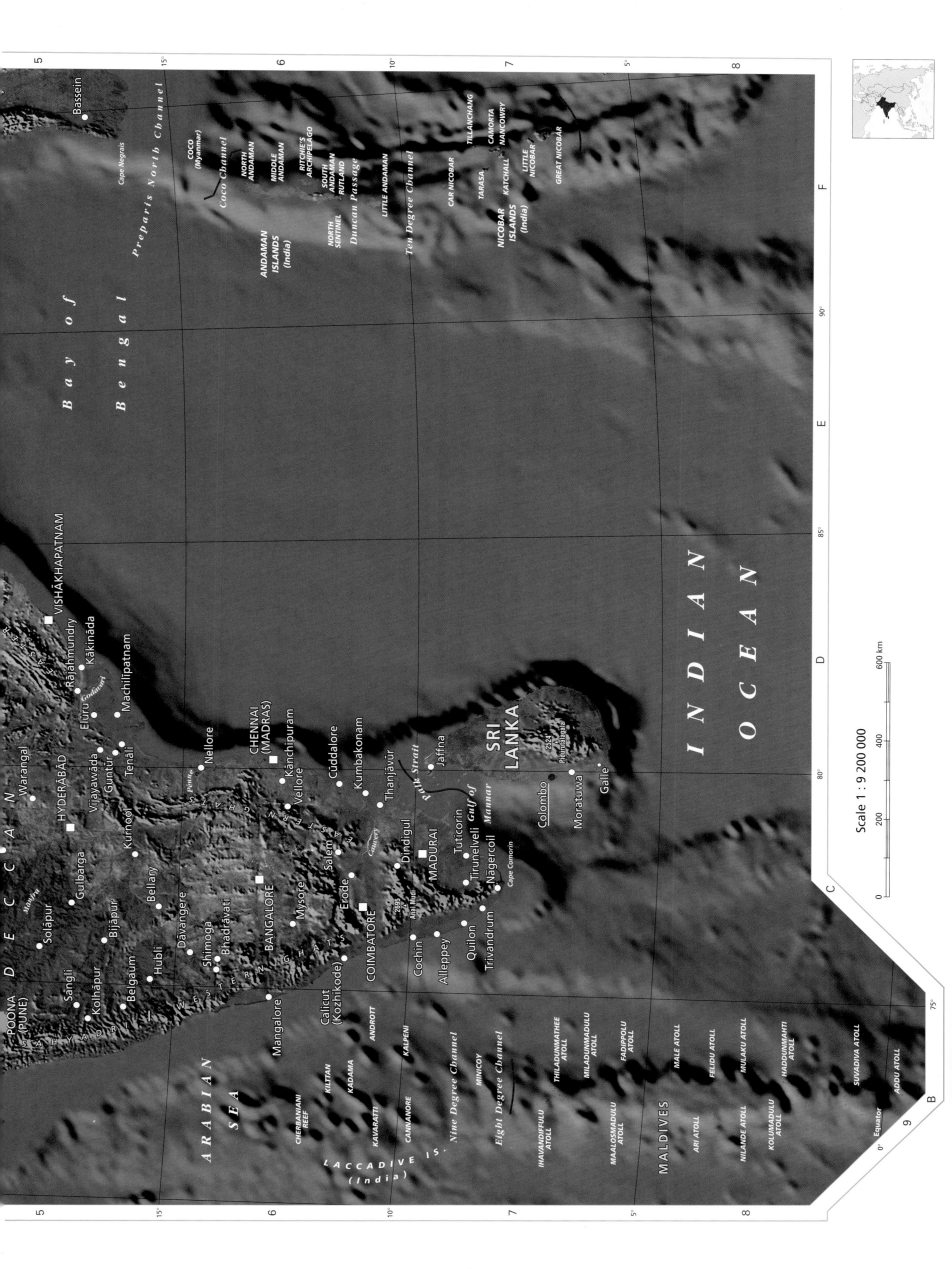

Bassein

Cape Negrais

Preparis North Channel

Bay

of

Bengal

COCO
(Myanmar)

Coco Channel

NORTH
ANDAMAN

MIDDLE
ANDAMAN

RITCHIE'S
ARCHIPELAGO

SOUTH
ANDAMAN
RUTLAND

Duncan Passage

LITTLE ANDAMAN

ANDAMAN
ISLANDS
(India)

NORTH
SENTINEL

Ten Degree Channel

TILLANCHANG

CAR NICOBAR

TARASA

CAMORTA
NANCOWRY

KATCHALL

LITTLE
NICOBAR

NICOBAR
ISLANDS
(India)

GREAT NICOBAR

F

90°

E

85°

INDIAN

OCEAN

VISHĀKHAPATNAM

D

75°

Scale 1 : 9 200 000

600 km

0   200   400   600 km

C

Rājahmundry
Kākināda
Elūru
Godāvari
Machilipatnam

Warangal

HYDERĀBĀD

Vijayawāda

Guntūr

Tenāli

Nellore

CHENNAI
(MADRAS)

Kānchipuram

Vellore

Cuddalore

Kumbakonam

Thanjāvūr

Palk Strait

Jaffna

SRI
LANKA

2524
Pidurutalagala

Colombo

Moratuwa

Galle

INDIAN

OCEAN

Solāpur

Gulbarga

Kurnool

Bellary

Dāvangere

Shimoga
Bhadrāvati

BANGALORE

Mysore

Erode

Salem

COIMBATORE

2695
Ānai Mudi

Dindigul

MADURAI

Tuticorin

Tirunelveli

Nāgercoil

Cape Comorin

Gulf of

Mannar

Cauvery

Ss. Pennar

D E C C A N

Poona
(PUNE)

Sāngli

Kolhāpur

Belgāum

Bijāpur

Hubli

SĀHYĀDRI

Mawla

Mangalore

Calicut
(Kozhikode)

ANDROTT

KALPENI

CANNANORE

CHERBANIANI
REEF

KILTAN

KADAMA

KAVARATTI

MINICOY

Nine Degree Channel

Eight Degree Channel

LACCADIVE IS.
(India)

Cochin

Alleppey

Quilon

Trivandrum

WESTERN GHATS

EASTERN GHATS

ARABIAN

SEA

IHAVANDIFFULU
ATOLL

THILADUNMATHEE
ATOLL

MILADUNMADULU
ATOLL

FADIPPOLU
ATOLL

MALE ATOLL

MAALOSMADULU
ATOLL

MALDIVES

ARI ATOLL

FELIDU ATOLL

NILANDE ATOLL

MULAKU ATOLL

KOLUMADULU
ATOLL

HADDUNMAHTI
ATOLL

SUVADIVA ATOLL

ADDU ATOLL

Equator

0°

9

75°

B

8

5°

7

10°

6

15°

5

105

Southeast Asia

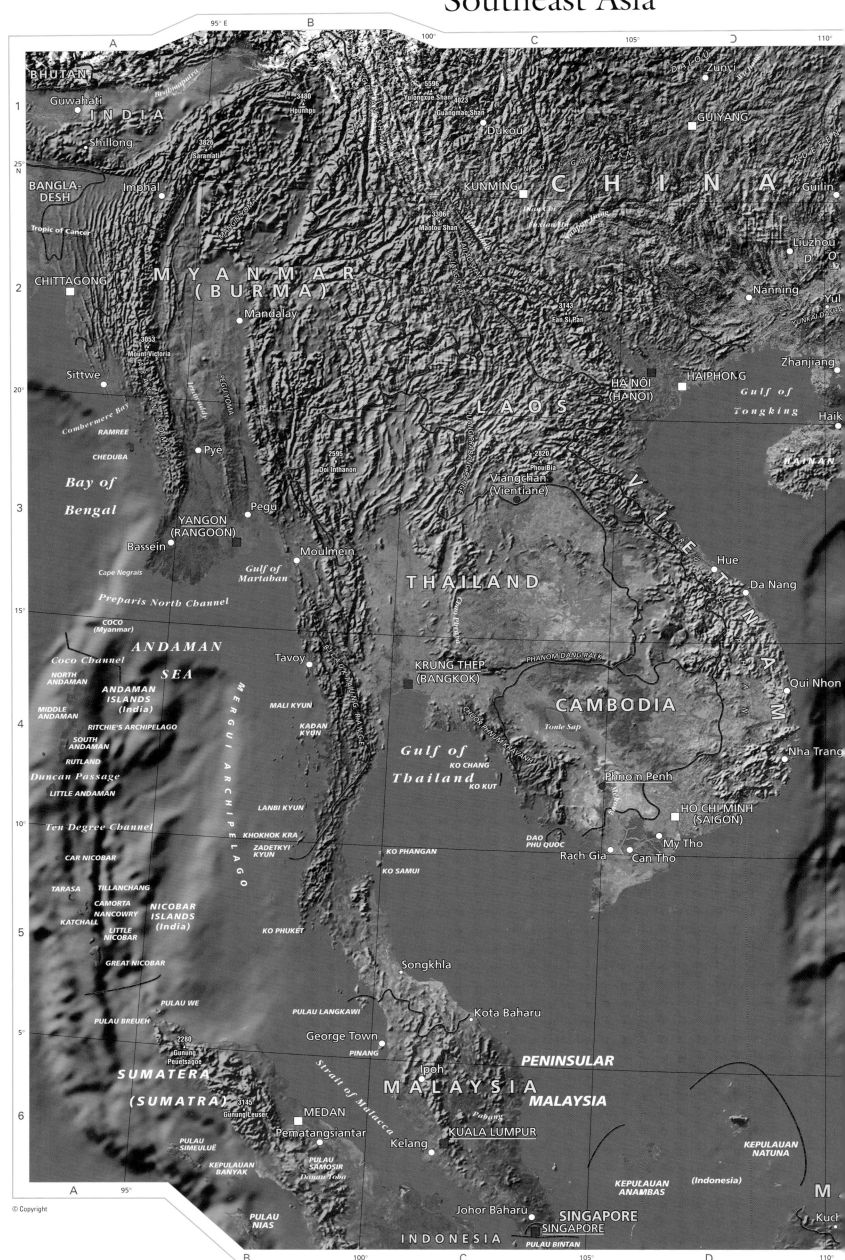

BHUTAN
Guwahati
Brahmaputra
INDIA
Shillong
3480
Hpunhpu
Yulongxue Shan
5596
4023
Guangmao Shan
Dukou
DA LOU
Zunyi
GUIYANG
25° N
BANGLA-
DESH
Imphal
3826
Saramati
KUNMING
CHINA
YUN-GUI GAOYUAN
Guilin
CHITTAGONG
MYANMAR
(BURMA)
Mandalay
3053
Mount Victoria
Maotou Shan
3306
Hei Chi
Hei Xian Hu
3143
Fan Si Pan
YUNKAI DASHA
Nanning
Liuzhou
Yul
Tropic of Cancer
20°
Sittwe
Combermere Bay
RAMREE
CHEDUBA
Pyé
Bay of
Bengal
2595
Doi Inthanon
HA NOI
(HANOI)
HAIPHONG
2820
Phou Bia
Viangchan
(Vientiane)
LAOS
Gulf of
Tongking
Zhanjiang
Haik
HAINAN
Cape Negrais
YANGON
(RANGOON)
Bassein
Pegu
Moulmein
Gulf of
Martaban
THAILAND
Hue
Da Nang
15°
Preparis North Channel
COCO
(Myanmar)
ANDAMAN
SEA
Tavoy
KRUNG THEP
(BANGKOK)
PHANOM DANG RAEK
CAMBODIA
Qui Nhon
NORTH
ANDAMAN
Coco Channel
ANDAMAN
ISLANDS
(India)
MALI KYUN
Tonle Sap
MIDDLE
ANDAMAN
RITCHIE'S ARCHIPELAGO
KADAN
KYUN
Gulf of
Thailand
KO CHANG
Phnom Penh
Nha Trang
SOUTH
ANDAMAN
RUTLAND
KO KUT
Duncan Passage
LITTLE ANDAMAN
LANBI KYUN
DAO
PHU QUOC
HO CHI MINH
(SAIGON)
Ten Degree Channel
KHOKHOK KRA
ZADETKYI
KYUN
KO PHANGAN
Rach Gia
Can Tho
My Tho
CAR NICOBAR
KO SAMUI
TARASA
TILLANCHANG
CAMORTA
NANCOWRY
KATCHALL
LITTLE
NICOBAR
NICOBAR
ISLANDS
(India)
KO PHUKET
GREAT NICOBAR
Songkhla
PULAU WE
PULAU LANGKAWI
Kota Baharu
5°
PULAU BREUEH
2280
Gunung
Peuetsagoe
George Town
PINANG
PENINSULAR
Ipoh
MALAYSIA
MALAYSIA
SUMATERA
(SUMATRA)
3145
Gunung Leuser
MEDAN
Pematangsiantar
Pahang
Kelang
KUALA LUMPUR
KEPULAUAN
NATUNA
PULAU
SIMEULUE
KEPULAUAN
BANYAK
PULAU
SAMOSIR
Danau Toba
KEPULAUAN
ANAMBAS
(Indonesia)
Johor Baharu
SINGAPORE
SINGAPORE
Kuch
PULAU
NIAS
INDONESIA
PULAU BINTAN

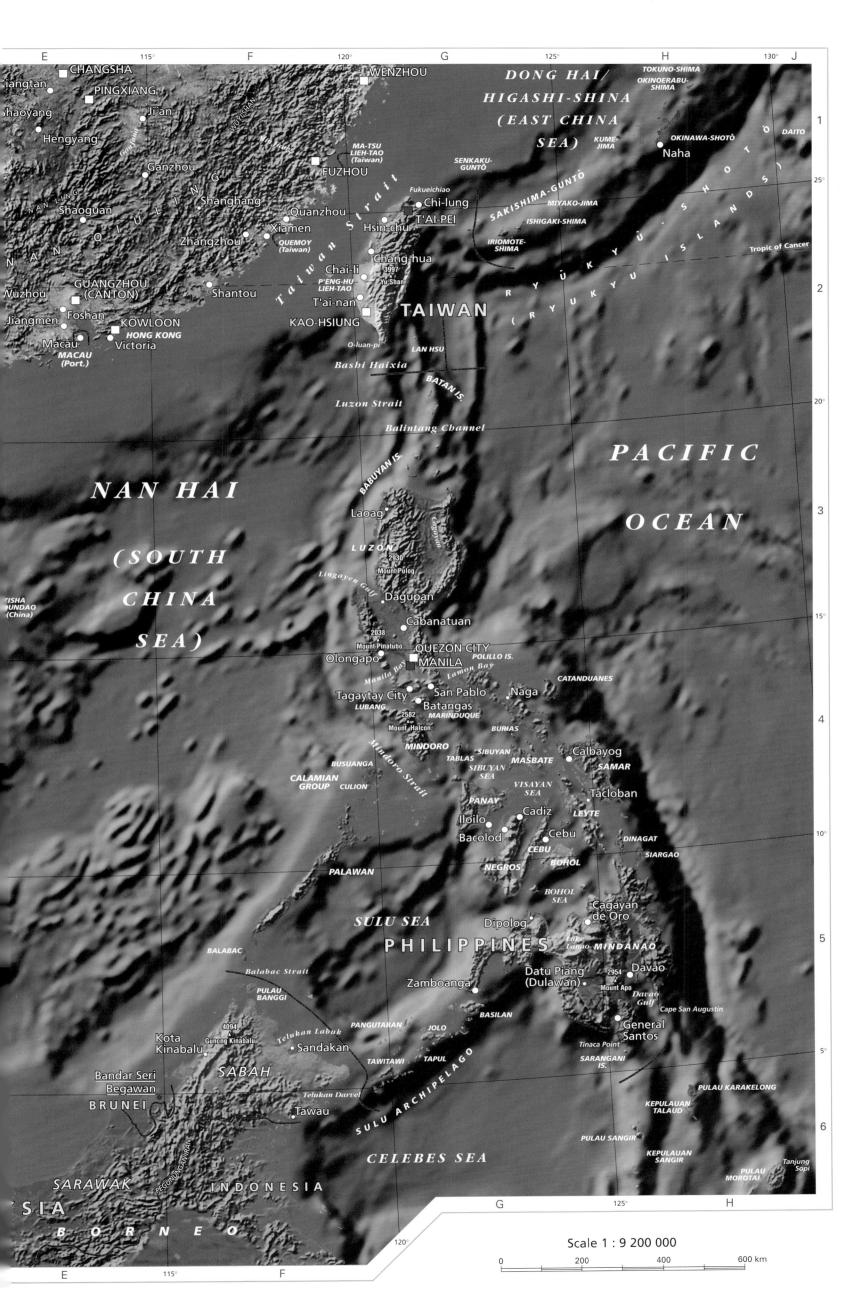

E   115°   F   120°   G   125°   H   130°   J

CHANGSHA
liangtan
PINGXIANG
Shaoyang   Ji'an
Hengyang
Ganzhou
Shanghang
Shaoguan
Wuzhou
**GUANGZHOU
(CANTON)**
Jiangmen   Foshan
KOWLOON
Macau   **HONG KONG**
MACAU   Victoria
(Port.)

WENZHOU

**DONG HAI/
HIGASHI-SHINA
(EAST CHINA
SEA)**

TOKUNO-SHIMA
OKINOERABU-
SHIMA

KUME-
JIMA

OKINAWA-SHOTŌ   DAITO
Naha

**MA-TSU
LIEH-TAO
(Taiwan)**
FUZHOU

Fukueichiao

SENKAKU-
GUNTŌ

SAKISHIMA-GUNTŌ
MIYAKO-JIMA
ISHIGAKI-SHIMA

Chi-lung
Quanzhou   Hsin-chu   **T'AI-PEI**
Xiamen
Zhangzhou   **QUEMOY
(Taiwan)**
Shantou   **P'ENG-HU
LIEH-TAO**

Chang-hua
Chai-li
3997
Yu Shan

IRIOMOTE-
SHIMA

Tropic of Cancer

25°

T'ai-nan
TAIWAN
KAO-HSIUNG

O-luan-pi
LAN HSU

Basbi Haixia

BATAN IS.

Luzon Strait

Balintang Channel

NAN HAI

(SOUTH

CHINA

SEA)

'ISHA
UNDAO
(China)

BABUYAN IS.
Laoag
LUZON
2930
Mount Pulog
Lingayen Gulf
Dagupan
Cabanatuan
2038
Mount Pinatubo
Olongapo   **QUEZON CITY**
MANILA
POLILLO IS.
Manila Bay   Lamon Bay
Tagaytay City   San Pablo   Naga
LUBANG   Batangas
2582   **MARINDUQUE**
Mount Halcon   **BURIAS**
MINDORO
BUSUANGA
**CALAMIAN
GROUP**   **CULION**
TABLAS   **SIBUYAN**
**SIBUYAN
SEA**
PANAY
**VISAYAN
SEA**
Iloilo   Cadiz
Bacolod   Cebu
NEGROS   **CEBU**
BOHOL

PALAWAN

**BOHOL
SEA**

SULU SEA
Dipolog
PHILIPPINES

BALABAC

Balabac Strait

**PULAU
BANGGI**

4094
Guncng Kinabalu
Kota
Kinabalu
PANGUTARAN
Telukan Labuk   Sandakan
SABAH
Telukan Darvel
**Bandar Seri
Begawan**
BRUNEI
Tawau

PANGUTARAN   **JOLO**
Zamboanga
TAWITAWI   **TAPUL**
BASILAN
SULU ARCHIPELAGO

CELEBES SEA

SARAWAK
INDONESIA
BORNEO

PACIFIC

OCEAN

RYŪKYŪ ISLANDS

(RYŪKYŪ-SHOTŌ)

CATANDUANES

Calbayog
SAMAR
MASBATE
Tacloban
LEYTE

DINAGAT
SIARGAO

Cagayan
de Oro
Lake
Lanao   **MINDANAO**
Datu Piang
(Dulawan)   2954   Davao
Mount Apo   **Davao
Gulf**
Cape San Augustin
General
Santos
Tinaca Point
**SARANGANI
IS.**

PULAU KARAKELONG

**KEPULAUAN
TALAUD**

PULAU SANGIR
**KEPULAUAN
SANGIR**
**PULAU
MOROTAI**
Tanjung
Sopi

1

2

3

4

5

6

20°

15°

10°

5°

5°

G   125°   H

E   115°   F   120°

Scale 1 : 9 200 000

0   200   400   600 km

China

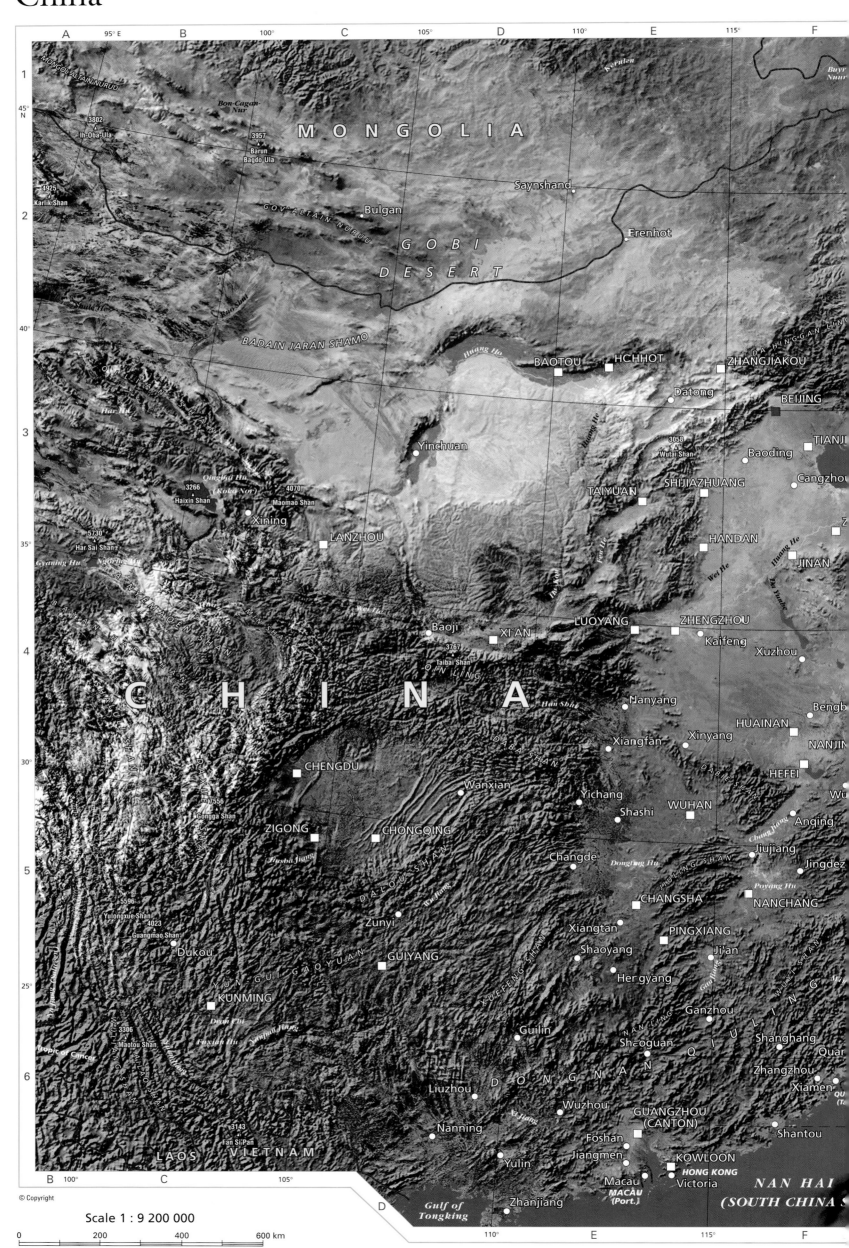

MONGOLIA

GOBI DESERT

Saynshand

Erenhot

Bulgan

Bon-Cagan-Nur

GOV'-ALTAIN NURUU

BADAIN JARAN SHAMO

Huang Ho

BAOTOU · HCHHOT · ZHANGJIAKOU

Datong

BEIJING

TIANJI

Yinchuan

3058 △ Wutai Shan

Baoding

Cangzhou

TAIYUAN · SHIJIAZHUANG

Z

Xining

Qinghai Hu (Koka Nor)

4070 △ Maomao Shan

LANZHOU

HANDAN

JINAN

Har Sai Shan

Gyaring Hu · Ngoring Hu

Wei He

LUOYANG · ZHENGZHOU

Baoji · XI'AN

Kaifeng · Xuzhou

3767 △ Taibai Shan

QIN LING

Han Shui

Nanyang

HUAINAN

Bengb

C H I N A

Xiangfan · Xinyang

NANJIN

DABA SHAN

CHENGDU

Wanxian

Yichang

WUHAN

HEFEI

Shashi

DABIE SHAN

Wu

7556 △ Gongga Shan

ZIGONG

CHONGQING

Chang Jiang

Anqing

Jiusha Jiang

Changde

Dongting Hu

Jiujiang

Jingdez

Zunyi

CHANGSHA

NANCHANG

5596 △ Yulongxue Shan

4023 △ Guangmao Shan

Dukou

GUIYANG

Xiangtan

Shaoyang

PINGXIANG

Ji'an

YUN-GUI GAOYUAN

XUEFENG SHAN

Her gyang

Ganjiang

KUNMING

Dean Hu

Ganzhou

3306 △ Maotou Shan

Fuxian Hu

Nanpan Jiang

Guilin

NAN LING

Shaoguan

Shanghang

Zhangzhou

DONGNAN

QIULING

Xiamen

3143 △ Fan Si Pan

Liuzhou

Wuzhou

GUANGZHOU (CANTON)

Shantou

Nanning

Xi Jiang

Foshan

Jiangmen

KOWLOON

LAOS · VIETNAM

Yulin

Macau

MACAU (Port.)

HONG KONG

Victoria

NAN HAI

Zhanjiang

Gulf of Tongking

(SOUTH CHINA S

© Copyright

Scale 1 : 9 200 000

0 · 200 · 400 · 600 km

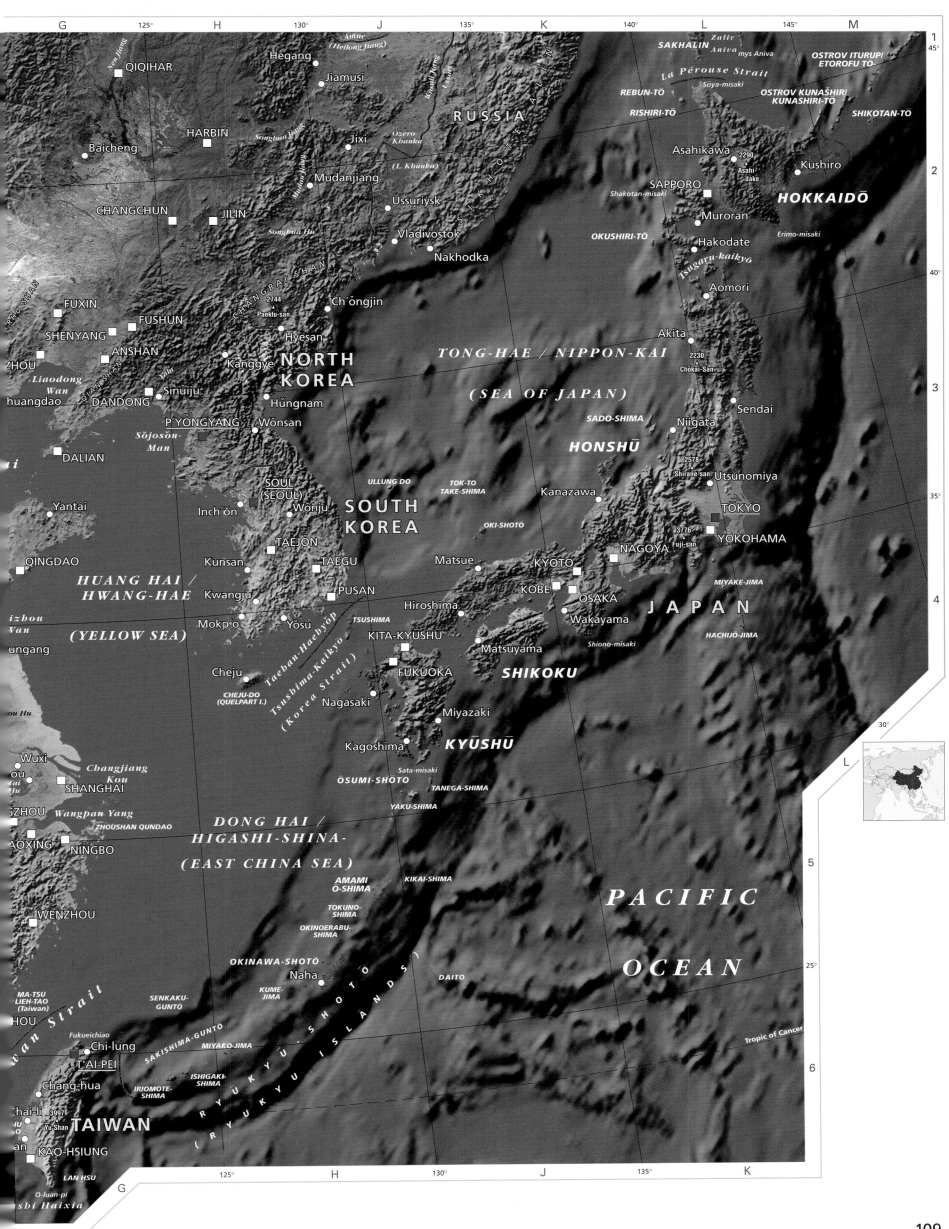

Japan and Korea

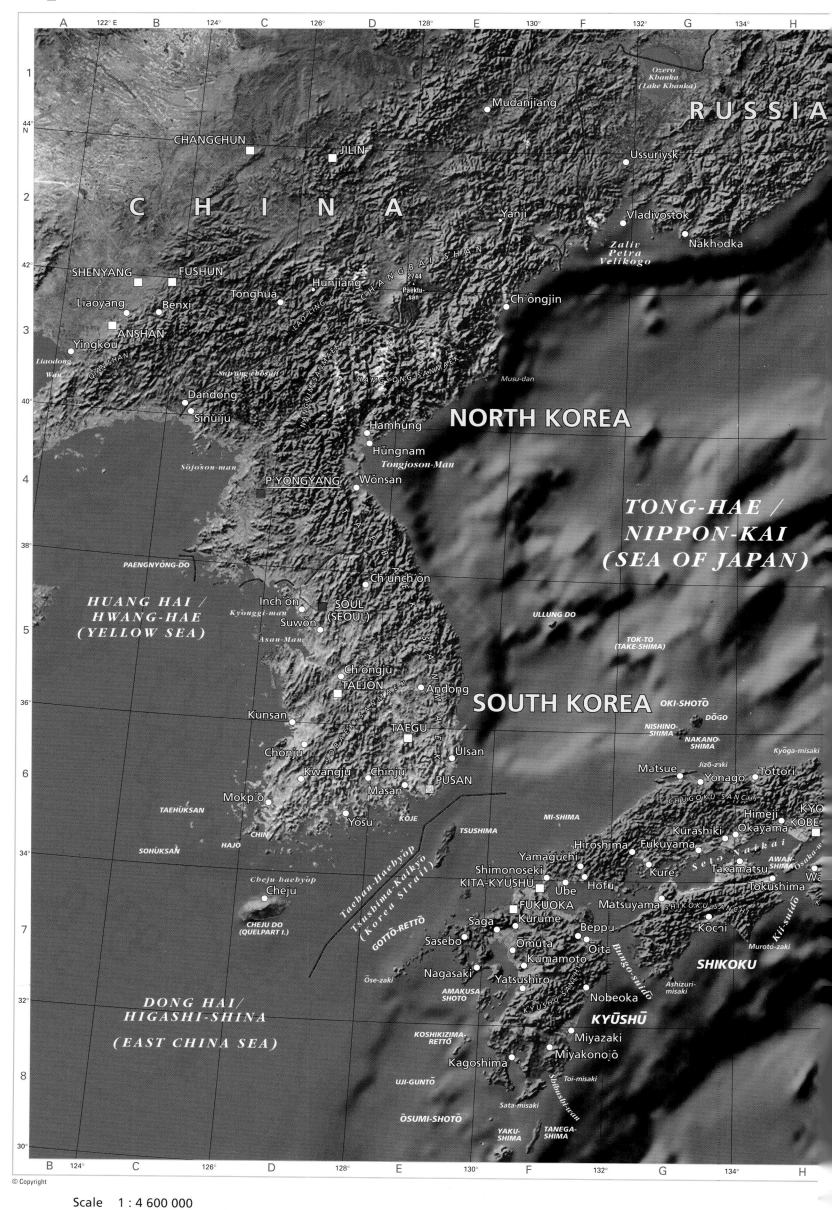

Scale   1 : 4 600 000

0   100   200   300 km

© Copyright

J   138°   K   140°   L   142°   M   144°   N   146°   P   148°   Q   150°   R

REBUN-TO

RISHIRI-TO

HOK-KAI
(SEA OF OKHOTSK)

Shiretoko-misaki

OSTROV ITURUP/
ETOROFU-TO

OSTROV KUNAŠIR/
KUNASHIRI-TO

SHIKOTAN-TŌ

KURIL TRENCH

Asahikawa

2290
Asahi-
dake

Ishikari-wan

Shakotan-misaki

Otaru

SAPPORO

Obihiro

Kushiro

HOKKAIDŌ

Shikotsu-Ko

Muroran

Uchiura-wan

OKUSHIRI-TO

Erimo-misaki

Hakodate

O-SHIMA

Tsugaru-kaikyō

Shiriya-zaki

Tappi-zaki

Mutsu-wan

Aomori

Hirosaki

Hachinohe

Nyūdō-zaki

Morioka

Akita

Todoga-saki

Sakata

Tsuruoka

AWA

Ishinomaki

Yamagata

Sendai

Kinka-san

SADO

Niigata

Sendai-wan

Fukushima

Aizu-
Wakamatsu

Koriyama

Suzu-misaki

Jōetsu

Nagaoka

HONSHŪ

Toyama-
wan

Iwaki

JAPAN TRENCH

...aoka   Toyama

Nagano

Utsunomiya

Hitachi

...zawa

3180
Yariga

Ueda

Maebashi

Mito

...ui

Matsumoto

Tsuchiura

Kasumiga-
ura

TŌKYŌ

Kofu

Chōshi

...ki   Gifu

KAWASAKI

Funabashi

JAPAN

3776
Fuji-san

Tokyo-wan

YOKOHAMA

NAGOYA

Numazu

Yokosuka

Okazaki

Sagami-
nada

PACIFIC

Toyohashi

Shizuoka

Ise-
wan

Hamamatsu

O-SHIMA

Ise

NII-JIMI

Daiō-zaki

KOZU-SHIMA

MIYAKE-JIMA

OCEAN

MIKURA-JIMA

HACHIJO-JIMA

Ramapo Deep
10374

111

Malaysia

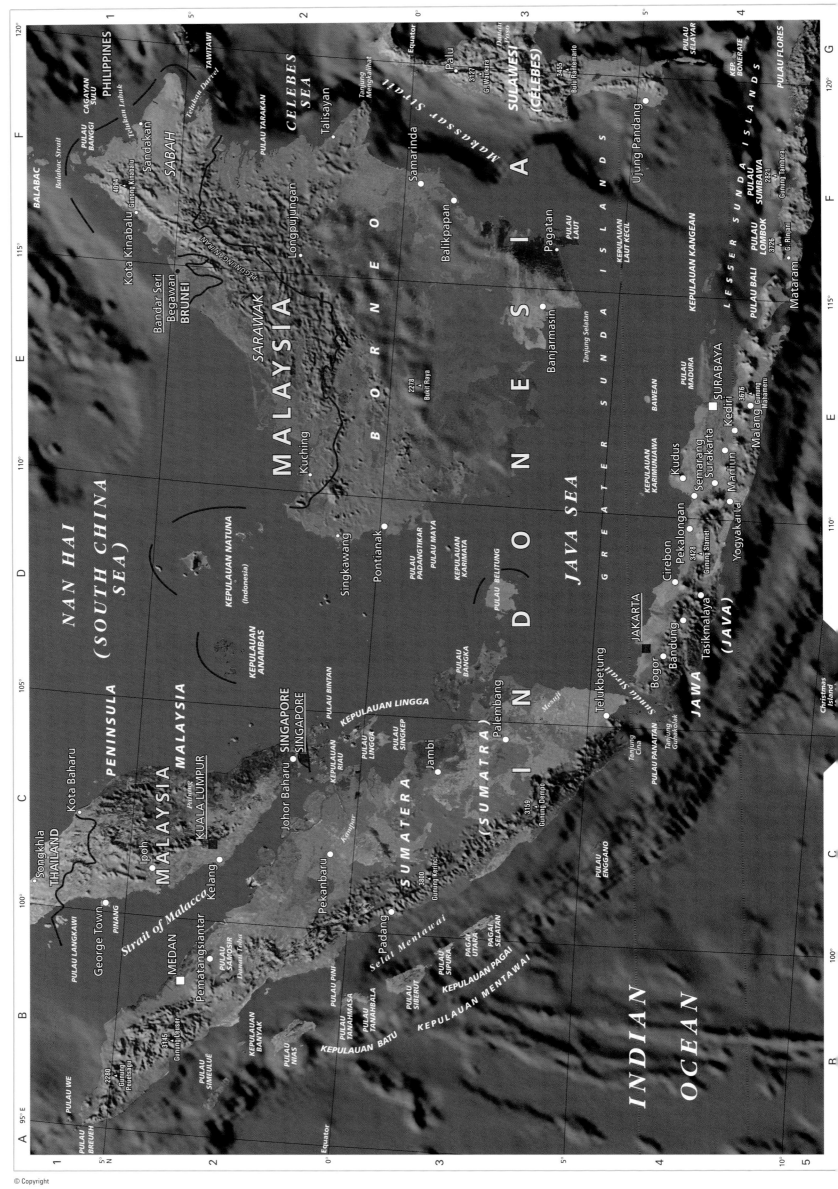

Scale 1 : 9 200 000

0   200   400   600 km

Indonesia

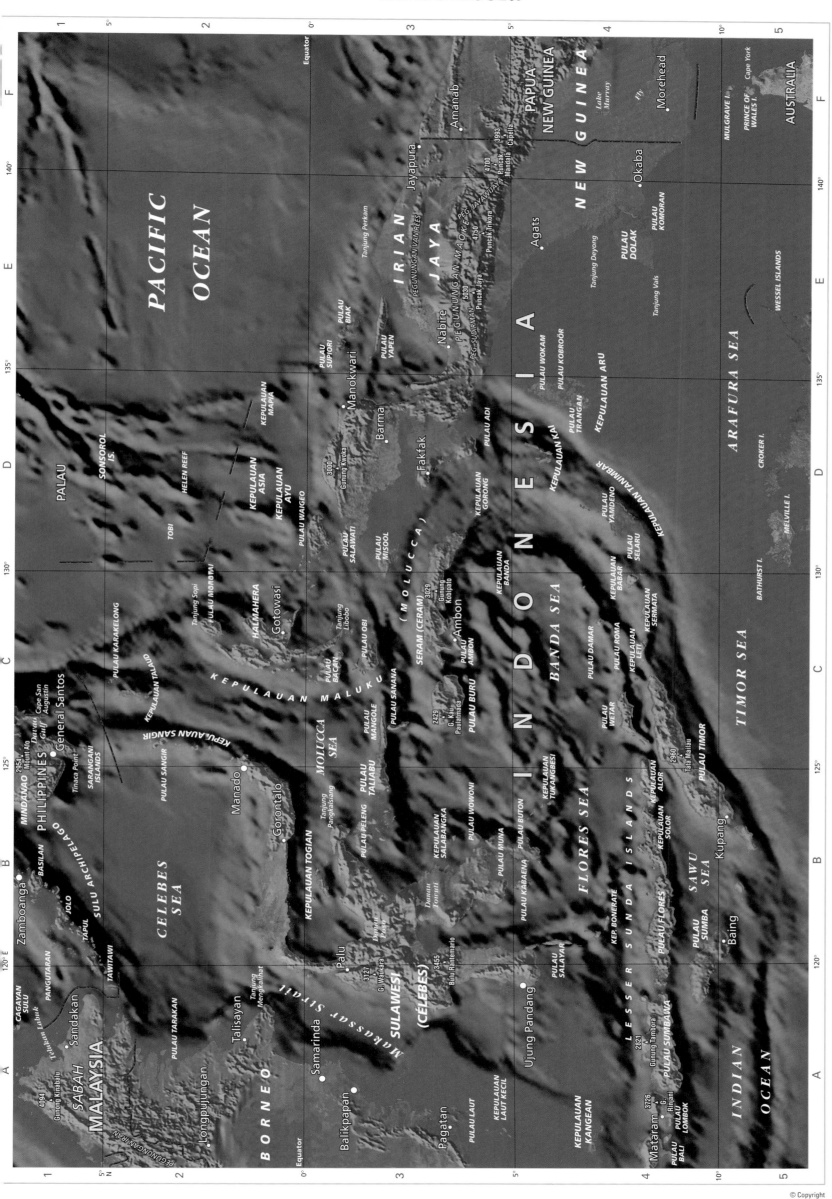

PACIFIC

OCEAN

PAPUA
NEW GUINEA

NEW GUINEA

AUSTRALIA

Amanab

Lake
Murray

Morehead

Fly

Okaba

MULGRAVE Is.
PRINCE OF
WALES I.
Cape York

Jayapura

PEGUNUNGAN VAN REES

IRIAN

JAYA

PEG. JAYAWIJAYA

4700 Puncak
Mandala
Capella 3993

PEG-SUDIRMAN 4750
Puncak Jaya
5030 Puncak Trikora

Agats

PEGUNUNGAN MAOKE

Tanjung Perkam

Nabire

Tanjung Deyong

PULAU
KOMORAN

PULAU
DOLAK

Tanjung Vals

ARAFURA SEA

PALAU

SONSOROL
IS.

HELEN REEF

TOBI

KEPULAUAN
MAPIA

KEPULAUAN
ASIA

KEPULAUAN
AYU

PULAU WAIGEO

PULAU
SUPIORI

PULAU
BIAK

PULAU
YAPEN

Manokwari

Barma

Fakfak

3000 Gunung Kwoka

PULAU
SALAWATI

PULAU
MISOOL

(M O L U C C A)

SERAM (CERAM)

PULAU ADI

KEPULAUAN
GORONG

KEPULAUAN
BANDA

KEPULAUAN KAI

PULAU KOBROÖR

PULAU WOKAM

PULAU
TRANGAN

KEPULAUAN ARU

WESSEL ISLANDS

CROKER I.

BATHURST I.

MELVILLE I.

Tanjung Sopi

Tanjung
Libobo

HALMAHERA

Gotowasi

PULAU MOROTAI

PULAU
BACAN

Tanjung
Obi

PULAU OBI

PULAU
MANGOLE

PULAU
TALIABU

KEPULAUAN TALAUD

PULAU KARAKELONG

KEPULAUAN SANGIR

KEPU.AUAN SANGIR

PULAU SANGIR

SARANGANI
ISLANDS

PULAU SANANA

2429
G. Kau
Praulamada

3029
Gunung
Kobijato

Ambon
PULAU
AMBON

PULAU BURU

KEPULAUAN
SULA

MOLUCCA
SEA

KEPULAUAN MALUKU

BANDA SEA

PULAU DAMAR

PULAU
WETAR

PULAU ROMA

KEPULAUAN
LETI

PULAU
YAMDENO

PULAU
SELARU

KEPULAUAN
BABAR

KEPULAUAN
SERMATA

KEPULAUAN TANIMBAR

TIMOR SEA

PHILIPPINES

MINDANAO
2954
Mount Apo
Danau
Cape San
Augustin

General Santos

Tinaca Point

2960
Tata Mailau

PULAU TIMOR

I N D O N E S I A

Zamboanga

BASILAN

JOLO

TAPUL

SULU

CAGAYAN
SULU

PANGUTARAN

TAWITAWI

SULU ARCHIPELAGO

Sandakan

SABAH
MALAYSIA

Gunung Kinabalu
4994

PEGUNUNGAN IRAN

Loŋgpujungan

BORNEO

Samarinda

Balikpapan

Pagatan

PULAU LAUT

KEPULAUAN
LAUT KECIL

KEPULAUAN
KANGEAN

Mataram
PULAU
BALI
G.
Rinjani 3726
PULAU
LOMBOK

INDIAN

OCEAN

2821
Gunung Tambora

PULAU SUMBAWA

L E S S E R S U N D A I S L A N D S

PULAU FLORES

Danau
Toruti

PULAU SUMBA

Baing

SAWU
SEA

Kupang

KEPULAUAN
ALOR

KEPULAUAN
SOLOR

FLORES SEA

KEP. BONERATE

KEP. BONERATÉ

PULAU
SALAYAR

PULAU KABAENA

PULAU BUTON

PULAU MUNA

PULAU WOWONI

KEPULAUAN
SALABANGKA

KEPULAUAN
TUKANGBESI

Ujung Pandang

Talisayan

Tanjung
Mengkalihat

Palu

3127

G. Watukara

3455
Bulu Rantemario

SULAWESI
(CÉLEBES)

Gorontalo

Manado

Tanjung
Pangkalaseang

KEPULAUAN TOGIAN

CELEBES
SEA

Makassar Strait

Equator

PALU

Palu

Makassar Strait

600 km

Scale 1 : 9 200 000

0   200   400   600 km

© Copyright

113

Oceania

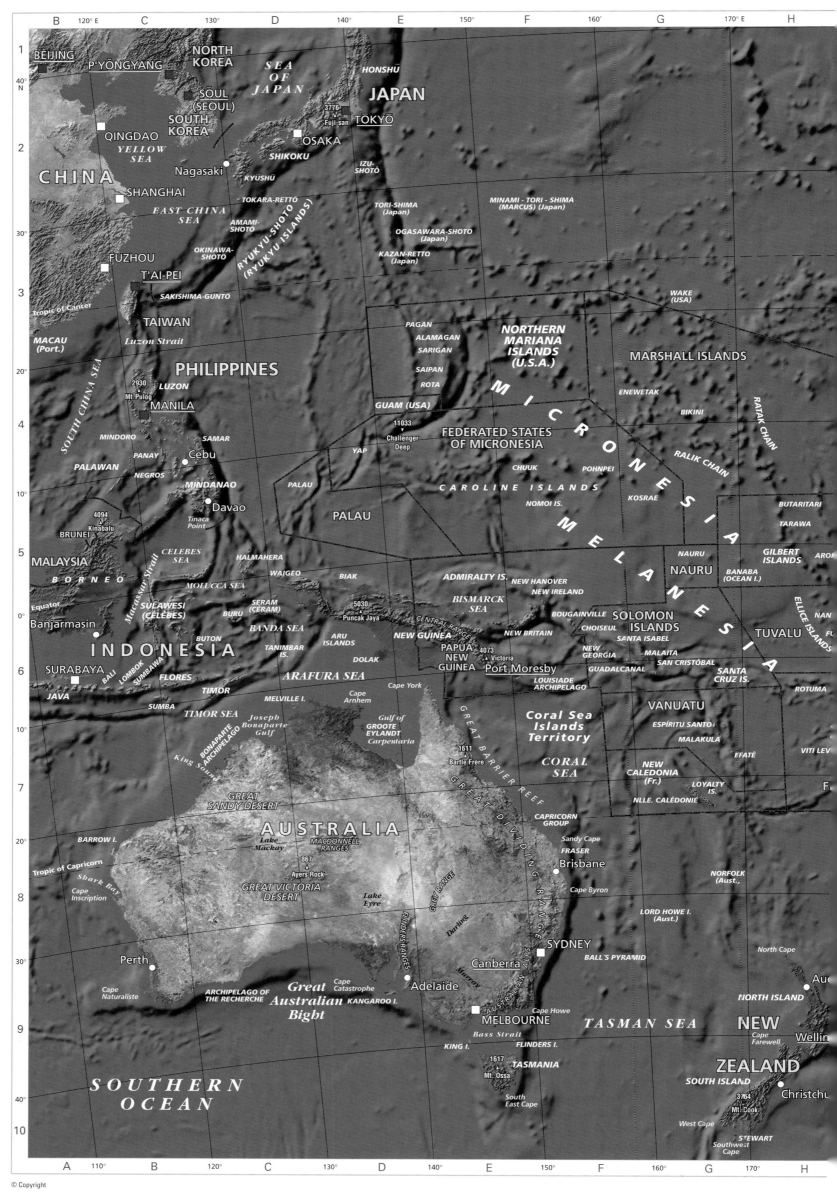

Scale 1 : 32 200 000

0   500   1000   1500   2000 km

© Copyright

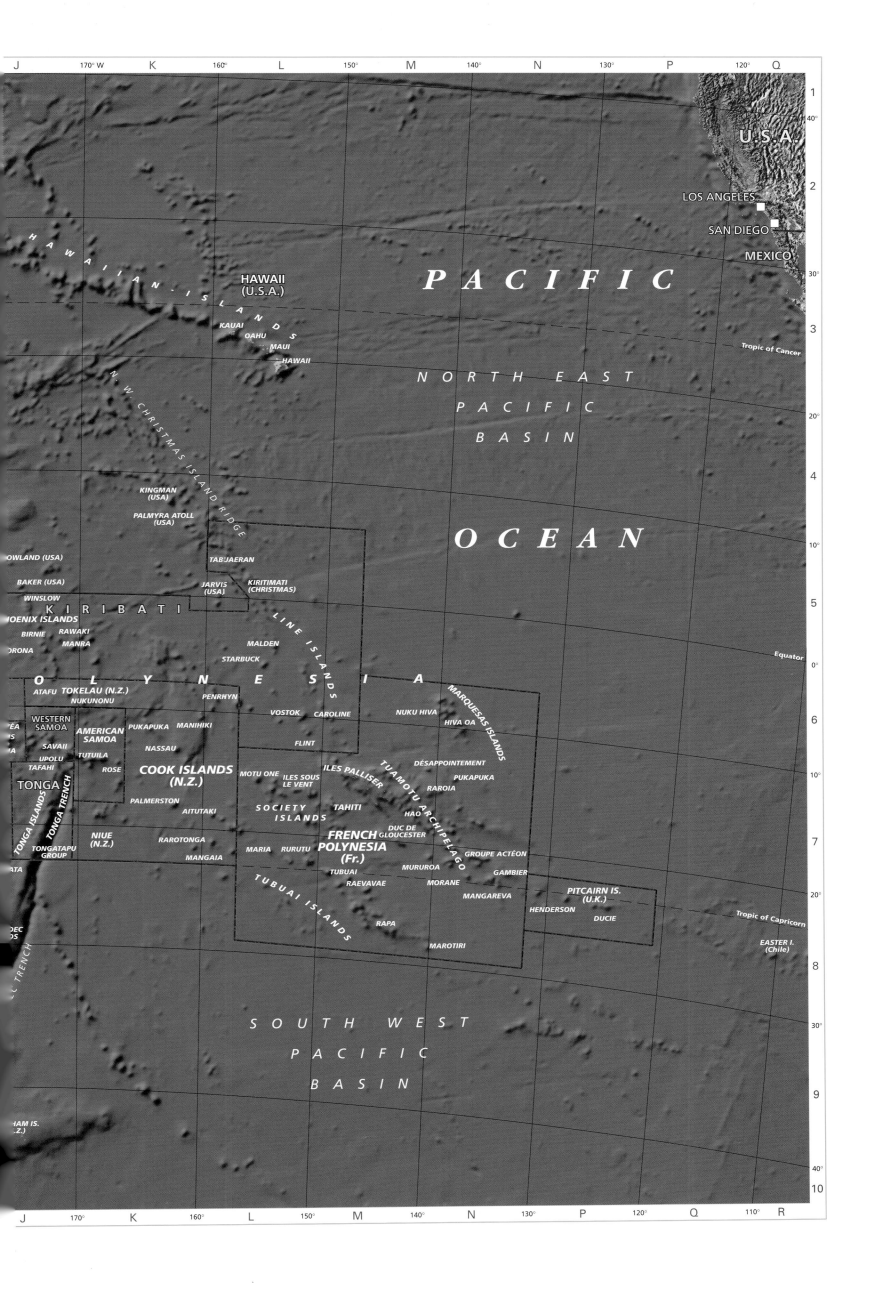

J   170° W   K   160°   L   150°   M   140°   N   130°   P   120°   Q

U.S.A.

1

40°

2

LOS ANGELES

SAN DIEGO

MEXICO

30°

P A C I F I C

Tropic of Cancer

3

HAWAIIAN ISLANDS

HAWAII
(U.S.A.)

KAUAI   OAHU

MAUI

HAWAII

N O R T H   E A S T

P A C I F I C

B A S I N

20°

4

N. W. CHRISTMAS ISLAND RIDGE

KINGMAN
(USA)

PALMYRA ATOLL
(USA)

O C E A N

10°

OWLAND (USA)

TAB·UAERAN

BAKER (USA)

JARVIS
(USA)

KIRITIMATI
(CHRISTMAS)

WINSLOW

K I R I B A T I

5

Equator

0°

HOENIX ISLANDS

L I N E   I S L A N D S

BIRNIE   RAWAKI

MALDEN

ORONA   MANRA

STARBUCK

P   O   L   Y   N   E   S   I   A

ATAFU   **TOKELAU (N.Z.)**

PENRHYN

M A R Q U E S A S   I S L A N D S

6

NUKUNONU

**WESTERN
SAMOA**

PUKAPUKA   MANIHIKI

VOSTOK   CAROLINE

NUKU HIVA

ÉA

**AMERICAN
SAMOA**

HIVA OA

SAVAII

NASSAU

FLINT

A

UPOLU   TUTUILA

DÉSAPPOINTEMENT

TAFAHI

ROSE

**COOK ISLANDS
(N.Z.)**

MOTU ONE   ILES SOUS
LE VENT

ILES PALLISER

PUKAPUKA

10°

TONGA

T U A M O T U   A R C H I P E L A G O

RAROIA

Tonga Trench

PALMERSTON

AITUTAKI

*SOCIETY
ISLANDS*

TAHITI

HAO

Tonga Islands

NIUE
(N.Z.)

RAROTONGA

**FRENCH
POLYNESIA
(Fr.)**

DUC DE
GLOUCESTER

7

TONGATAPU
GROUP

MANGAIA

MARIA   RURUTU

GROUPE ACTÉON

ATA

TUBUAI ISLANDS

TUBUAI

MURUROA

GAMBIER

RAEVAVAE

MORANE

20°

DEC
OS

RAPA

MANGAREVA

**PITCAIRN IS.
(U.K.)**

HENDERSON

DUCIE

Tropic of Capricorn

EASTER I.
(Chile)

MAROTIRI

8

C TRENCH

IAM IS.
.Z.)

S O U T H   W E S T

30°

P A C I F I C

9

B A S I N

40°

10

J   170°   K   160°   L   150°   M   140°   N   130°   P   120°   Q   110°   R

Australia

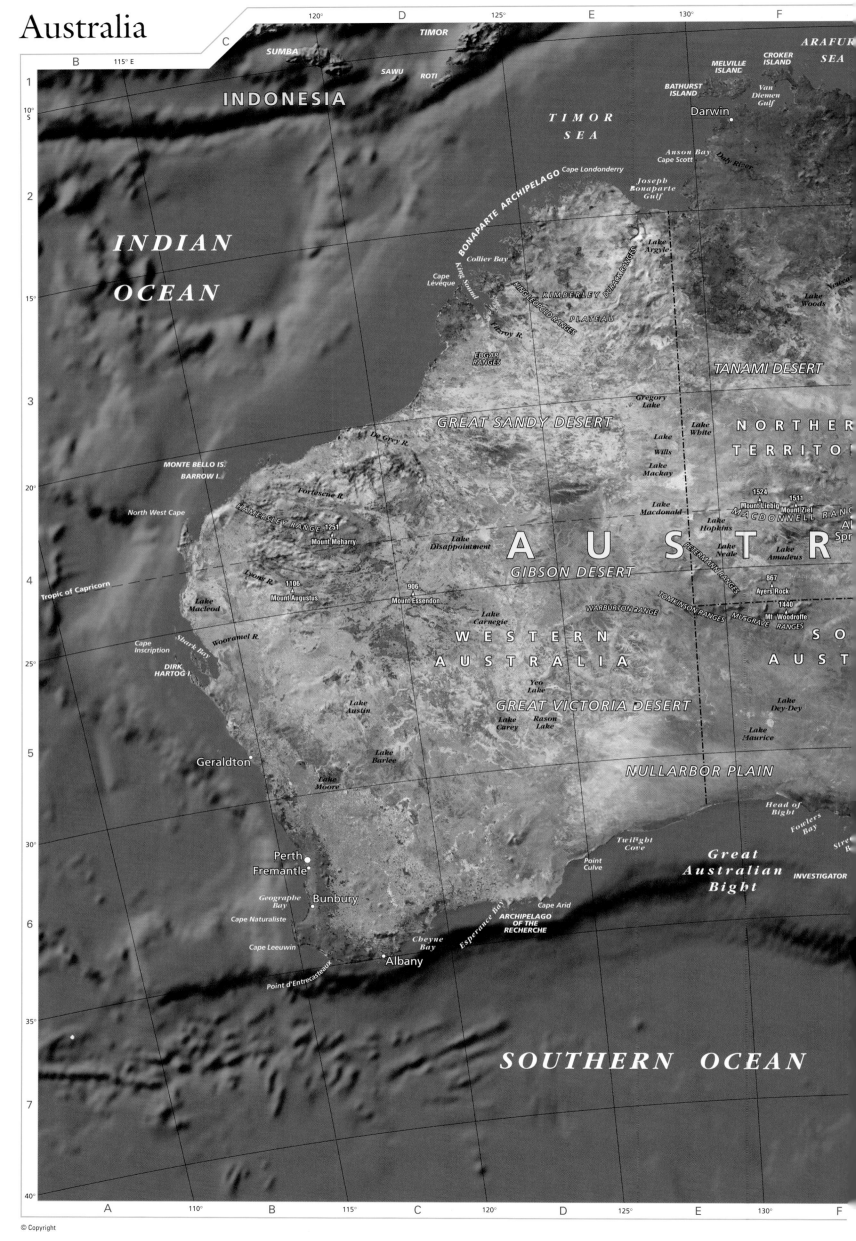

INDONESIA

SUMBA   TIMOR

SAWU   ROTI

TIMOR
SEA

MELVILLE
ISLAND   CROKER
ISLAND

ARAFUR
SEA

BATHURST
ISLAND   Van
Diemen
Gulf

Darwin

Anson Bay
Cape Scott   Daly River

INDIAN

OCEAN

BONAPARTE ARCHIPELAGO   Cape Londonderry

Joseph
Bonaparte
Gulf

Lake
Argyle

Collier Bay

Cape
Lévêque

King Sound

KIMBERLEY   DURACK RANGES

KING LEOPOLD RANGES

PLATEAU

Lake
Woods

Fitzroy R.

EDGAR
RANGES

TANAMI DESERT

De Grey R.

GREAT SANDY DESERT

Gregory
Lake

Lake
White   NORTHER

TERRITO

MONTE BELLO IS.
BARROW I.

North West Cape

Fortescue R.

HAMERSLEY RANGE

1251
Mount Meharry

Lake
Wills

Lake
Mackay

Lake
Macdonald

1524
Mount Liebig   1511
Mount Ziel

MACDONNELL RANG   Al
Spr

Lake
Disappointment

A U S T R

Lake
Hopkins

Lake
Neale   Lake
Amadeus

Tropic of Capricorn

Lyons R.   1106
Mount Augustus

906
Mount Essendon

GIBSON DESERT

PETERMANN RANGES

867
Ayers Rock

1440
Mt. Woodroffe

SO

Lake
Macleod

Lake
Carnegie

WARBURTON RANGE

TOMKINSON RANGES   MUSGRAVE RANGES

AUST

Cape
Inscription

Shark Bay

Wooramel R.

W E S T E R N

A U S T R A L I A

Lake
Dey-Dey

DIRK
HARTOG I.

Lake
Austin

Yeo
Lake

GREAT VICTORIA DESERT

Lake
Carey   Rason
Lake

Lake
Maurice

Lake
Barlee

NULLARBOR PLAIN

Head of
Bight   Fowlers
Bay

Geraldton

Lake
Moore

Twilight
Cove

Great
Australian
Bight

Stre
R

Perth
Fremantle

Point
Culve

INVESTIGATOR

Geographe
Bay   Bunbury

Cape Naturaliste

Cape Arid

ARCHIPELAGO
OF THE
RECHERCHE

Cape Leeuwin

Cheyne
Bay

Esperance Bay

Albany

Point d'Entrecasteaux

SOUTHERN   OCEAN

© Copyright

Scale 1 : 11 040 000

0   200   400   600 km

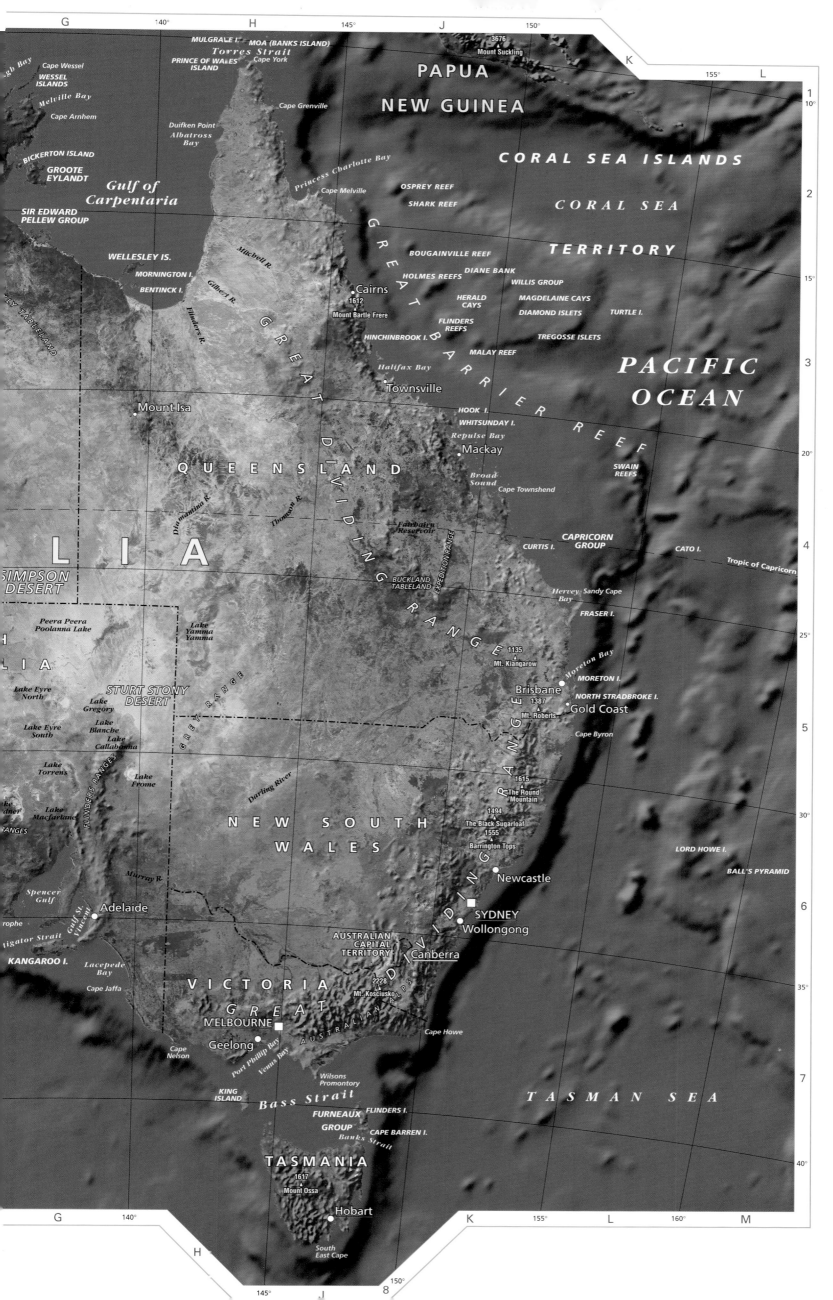

MULGRAVE I.　MOA (BANKS ISLAND)
PRINCE OF WALES
ISLAND
Torres Strait　Cape York

Cape Grenville

PAPUA
NEW GUINEA

3676
Mount Suckling

Duifken Point
Albatross
Bay

Princess Charlotte Bay
Cape Melville

CORAL SEA ISLANDS

Cape Wessel
**WESSEL
ISLANDS**
Melville Bay
Cape Arnhem

OSPREY REEF

SHARK REEF

CORAL SEA

BICKERTON ISLAND
**GROOTE
EYLANDT**

*Gulf of
Carpentaria*

TERRITORY

BOUGAINVILLE REEF

DIANE BANK

**SIR EDWARD
PELLEW GROUP**

HOLMES REEFS

WILLIS GROUP

HERALD
CAYS

MAGDELAINE CAYS

WELLESLEY IS.

Mitchell R.

MORNINGTON I.

Cairns

DIAMOND ISLETS

TURTLE I.

BENTINCK I.

Gilbert R.

1612
Mount Bartle Frere

FLINDERS
REEFS

TREGOSSE ISLETS

Flinders R.

HINCHINBROOK I.

MALAY REEF

PACIFIC
OCEAN

Halifax Bay

Townsville

Mount Isa

HOOK I.

WHITSUNDAY I.

Repulse Bay

QUEENSLAND

Mackay

*Broad
Sound*

SWAIN
REEFS

Cape Townshend

Diamantina R.

Thomson R.

*Fairbairn
Reservoir*

CAPRICORN
GROUP

CURTIS I.

CATO I.

Tropic of Capricorn

**SIMPSON
DESERT**

*BUCKLAND
TABLELAND*

*Hervey Sandy Cape
Bay*

FRASER I.

Peera Peera
Poolanna Lake

*Lake
Yamma
Yamma*

1135
Mt. Kiangarow

Moreton Bay

MORETON I.

*Lake Eyre
North*

**STURT STONY
DESERT**

Brisbane

NORTH STRADBROKE I.

1387
Mt. Roberts

Gold Coast

*Lake
Gregory*

*Lake
Blanche*

*Lake
Callabonna*

Cape Byron

*Lake Eyre
South*

*Lake
Torrens*

*Lake
Frome*

Darling River

1615
The Round
Mountain

LORD HOWE I.

*Lake
Macfarlane*

NEW SOUTH
WALES

1494
The Black Sugarloaf
1555
Barrington Tops

BALL'S PYRAMID

*Spencer
Gulf*

Murray R.

Newcastle

Adelaide

SYDNEY
Wollongong

KANGAROO I.

*Lacepede
Bay*

**AUSTRALIAN
CAPITAL
TERRITORY**

Canberra

Cape Jaffa

VICTORIA

2228
Mt. Kosciusko

GREAT

MELBOURNE

Cape Howe

Geelong

Cape
Nelson

Port Phillip Bay
Venus Bay

*Wilsons
Promontory*

TASMAN SEA

KING
ISLAND

Bass Strait

FLINDERS I.

**FURNEAUX
GROUP**

CAPE BARREN I.

Banks Strait

TASMANIA

1617
Mount Ossa

Hobart

South
East Cape

New Zealand

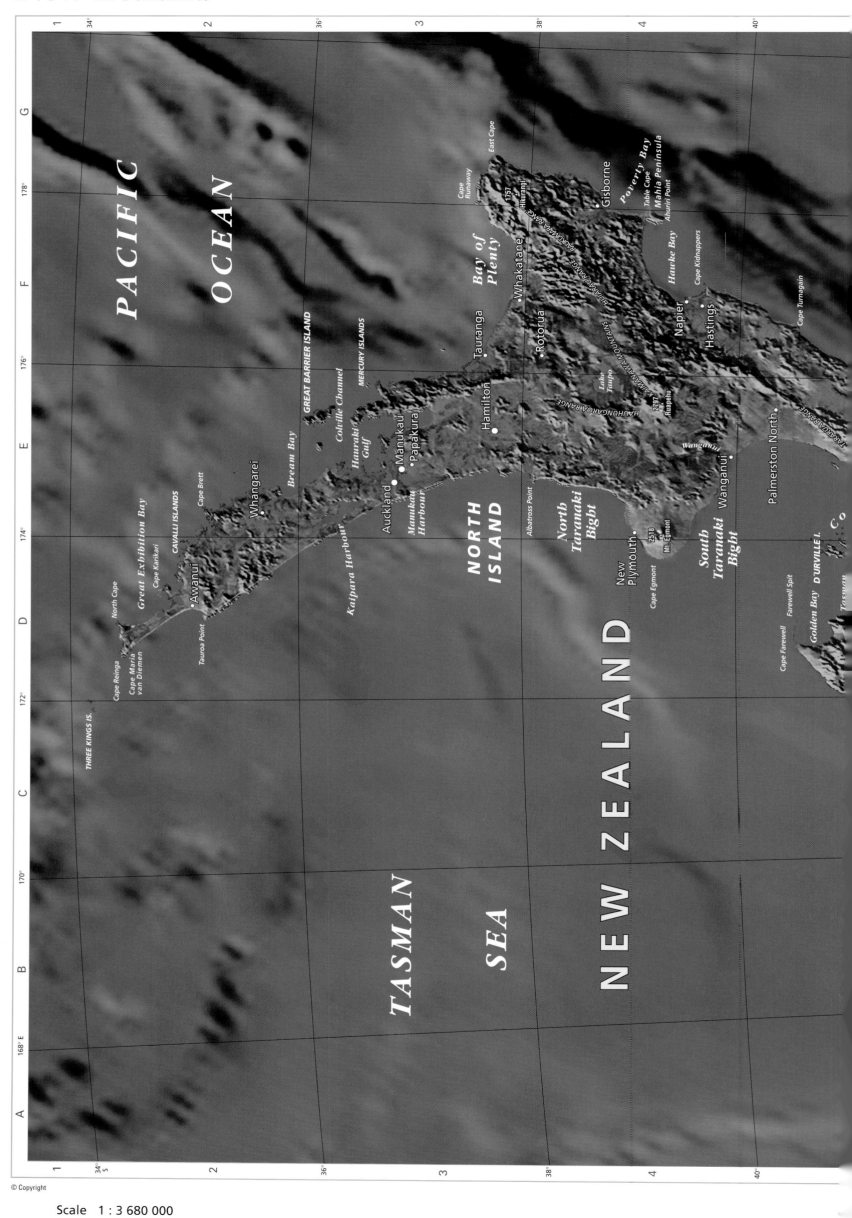

Scale   1 : 3 680 000

0   100   200 km

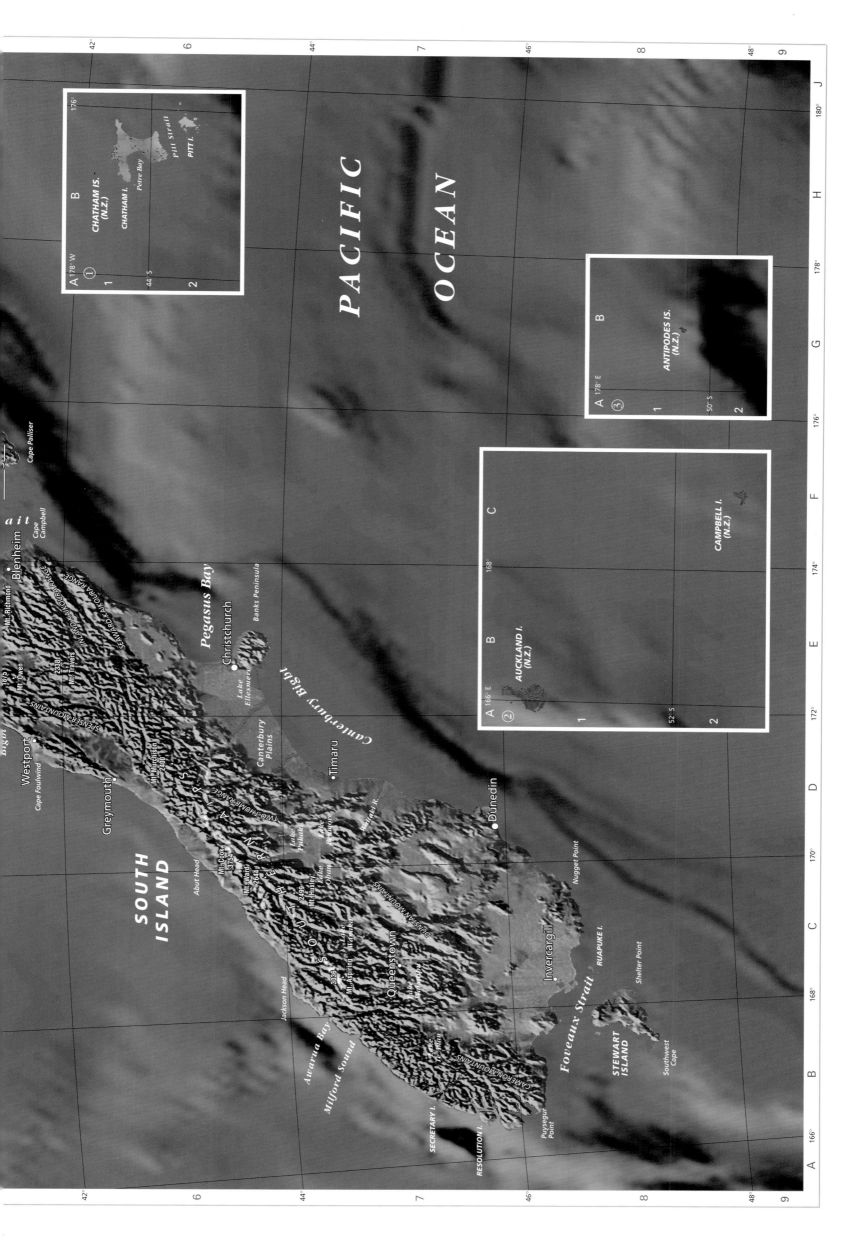

PACIFIC

OCEAN

SOUTH
ISLAND

Polar Regions

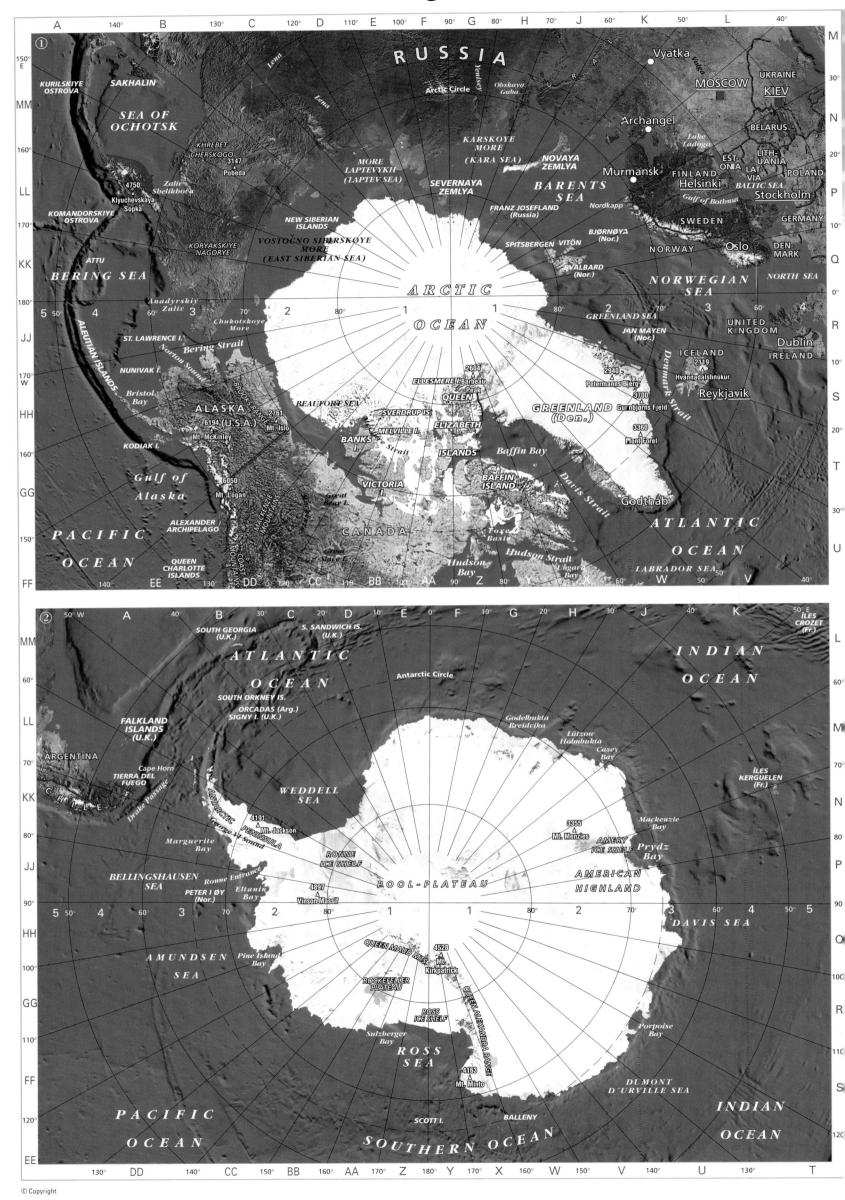

Scale 1 : 40 480 000

0   500   1000   1500   2000 km

© Copyright

Satellite Atlas
OF THE
WORLD

Using the Index

All the placenames and features appearing in this atlas are included in this index. The same feature name may appear on several different pages. In order to avoid duplication, the name will generally be referred to the largest scale map on which the feature appears.

Explanation of symbols used

▨	Physical region, feature		■	Capital City
⬚	Island or Island group, Rocky reef, Coral reef		○	State capital
▲	Mountain, volcano, peak		A	Country names
▲	Mountain range		a	State or province name
⌐	Cape, point		✔	Lake or salt lake
∕	River, canal		▬	Sea, ocean
●	Place name		►	Gulf, strait, bay
			✳	Point/Place of interest

Facts and Figures

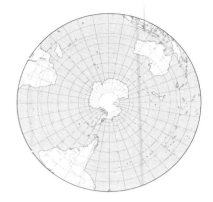

Dimensions of the Earth

Circumference of the Equator 40,076 km

Total surface area of the Earth 510,100,933 km²

Area of dry land (29.2%) 149,408,563 km²

Area of sea (70.8%) 360,692,370 km²

Continental Land Surface

1.	Asia	43,608,000 km²
2.	Africa	30,335,000 km²
3.	North America	25,349,000 km²
4.	South America	17,611,000 km²
5.	Antarctica	13,340,000 km²
6.	Europe	10,498,000 km²
7.	Australia and Oceania	8,923,000 km²

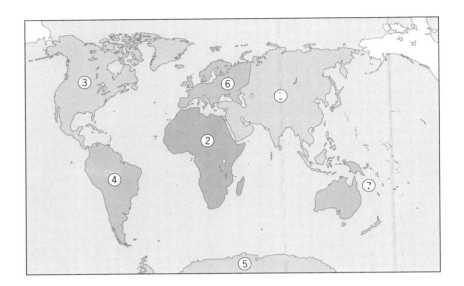

Largest Countries according to area

1.	Russia	17,100,000 km²
2.	Canada	9,976,139 km²
3.	China	9,572,980 km²
4.	United States	9,363,166 km²
5.	Brazil	8,511,996 km²
6.	Australia	7,682,300 km²
7.	India	3,166,829 km²
8.	Argentina	2,780,092 km²
9.	Sudan	2,505,813 km²
10.	Algeria	2,381,740 km²

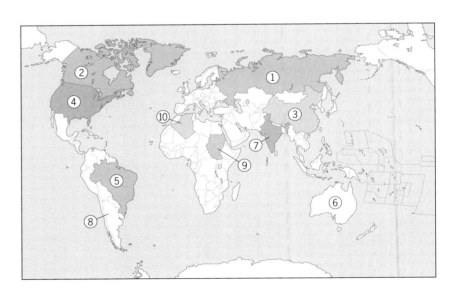

Oceans and largest inland waters

1.	Caspian Sea (Salt) (Asia)	371,000 km²
2.	Lake Superior (N. America)	83,270 km²
3.	Lake Victoria (Africa)	68,800 km²
4.	Lake Huron (N. America)	60,700 km²
5.	Lake Michigan (N. America)	58,020 km²
6.	Aral Sea (Salt) (Asia)	36,000 km²
7.	Lake Tanganyika (Africa)	32,900 km²
8.	Great Bear Lake (N. America)	31,790 km²
9.	Lake Baikal (Asia)	30,500 km²
10.	Great Slave Lake (N. America)	28,440 km²

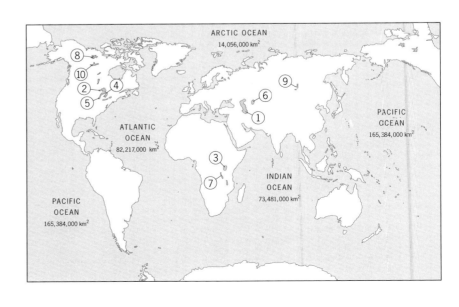

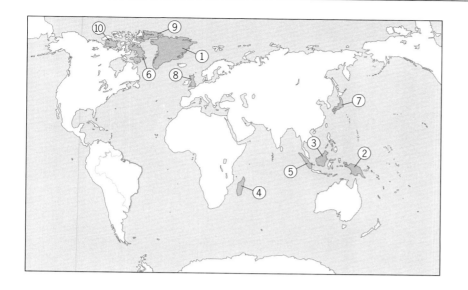

Largest islands of the world

1.	Greenland	2,175,600 km^2
2.	New Guinea	808,510 km^2
3.	Borneo	757,050 km^2
4.	Madagascar	594,180 km^2
5.	Sumatra	524,100 km^2
6.	Baffin Island	476,070 km^2
7.	Honshu	230,455 km^2
8.	Great Britain	229,870 km^2
9.	Ellesmere Island	212,690 km^2
10.	Victoria Island	212,200 km^2

Longest rivers of the world

1.	Nile (Africa)	6,695 km
2.	Amazon (S. America)	6,515 km
3.	Chang-Jiang/Yangtze (Asia)	6,380 km
4.	Mississippi-Missouri (N. America)	6,019 km
5.	Ob-Irtysh (Asia)	5,570 km
6.	Jenisey-Angara (Asia)	5,550 km
7.	Huang He-Yellow River (Asia)	5,464 km

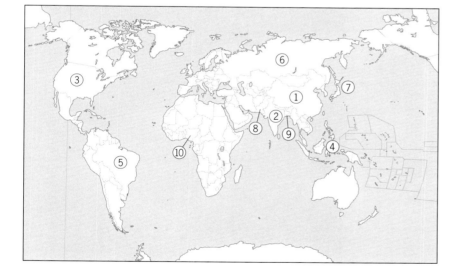

Largest countries according to population

1.	China	1,185,000,000
2.	India	903,000,000
3.	United States	257,000,000
4.	Indonesia	188,000,000
5.	Brazil	159,000,000
6.	Russia	150,000,000
7.	Japan	124,900,000
8.	Pakistan	122,400,000
9.	Bangladesh	122,280,000
10.	Nigeria	92,800,000

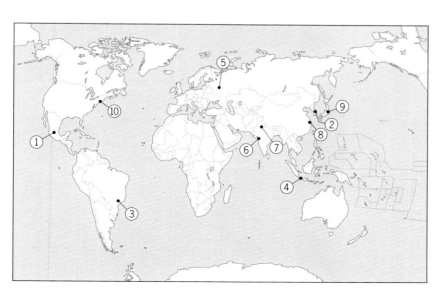

Largest cities of the world

1.	Mexico City	15,047,000
2.	Seoul	10,628,000
3.	Sao Paulo	9,480,427
4.	Jakarta	9,000,000
5.	Moscow	8,967,000
6.	Bombay	8,400,000
7.	Delhi	8,380,000
8.	Shanghai	8,214,436
9.	Tokyo	7,976,000
10.	New York	7,322,564

Index

SATELLITE ATLAS OF THE WORLD

Amundsen Sea	Antarctica	112	(2)GG4
Amur (Heilong Jiang)	China / Russia	72	M6
Amvrakikos Kólpos	Greece	78	C6
An Nafud	Saudi Arabia	82	C4
An Najaf	Iraq	82	D3
An Nasiryah	Iraq	82	E3
Anabar	Russia	102	J2
Anabarskoye Ploskogorye	Russia	102	H2
Anadyr	Russia	103	V3
Anadyr	Russia	103	X4
Anadyrskiy Zaliv	Russia	103	Y4
Anadyrskoye Ploskogorye	Russia	103	V3
Anafi	Greece	78	H8
Anai Mudi	India	105	C6
Anamur Burun	Turkey	80	E6
Anchorage	Alaska (U.S.)	29	(1)H3
Ancona	Italy	74	H5
Andújar	Spain	70	F6
Andalusia	United States	35	J5
Andaman Islands	India (Indian Ocean)	105	F6
Andaman Sea	South East Asia	106	A4
Andernach	Germany	65	C6
Anderson	United States	35	K5
Andikithira	Greece	78	F9
Andizhan	Uzbekistan	101	N9
Andong	South Korea	110	E5
Andorra	Europe	69	G11
Andorra la Vella	Andorra	71	M2
Andover	United Kingdom	56	B3
Andradina	Brazil	50	G8
Andreanof Islands	Alaska (U.S.)	29	(3)C1
Andrews	United States	33	F5
Andria	Italy	76	D8
Andros	Bahamas	47	J4
Andrott	Laccadive Islands (India)	105	B6
Andselv	Norway	58	K2
Andya	Norway	58	H2
Angara	Russia	102	F5
Angarsk	Russia	102	G6
Angathonisi	Greece	79	J7
Ånge	Sweden	58	H5
Ängelholm	Sweden	62	B1
Angers	France	68	E6
Ångesön	Sweden	58	L5
Anglesey	United Kingdom	67	J8
Angmagssa	Greenland	44	Z3
Angola	Southern Africa	96	B2
Angoulême	France	69	F8
Anguilla	Caribbean	47	M5
Anholt	Denmark	59	F8
Anjouani	Comoros	95	G6
Ankara	Turkey	80	E3
Ankaratra	Madagascar	97	H3
Anklam	Germany	64	J3
Ann Arbor	United States	36	K3
Annaba	Algeria	89	G1
Annecy	France	69	M8
Annobón (Pagalu)	Equatorial Guinea	93	F5
Anqing	China	108	F4
Ansbach	Germany	65	F7
Anshan	China	109	G2
Anson Bay	Australia	116	E2
Antakya	Turkey	80	G5
Antalya	Turkey	80	D5
Antalya Körfezi	Turkey	80	D5
Antananarivo	Madagascar	97	H3
Antequera	Spain	70	F7
Anti-Atlas	Morocco	88	D3
Antigua	Caribbean	47	M5
Antigua and Barbuda	Caribbean	47	M5
Antipodes Islands	New Zealand	119	(3)B1
Antofagasta	Chile	52	G3
Antrim Mountains	United Kingdom	67	G6
Antsiranana	Madagascar	95	H6
Antwerpen	Belgium	57	H3
Anzhero-Sudzhensk	Russia	101	R6
Aomori	Japan	111	L3
Aosta/Aoste	Italy	72	C5
Aoukale	Central Africa	94	C1
Aoukâr	Mauritania	88	D5
Apalachee Bay	United States	35	K6
Apeldoorn	Netherlands	57	K2
Apennini (Apennines)	Italy	72	F6
Api	Nepal	104	D2
Apolda	Germany	65	G5
Apostle Islands	United States	36	H2
Appalachian Mountains	United States	35	K4
Appennino Calabro	Italy	75	L10
Appennino Campano	Italy	75	K8
Appennino Ligure	Italy	72	D6
Appennino Lucano	Italy	75	L8
Appennino Napoletano	Italy	76	C8
Appennino Tosco-Emiliano	Italy	74	E4
Appleton	United States	36	J3
Apuka	Russia	103	V4
Apure	South America	50	D2
Aqaba	Jordan	84	C7
Ar Ra´s al Abyad	Saudi Arabia	82	C5
Ar Rayn	Saudi Arabia	85	A5
Ar Riyad (Riyadh)	Saudi Arabia	82	E5
Arabian Sea	Middle East	83	H6
Arad	Romania	76	J3
Arafura Sea	Oceania	114	D6
Aragats	Armenia	81	L3
Aragon	Spain	71	J2
Araguacema	Brazil	51	H5
Arak	Algeria	89	F3
Arak	Iran	82	E3
Arakan Yoma	South East Asia	106	A2
Araks	Middle East	82	E2
Aral Sea	Kazakhstan / Uzbekistan	101	K9
Aralsk	Kazakhstan	61	N5
Aran Island	Ireland	67	E6
Aran Islands	Ireland	67	D8
Aranda de Duero	Spain	70	G3
Aranjuez	Spain	70	G4
Aras	Asia	81	M4
Arcachon	France	69	D9
Arcata	United States	29	B2
Archangel	Russia	60	J2
Arches National Park	United States	30	E4
Archipel des Comores	Comoros	95	G6
Archipelago of the Recherche	Australia	116	D6
Archipiélago de la Reina Adelaida	Chile	52	F9
Archipiélago de Los Chonos	Chile	52	F8
Arctic Ocean	Canada	24	C1
Arda	Bulgaria	78	H3
Årdalstangen	Norway	59	D6
Ardennes	Belgium	57	J4
Ardila	Spain / Portugal	70	C6
Ardmore	United States	34	G5
Arendal	Norway	59	E7
Arequipa	Peru	50	C7
Åreskutan	Sweden	58	G5
Arezzo	Italy	73	G7
Argenta	Italy	73	G6
Argenteuil	France	68	G4
Argentina	South America	52	H4
Arges	Romania	77	N5
Argonne	France	57	J5
Argun	China / Russia	102	K6
Århus	Denmark	59	F8
Ari Atoll	Maldives	105	B8
Arica	Chile	50	C7
Ariège	France	69	G10
Aripuanã	Brazil	50	E5
Arizona	United States	32	D5
Arkadelphia	United States	34	H5
Arkalyk	Kazakhstan	61	P4
Arkansas	United States	34	H5
Arkansas City	United States	33	G4
Arkansas River	United States	34	H4
Arkatag	China	101	R10
Arles	France	69	K10
Arlit	Niger	89	G5
Arlon	Belgium	57	J5
Armavir	Russia	81	J1
Armenia	Asia	81	L4
Arnhem	Netherlands	57	J3
Arno	Italy	72	F7
Arnstadt	Germany	65	F6
Arny	Norway	58	L1
Aroostook	Canada	37	N2
Arorae	Kiribati (Pacific Ocean)	114	H6
Arran	United Kingdom	66	H6
Arras	France	56	F4
Artesia	United States	32	F5
Artillery Lake	Canada	42	K4
Aru Islands	Indonesia	114	D6
Aruba	Central America	47	K6
Arusha	Tanzania	95	F4
Arvika	Sweden	59	G7
Arzano	Croatia	76	D6
Arzew	Algeria	71	K9
Arzipe	Mexico	32	D5
As Sahra´ al Janubiyah	Egypt	90	E3
As Sahra´ al Libiyah (Libyan Desert)	Libya	90	D2
As Sahra´ an Nubiyah (Nubian Desert)	Sudan	91	F3
As Sahra´ ash Sharqiyah (Eastern Desert)	Egypt	91	F2
As Sidrah	Libya	89	J2
As Sudd	Sudan	94	D2
As Sulaymaniyah	Iraq	81	L6
As Sulayyil	Saudi Arabia	82	E5
As Sulb	Saudi Arabia	85	B3
As Summan	Saudi Arabia	85	B3
As Suways (Suez)	Egypt	91	F1
Asahi	Japan	111	M2
Asahi-dake	Japan	103	Q8
Asahikawa	Japan	111	M2
Asan-Man	South Korea	110	D5
Asansol	India	104	E4
Ascension	U.K. (Atlantic Ocean)	92	B6
Aschaffenburg	Germany	65	E7
Asenovgrad	Bulgaria	77	M7
Ash Shallal al Khamis	Egypt	91	F4
Ash Shallal ar Rab	Egypt	91	F4
Ash Shallal as Sablukah	Egypt	91	F4
Ash Shallal ath Thalith	Egypt	91	F4
Ash Shallal ath Than	Egypt	91	F3
Ash Shallal Sadd el Aali	Egypt	91	F3
Ash Shariqah (Sharjah)	United Arab Emirates	83	F4
Ash Sharqi	Lebanon / Syria	84	D3
Ash Shumlul	Saudi Arabia	85	B3
Asheville	United States	35	K4
Ashgabat (Ashkhabad)	Turkmenistan	83	G2
Ashizuri-Misaki	Japan	110	G7
Ashkhabad (Ashgabat)	Turkmenistan	83	G2
Ashtabula	United States	36	K3
Asilah	Morocco	88	D9
Asinara	Sardinia (Italy)	75	C7
Asir	Saudi Arabia	82	D5
Asmara	Eritrea	91	G4
Åsnen	Sweden	62	D1
Assab	Eritrea	91	H5
Assen	Netherlands	57	K2
Assumption	Seychelles	97	(2) A2
Asti	Italy	72	D6
Astipálaia	Greece	78	H8
Astoria	United States	28	B1
Astove	Seychelles	97	(2)A3
Astrachan	Russia	61	K5
Aswân	Egypt	82	B5
Asyt	Egypt	82	B4
At Ta´if	Saudi Arabia	82	D5
At Taff	United Arab Emirates	85	F5
Ata	Tonga	115	J8
Atafu	Tokelau (N.Z.)	115	J6
Atâr	Mauritania	88	C4
Atasu	Kazakhstan	61	Q5
Atbarah	Sudan	82	B6
Atbasar	Kazakhstan	61	P4
Atchison	United States	31	H4
Athabasca Lake	Canada	42	J5
Athabasca River	Canada	41	H6
Athínai (Athens)	Greece	78	F7
Athens	United States	35	K5
Athens (Athínai)	Greece	78	F7
Athlone	Ireland	67	F8
Athos	Greece	78	G4
Ati	Chad	90	C5
Atienzo	Spain	71	H3
Atka Island	Alaska (U.S.)	29	(3)C1
Atlanta	United States	35	K5
Atlantic City	United States	37	M4
Atlantic Ocean	Europe	54	B3
Atlin Lake	Canada	40	E4
Ätran	Sweden	59	G8
Attawapiskat	Canada	43	Q6
Attersee	Austria	73	J3
Attu Island	Alaska (U.S.)	29	(3)A1
Atyrau	Kazakhstan	101	J8
Auas Mountains	Namibia	96	B4
Auburn	United States	37	M3
Auckland	New Zealand	118	E3
Auckland Island	New Zealand	119	(2)B1
Audo	Ethiopia	95	G2
Aue	Germany	63	B7
Augrabies Falls	South Africa	96	C5
Augsburg	Germany	65	F8
Augusta (GA)	United States	35	K5
Augusta (ME	United States	37	N3
Aumale	France	56	E5
Aurangabad	India	104	B4
Auron	France	72	B6
Austin	United States	30	C4
Austin (TX)	United States	33	G5
Australia	Oceania	116	F4
Australian Alps	Australia	117	J7
Australian Capital Territory	Australia	117	J7
Austria	Europe	73	K3
Austvågy	Norway	58	H2
Auxerre	France	68	J6
Auyán Tepuy	Venezuela	50	E2
Aveiro	Portugal	70	B4
Avesta	Sweden	59	J6
Avezzario	Italy	74	H7
Avignon	France	69	K10
Avilés	Spain	70	E1
Avon	United Kingdom	56	B4
Avranches	France	56	B6
Avrillac	France	69	H9
Awa	Japan	111	K4
Awaji-Shima	Japan	110	H6
Awanui	New Zealand	118	D2
Awarua Bay	New Zealand	119	B7
Awash	Ethiopia	95	G1
Awbari´ Sahra´	Libya	90	B2
Axios	Greece	78	E4
Ayamonte	Spain	70	C7
Aydin	Turkey	79	K7
Aydin Daglari	Turkey	79	K6
Ayers Rock	Australia	116	F5
Aylesbury	United Kingdom	56	B3
Ayon el Atros	Mauritania	88	D5
Ayr	United Kingdom	66	J6
Az Zahirah	Oman	85	G5
Az Zarqa	Jordan	84	D4
Az Zuqar	Yemen	91	H5
Azaila	Spain	71	K3
Azaouâd	Mali	88	E5
Azare	Switzerland	72	C3
Azbine (Aïr)	Niger	89	G5
Azerbaijan	Asia	81	M3
Azores (Açores)	Portugal	88	(1)B2
Azuaga	Spain	70	E6

B

Ba´qubah	Iraq	82	D3
Bab al Mandab	Indian Ocean	91	H5
Baba Burun	Turkey	79	P3
Baba Burun	Turkey	78	H5
Babine Lake	Canada	38	F6
Babol	Iran	82	F2
Babuyan Islands	Philippines	107	G3
Bacau	Romania	77	P3
Backnang	Germany	65	E8
Bacolod	Philippines	107	G4
Bad Hersfeld	Germany	65	E6
Bad Ischal	Austria	62	C10
Bad Kissingen	Germany	65	F6
Bad Kreuznach	Germany	57	L5
Bad Salzungen	Germany	65	F6
Badain Jaran Shamo	China	108	C2
Badajoz	Spain	70	D6
Badalona	Spain	71	N3
Baden-Baden	Germany	65	D8
Badiet esh Sham (Syrian Desert)	Syria	84	E3
Badlands National Park	United States	31	F3
Baffin Bay	North America	42	T2
Baffin Island	Canada	42	Q2
Bafing	West Africa	92	B2
Bafra Burun	Turkey	80	F3
Bagdad (Baghdad)	Iraq	82	D3
Baghdad (Bagdad)	Iraq	82	D3
Bahía Blanca	Argentina	52	J6
Bahía Blanca	Argentina	52	J6
Bahía de Alcudia	Spain	71	P5
Bahía de Algeciras	Spain	70	E8
Bahía de Campeche	Mexico	46	F4
Bahía de Manta	Ecuador	50	A4
Bahía de Palma	Spain	71	N5
Bahía de Santander	Spain	70	G1
Bahía de Sechura	Peru	50	A5
Bahía Grande	Argentina	52	H9

Bahamas	*Atlantic Ocean*	47	J3
Bahawalpur	*Pakistan*	83	K4
Bahia	*Honduras*	47	G5
Bahia de Rio de Oro	*Western Sahara*	88	B4
Bahr al Jabal (White Nile)	*Central Africa*	94	E2
Bahr al Mill	*Iraq*	82	D3
Bahr Aouk	*Central Africa*	94	B2
Bahr el Abiad	*Africa*	91	F5
Bahr el Ghazal	*Central Africa*	90	C5
Bahr Salamat	*Chad*	93	H3
Bahrain	*Middle East*	85	D3
Bahrat Hims	*Syria*	84	D2
Baía do Bengo	*Angola*	93	G6
Baía de Inhambane	*Mozambique*	97	F4
Baía de Maputo	*Mozambique*	97	E5
Baía de Marajó	*Brazil*	51	H4
Baía de Memba	*Mozambique*	97	G2
Baía de Setúbal	*Spain*	70	A6
Baía de São Marcos	*Brazil*	51	J4
Baía de Sofala	*Mozambique*	97	F4
Baía de Todos os Santos	*Brazil*	51	K6
Baia Mare	*Romania*	77	L2
Baicheng	*China*	109	G1
Baie d'Antongil	*Madagascar*	97	H3
Baie d'Audierne	*France*	68	A6
Baie de Bourgneuf	*France*	68	C6
Baie de la Seine	*France*	68	E4
Baie de Saint Augustin	*Madagascar*	97	G4
Baie de St.-Brieuc	*France*	68	C5
Baie des Chaleurs	*Canada*	39	T7
Baie du Cap Lopez	*Gabon*	93	F5
Baikalskiy Khrebet	*Russia*	102	H5
Baile tha Cliath	*Ireland*	67	G8
Baile tha Cliath (Dublin)	*Ireland*	67	H8
Bailleul	*France*	56	F4
Bainbridge	*United States*	35	K5
Baing	*Indonesia*	113	B5
Bairin Zuoqi	*China*	102	K8
Baja	*Hungary*	76	F3
Baja California	*Mexico*	46	B3
Bakadzicite	*Bulgaria*	79	J2
Baker	*United States*	115	J5
Baker	*United States*	28	C2
Baker (MT)	*United States*	31	F2
Baker Lake	*Canada*	42	N4
Bakersfield	*United States*	29	C3
Bakhtaran	*Iran*	81	M6
Baki (Baku)	*Azerbaijan*	81	N3
Bakir	*Turkey*	79	J5
Bakony	*Hungary*	76	F2
Balabac	*Philippines*	112	F1
Balabac Strait	*Malaysia*	112	F1
Balaguer	*Spain*	71	L3
Balakovo	*Russia*	61	K4
Balashov	*Russia*	60	J4
Balaton	*Hungary*	73	N4
Baldy Peak	*United States*	46	C2
Balearic Isles (Islas Baleares)	*Spain*	71	M5
Bali	*Indonesia*	112	E4
Balikpapan	*Indonesia*	112	F3
Balintang Channel	*South East Asia*	107	G2
Balkesir	*Turkey*	80	B4
Balleny	*Antarctica*	120	(2)X3
Balls Pyramid	*Australia*	117	L6
Balta	*Ukraine*	77	S2
Baltic Sea	*Europe*	59	J9
Baltijssk	*Russia*	63	J3
Baltimore	*United States*	37	L4
Baltrum	*Germany*	64	C3
Bam	*Iran*	85	H2
Bamako	*Mali*	92	C2
Bamberg	*Germany*	65	F7
Bamenda	*Cameroon*	93	G3
Bampur	*Iran*	83	G4
Banaadir	*Somalia*	95	G3
Banaba (Ocean Island)	*Kiribati (Pacific Ocean)*	114	G6
Banbury	*United Kingdom*	56	B2
Banda Sea	*Indonesia*	113	C4
Bandama	*West Africa*	92	C3
Bandar Seri Begawan	*Brunei*	112	E2
Bandar-e Abbas	*Iran*	85	G3
Bandar-e Lengeh	*Iran*	85	F3
Bandirma	*Turkey*	79	L4
Bandirma Körfezi	*Turkey*	79	L4
Bandundu	*Democratic Republic Of Congo*	94	B4
Bandung	*Indonesia*	112	D4
Banff	*Canada*	41	H6
Bangalore	*India*	105	C6
Bangang Co	*China*	104	C2
Bangassou	*Central African Republic*	94	C3
Banghazi (Benghazi)	*Libya*	90	C1
Bangkok (Krung Thep)	*Thailand*	106	C4
Bangladesh	*Southern Asia*	104	E4
Bangor	*United States*	37	N3
Bangui	*Central African Republic*	94	B3
Bani Walid	*Libya*	90	B1
Baniyas	*Syria*	84	C1
Banja Luka	*Bosnia-Herzegovina*	73	N6
Banjarmasin	*Indonesia*	112	E3
Banjul	*Gambia*	88	B6
Banks Island	*Canada*	40	G2
Banks Island (Moa)	*Australia*	117	H2
Banks Peninsula	*New Zealand*	119	E 6
Banks Strait	*Australia*	117	J8
Bann	*United Kingdom*	67	G6
Bantry Bay	*Ireland*	67	D10
Baoding	*China*	108	F3
Baoji	*China*	108	D4
Baotou	*China*	108	E2
Baracaldo	*Spain*	69	B10
Baranof Island	*Alaska (U.S.)*	29	(1)K4
Baranovichi	*Belarus*	59	P10
Barbados	*Caribbean*	47	N6
Barbeau Peak	*Canada*	120	(1)Y1
Barbuda	*Caribbean*	47	M5

Barcelona	*Spain*	71	N3
Barcelona	*Venezuela*	50	E1
Barcotta	*Spain*	70	D6
Bareilly	*India*	104	C3
Barents Sea	*Northern Asia*	100	D3
Barguzinskiy Khrebet	*Russia*	102	H6
Bari	*Italy*	75	L7
Barinas	*Venezuela*	50	C2
Barisal	*Bangladesh*	104	F4
Barkly Tableland	*Australia*	117	G3
Barletta	*Italy*	76	D8
Barma	*Indonesia*	113	D3
Barnaul	*Russia*	101	Q7
Barnstaple	*United Kingdom*	68	B2
Barnstaple or Bideford Bay	*United Kingdom*	67	J10
Barqah al Bahriyah	*Egypt*	90	E1
Barquisimeto	*Venezuela*	50	D1
Barra	*United Kingdom*	66	F4
Barracaldo	*Spain*	70	G8
Barragem de Sobradinho	*Brazil*	51	J6
Barranquilla	*Colombia*	50	C1
Barre des Ecrins	*France*	69	M8
Barreiro	*Portugal*	70	A6
Barrie	*Canada*	37	L3
Barrieras	*Brazil*	51	J6
Barrington Tops	*Australia*	117	K6
Barrow Island	*Australia*	116	B4
Barstow	*United States*	29	C4
Barth	*Germany*	64	H2
Bartle Frere	*Australia*	114	E7
Bartoszyce	*Poland*	62	K4
Barun Bagdo-Ula	*Mongolia*	108	C1
Basel	*Switzerland*	72	C3
Bashi Haixia	*Taiwan / Philippines*	109	F6
Basilan	*Philippines*	113	B1
Basildon	*United Kingdom*	67	P10
Basingstoke	*United Kingdom*	56	B3
Basra (Al Basrah)	*Iraq*	82	E3
Bass Strait	*Australia*	117	H8
Bassano d.Grappa	*Italy*	73	G5
Bassas da India (Réunion)	*Southern Africa*	97	F4
Bassein	*Myanmar (Burma)*	106	A3
Bassum	*Germany*	64	D4
Bastia	*France*	74	D6
Bastogne	*Belgium*	57	J4
Bastrop	*United States*	34	H5
Bataklk Gölü	*Turkey*	79	R7
Batan Islands	*Philippines*	107	G2
Batangos	*Philippines*	107	G4
Batavia	*United States*	37	L3
Bath	*United Kingdom*	68	C2
Bath	*United States*	37	N3
Bathurst	*Canada*	45	T7
Bathurst Inlet	*Canada*	42	K2
Bathurst Island	*Australia*	116	E2
Bathurst Island	*Canada*	42	L1
Batna	*Algeria*	89	G1
Baton Rouge	*United States*	34	H5
Battle Creek	*United States*	36	J3
Battle Mountain	*United States*	29	C2
Batumi	*Georgia*	81	J3
Bauru	*Brazil*	51	H8
Bautzen	*Germany*	65	K5
Bawean	*Indonesia*	112	E4
Bay City (MI)	*United States*	36	K3
Bay City (TX)	*United States*	33	G6
Bay of Bengal	*India*	105	E5
Bay of Biscay	*France / Spain*	70	F1
Bay of Fundy	*Canada*	39	T8
Bay of Islands	*Canada*	39	V7
Bay of Plenty	*New Zealand*	118	F3
Bayan Har Shan	*China*	108	B4
Baydaratskaya Guba	*Russia*	100	L4
Baydhabo	*Somalia*	95	G3
Bayerische Alpen	*Germany*	73	G3
Bayerischer Wald	*Germany*	65	H7
Bayeux	*France*	56	C5
Baykit	*Russia*	102	F4
Baynunah	*United Arab Emirates*	85	E5
Bayn Nuur	*Mongolia*	102	K7
Bayreuth	*Germany*	65	G7
Baytik Shan	*China*	101	R8
Bayy al Kabr	*Libya*	90	B1
Baza	*Spain*	70	H7
Beachy Head	*United Kingdom*	68	F3
Beacon	*United States*	37	M3
Bear Lake	*United States*	30	D3
Bearskin Lake	*Canada*	38	N6
Beas de Segura	*Spain*	70	H6
Beatrice	*United States*	31	G3
Beaufort Sea	*North Pole*	38	E2
Beaumont	*France*	57	J6
Beaumont	*United States*	34	H6
Beauvais	*France*	56	F5
Beaver	*United States*	32	D4
Beaver Island	*United States*	36	J2
Becej	*Yugoslavia*	76	H4
Béchar	*Algeria*	89	E2
Beckley	*United States*	36	K4
Beda	*Spain*	70	G6
Bedford	*United Kingdom*	56	C2
Beersheba	*Israel*	84	B5
Beijing	*China*	108	F2
Beira	*Mozambique*	97	F3
Beirut	*Lebanon*	84	C3
Beirut (Beyrouth)	*Lebanon*	84	C3
Beius	*Romania*	77	K3
Béja	*Tunisia*	75	C12
Beja	*Portugal*	70	C6
Béjar	*Spain*	70	E3
Békéscsaba	*Hungary*	76	J3
Belarus	*Europe*	60	F4
Belaya	*Russia*	103	W3
Belcher Islands	*Canada*	43	Q5
Belém	*Brazil*	51	H4
Belfast	*United Kingdom*	67	H7
Belfort	*France*	68	M6

Belgaum	*India*	105	B5
Belgium	*Europe*	57	H4
Belize	*Central America*	46	G5
Bellary	*India*	105	C5
Belle Isle	*Canada*	39	W6
Belle Ile	*France*	68	B6
Belleville	*Canada*	45	R8
Bellingshausen Sea	*Antarctica*	120	(2)JJ5
Bellinzona	*Switzerland*	72	E4
Belluno	*Italy*	73	H4
Belmopan	*Belize*	46	G5
Belo Horizonte	*Brazil*	51	J7
Belovo	*Russia*	101	R7
Beloye More (White Sea)	*Russia*	60	H1
Belozersk	*Russia*	60	H2
Beltsy	*Moldova*	77	R2
Bemidji	*United States*	31	H2
Ben Klibreck	*United Kingdom*	66	J3
Ben Macdhui	*United Kingdom*	66	K4
Ben Nevis	*United Kingdom*	66	H5
Benabarre	*Spain*	71	L2
Benavente	*Spain*	70	E3
Bend	*United States*	28	B2
Benevento	*Italy*	75	J7
Bengbu	*China*	108	F4
Benghazi (Banghazi)	*Libya*	90	C1
Benguela	*Angola*	96	A2
Benguela	*Angola*	94	A6
Beni Mellal	*Morocco*	88	D2
Beni-Abbès	*Algeria*	89	E2
Benin	*West Africa*	93	E2
Benin-City	*Nigeria*	93	F3
Benoni	*South Africa*	96	D5
Bensheim	*Germany*	65	D7
Bentinck Island	*Australia*	117	G3
Benton	*United States*	34	H5
Benton Harbor	*United States*	36	J3
Benue	*West Africa*	93	F3
Benwee Head	*Ireland*	67	D7
Benxi	*China*	110	C3
Beograd (Belgrade)	*Yugoslavia*	76	H5
Beppu	*Japan*	110	F7
Berat	*Albania*	78	C4
Berbérati	*Central African Republic*	93	H4
Berbera	*Somalia*	95	H1
Berck	*France*	56	E4
Berdyansk	*Ukraine*	60	H5
Beregovo	*Ukraine*	77	K1
Berezniki	*Russia*	100	K6
Berezovo	*Russia*	61	N2
Berga	*Spain*	71	M2
Bergama	*Turkey*	79	K5
Bergamo	*Italy*	74	D3
Bergen	*Norway*	59	C6
Bergen op.Zoom	*Netherlands*	57	H3
Bergerac	*France*	69	F9
Bering Sea	*Pacific Ocean*	29	(1)C3
Beringov Proliv / Bering Strait	*Russia / United States*	29	(1)D2
Berlevåg	*Norway*	58	Q1
Berlin	*Germany*	64	J4
Berlin	*United States*	37	M3
Bermejo	*Argentina*	52	K4
Bermuda	*Atlantic Ocean*	47	M2
Bern	*Switzerland*	72	C4
Bernay	*France*	56	D5
Berner Alpen	*Switzerland*	72	C4
Bernina	*Switzerland / Italy*	72	E4
Berounka	*Czech Republic*	63	C8
Bertix	*Belgium*	57	J5
Bertoua	*Cameroon*	93	G3
Besançon	*France*	68	M6
Beskid Niski	*Poland*	63	L8
Beskiden	*Poland*	63	H8
Béthune	*France*	56	F4
Bettola	*Italy*	72	E6
Bey Daglari	*Turkey*	80	C5
Beykoz	*Turkey*	79	M3
Beyrouth (Beirut)	*Lebanon*	84	C3
Beysehir Gölü	*Turkey*	80	D5
Béziers	*France*	69	J10
Bhadravati	*India*	105	C6
Bhagalpur	*India*	104	E3
Bharuch	*India*	104	B4
Bhatpara	*India*	104	E4
Bhavnagar	*India*	104	B4
Bhopal	*India*	104	C4
Bhubaneshwar	*India*	104	E4
Bhutan	*Southern Asia*	104	F3
Biak	*Indonesia*	114	D6
Bialystok	*Poland*	62	N4
Biarritz	*France*	69	D10
Biata Podlaska	*Poland*	63	N7
Biatystock	*Poland*	59	M10
Biberach	*Germany*	65	E8
Bicaj	*Albania*	76	H8
Bickerton Island	*Australia*	117	G2
Bida	*Nigeria*	93	F3
Biebrza	*Poland*	62	M4
Biel	*Switzerland*	72	C3
Bielefeld	*Germany*	64	D4
Bieler See	*Switzerland*	72	C3
Biella	*Italy*	72	D5
Bielsko-Biala	*Poland*	63	J8
Bieszczady	*Poland*	63	M8
Big Bend Dam	*United States*	31	G3
Big Horn Lake	*United States*	30	E2
Big Horn Mountains	*United States*	30	E3
Big Quill Lake	*Canada*	43	L6
Big Rapids	*United States*	36	J3
Big Spring	*United States*	33	F5
Big Trout Lake	*Canada*	43	N6
Bighorn	*United States*	30	E2
Bighorn River	*United States*	30	E2
Bight of Benin	*Atlantic Ocean*	93	E3
Bihac	*Bosnia Herzegovina*	76	C5
Bihar	*India*	104	E3
Bijapur	*India*	105	C5

Bijeljina	Bosnia Herzegovina	76	G5
Bikaner	India	104	B3
Bikini	Marshall Islands	114	G4
Bilaspur	India	104	D4
Bilauktaung Range	Myanmar (Burma) / Thailand	106	B4
Bilbao	Spain	70	H1
Bilibino	Russia	103	V3
Billings	United States	30	E2
Bilma	Niger	89	H5
Bilogora	Croatia	76	D3
Biloku	Guyana	51	F3
Bioko (Fernando Póo)	Equatorial Guinea	93	F4
Biokovo	Bosnia-Herzegovina / Croatia	76	E6
Birao	Central African Republic	90	D5
Bîrlad	Romania	77	Q3
Birmingham	United Kingdom	67	M9
Birmingham	United States	35	J5
Bîr Mogreïn	Mauritania	88	C3
Birnie Atoll	Kiribati (Pacific Ocean)	115	J6
Birnin-Kebbi	Nigeria	93	E2
Birzai	Lithuania	59	N8
Bisevo	Croatia	76	C7
Bishkek	Kyrgyzstan	101	P9
Biskra	Algeria	89	G2
Bismarck	United States	31	F2
Bismarck Sea	Papua New Guinea	114	E6
Bissau	Guinea-Bissau	92	A2
Bistcho Lake	Canada	41	H5
Bistrita	Romania	77	M2
Bitburg	Germany	65	B7
Bitola	Macedonia	78	D3
Bitonto	Italy	76	D8
Bitterroot Range	United States	28	C1
Biwa-Ko	Japan	111	J6
Biysk	Russia	101	R7
Bizerte	Tunisia	75	D11
Bjelovar	Croatia	76	D4
Bjeshkët e Nemuna	Yugoslavia / Albania	76	G7
Bjrnevatn	Norway	58	Q2
Bjrnya	Norway	120	(1)N2
Black Forest	Germany	72	D3
Black Hills	United States	30	E3
Black Mountains	United States	32	D4
Black Rock Desert	United States	29	C2
Black Sea	Europe	80	D2
Black Volta (Mouhoun)	West Africa	92	E3
Blackburn	United Kingdom	67	L8
Blackpool	United Kingdom	67	K8
Blacksod Bay	Ireland	67	C8
Blagoevgrad	Bulgaria	78	F2
Blagoveshchensk	Russia	102	M6
Blanca Peak	United States	32	E4
Blanes	Spain	71	N3
Blantyre	Malawi	97	E3
Blåvands Huk	Denmark	59	D9
Blenheim	New Zealand	119	E5
Bletchley	United Kingdom	56	C3
Blida	Algeria	71	P8
Blida	Algeria	89	F1
Bloemfontein	South Africa	96	D5
Blois	France	68	G6
Blönduós	Iceland	58	(1)D2
Bloomington	United States	36	J3
Blue Mountains	United States	29	C3
Blue Nile (El Bahr el Azraq)	Africa	91	F5
Blue Ridge	United States	35	K4
Bluewater	United States	32	E4
Blyot Island	Canada	39	R2
Blytheville	United States	34	J4
Bmlo	Norway	59	C7
Bo	Sierra Leone	92	B3
Bo Hai	China	109	F3
Boa Vista	Brazil	50	E3
Boa Vista	Cape Verde	92	(1)B1
Bobo Dioulasso	Burkina Faso	88	E6
Bóbr	Poland	62	E6
Bobruysk	Belarus	60	F4
Boca Raton	United States	35	K6
Bocholt	Germany	64	B5
Bochum	Germany	64	C5
Bodega Bay	United States	29	B3
Bodelé	Chad	89	J5
Boden	Sweden	58	L4
Bodensee	Germany / Switzerland	65	E9
Bodo	Norway	58	H3
Boende	Democratic Republic Of Congo	94	C4
Bogalusa	United States	34	J5
Bogda Feng	China	101	R9
Bogda Shan	China	101	R9
Bogor	Indonesia	112	D4
Bogotá	Colombia	50	C3
Bohol	Philippines	107	G5
Bohol Sea	Philippines	107	G5
Boise	United States	28	C2
Boizenburg	Germany	64	F3
Boknafjorden	Norway	59	C7
Bolaçu	Brazil	50	E4
Boleslawiec	Poland	63	E6
Bolgatanga	Ghana	92	D2
Bolivia	South America	50	D7
Bollnäs	Sweden	59	J6
Bolmen	Sweden	59	G8
Bologna	Italy	74	F4
Bolognesi	Peru	50	C5
Bolsoj Kavkaz	Russia / Georgia	81	H2
Bolsón de Mapimi	Mexico	32	E6
Boltaña	Spain	71	L2
Bolton	United Kingdom	67	L8
Bolu	Turkey	79	P4
Bolu Daglari	Turkey	80	E3
Bolzano	Italy	72	G4
Bomu	Central Africa	94	D3
Bon-Cagan-Nur	Mongolia	108	B1
Bonaire	Central America	47	L6
Bonaparte Archipelago	Australia	116	D3
Bondo	Democratic Republic Of Congo	94	C3
Bondoukou	Côte dIvoire	92	D3
Bongolava	Madagascar	97	H3
Bongor	Chad	90	C5
Bonn	Germany	65	C6
Boone	United States	31	H3
Bor	Yugoslavia	77	K5
Bor Dagi	Turkey	80	C5
Borah Peak	United States	30	D3
Borazjan	Iran	85	D2
Bordeaux	France	69	E9
Bordj Mokhtar	Algeria	89	F4
Borgarnes	Iceland	58	C2
Borislav	Ukraine	63	N8
Borja	Peru	50	B4
Borkou	Chad	90	C4
Borkum	Germany	64	B3
Borlänge	Sweden	59	H6
Borneo	South East Asia	112	E2
Bornes	Indonesia	113	A2
Bornholm	Denmark	59	H9
Bornholmsgattet	Europe	62	D2
Borovichi	Russia	60	G3
Bosna	Croatia	74	M4
Bosnia-Herzegovina	Europe	76	E5
Bosporus (Karadeniz Bogazi)	Turkey	80	C3
Bossangoa	Central African Republic	93	H3
Boston	United Kingdom	56	C2
Boston	United States	37	M3
Boston Mountains	United States	33	H4
Botosani	Romania	77	P2
Botswana	Southern Africa	96	C4
Botte Donato	Italy	75	L9
Bottrop	Germany	65	B5
Bouaké	Côte dIvoire	92	D3
Bouar	Central African Republic	94	B2
Bougainville	Papua New Guinea	114	F6
Bougainville Reef	Australia	117	J3
Bouira	Algeria	71	P8
Boulogne	France	68	G3
Bouna	Côte dIvoire	92	D3
Bourg-en-Bresse	France	69	L7
Bourges	France	69	H6
Bournemouth	United Kingdom	67	L11
Bovec	Slovenia	63	C11
Bowling Green	United States	36	K3
Boxmeer	Netherlands	57	J3
Boyoma Falls	Democratic Republic Of Congo	94	D3
Boz Burun	Turkey	80	C3
Boz Daglari	Turkey	79	K6
Bozburun Dag	Turkey	79	N7
Bozca Ada	Turkey	78	H5
Bozeman	United States	30	D2
Bozoum	Central African Republic	93	H3
Br Sa'id (Port Said)	Egypt	91	F1
Brac	Croatia	76	D6
Bracki Kanal	Croatia	76	D6
Brad	Romania	63	M12
Bradford	United Kingdom	67	L8
Bradford	United States	37	L3
Bragança	Portugal	70	D3
Brahmapur	India	105	D5
Brahmaputra	Southern Asia	104	E3
Braila	Romania	77	Q4
Brandberg	Namibia	96	A4
Branden	Canada	43	L7
Brandenburg	Germany	64	H4
Brandon	Canada	31	F2
Brasília	Brazil	51	H7
Brasov	Romania	77	N4
Bratislava	Slovakia	63	G9
Bratsk	Russia	102	G5
Bratskoye Vdkhr.	Russia	102	G5
Brattleboro	United States	37	M3
Braunau	Austria	73	J2
Braunschweig	Germany	64	F4
Brava	Cape Verde	92	(1)A2
Bravo	Europe	76	G4
Bray Island	Canada	42	R3
Brayança	Brazil	50	H4
Brazil	South America	50	D5
Brazilian Highlands (Planalto do Brasil)	Brazil	51	J7
Brazos River	United States	46	E2
Brazzaville	Congo	93	G5
Bream Bay	New Zealand	118	E2
Breaza	Romania	77	N2
Breclav	Slovakia	73	M2
Breclav	Czech Republic	63	F9
Brecon Beacons	United Kingdom	67	K10
Breda	Netherlands	57	H3
Breida Fjördur	Iceland	58	(1)B2
Breivikbotn	Norway	58	M1
Brekken	Norway	58	F5
Bremen	Germany	64	D3
Bremerhaven	Germany	64	D3
Brenta	Italy	74	F3
Brescia	Italy	74	E3
Brest	France	68	A5
Brest	Belarus	60	E4
Breteuil	France	56	F5
Brgefjellet	Norway	58	G4
Bria	Central African Republic	94	C5
Briançon	France	69	M9
Bridgeport	United States	37	M3
Bridgetown	Barbados	47	N6
Bridgwater	United Kingdom	68	B2
Brienzer See	Switzerland	72	C4
Brigham City	United States	30	D3
Brighton	United Kingdom	67	N11
Brignoles	France	72	B7
Brisbane	Australia	117	K5
Bristol	United Kingdom	67	L10
Bristol Bay	United States	112	(1)HH4
Bristol Channel	United Kingdom	37	J10
British Columbia	Canada	38	F5
Brive-la-Gaillarde	France	69	G8
Brno	Czech Republic	63	F8
Broad Sound	Australia	117	J4
Broadwater	United States	31	F3
Brocken	Germany	64	F5
Brookings	United States	28	B2
Brooks Range	Alaska (U.S.)	29	(1)F2
Brownfield	United States	33	F5
Browns Valley	United States	31	G2
Brownsville	United States	33	G6
Brownwood	United States	33	G5
Bruce Peninsula	Canada	36	K2
Bruchsal	Germany	65	D7
Brugge	Belgium	56	G3
Brule	United States	31	F3
Bruncu Spina	Sardinia (Italy)	75	D9
Brunei	Asia	112	E2
Brunswick (GA)	United States	35	K5
Brunswick (ME)	United States	37	N3
Bruxelles / Brüssel (Brussels)	Belgium	57	H4
Bryan	United States	33	G5
Bryansk	Russia	60	G4
Bryce Canyon	United States	32	D4
Brzeg	Poland	62	G6
Bubiyan	Kuwait	85	C2
Bucaramanga	Colombia	50	C2
Bucharest (Bucuresti)	Romania	77	P5
Buckland Tableland	Australia	117	J4
Bucuresti (Bucharest)	Romania	77	P5
Budapest	Hungary	76	G2
Bude Bay	United Kingdom	67	J11
Budennovsk	Russia	60	J6
Büdingen	Germany	65	E6
Buenaventura	Colombia	50	B3
Buenos Aires	Argentina	53	K5
Buffalo (NY)	United States	37	L3
Buffalo (WY)	United States	30	E3
Buffalo Lake	Canada	42	J5
Buffalo Narrows	Canada	43	K5
Bug	Ukraine / Poland	60	E4
Bugrino	Russia	61	K1
Buhayrat al Asad	Syria	81	H5
Bujumbura	Burundi	94	D4
Bukavu	Democratic Republic Of Congo	94	D4
Bukhara	Uzbekistan	101	L10
Bukit Raya	Indonesia	112	E3
Bulawayo	Zimbabwe	96	D4
Bulgaria	Europe	77	L7
Bulgen	Mongolia	102	G8
Bulu Rantemario	Indonesia	112	G3
Bumba	Democratic Republic Of Congo	94	C3
Bunbury	Australia	116	C6
Bungo-Suido	Japan	110	G7
Bur Sudan (Port Sudan)	Sudan	91	G4
Burao	Somalia	95	H2
Burdur	Turkey	79	N7
Burdur Gölü	Turkey	79	N7
Bureinskiy Khrebet	Russia	102	N7
Burfjord	Norway	58	M2
Burg	Germany	64	G5
Burgas	Bulgaria	77	Q7
Burgaski Zaliv	Bulgaria	79	K2
Burgos	Spain	70	G2
Burhanpur	India	104	C4
Burias	Philippines	107	G4
Burkina Faso	West Africa	92	D2
Burlington (IA)	United States	36	H3
Burlington (VT)	United States	37	M3
Bursa	Turkey	80	C3
Buru	Indonesia	113	C3
Burundi	Central Africa	94	D4
Bury St.Edmunds	United Kingdom	56	D2
Busau	Romania	77	P4
Bushehr	Iran	85	D2
Busko-Zdrój	Poland	62	K7
Busuanga	Philippines	107	F4
Buta	Democratic Republic Of Congo	94	C3
Butaritari	Kiribati (Pacific Ocean)	114	H5
Bute	United Kingdom	66	H6
Buton	Indonesia	113	C3
Butte	United States	30	D2
Buy	Russia	60	H2
Buyr Nur	China / Mongolia	102	K7
Büyük Agr Dag (Mount Ararat)	Turkey	81	L4
Büyük Menderes	Turkey	80	B5
Buzancy	France	57	H5
Bydgoszcz	Poland	62	H4
Bygland	Norway	59	D7
Bytom	Poland	63	H7
Bytów	Poland	62	G3

C

Caaguazú	Paraguay	53	K4
Cabanatuan	Philippines	107	G3
Cabimas	Venezuela	50	C1
Cabinda	West Africa	93	G6
Cabo Beata	Dominican Republic	47	K5
Cabo Blanco	Spain	71	N5
Cabo Bojador	Western Sahara	88	B3
Cabo Camarón	Honduras	47	H5
Cabo Carvoeiro	Portugal	70	A5
Cabo Corrientes	Colombia	50	B2
Cabo da Roca	Portugal	70	A6
Cabo de Ajo	Spain	69	B10
Cabo de Caballeria	Spain	71	P4
Cabo de Cala Figuera	Spain	71	M5
Cabo de Creus	Spain	71	P2
Cabo de Formentor	Spain	71	P4
Cabo de Gata	Spain	71	H8
Cabo de Hornos (Cape Horn)	Chile	52	H10

Cesky Les	Czech Republic	63	B8
Ceuta	Spain	70	E9
Cévennes	France	69	J10
Ch'ongjin	North Korea	110	E3
Ch'ongju	South Korea	110	D5
Ch'unch'on	South Korea	110	D5
Chablais	France	72	B4
Chaco Austral	Argentina	52	J4
Chaco Boreal	Paraguay	52	J3
Chad	West Africa	90	C4
Chëshskaya Guba	Russia	100	H4
Chagai Hills	Pakistan	83	H4
Chai-li	Taiwan	109	F6
Chaîne des Albères	France	71	N2
Chalbi Desert	Kenya	95	F3
Chalk River	Canada	37	L2
Challenger Deep	Oceania	114	E4
Châlons-sur-Marne	France	57	H6
Chalon-sur-Saône	France	69	K7
Cham	Germany	65	H7
Chambal	India	104	C3
Chambery	France	69	L8
Champaign	United States	36	J4
Champaqui	Argentina	52	J5
Chandigarh	India	104	C2
Chang Jiang	China	108	F4
Chang-hua	Taiwan	107	G2
Changbai Shan	East Asia	110	D3
Changchun	China	109	G2
Changde	China	108	E5
Changjiang Kou	China	109	G4
Changsha	China	108	E5
Channel Islands	United Kingdom	67	K12
Chanute	United States	34	G4
Chao Phraya	South East Asia	106	C3
Chapada Damantina	Brazil	48	G4
Chapayevo	Kazakhstan	61	L4
Chapleau	Canada	36	K2
Chardzhou	Turkmenistan	101	L10
Charente	France	69	F8
Chari	Africa	90	C5
Charleroi	Belgium	57	H4
Charles Island	Canada	44	S4
Charleston (SC)	United States	35	L5
Charleston (WV)	United States	36	K4
Charleston Peak	United States	29	C4
Charleville-Mézières	France	57	H5
Charlotte	United States	35	K4
Charlottesville	United States	35	L4
Charlottetown	Canada	45	U7
Chartres	France	68	G5
Châteauroux	France	69	G7
Châteauxbriant	France	68	D6
Châtellerault	France	69	F7
Châteux-Thierry	France	56	G5
Chatham	Canada	36	K3
Chatham Island	New Zealand	119	(1)B1
Chatham Islands	New Zealand	119	(1)B1
Chatkalskiy Khrebet	Kyrgyzstan	101	N9
Chattanooga	United States	35	J4
Chaumont	France	68	L5
Chaunskaya Guba	Russia	103	V3
Chavantina	Brazil	51	G6
Chaves	Portugal	70	C3
Cheb	Czech Republic	65	H6
Cheboksary	Russia	61	K3
Cheduba	Myanmar (Burma)	106	A3
Cheju	South Korea	110	D7
Cheju Do (Quelpart I.)	South Korea	110	D7
Cheju-Haehyop	East Asia	110	D7
Chelif	Algeria	89	F1
Chelkar	Kazakhstan	61	M5
Chelm	Poland	63	N6
Chelmsford	United Kingdom	56	D3
Chelyabinsk	Russia	61	N3
Chemnitz	Germany	65	J6
Chenachane	Algeria	88	E3
Chengdu	China	108	C4
Chennai (Madras)	India	105	D6
Chentijn Nuruu	Mongolia	102	H7
Cherbaniani Reef	India	105	B6
Cherbourg	France	68	D4
Cherepovets	Russia	60	H3
Cherkassy	Ukraine	60	G5
Cherkessk	Russia	81	K1
Cherlak	Russia	61	Q4
Chernaya	Russia	61	M1
Chernigov	Ukraine	60	G4
Chernovtsy	Ukraine	60	F5
Cherski	Russia	103	U3
Cherzhell	Algeria	71	N8
Chesapeake Bay	United States	37	L4
Chesterfield	United Kingdom	56	B1
Chesterfield Inlet	Canada	42	N4
Chett el Jerd	Tunisia	89	G2
Cheviot	United Kingdom	67	K6
Chew Bahir	Ethiopia	95	F3
Cheyenne	United States	31	F3
Cheyne Bay	Australia	116	C6
Chi-lung	Taiwan	107	G1
Chia-li	Taiwan	107	G2
Chiavari	Italy	72	E6
Chibougamou	Canada	37	M2
Chicago	United States	36	J3
Chichagof	Alaska (U.S.	29	(1)K4
Chickasha	United States	34	G4
Chiclana de la Frontera	Spain	70	D8
Chiclayo	Peru	50	B5
Chico	United States	29	B3
Chicoutimi	Canada	45	S7
Chiemsee	Germany	65	H9
Chier	Italy	72	C5
Chigu Co	China	104	F3
Chihuahua	Mexico	32	E6
Chile	South America	52	H4
Chile Chico	Chile	52	G8
Chillán	Chile	52	G6
Chillicothe	United States	36	K4
Chiltern Hills	United Kingdom	67	M10
Chimanimari	Zimbabwe	97	E3
Chimbote	Peru	50	B5
Chimkent	Kazakhstan	101	M9
Chin	North Korea	110	D6
China	East Asia	108	B4
Chingola	Zambia	96	D2
Chingola	Zambia	94	D6
Chinguetti	Mauritania	88	C4
Chinju	South Korea	110	E6
Chioggia	Italy	75	H5
Chipata	Zambia	95	E6
Chipawyan	Canada	41	J5
Chippawa Falls	United States	36	H3
Chirinda	Russia	102	G3
Chisinau	Moldova	60	F5
Chita	Russia	102	J6
Chitato	Angola	94	C5
Chittagong	Bangladesh	104	F4
Chivasso	Italy	72	C5
Chivilcoy	Argentina	52	K6
Chobe	South Africa	96	C3
Choiseul	Solomon Islands	114	F6
Chojnice	Poland	62	G3
Chokai-San	Japan	109	K3
Choke	Ethiopia	95	F1
Chokurdah	Russia	103	R2
Cholet	France	69	E6
Chomutov	Czech Republic	63	C7
Chongqing	China	108	D5
Chonju	South Korea	110	D6
Choshi	Japan	111	L6
Chott Ech Chergui	Algeria	89	E2
Chott el Hodna	Algeria	89	G1
Choybalsan	Mongolia	102	J7
Christchurch	New Zealand	119	E6
Christmas Island	Australia	112	D5
Chubut	Argentina	52	H7
Chugoku-Sanchi	Japan	110	G6
Chugwater	United States	31	F3
Chukeni Sea (Chukotskoye More)	Russia	103	Z3
Chukotskoye More (Chukeni Sea)	Russia	103	Z3
Chuor Phnum Krâvanh	South East Asia	106	C4
Chur	Switzerland	72	E4
Churches Ferry	United States	31	G2
Churchill	Canada	43	N5
Churchill Falls	Canada	45	U6
Churchill Lake	Canada	42	J5
Churchill River	Canada	43	M5
Chutes de Livingstone	Democratic Republic Of Congo	93	G6
Chuuk	Micronesia	114	F5
Cicarija	Croatia	76	B4
Ciechanowiec	Poland	62	M5
Ciechanów	Poland	62	K5
Cienfuegos	Cuba	47	H4
Ciezq	Spain	71	J6
Cihanbeyli Platosu	Turkey	79	Q6
Cilo Dag	Turkey	81	L5
Cimarron	United States	31	G3
Cimone	Italy	74	E4
Cîmpina	Romania	77	N4
Cîmpulung	Romania	77	N4
Cincar	Bosnia-Herzegovina	76	E6
Cincinnati	United States	36	K4
Circle Egvekenot	Russia	29	(1)B2
Cirebon	Indonesia	112	D4
Citlaltépetl	Mexico	46	E5
Città di Castello	Italy	73	H7
Ciudad Bolivar	Venezuela	50	E2
Ciudad de Mexico (Mexico City)	Mexico	46	D5
Ciudad Guayana	Venezuela	50	E2
Ciudad Juárez	Mexico	46	C2
Ciudad Madero	Mexico	46	G4
Ciudad Mante	Mexico	34	G7
Ciudad Obregón	Mexico	46	C3
Ciudad Real	Spain	70	G6
Ciudad Valles	Mexico	34	G7
Ciudad Victoria	Mexico	46	E4
Ciudadela	Spain	71	P5
Clacton-on-Sea	United Kingdom	56	E3
Clare	Ireland	67	C8
Claremont	United States	37	M3
Clarksburg	United States	37	K4
Clarksdale	United States	34	H5
Clarksville	United States	35	J4
Clermont-Ferrand	France	69	J8
Cleveland (MS)	United States	34	H5
Cleveland (OH)	United States	36	K3
Clew Bay	Ireland	67	D8
Clinton	United States	36	H3
Clinton-Golden Lake	Canada	42	K4
Clipperton	France	46	C6
Cloppenburg	Germany	64	D4
Cloud Peak	United States	30	E3
Clovis	United States	33	F5
Cluj Napoca	Romania	77	L3
Cluses	France	69	M7
Clyde	United Kingdom	66	K6
Clyde	Canada	42	T2
Coakley Town	Bahamas	35	L7
Coalville	United Kingdom	56	B2
Coari	Brazil	50	E4
Coast Mountains	Canada	41	F6
Coast Range	United States	28	B2
Coastal Plains	United States	3435	J5
Coats Island	Canada	42	Q4
Coatzacoalcos	Mexico	46	F5
Coburg	Germany	65	F6
Cobourg	Canada	37	L3
Cochabamba	Bolivia	50	D7
Cochem	Germany	65	C6
Cochin	India	105	C7
Cochrane	Canada	43	Q7
Coco Channel	Andaman Islands	105	F6
Coco Islands	Myanmar	105	F6
Cocoa Beach	United States	35	K6
Cody	United States	30	E3
Coetivy	Seychelles	97	(2)C2
Coeur d'Alene	United States	30	C2
Coiba	Panama	50	A2
Coimbatore	India	105	C6
Coimbra	Portugal	70	B4
Colchester	United Kingdom	56	D3
Coll	United Kingdom	66	G5
College Station	United States	34	G5
Collier Bay	Australia	116	D3
Collines de Normandie	France	68	E5
Collines du Perche	France	56	D6
Colmar	France	72	C2
Cologne (Köln)	Germany	65	B6
Colombia	South America	50	C3
Colombo	Sri Lanka	105	C7
Colón	Panama	50	B2
Colonsay	United Kingdom	66	G5
Colorado	United States	32	E4
Colorado City	United States	32	F4
Colorado Plateau	United States	32	D4
Colorado River	United States	32	D4
Colorado Springs	United States	31	F4
Columbia (MO)	United States	33	H4
Columbia (SC)	United States	35	K5
Columbia (TN)	United States	35	J4
Columbia Mountains	Canada	41	G6
Columbia Plateau	United States	28	C2
Columbia River	United States	28	B1
Columbus (GA)	United States	35	K5
Columbus (MS)	United States	34	J5
Columbus (NE)	United States	31	G3
Columbus (OH)	United States	36	K4
Colville	Alaska (U.S.)	29	(1)F2
Colville Channel	New Zealand	118	E3
Comacchio	Italy	73	H6
Combermere Bay	Myanmar	106	A3
Como	Italy	72	E5
Comodoro Rivodaavia	Argentina	52	H8
Comoros	Indian Ocean	97	G2
Compiègne	France	56	F5
Comrat	Moldova	77	R3
Conakry	Guinea	92	B3
Concepción	Chile	52	G6
Concepción	Paraguay	51	F8
Conchas Lake	United States	33	F4
Concord	United States	37	M3
Conegliano	Italy	73	H5
Congo	Congo	94	B4
Congo	West Africa	93	H4
Congo	West Africa	93	H5
Connecticut	United States	37	M3
Constanta	Romania	77	R5
Constantina	Spain	70	E7
Constantine	Algeria	89	G1
Contwoyto Lake	Canada	42	J3
Cook Inlet	Alaska (U.S.)	29	(1)G3
Cook Islands	New Zealand	115	K7
Cook Strait	New Zealand	118	E5
Cookeville	United States	35	J4
Coolidge	United States	33	F4
Coos Bay	United States	28	B2
Copenhagen (Kbenhavn)	Denmark	59	F9
Copiapó	Chile	52	G4
Copper Canyon	Mexico	32	E6
Copperas	United States	33	G5
Coral Gables	United States	35	K6
Coral Sea	Australia	117	K2
Coral Sea Islands Territory	Micronesia	114	E7
Corby	United Kingdom	56	C2
Corcaigh (Cork)	Ireland	67	E10
Cordele	United States	35	K5
Cordillera Cantábrica	Spain	70	D2
Cordillera Central	Colombia	50	B3
Cordillera de la Costa	Venezuela	50	D2
Cordillera de Merida	Venezuela	50	C2
Cordillera Isabella	Nicaragua	47	G6
Cordillera los Andes	South America	50	B5
Cordillera Occidental	Colombia	50	B3
Cordillera Occidental	Chile	52	H2
Cordillera Oriental	South America	50	D7
Cordillera Oriental	Colombia	50	C3
Córdoba	Spain	70	F7
Córdoba	Argentina	52	J5
Corfu (Kérkira)	Greece	78	B5
Coria	Spain	70	D5
Corinth	United States	34	J5
Cork (Corcaigh)	Ireland	67	E10
Corlu	Turkey	79	K3
Corning	United States	37	L3
Corno Grande	Italy	74	H6
Cornwall	Canada	45	S7
Cornwallis Island	Canada	42	M2
Coronation Gulf	Canada	42	J3
Corpus Christi	United States	33	G6
Corrientes	Argentina	53	K4
Corse (Corsica)	France	74	C6
Corsica (Corse)	France	74	C6
Corsicana	United States	33	G5
Corumbá	Brazil	51	F7
Corvo	Azores (Portugal)	88	(1)A2
Cosenza	Italy	75	L9
Cosmoledo Group	Seychelles	97	(2) A2
Cosne-sur-Loire	France	68	H6
Costa Rica	Central America	47	G6
Côte d'Ivoire	West Africa	92	C3
Cotonou	Benin	93	E3
Cotswold Hills	United Kingdom	67	L10
Cottbus	Germany	65	K5
Coulommiers	France	56	G6
Council Bluffs	United States	31	G3
Coutances	France	56	B5
Couvin	Belgium	57	H4
Coventry	United Kingdom	67	M9

D

Dungeness	United Kingdom	67	P11
Dungu	Democratic Republic Of Congo	94	D3
Dunkerque	France	56	F3
Dunkery Beacon	United Kingdom	67	K10
Dunmore Town	Bahamas	35	L6
Dunnet Head	United Kingdom	66	K3
Dunstan Mountains	New Zealand	119	C7
Duqm	Oman	83	G6
Durack Ranges	Australia	116	E3
Durance	France	69	M9
Durango	United States	32	E4
Durban	South Africa	97	E5
Düren	Germany	65	B6
Durgapur	India	104	E4
Durham	United States	35	L4
Durmitor	Yugoslavia	76	G6
Durrës	Albania	78	B3
Durresi	Albania	76	G8
D'Urville Island	New Zealand	118	D5
Dushanbe	Tajikistan	83	J2
Düsseldorf	Germany	65	B5
Düzce	Turkey	79	P4
Dvinskaya Guba	Russia	60	H1
Dyersburg	United States	34	J4
Dytiki Rodópi	Greece	78	G3
Dzhambul	Kazakhstan	101	N9
Dzhetygara	Kazakhstan	61	N4
Dzhezkazgan	Kazakhstan	101	M8
Dzhizak	Uzbekistan	83	J1
Dzhusaly	Kazakhstan	61	N6

E

Eagle Pass	United States	33	F6
Earn	United Kingdom	66	K5
East Cape	New Zealand	118	G3
East Chinja Sea (Dong Hai / Higashi-Shina-Kai)	South East Asia	109	H5
East Falkland	South Atlantic Ocean	53	K9
East Grand Forks	United States	31	G2
East London	South Africa	96	D6
East Siberian Sea (Vostocno-Sibirskoye More)	Russia	103	T2
East St. Louis	United States	36	H4
Eastbourne	United Kingdom	56	D4
Easter Island	Chile	115	Q8
Eastern Desert (As Sahra' ash Sharqiyah)	Egypt	91	F3
Eastern Ghats	India	105	D5
Eau Claire	United States	36	H3
Eber Gölü	Turkey	79	P6
Eberswalde	Germany	64	J4
Ebro	Spain	71	K3
Ech Cheliff	Algeria	71	M8
Echo Bay	Canada	40	H3
Écija	Spain	70	E7
Ecuador	South America	50	B4
Eday	United Kingdom	66	L2
Ede	Netherlands	57	J2
Edgar Ranges	Australia	116	D3
Edgell Island	Canada	44	U4
Edinburgh	United Kingdom	66	K6
Edirne	Turkey	78	J3
Edmonton	Canada	41	H6
Edmundston	Canada	37	N2
Edremit	Turkey	79	K5
Edremit Körfezi	Turkey	79	J5
Edwards Plateau	United States	33	G5
Efaté	Vanuatu	114	G7
Effingham	United States	36	J4
Eger	Hungary	76	H2
Egersund	Norway	59	C7
Egridir Gölü	Turkey	80	D4
Egypt	North Africa	90	E3
Eibar	Spain	71	H1
Eifel	Germany	65	B6
Eigg	United Kingdom	66	G5
Eight Degree Channel	Arabian Sea	105	B7
Einbeck	Germany	64	E5
Eindhoven	Netherlands	57	J3
Eirunepé	Brazil	50	D5
Eisenach	Germany	65	F6
Eisenhüttenstadt	Germany	64	K4
Eisleben	Germany	64	G5
El Acaba	Mauritania	92	B1
El Bahr el Azraq (Blue Nile)	Africa	91	F5
El Centro	United States	32	C5
El Djouf	Mauritania / Mali	88	D4
El Dorado	United States	33	G4
El Eglab	Algeria	88	D3
El Faiym	Egypt	91	E2
El Fasher	Sudan	90	E5
El Ferrol	Spain	70	B1
El Geneira	Sudan	90	D5
El Gezira	Sudan	91	F5
El Goléa	Algeria	89	F2
El Gîza (Giza)	Egypt	91	E1
El Iskandarîyah (Alexandria)	Egypt	91	E1
El Kef	Tunisia	75	C12
El Khârga	Egypt	91	F2
El Khartum (Khartoum)	Sudan	91	F4
El Khartum Bahri	Sudan	91	F4
El Mahallah El Kubrá	Egypt	82	B3
El Milk	Sudan	91	E4
El Minyâ	Egypt	91	E2
El Mreyyé	Mauritania / Mali	88	D5
El Navado	Argentina	52	H6
El Obeid	Sudan	91	F5
El Oued	Algeria	89	G2
El Paso	United States	32	E5
El Qâhira (Cairo)	Egypt	91	F2
El Reno	United States	34	G4
El Rosario	Mexico	32	C6
El Salvador	Central America	46	F6
El Suweis	Egypt	82	B3
El Wâhât el Khârga	Egypt	91	F2
Elat	Israel	84	B7
Elâzg	Turkey	81	H4
Elba	Italy	74	E6
Elbasan	Albania	78	C3
Elbe	Germany / Czech Republic	65	J5
Elbe (Labe)	Germany / Czech Republic	65	K6
Elbeuf	France	56	E5
Elblag	Poland	60	D4
Elburz	Iran	82	E2
Elche	Spain	71	K6
Elda	Spain	71	K6
Elephant Butte	United States	32	E5
Eleuthera	Bahamas	35	L6
Elgon	Uganda / Kenya	95	E3
Elista	Russia	60	J5
Elizabethtown	United States	36	J4
Elk	Poland	62	M4
Elko	United States	29	C2
Ellesmere Island	Canada	120 (1)	CC1
Ellice Islands	Micronesia	114	H6
Elliot Lake	Canada	43	Q7
Elmira	United States	37	L3
Elsen Nur	China	104	F1
Elsenerz	Austria	63	D9
Eltanin Bay	Antarctica	120 (2)	JJ2
Eluru	India	105	D5
Ely	United Kingdom	56	D2
Ely	United States	30	D4
Emån	Sweden	59	J8
Emba	Kazakhstan	101	K8
Embalse de Alcántara	Spain	70	D5
Embalse de Almendra	Spain	70	D3
Embalse de Cijara	Spain	70	F5
Embalse de Guri	Venezuela	50	E2
Embalse de Mequinenza	Spain	71	K3
Embalse de Ricabayo	Spain	70	E3
Embalse de Valdecañas	Spain	70	E5
Embalse de Yesa	Spain	71	J2
Embalse del Ebro	Spain	70	G1
Embalse del Río Negro	Uruguay	53	K5
Embalse del Zújar	Spain	70	E6
Emden	Germany	64	C3
Emery	United States	32	D4
Emi Koussi	Chad	90	C4
Emmen	Netherlands	57	K2
Empoli	Italy	72	G7
Emporia	United States	33	G4
Ems	Germany	64	C4
Encantada	Mexico	26	C5
Encarnación	Paraguay	53	K4
Endicott	United States	37	L3
Enentokiö	Finland	58	M2
Enewetak	Marshall Islands	114	G4
Enez Körfezi	Greece	78	H4
Engels	Russia	60	K4
England	United Kingdom	67	L9
English Channel / La Manche	United Kingdom	67	L11
Enid	United States	33	G4
Ennadal	Canada	42	L4
Ennedi	Chad	90	D4
Enos	Greece	78	C6
Enschede	Netherlands	57	K2
Ensenada	Mexico	26	C5
Enterprise	United States	35	J5
Enugu	Nigeria	93	F3
Épernay	France	57	G5
Épinal	France	68	M5
Epupa Falls	Angola / Namibia	96	A3
Equatorial Guinea	West Africa	93	F4
Er Rachidia	Morocco	88	E2
Erbeskopf	Germany	65	C7
Erciyas Dag	Turkey	80	F4
Erd	Hungary	76	F2
Erdek Körfezi	Turkey	80	B3
Erdi	Chad	90	D4
Erdi Ma	Chad	90	D4
Erechim	Brazil	53	L3
Erenhot	China	102	L6
Erfurt	Germany	65	G6
Erg Chech	Mali / Algeria	88	E4
Erg du Djourab	Chad	93	H1
Erg du Ténéré	Niger	89	H5
Erg Iguidi	Mauritania / Algeria	88	D3
Ergene	Turkey	78	J3
Ergun He	China	102	L6
Ergun Zuoqi	China	102	L6
Erie	United States	39	Q8
Erimanthos	Greece	78	D7
Erimo-Misaki	Japan	111	M3
Eritrea	Africa	91	G4
Erlangen	Germany	65	G7
Ermeraldas	Equador	50	B3
Erode	India	105	C6
Erzgebirge	Germany	65	J6
Erzurum	Turkey	81	J4
Es Semara	Western Sahara	88	C3
Esbjerg	Denmark	59	E9
Escanaba	United States	36	J2
Escaut	France	56	G4
Esch-sur-Alzett	Luxembourg	57	J5
Esfahan (Isfahan)	Iran	82	F3
Eshwege	Germany	65	F5
Eskilstuna	Sweden	59	J7
Eskimo Lake	Canada	40	E3
Eskisehir	Turkey	80	C4
Esler Dag	Turkey	79	M7
Espíritu Santo	Vanuatu	114	G7
Espanola	Canada	36	K2
Española	Ecuador	50 (1)	B2
Esperance Bay	Australia	116	D6
Espoo / Esbo	Finland	59	M6
Esquel	Argentina	52	G7
Essen	Germany	65	C5
Estonia	Europe	59	N7
Estrecho de Magallanes	South America	52	G9
Esztergom	Hungary	63	H10
Étaples	France	56	E4
Eternity Range	Antarctica	120 (2)	LL3
Ethiopia	Central Africa	95	F2
Etna	Sicily (Italy)	75	J11
Etolin Island	Canada	41	E6
Etosha Pan	Namibia	96	B3
Eugene	United States	28	B2
Euphrates (Al Furat)	Middle East	82	C2
Eureka	United States	30	C4
Euskirchen	Germany	65	B6
Evans Strait	Canada	42	Q4
Evanston	United States	30	D3
Evansville	United States	36	J4
Evaz	Iran	85	F3
Everett	United States	28	B1
Everglades	United States	35	K6
Évora	Portugal	70	C6
Évreux	France	56	E5
Évros	Greece / Turkey	80	B3
Evvoïkos Kólpos	Greece	78	F6
Exe	United Kingdom	67	K11
Exeter	United Kingdom	67	K11
Exmoor	United Kingdom	68	B2
Expedition Range	Australia	117	J5

F

Faber Lake	Canada	38	H4
Fabriano	Italy	74	G5
Fadippolu Atoll	Maldives	105	B7
Faeroes	Denmark	54	D1
Fafen Shet	Ethiopia	91	H6
Fagaras	Romania	77	M4
Faial	Azores (Portugal)	88 (1)	B2
Fair Isle	United Kingdom	66	M2
Fairbairn Reservoir	Australia	117	J4
Fairbanks	Alaska (U.S.)	29 (1)	H3
Fairmont	United States	31	H3
Faisalabad	Pakistan	83	K3
Faizabad	India	104	D3
Fakfak	Indonesia	113	D3
Fakse Bugt	Denmark	64	H1
Falaise	France	56	C6
Falaise de Tiguidit	Niger	89	G5
Falcon Reservoir	United States	33	F6
Falkensee	Germany	64	J4
Falkland Islands	South Atlantic Ocean	53	K9
Falster	Denmark	59	G9
Falterona	Italy	73	G7
Falun	Sweden	59	H6
Famagusta	Cyprus	79	S9
Fan	Denmark	59	E9
Fan Si Pan	Vietnam	106	C2
Fano	Italy	73	J7
Farewell Spit	New Zealand	118	D5
Fargo	United States	31	G2
Farmington	United States	32	E4
Faro	Portugal	70	C7
Faro	Canada	40	E4
Fårö	Sweden	59	K7
Farquhar Group	Seychelles	97 (2)	B2
Farrukhabad	India	104	C3
Fassano	Italy	76	E9
Favignana	Sardinia (Italy)	75	G11
Faxaflói	Iceland	58 (1)	B2
Faxälven	Sweden	58	H5
Faya	Chad	90	C4
Fayetteville	United States	34	H4
Fécamp	France	56	E5
Federal States of Micronesia	Oceania	114	E4
Fehmarn	Germany	64	F2
Fehmarnbelt	Germany	64	F2
Feira de Santana	Brazil	51	K6
Felanitx	Spain	71	P5
Feldberg	Germany	65	D9
Felidu Atoll	Maldives	105	B8
Feltre	Italy	73	G4
Femer Blt	Denmark	64	F2
Femund	Norway	59	F5
Fen He	China	108	E3
Fergana	Uzbekistan	101	N9
Fermo	Italy	74	H5
Fernandina	Ecuador	50 (1)	A2
Fernando Póo (Bioko)	Equatorial Guinea	93	F4
Ferrara	Italy	74	F4
Fès	Morocco	88	E2
Fethiye Körfezi	Turkey	79	L8
Fetlar	United Kingdom	66	N1
Fezzân	Libya	90	B2
Fiambala	Argentina	52	H4
Fichtelgebirge	Germany	65	G6
Fidenza	Italy	72	F6
Fife Ness	United Kingdom	66	L5
Figueras	Spain	71	N2
Fiha al Inab	Saudi Arabia	84	D7
Fiji	Oceania	114	H8
Filicudi	Italy	75	J10
Fimania	Greece	78	J7
Finger Lakes	United States	37	L3
Finland	Europe	58	P3
Finstenwalde	Germany	64	J4
Finsteraarhorn	Switzerland	72	D4
Firat	Turkey	81	H5
Firenze (Florence)	Italy	74	F5
Firozabad	India	104	C3
Firth of Clyde	United Kingdom	66	H6
Firth of Forth	United Kingdom	66	L5
Firth of Lorn	United Kingdom	66	H5
Firuzabad	Iran	85	E2
Fisher Strait	Canada	42	P4
Fitzroy River	Australia	116	D3
Fivizzano	Italy	72	F6
Fjtjar	Norway	59	C7
Flagstaff	United States	32	D4
Flaming Gorge National Park	United States	30	E3
Flåsjön	Sweden	58	J4

Flathead Lake	United States	30	D2
Flensburg	Germany	64	E2
Flers	France	56	C6
Flin Flon	Canada	43	L6
Flinders Island	Australia	117	J7
Flinders Ranges	Australia	117	G6
Flinders Reefs	Australia	117	J3
Flinders River	Australia	117	H3
Flint	Kiribati (Pacific Ocean)	115	L7
Flint	United States	43	Q8
Flora	Norway	59	C6
Florence	United States	34	J5
Florence (Firenze)	Italy	74	F5
Flores	Indonesia	113	B4
Flores	Azores (Portugal)	88	(1)A2
Flores Sea	Indonesia	113	B4
Floriano	Brazil	51	J5
Florianópolis	Brazil	53	M4
Florida	United States	35	K6
Florida Keys	United States	35	K7
Fluviá	Spain	69	H11
Fly	South East Asia	113	F4
Foci del Po	Italy	74	G4
Focsani	Romania	77	Q4
Foggia	Italy	75	K7
Fogo	Cape Verde	92	(1)B1
Fogo	Canada	45	W7
Fohnsdorf	Austria	73	K3
Föhr	Germany	64	D2
Foix	France	69	G11
Foley Island	Canada	42	R3
Folkestone	United Kingdom	56	E3
Fond du Lac	United States	36	J3
Fonsagrada	Spain	70	C1
Fonte Boa	Brazil	50	D4
Fontur	Iceland	58	(1)F1
Forbach	France	57	K5
Forges les-Eux	France	56	E5
Forli	Italy	74	G4
Formentera	Spain	71	M6
Formia	Italy	75	H7
Formies	France	57	H4
Formigas	Azores (Portugal)	88	(1)C2
Formosa	Argentina	53	K4
Forrest City	United States	34	H4
Forssa	Finland	59	M6
Fort Albany	Canada	43	Q6
Fort Bragg	United States	29	B3
Fort Collision	Canada	42	H2
Fort Dodge	United States	31	H3
Fort Franklin	Canada	37	N5
Fort Good Hope	Canada	40	F3
Fort Lauderdale	United States	35	K6
Fort MacPherson	Canada	40	E3
Fort Madison	United States	36	H3
Fort McMurray	Canada	42	J5
Fort Myers	United States	35	K6
Fort Nelson	Canada	41	G5
Fort Peck Lake	United States	30	E2
Fort Pierce	United States	35	K6
Fort Severn	Canada	43	P5
Fort Simpson	Canada	40	G4
Fort Smith	United States	33	H4
Fort Wayne	United States	36	J3
Fort Worth	United States	33	G5
Fort Yates	United States	31	F2
Fort-de-France	Martinique	47	M5
Fortaleza	Brazil	51	K4
Fortescue River	Australia	116	C4
Fortune Bay	Canada	45	V7
Foshan	China	107	E2
Fougères	France	68	D5
Foula	United Kingdom	66	L1
Foulness Island	United Kingdom	68	G2
Fouta Djallon	Guinea	92	B2
Foveaux Strait	New Zealand	119	B8
Fowlers Bay	Australia	116	F6
Foxe Basin	Canada	42	R3
Foxe Channel	Canada	42	Q4
Fralovo	Russia	60	J5
France	Europe	68	F6
Francistown	Botswana	96	D4
Frankenwald	Germany	65	G6
Frankfort (KY)	United States	35	K4
Frankfort (TN)	United States	47	G1
Frankfurt	Germany	64	K4
Frankfurt am Main	Germany	65	D6
Fränkische Alb	Germany	65	F8
Franklin Bay	Canada	40	F3
Franklin Mountains	Canada	40	G4
Franklin Strait	Canada	42	M2
Frans-Jozef-Land	Russia	120	(1)J1
Fraser	Australia	114	F8
Fraser	Canada	28	B1
Fraser Island	Australia	117	K5
Fredericksburg	United States	35	L4
Fredericton	Canada	45	T7
Frederikshavn	Denmark	59	F8
Fredonia	United States	37	L3
Freeport	Bahamas	35	L6
Freeport	United States	33	G6
Freetown	Sierra Leone	92	B3
Freiberg	Germany	65	J6
Freiburg im Breisgau	Germany	65	C8
Freising	Germany	65	G8
Fréjus	France	69	M10
Fremantle	Australia	116	C6
Fremont (NE)	United States	31	G3
Fremont (OH)	United States	36	K3
French Guiana	South America	51	G3
French Polynesia	France	115	M7
Fresnillo de Gonzáles Echeverria	Mexico	33	F7
Fresno	United States	29	C3
Fribourg	Switzerland	72	C4
Friedberg	Austria	63	F10
Friedrichshafen	Germany	65	E9
Frobisher Bay	Canada	44	T4

Frobisher Lake	Canada	42	J5
Fruska Gora	Yugoslavia	76	G4
Frya	Norway	58	D5
Fuentesaúco	Spain	70	E3
Fuerteventura	Canary Islands (Spain)	88	C3
Fuji-San	Japan	111	K6
Fukueichiao	Taiwan	109	G5
Fukui	Japan	111	J5
Fukuoka	Japan	110	F7
Fukushima	Japan	111	L5
Fukuyama	Japan	110	G6
Fulda	Germany	65	E5
Funabashi	Japan	111	L6
Funafuti	Tuvalu	114	H6
Funchal	Madeira	88	B1
Furneaux Group	Australia	117	J8
Fürstenwalde	Germany	64	K4
Fürth	Germany	65	F7
Fushun	China	109	G2
Fuxian Hu	China	106	C2
Fuxin	China	109	G2
Fuzhou	China	109	F5
Fyn	Denmark	59	F9

G

G.Rantamerio	Sulewesi	113	A3
Gabes	Tunisia	89	G2
Gabon	West Africa	93	G5
Gaborone	Botswana	96	D4
Gabriel Strait	Canada	44	T4
Gäddede	Sweden	58	H4
Gadsden	United States	35	J5
Gaffney	United States	35	K4
Gaggenau	France	57	M6
Gailtaler Alpen	Austria	73	J4
Gainesville (FL)	United States	35	K6
Gainsville (GA)	United States	35	K5
Gainsville (TX)	United States	34	G5
Galápagos Islands (Islas Galápagos)	Ecuador	50	(1)A1
Galati	Romania	77	Q4
Galesburg	United States	36	H3
Gallarate	Italy	72	D5
Galle	Sri Lanka	105	C7
Gällivare	Sweden	58	L3
Gallup	United States	32	E4
Galveston	United States	34	H6
Galveston Bay	United States	34	H6
Galway	Ireland	67	E8
Galway Bay	Ireland	67	D8
Gambia	Gambia	92	B2
Gambia	West Africa	92	A2
Gambier	French Polynesia	115	N8
Gamvik	Norway	58	Q1
Gan Jiang	China	108	E5
Gandajika	Democratic Republic Of Congo	94	C5
Gandak	Southern Asia	104	D3
Gander	Canada	45	W7
Gandia	Spain	71	K6
Ganga (Ganges)	Southern Asia	104	D3
Ganjang	China	107	E2
Gannett Peak	United States	30	E3
Ganzhou	China	108	E5
Gao	Mali	88	E5
Gaoyou Hu	China	109	F4
Gap	France	69	M9
Gardelegen	Germany	64	G4
Garden City	United States	31	F4
Garden Peninsula	United States	36	J2
Garissa	Kenya	95	F4
Garmisch-Partenkirchen	Germany	65	G8
Garonne	France	69	E9
Garoua	Cameroon	93	G3
Gary	United States	36	J3
Gaspe	Canada	45	U7
Gävle	Sweden	59	J6
Gawler Ranges	Australia	117	G6
Gaya	India	104	D4
Gayny	Russia	61	L2
Gaza	Israel	84	B5
Gaziantep	Turkey	80	G5
Gbarnga	Liberia	92	C3
Gdansk (Danzig)	Poland	62	H3
Gdynia	Poland	59	K9
Gediz	Turkey	79	K6
Geel	Belgium	57	H3
Geelong	Australia	117	H7
Geesthacht	Germany	64	F3
Geilo	Norway	59	E6
Gela	Italy	75	J11
Gelsenkirchen	Germany	64	C5
Gemena	Democratic Republic Of Congo	94	C3
Gemlik Körfezi	Turkey	79	L4
Genève (Geneva)	Switzerland	72	A4
General Roca	Argentina	52	H6
General Santos	Philippines	113	C1
Geneva	United States	37	L3
Geneva (Genève)	Switzerland	72	A4
Genil	Spain	70	E7
Genoa (Génova)	Italy	74	C4
Gênova (Genoa)	Italy	74	C4
Genovesa	Ecuador	50	(1)B1
Gent	Belgium	57	G3
Geographe Bay	Australia	116	B6
George	South Africa	96	C6
George River	Canada	44	T5
George Town	Malaysia	112	C1
George VI Sound	Antarctica	120	(2)LL3
George West	United States	33	G6
Georgetown	Guyana	51	F2
Georgetown	United States	35	L5
Georgia	Asia	81	K3
Georgia	United States	35	K5

Georgian Bay	Canada	36	K2
Gera	Germany	65	H6
Geraldton	Australia	116	B5
Geraldton	Canada	36	J2
Gering	United States	31	F3
Gerlachovsky	Slovakia	63	K8
Germany	Europe	64	E4
Germiston	South Africa	96	D5
Geroardsbergen	Belgium	57	G4
Gerona	Spain	71	N3
Getafe	Spain	70	G4
Gettysburg	United States	31	G3
Geyik Dag	Turkey	80	E5
Ghadamis	Libya	90	A2
Ghaghara	Southern Asia	104	D3
Ghana	West Africa	92	D3
Ghanzi	Botswana	96	C4
Ghard Abu Muharik	Egypt	91	E2
Ghardaïa	Algeria	89	F2
Gharyan	Libya	90	B1
Ghat	Libya	90	B2
Gheorghe Gheorghiu-Dej	Romania	77	P3
Gheorghieni	Romania	77	N3
Ghubbat Sawqirah	Oman	83	G6
Gibraltar	United Kingdom	70	E8
Gibson Desert	Australia	116	D4
Gien	France	68	H6
Giessen	Germany	65	D6
Gifu	Japan	111	J6
Giglio	Italy	74	E6
Gijón	Spain	70	E1
Gilbert Islands	Kiribati (Pacific Oean)	114	H5
Gilbert River	Australia	117	H3
Gilbués	Brazil	51	H5
Gillette	United States	31	E3
Gímsstadir	Iceland	58	E2
Ginzo de Limra	Spain	70	C2
Gironde	France	69	E8
Gisborne	New Zealand	118	G4
Gisors	France	56	E5
Giurgiu	Romania	77	N6
Giza (El Gîza)	Egypt	91	E1
Gizhiga	Russia	103	U4
Gizhiginskaya Guba	Russia	103	T4
Gji i Durrësit	Albania	78	B3
Gji i Lalzës	Albania	78	B3
Gjvik	Norway	59	F6
Glacier National Park	United States	30	D2
Glåma	Norway	59	F6
Glamoc	Bosnia-Herzegovina	76	D5
Glarner Alpen	Switzerland	74	C2
Glasgow	United Kingdom	66	J6
Glasgow (KY)	United States	35	J4
Glasgow (MT)	United States	30	E2
Glazov	Russia	61	L3
Glen Canyon	United States	32	D4, E4
Glendive	United States	31	F2
Glens Falls	United States	37	M3
Glittertind	Norway	59	E6
Gliwice	Poland	63	H7
Glogów	Poland	62	F6
Glommersträst	Sweden	58	K4
Glorieuses (Réunion)	South Africa	97	H2
Gloucester	United Kingdom	68	C2
Gmunden	Austria	73	J3
Gniezno	Poland	62	G3
Goba	Ethiopia	95	G2
Gobi Desert	China / Mongolia	108	D2
Goch	Germany	64	B5
Godavari	India	104	C5
Godelbukta Breidvika	Antarctica	120	(2)H3
Godhaun	Greenland	39	W3
Godthåb	Greenland	39	W4
Goelette	Seychelles	97	(2) B3
Goes	Netherlands	57	G3
Gogebic Range	United States	36	H2
Goiânia	Brazil	51	H7
Gök Tepe	Turkey	79	M8
Gökçeada	Turkey	78	H4
Gökora Körfezi	Turkey	79	K8
Gökrmak	Turkey	80	E3
Golan Heights	Israel	84	C3
Gold Beach	United States	28	B2
Gold Coast	Australia	117	K5
Goldap	Poland	62	M3
Golden Bay	New Zealand	118	D5
Golfe dArzew	Algeria	71	K9
Golfe de Gascogne	France	69	C10
Golfe de Saint-Malo	France	68	C5
Golfe de Valinco	Corsica (France)	74	C7
Golfe di Sagone	Corsica (France)	74	C6
Golfe du Lion	France / Spain	69	K10
Golfo de Alicante	Spain	71	L6
Golfo de Almería	Spain	71	H8
Golfo de Arica	South America	52	G2
Golfo de Batabanó	Cuba	47	H4
Golfo de Cádiz	Spain / Portugal	70	C8
Golfo de Fonseca	El Salvador	46	G6
Golfo de Guayaquil	Ecuador	50	A4
Golfo de Honduras	Honduras	47	G5
Golfo de los Mosquitos	Central America	47	H6
Golfo de Mazarrón	Spain	71	J7
Golfo de Panamá	Panama	47	J7
Golfo de Rosas	Spain	71	P2
Golfo de San Jorge	Spain	71	L4
Golfo de San Jorge	Argentina	52	H8
Golfo de Tehuantepec	Mexico	46	F5
Golfo de Valencia	Spain	71	L5
Golfo de Venezuela	Venezuela	50	C1
Golfo del Darién	Central America	50	B2
Golfo dell Asinara	Sardinia (Italy)	75	C7
Golfo di Gaeta	Italy	75	H7
Golfo di Cagliari	Sardinia (Italy)	75	D9
Golfo di Castellammare	Sicily (Italy)	75	G10
Golfo di Catània	Sicily (Italy)	75	K11
Golfo di Genova	Italy	72	D6
Golfo di Manfredonia	Italy	75	L7

Golfo di Napoli	*Italy*	75	H8
Golfo di Oristano	*Sardinia (Italy)*	75	C9
Golfo di Orosei	*Sardinia (Italy)*	75	D8
Golfo di Policastro	*Italy*	75	K9
Golfo di Salerno	*Italy*	75	J8
Golfo di Sant Eufemia	*Italy*	75	K10
Golfo di Squillace	*Italy*	75	L10
Golfo di Taranto	*Italy*	75	L8
Golfo di Trieste	*Italy*	73	J5
Golfo di Venezia	*Italy*	74	G3
Golfo San Matias	*Argentina*	52	J7
Gomel	*Belarus*	60	G4
Gomera	*Canary Islands (Spain)*	88	B3
Gonder	*Ethiopia*	91	G5
Gongga Shan	*China*	108	C5
Gongola	*Central Africa*	90	B5
Goodland	*United States*	31	F4
Goose Bay	*Canada*	44	U6
Goose Lake	*United States*	28	B2
Göppingen	*Germany*	65	E8
Gora Belukha	*Russia*	101	R8
Gora Burun-Sabartuj	*Russia*	102	H7
Gora Denezkin Kamen	*Russia*	61	M2
Gora Dykh Tau	*Russia / Georgia*	81	K2
Gora Elbrus	*Russia / Georgia*	81	J2
Gora Golets-Skalistyy	*Russia*	102	K5
Gora Jamantau	*Russia*	61	M4
Gora Munku Sardyk	*Russia*	102	G6
Gora Narodnaya	*Russia*	61	N1
Gora Payyer	*Russia*	61	N1
Gora Telpoziz	*Russia*	61	M2
Gorakhpur	*India*	104	D3
Gorgona	*Italy*	74	D5
Gorgona	*Colombia*	50	B3
Gorinchem	*Netherlands*	57	H3
Gorizia	*Italy*	73	J5
Gorjanci	*Slovakia/ Croatia*	76	C4
Gorki	*Russia*	61	P1
Gorkovskoye Vdkhr.	*Russia*	60	J3
Görlitz	*Germany*	65	K5
Gorlovka	*Ukraine*	60	H5
Gorna Oryahovitsa	*Bulgaria*	77	N6
Gorontalo	*Indonesia*	113	B2
Gory Byrranga	*Russia*	100	S3
Gory Putorana	*Russia*	100	S4
Góry Swietokrzyskie	*Poland*	63	K6
Gorzów Wielkopolski	*Poland*	62	E5
Goshen	*United States*	36	J3
Goslar	*Germany*	64	F5
Göta älv	*Sweden*	59	F8
Gotel Mountains	*Nigeria*	93	G3
Gotha	*Germany*	65	F6
Gotland	*Sweden*	59	K8
Gotowasi	*Indonesia*	113	C2
Gotska Sandön	*Sweden*	59	K7
Göttingen	*Germany*	64	F5
Gotto-Retto	*Japan*	110	E7
Gouda	*Netherlands*	57	H2
Gough Is.	*Atlantic Ocean*	87	B10
Gourma	*Mali*	92	D1
Govaltain Nuruu	*Mongolia*	108	C2
Governador Valadares	*Brazil*	51	J7
Gozo	*Malta*	75	J12
Gracac	*Croatia*	76	C5
Graciosa	*Azores (Portugal)*	88	(1)B2
Graham Island	*Canada*	29	(1)L5
Grampian Mountains	*United Kingdom*	66	J5
Gran Canaria	*Canary Islands (Spain)*	88	B3
Gran Chaco	*Argentina / Paraguay*	52	J3
Gran Paradiso	*Italy*	72	C5
Gran Pilastro	*Austria / Italy*	73	G4
Granada	*Spain*	70	G7
Granby	*Canada*	37	M2
Grand Bahama	*Bahamas*	47	J3
Grand Ballon dAlsace	*France*	65	C9
Grand Canyon	*United States*	32	D4
Grand Coulee Dam	*United States*	28	C1
Grand Erg de Bilma	*Niger*	90	B4
Grand Erg Occidental	*Algeria*	89	E3
Grand Erg Oriental	*Algeria*	89	F3
Grand Forks	*United States*	31	G2
Grand Junction	*United States*	30	E4
Grand Prairie	*Canada*	41	H5
Grand Rapids (MI)	*United States*	36	J3
Grand Rapids (MN)	*United States*	31	H2
Grand Teton	*United States*	41	J8
Grande Casse	*France*	72	B5
Grande Comore (Njazidja)	*Comoros*	97	G2
Grândola	*Portugal*	70	B6
Granite Peak	*United States*	29	C2
Grant Pass	*United States*	28	B2
Grantham	*United Kingdom*	56	C2
Granville	*France*	68	D5
Grasse	*France*	72	B7
Grassrange	*United States*	30	E2
Grays	*United Kingdom*	56	D3
Graz	*Austria*	73	L3
Great Abaco	*Bahamas*	47	J3
Great Australian Bight	*Australia*	116	E6
Great Barrier Island	*New Zealand*	118	E3
Great Barrier Reef	*Australia*	117	J3
Great Bear Lake	*Canada*	40	G3
Great Bend	*United States*	31	G4
Great Dividing Range	*Australia*	117	H3
Great Exhibition Bay	*New Zealand*	118	D2
Great Exuma	*Bahamas*	47	J4
Great Falls	*United States*	30	D2
Great Inagua	*Caribbean*	47	K4
Great Karoo	*South Africa*	96	C6
Great Nicobar	*India*	105	F7
Great Plains	*United States*	31	F2
Great Salt Lake	*United States*	30	D3
Great Salt Lake Desert	*United States*	30	D3
Great Sandy Desert	*Australia*	116	D4
Great Sandy Desert	*United States*	28	B2
Great Slave Lake	*Canada*	38	H4
Great Smokey Mountain Nat. Pk.	*United States*	35	K4

Great Victoria Desert	*Australia*	116	D5
Great Yarmouth	*United Kingdom*	56	E2
Greater Antilles	*Caribbean*	47	J4
Greater Sunda Islands	*Indonesia*	112	D4
Greece	*Europe*	78	D5
Greeley	*United States*	31	F3
Green Bay	*United States*	36	J3
Green River	*United States*	32	D4
Greenland (Denmark)	*North Atlantic Ocean*	39	X3
Greenland Sea	*Iceland*	58	B1
Greensboro	*United States*	35	L4
Greenville (MS)	*United States*	34	H5
Greenville (NC)	*United States*	35	L4
Greenville (SC)	*United States*	35	K5
Greers Ferry Lake	*United States*	33	H4
Gregory Lake	*Australia*	116	E4
Greifswalder Bodden	*Germany*	64	J2
Gremikha	*Russia*	60	H1
Grenada	*Caribbean*	47	M6
Grenada	*United States*	34	J5
Grenen	*Denmark*	59	F8
Grenoble	*France*	69	L8
Greven	*Germany*	64	C4
Grey Islands	*Canada*	39	V6
Grey Range	*Australia*	117	H5
Greymouth	*New Zealand*	119	D6
Griefswald	*Germany*	64	J2
Grimsby	*United Kingdom*	67	N8
Grímsey	*Iceland*	58	(1)E1
Griz	*Germany*	65	G6
Grmec	*Bosnia-Herzegovina*	76	D5
Grodno	*Belarus*	59	N10
Groningen	*Netherlands*	57	K1
Groot Karas Berg	*Namibia*	96	B5
Groote Eylandt	*Australia*	117	G2
Großer Arber	*Germany*	65	J7
Großer Beerberg	*Germany*	65	F6
Großglockner	*Austria*	73	H3
Großvenediger	*Austria*	74	G1
Grosseto	*Italy*	74	F6
Grotli	*Norway*	59	D6
Groupe Acteón	*French Polynesia*	115	N8
Groznyy (Grosny)	*Russia*	81	L2
Grudziadz	*Poland*	62	H4
Guadalajara	*Spain*	70	G4
Guadalajara	*Mexico*	46	D4
Guadalcanal	*Solomon Islands*	114	F7
Guadalimar	*Spain*	70	G6
Guadalquivir	*Spain*	70	E7
Guadalupe	*Mexico*	32	E6
Guadeloupe	*Caribbean*	47	M5
Guadelupe	*Spain*	70	E5
Guadiana	*Spain / Portugal*	70	C7
Guadix	*Spain*	70	G7
Guajará Mirim	*Brazil*	50	D6
Guam	*U.S. (Pacific Ocean)*	114	E4
Guangmao Shan	*China*	106	C1
Guangzhou (Canton)	*China*	108	E6
Guantamo Bay	*U.S. (Caribbean)*	47	K5
Guarda	*Portugal*	70	C4
Guardo	*Spain*	70	F2
Guatemala	*Central America*	46	F5
Guatemala City	*Guatemala*	46	F6
Guayaquil	*Ecuador*	50	A4
Guaymas	*Mexico*	32	D6
Guba Buorkhaya	*Russia*	102	M2
Guba Gusinaya	*Russia*	103	S2
Gubakha	*Russia*	61	M3
Guban	*Somalia*	95	G1
Guben	*Germany*	64	K5
Gueda	*Spanje / Portugal*	70	D4
Guelmine	*Morocco*	88	C3
Guéret	*France*	69	G7
Guernsey	*United Kingdom*	67	L12
Guerrero Negro	*Mexico*	32	D6
Gueru	*Zimbabwe*	96	D3
Guge	*Ethiopia*	95	F2
Guiana Highlands	*South America*	50	E3
Guildford	*United Kingdom*	56	C3
Guilin	*China*	108	E5
Guinea	*West Africa*	92	B2
Guinea-Bissau	*West Africa*	92	A2
Guise	*France*	57	G5
Guiyang	*China*	108	D5
Gujranwala	*Pakistan*	83	K3
Gujrat	*Pakistan*	104	B2
Gulbarga	*India*	105	C5
Gulbere	*Latvia*	59	P8
Gulf of Aden	*Middle East*	91	J5
Gulf of Alaska	*North Pacific Ocean*	40	D5
Gulf of Aqaba	*Saudi Arabia / Egypt*	91	F2
Gulf of Boothia	*Canada*	42	N2
Gulf of Bothnia	*Sweden / Finland*	58	K6
Gulf of California	*Mexico*	46	B3
Gulf of Carpentaria	*Australia*	117	G2
Gulf of Finland	*Finland / Estonia / Russia*	59	N7
Gulf of Gdansk	*Poland*	62	J3
Gulf of Guinea	*Atlantic Ocean*	93	E4
Gulf of Kachchh	*India*	104	A4
Gulf of Khambhat	*India*	104	B4
Gulf of Maine	*United States*	45	T8
Gulf of Mannar	*India / Sri Lanka*	105	C7
Gulf of Martaban	*South East Asia*	106	B3
Gulf of Mexico	*Central America*	46	F3
Gulf of Oman	*Middle East*	83	G4
Gulf of Riga	*Lithuania*	59	M8
Gulf of Sirte (Khalij Surt)	*Tunisia*	90	C1
Gulf of St. Lawrence	*Canada*	45	U7
Gulf of Suez	*Egypt*	82	B4
Gulf of Thailand	*South East Asia*	106	C4
Gulf of Tongking	*South East Asia*	106	D2
Gulf St. Vincent	*Australia*	117	G7
Gulfport	*United States*	34	J5
Gull Bay	*Canada*	36	J2
Gulu	*Uganda*	94	E3
Gummersbach	*Germany*	65	C5
Guna Terara	*Ethiopia*	91	G5

Güney Dogu Toroslar	*Turkey*	80	G4
Gunnbjrns Fjeld	*Greenland*	120	(1)U3
Gunnison (CO)	*United States*	32	E4
Gunnison (UT)	*United States*	32	D4
Gunong Kinabalu	*Malaysia*	112	F1
Guntur	*India*	105	C5
Gunung Dempo	*Indonesia*	112	C3
Gunung Kau Paulatmada	*Indonesia*	113	C3
Gunung Kerinci	*Indonesia*	112	C3
Gunung Kinabalu	*Malaysia*	113	A1
Gunung Kobipato	*Indonesia*	113	C3
Gunung Kwoka	*Indonesia*	113	D3
Gunung Leuser	*Indonesia*	112	B2
Gunung Mahameru	*Indonesia*	112	E4
Gunung Peuetsagoe	*Indonesia*	106	B6
Gunung Peuetsagu	*Indonesia*	112	B2
Gunung Rinjani	*Indonesia*	112	F4
Gunung Slamet	*Indonesia*	112	D4
Gunung Tambora	*Indonesia*	112	F4
Gunung Waukara	*Indonesia*	112	F3
Gunzenhausen	*Germany*	65	F7
Gurktaler Alpen	*Austria*	73	J4
Gursky	*Norway*	59	C5
Gurupi	*Brazil*	51	H6
Gusau	*Nigeria*	93	F2
Güstrow	*Germany*	64	H3
Gütersloh	*Germany*	64	D5
Güzelyurt Körfezi	*Cyprus*	79	Q9
Guwahati	*India*	104	F3
Guyana	*South America*	51	F2
Gwalior	*India*	104	C3
Gweebarra Bay	*Ireland*	67	E7
Gyandzha	*Azerbaijan*	81	M3
Gyaning Hu	*China*	104	G2
Gyaring Co	*China*	104	E2
Gyöngyös	*Hungary*	76	G2
Györ	*Hungary*	76	E2
Gyula	*Hungary*	76	J3

H

Ha Nôi (Hanoi)	*Vietnam*	106	D2
Haapsalu	*Estonia*	59	M7
Haardt	*Germany*	65	C7
Haarlem	*Netherlands*	57	H2
Habana (Havana)	*Cuba*	47	H4
Hachijo-Jima	*Japan*	111	K7
Hachinohe	*Japan*	111	L3
Hadded	*Somalia*	95	H1
Haddunmahti Atoll	*Maldives*	105	B8
Hadejia	*West Africa*	93	G2
Hadhramaut	*Yemen*	82	E6
Hafar al Batin	*Saudi Arabia*	85	B2
Hagen	*Germany*	65	C5
Hagerstown	*United States*	37	L4
Haifa (Hefa)	*Israel*	84	B4
Haikou	*China*	106	E2
Hailuoto	*Finland*	58	N4
Hainan	*China*	106	D3
Haiphong	*Vietnam*	106	D2
Haiti	*Caribbean*	47	K5
Haixin Shan	*China*	108	C3
Haizhou Wan	*China*	109	F3
Hajdúböszörmény	*Hungary*	76	J2
Hajnówka	*Poland*	63	N5
Hajo	*South Korea*	110	C6
Hakodate	*Japan*	111	L3
Halab (Aleppo)	*Syria*	80	G5
Halden	*Norway*	59	F7
Halifax	*Canada*	45	U8
Halifax Bay	*Australia*	117	J3
Halle	*Belgium*	57	H4
Halle	*Germany*	65	H5
Hallingskarvet	*Norway*	59	D6
Halmahera	*Indonesia*	113	C2
Halmstad	*Sweden*	59	G8
Hamada Mangueni	*Niger*	89	H4
Hamadan	*Iran*	82	E3
Hamah	*Syria*	84	D1
Hamamatsu	*Japan*	111	J6
Hamburg	*Germany*	64	F3
Hameln	*Germany*	64	E4
Hamersley Range	*Australia*	116	C4
Hamgyong-Sanmaek	*North Korea*	110	D3
Hamhung	*North Korea*	110	D3
Hami	*China*	101	S9
Hamilton	*New Zealand*	118	E3
Hamilton	*Canada*	37	L3
Hamm	*Germany*	64	C5
Hammadat Tingharat	*Libya / Algeria*	90	A2
Hammerfest	*Norway*	58	M1
Hammond	*United States*	34	H5
Hamphreys Peak	*United States*	32	D4
Hamun-e Jaz Muran	*Iran*	85	H3
Han Shui	*China*	108	E4
Handan	*China*	108	E3
Hangzhou	*China*	109	F4
Hanksville	*United States*	30	D4
Hannibal	*United States*	36	H4
Hannover	*Germany*	64	E4
Hanoi (Ha Nôi)	*Vietnam*	106	D2
Hanöbukt	*Sweden*	62	D2
Hao	*French Polynesia*	115	M7
Har Hu	*China*	108	B3
Har Sai Shan	*China*	108	B3
Harad	*Saudi Arabia*	85	C4
Héradsvötn	*Iceland*	58	(1)D2
Harare	*Zimbabwe*	97	E3
Harbin	*China*	109	H1
Hardangerfjorden	*Norway*	59	C7
Hardangervidda	*Norway*	59	D6
Hardenberg	*Netherlands*	57	K2
Harderwijk	*Netherlands*	57	J2
Hargeysa	*Somalia*	91	H6
Harleston	*United Kingdom*	56	E2
Harlingen	*United States*	33	G6

Lough Corrib	*Ireland*	67	D8
Lough Derg	*Ireland*	67	E9
Lough Foyle	*United Kingdom / Ireland*	67	F6
Lough Mask	*Ireland*	67	D8
Lough Neagh	*United Kingdom*	67	G7
Lough Ree	*Ireland*	67	E8
Lough Swilly	*Ireland*	67	F6
Louisiade Archipelago	*Papua New Guinea*	114	F7
Louisiana	*United States*	34	H5
Louisville	*United States*	36	J4
Loukhi	*Russia*	58	S3
Lovech	*Bulgaria*	77	M6
Loveland	*United States*	31	F3
Lovelock	*United States*	29	C2
Lovozero	*Russia*	58	T2
Lower Lough Erne	*United Kingdom*	67	F7
Lower Post	*Canada*	37	M6
Lower Red Lake	*United States*	31	H2
Lowestoft	*United Kingdom*	56	E2
Lowicz	*Poland*	62	J5
Loyalty Islands	*France*	114	G8
Ls	*Denmark*	59	F8
Luachimo	*Central Africa*	94	C5
Luanda	*Angola*	94	A5
Luang Prabang Range	*South East Asia*	106	C2
Luanginga	*South Africa*	96	C2
Luangwa	*South Africa*	96	E2
Luanshya	*Zambia*	94	D6
Luapula	*Central Africa*	94	D6
Luarca	*Spain*	70	D1
Lubang	*Philippines*	107	F4
Lubango	*Angola*	96	A3
Lubbock	*United States*	33	F5
Lübeck	*Germany*	64	F3
Lübecker Bucht	*Germany*	64	G2
Lubenec	*Czech Republic*	65	J6
Lubin	*Poland*	62	F6
Lublin	*Poland*	60	E4
Lubumbashi	*Democratic Republic Of Congo*	94	D6
Lucca	*Italy*	72	F7
Luce Bay	*United Kingdom*	67	J7
Lucena	*Spain*	70	F7
Lucenec	*Slovakia*	63	J9
Lucera	*Italy*	76	C8
Luckenwalde	*Germany*	64	J4
Lucknow	*India*	104	D3
Lüdenscheid	*Germany*	57	L3
Lüderitz	*Namibia*	96	B5
Lüderitz Bay	*Namibia*	96	A5
Ludhiana	*India*	104	C2
Ludington	*United States*	36	J3
Ludogorsko Plato	*Bulgaria*	77	P6
Ludvika	*Sweden*	59	H6
Ludwigshafen	*Germany*	65	D7
Ludwigslust	*Germany*	64	G3
Luena	*Angola*	94	B6
Lufkin	*United States*	34	H5
Luga	*Russia*	60	G2
Lugansk	*Ukraine*	60	H5
Lugnaguillia	*Ireland*	67	G9
Lugo	*Spain*	70	C1
Lugo	*Italy*	73	G6
Lugoj	*Romania*	76	J4
Lukenie	*Democratic Republic Of Congo*	94	B4
Lulea	*Sweden*	58	M4
Lüleburgaz	*Turkey*	79	K3
Lulonga	*Central Africa*	94	B3
Lulonga	*Democratic Republic Of Congo*	93	H4
Lumajangdong Co	*China*	104	D2
Lüneburg	*Germany*	64	F3
Lunéville	*France*	72	B2
Luoyang	*China*	108	E3
Lupeni	*Romania*	77	L4
Lurio	*Mozambique*	97	F2
Lusaka	*Zambia*	96	D3
Lusambo	*Democratic Republic Of Congo*	94	C4
Luton	*United Kingdom*	67	N10
Lützow-Holmbukta	*Antarctica*	120	(2)J3
Luxembourg	*Europe*	57	J5
Luxembourg	*Luxembourg*	57	K5
Luxor	*Egypt*	82	B4
Luzern	*Switzerland*	69	M7
Luzon	*Philippines*	107	G3
Luzon Strait	*Philippines*	114	C3
Lviv	*Ukraine*	60	E5
Lycksele	*Sweden*	58	K4
Lyme Bay	*United Kingdom*	67	K11
Lymington	*United Kingdom*	56	B4
Lyna	*Poland*	62	K3
Lyngeidet	*Norway*	58	L2
Lynn Lake	*Canada*	43	L5
Lyon	*France*	69	K8
Lyons River	*Australia*	116	C4

M

Ma-tsu Lieh-Tao	*Taiwan*	109	G5
Maalosmadulu Atoll	*Maldives*	105	B7
Maan	*Jordan*	84	C6
Maas	*Central Europe*	64	B5
Maastricht	*Netherlands*	57	J4
Macapá	*Brazil*	51	G3
Macau	*South East Asia*	107	E2
Macau	*South East Asia*	107	E2
Macdonnell Ranges	*Australia*	116	F4
Macedonia	*Europe*	78	C3
Maceió	*Brazil*	51	K5
Macgillycuddys Reeks	*Ireland*	67	C10
Machilpatnam	*India*	105	D5
Macina	*Mali*	92	D2
Macizo Galaico	*Spain*	70	C3
Mackenzie	*Canada*	29	(1)M2
Mackenzie Bay	*Antarctica*	120	(2)M3
Mackenzie Bay	*Canada*	40	D3
Mackenzie Mountains	*Canada*	29	(1)K3
Mackenzie River	*Canada*	38	F3
Mackinaw City	*United States*	36	K2
Macomb	*United States*	36	H3
Macon	*United States*	35	K5
Mâcon	*France*	69	K7
Macujer	*Colombia*	50	C3
Macuzari	*Mexico*	32	D6
Madagascar	*Southern Africa*	97	G4
Madama	*Niger*	89	H4
Maddalena	*Sardinia (Italy)*	75	D7
Madeira	*Portugal*	88	B2
Madeira	*South America*	50	E4
Madeira (Ilhas Selvagens)	*Portugal*	88	B2
Madison (IN)	*United States*	36	J4
Madison (WI)	*United States*	36	J3
Madisonville	*United States*	35	J4
Madras (Chennai)	*India*	105	D6
Madrid	*Spain*	70	G4
Madurai	*India*	105	C7
Madyan	*Saudi Arabia*	82	C4
Maebashi	*Japan*	111	K5
Mafia	*Tanzania*	95	G5
Mafikeng	*South Africa*	96	D5
Magadan	*Russia*	103	S5
Magdalena	*Colombia*	50	C2
Magdalena	*Mexico*	32	D5
Magdeburg	*Germany*	64	G4
Magdelaine Cays	*Australia*	117	K3
Magerya	*Norway*	58	N1
Magnitogorsk	*Russia*	61	M4
Magnolia	*United States*	34	H5
Magog	*Canada*	37	M2
Mahajanga	*Madagascar*	97	H3
Mahanadi	*India*	104	D4
Mahé	*Seychelles*	97	(2)C1
Mahia Peninsula	*New Zealand*	118	G4
Mahón	*Spain*	71	Q5
Maidenhead	*United Kingdom*	56	C3
Maidstone	*United Kingdom*	56	D3
Maiduguri	*Nigeria*	93	G2
Main	*Germany*	65	D6
Maine	*United States*	37	N2
Mainland (Orkney Islands)	*United Kingdom*	66	K2
Mainland (Shetland Islands)	*United Kingdom*	66	M1
Mainz	*Germany*	65	D7
Maio	*Cape Verde*	92	(1)B1
Majerten	*Somalia*	95	H2
Majevica	*Bosnia-Herzegovina*	76	F5
Makassar Strait	*Indonesia*	113	A3
Makgadikgadi Pans	*Botswana*	96	D4
Makhachkala	*Russia*	81	M2
Makkah (Mecca)	*Saudi Arabia*	82	D5
Makó	*Hungary*	76	H3
Makurdi	*Nigeria*	93	F3
Mala Kapela	*Croatia*	76	C5
Malé Karpaty	*Slovakia*	73	N2
Malabo	*Equatorial New Guinea*	93	F4
Malacky	*Slovakia*	73	N2
Málaga	*Spain*	70	F8
Malaita	*Solomon Islands*	114	G6
Malakula	*Vanuatu*	114	G7
Malang	*Malaysia*	112	E4
Malanje	*Angola*	93	H6
Mälaren	*Sweden*	59	J7
Malatya	*Turkey*	81	H4
Malawi	*Southern Africa*	97	E2
Malay Reef	*Australia*	117	J3
Malaysia	*Asia*	112	C2
Malden	*Kiribati*	115	L6
Maldives	*Indian Ocean*	105	B8
Male Atoll	*Maldives*	105	B8
Malegaon	*India*	83	K5
Malgomaj	*Sweden*	58	H4
Malheur Lake	*United States*	28	C2
Mali	*West Africa*	88	E5
Mali Kyun	*Myanmar (Burma)*	106	B4
Malin Head	*Ireland*	66	F6
Maljen	*Yugoslavia*	76	H5
Mallorca	*Spain*	71	P5
Malmédy	*Belgium*	57	K4
Malmö	*Sweden*	59	G9
Malpelo	*Colombia*	50	A3
Malse	*Austria / Czech Republic*	73	K2
Malta	*Europe*	75	J13
Malta	*United States*	30	E2
Malta Channel	*Italy/Malta*	75	J12
Malvern	*United Kingdom*	68	C1
Man	*Côte dIvoire*	92	C3
Manado	*Indonesia*	113	B2
Managua	*Nicaragua*	47	G6
Manama (Al Manamah)	*Bahrain*	85	D3
Manaus	*Brazil*	50	E4
Manchester	*United Kingdom*	67	L8
Manchester	*United States*	37	M3
Mandal	*Norway*	59	D7
Mandalay	*Myanmar (Burma)*	106	B2
Mandalya Körfezi	*Turkey*	79	K7
Mandan	*United States*	31	F2
Manfredonia	*Italy*	76	C8
Manga	*Niger*	89	H6
Mangaia	*Cook Islands*	115	K8
Mangalore	*India*	105	B6
Mangareva	*French Polynesia*	115	N8
Mangin Yoma	*Myanmar (Burma)*	106	B2
Manhatten	*United States*	31	G4
Manicouagan Réservoir	*Canada*	45	T6
Manihiki	*Cook Islands*	115	K7
Manila	*Philippines*	107	G4
Manila Bay	*Philippines*	107	G4
Manisa	*Turkey*	80	B4
Manitoba	*Canada*	38	L6
Manitoulin Island	*Canada*	36	K2
Manitowoc	*United States*	36	J3
Maniwaki	*Canada*	37	L2
Manjra	*India*	105	C5
Mankato	*United States*	31	H3
Mannheim	*Germany*	65	D7
Manning	*Canada*	41	H5
Manokwari	*Indonesia*	113	D3
Manra	*Kiribati (Pacific Ocean)*	115	J6
Manresa	*Spain*	71	M3
Mansa	*Zambia*	96	D2
Mansel Island	*Canada*	42	Q4
Mansfield	*United Kingdom*	56	B1
Mansfield	*United States*	36	K3
Mantes-la-Jolie	*France*	56	E5
Mantova	*Italy*	72	F5
Manukau	*New Zealand*	118	E3
Manukau Harbour	*New Zealand*	118	E3
Manzano Peak	*United States*	32	E5
Maomao Shan	*China*	108	C3
Maotou Shan	*China*	106	C2
Maputo	*Mozambique*	97	E5
Mar Cantábrico	*Spain*	70	D1
Mar del Plata	*Argentina*	53	K6
Mar Menor	*Spain*	71	K7
Maraba	*Brazil*	51	H5
Maracaibo	*Venezuela*	50	C1
Maracay	*Venezuela*	50	D1
Maradi	*Niger*	89	G6
Marahuaca	*Venezuela*	50	D3
Marathon	*Canada*	36	J2
Marbella	*Spain*	70	F8
Marburg	*Germany*	65	D6
March	*United Kingdom*	56	D2
Marchena	*Ecuador*	50	(1)A1
Mardan	*Pakistan*	83	K3
Mardin Daglari	*Turkey*	81	J5
Mare Tirreno (Tyrrhenian Sea)	*Italy*	75	G9
Marettimo	*Sardinia (Italy)*	75	F11
Margarita	*Central America*	50	E1
Marguerite Bay	*Antarctica*	120	(2)KK3
Maria	*French Polynesia*	115	L8
Maribor	*Slovakia*	76	C3
Marica	*Bulgaria*	77	N7
Mariestad	*Sweden*	59	G7
Marietta	*United States*	36	K4
Marijampole	*Lithuania*	59	M9
Marinduque	*Philippines*	107	G4
Marinette	*United States*	36	J2
Marion	*United States*	34	J4
Mariupol	*Ukraine*	60	H5
Marlow	*United Kingdom*	56	D3
Marmande	*France*	69	F9
Marmara	*Turkey*	80	B3
Marmara Denizi (Sea of Marmara)	*Turkey*	80	B3
Marmara Gölü	*Turkey*	79	K6
Marmolada	*Italy*	74	F2
Marne	*France*	68	J4
Maro	*Chad*	89	J5
Maromokotro	*Madagascar*	97	H2
Marotiri	*French Polynesia*	115	M8
Maroua	*Cameroon*	90	B5
Marquesas Islands	*French Polynesia*	115	N6
Marquette	*United States*	36	J2
Marradi	*Italy*	73	G6
Marrakech	*Morocco*	88	D2
Marsala	*Italy*	75	G11
Marsberg	*Germany*	65	D5
Marseille	*France*	69	L10
Marshall (MO)	*United States*	33	H4
Marshall (TX)	*United States*	34	H5
Marshall Islands	*Oceania*	114	G4
Martha's Vineyard	*United States*	37	M3
Martigues	*France*	69	L10
Martin	*Slovakia*	63	H8
Martinique	*Caribbean*	47	M6
Martinsburg	*United States*	37	L4
Maryland	*United States*	37	L4
Maryville	*United States*	31	H3
Masan	*South Korea*	110	E6
Masbate	*Philippines*	107	G4
Maseru	*Lesotho*	96	D5
Mashabih	*Saudi Arabia*	91	G2
Mashhad	*Iran*	83	G2
Maskovo	*Bulgaria*	77	N8
Mason City	*United States*	43	N8
Masqat (Muscat)	*Oman*	85	H5
Masringo	*Zimbabwe*	96	E4
Massa	*Italy*	72	F7
Massachusetts	*United States*	37	M3
Massena	*United States*	37	M2
Massenya	*Chad*	90	C5
Massif Central	*France*	69	H8
Massif dAbo	*Chad*	90	C3
Massif dAfafi	*Chad*	90	C3
Massif de lIsalo	*Madagascar*	97	G3
Massif de lItremo	*Madagascar*	97	H4
Massif de lOuarsenis	*Algeria*	71	M9
Massif de Termit	*Niger*	89	H5
Massif des Bongos	*Central African Republic*	94	C2
Massif du Chaillu	*Gabon*	93	G5
Massif du Kapka	*Chad*	90	D5
Massif du Pelvoux	*France*	72	B5
Massif du Tamgué	*Guinea*	92	B2
Massif du Yadé	*Central African Republic*	93	G3
Matadi	*Democratic Republic Of Congo*	94	A5
Matagami	*Canada*	37	L2
Matagorda	*United States*	33	G6
Matamoros	*Mexico*	46	E3
Mataram	*Indonesia*	112	F4
Mataró	*Spain*	71	N3
Matehula	*Mexico*	32	E7
Mateni	*Sierra Leone*	92	B3
Mathura	*India*	104	C3
Mato Grosso	*Brazil*	51	F6
Matra	*Hungary*	63	J10
Matsue	*Japan*	110	G6
Matsumoto	*Japan*	111	K5

Matsuyama	*Japan*	110	G7
Matterhorn	*Italy / Switzerland*	72	C5
Mattoon	*United States*	36	J4
Maturin	*Venezuela*	50	E2
Maubeuge	*France*	57	G4
Maui	*Hawaii (U.S.)*	29	(2)E3
Maun	*Botswana*	96	C3
Mauna Kea	*Hawaii (U.S.)*	29	(2)F4
Mauna Loa	*Hawaii (U.S.)*	29	(2)F4
Mauritania	*West Africa*	88	C5
Mauritius	*Indian Ocean*	97	(1)B2
Mayaguana	*Caribbean*	47	K4
Mayenne	*France*	68	E6
Mayfield	*United States*	34	J4
Maykop	*Russia*	60	J6
Maykop	*Russia*	81	J1
Mayotte (France)	*Indian Ocean*	97	H2
Mazar-e-Sharf	*Afghanistan*	83	J2
Mazatlán	*Mexico*	46	C4
Mazeikiai	*Lithuania*	62	M1
Mbabane	*Mozambique*	97	E5
Mbaiki	*Central African Republic*	93	H4
Mbandaka	*Democratic Republic Of Congo*	94	B4
Mbanza Congo	*Angola*	93	G6
Mbeya	*Tanzania*	95	E5
Mbomou	*Central Africa*	94	D2
Mbuji-Mayi	*Democratic Republic Of Congo*	94	C5
McAlester	*United States*	34	G5
McCamey	*United States*	33	F5
McClintock Channel	*Canada*	42	L2
McClure Strait	*Canada*	42	H2
McComb	*United States*	34	H5
McCook	*United States*	31	F3
Mcherrah	*Algeria*	88	E3
McLean's Town	*Bahamas*	35	L6
McMinnville	*United States*	35	J4
McPherson	*United States*	31	G4
Mdennah	*Mali / Algeria*	88	E4
Meadow	*United States*	31	F2
Meaux	*France*	56	F6
Mecca (Makkah)	*Saudi Arabia*	82	D5
Mechelen	*Belgium*	57	H3
Mecklenburger Bucht	*Germany*	64	G2
Mecsek	*Hungary*	63	H11
Médéa	*Algeria*	71	N8
Medan	*Indonesia*	112	B2
Medellín	*Colombia*	50	B2
Medford	*United States*	28	B2
Medgidia	*Romania*	77	R5
Medias	*Romania*	77	M3
Medina (Al Madnah)	*Saudi Arabia*	82	C5
Medina del Campo	*Spain*	70	F3
Medina Gounas	*Senegal*	88	C6
Mediterranean Sea	*Europe*	69	K11
Medora	*United States*	31	F2
Medvednica	*Croatia*	76	C4
Medvezhyegorsk	*Russia*	60	G2
Meerut	*India*	104	C3
Megísti	*Greece*	79	M8
Mehran	*Iran*	85	F3
Meiningen	*Germany*	65	F6
Meißen	*Germany*	65	J5
Meknès	*Morocco*	88	D2
Mekong	*South East Asia*	106	D4
Melanesia	*Oceania*	114	F5
Melbourne	*Australia*	117	H7
Melbourne	*United States*	35	K6
Melilla	*Spain*	70	H9
Mellum	*Germany*	64	D3
Melun	*France*	68	H5
Melville Bay	*Australia*	117	G2
Melville Hills	*Canada*	40	G3
Melville Island	*Australia*	116	F2
Melville Island	*Canada*	42	J2
Memmert	*Germany*	64	B3
Memphis	*United States*	34	J4
Mende	*France*	69	J9
Mendebo	*Ethiopia*	95	F2
Mendocino	*United States*	29	B3
Mendoza	*Argentina*	52	H5
Menorca	*Spain*	71	Q5
Mentawai Is.	*Indonesia*	112	B3
Menton	*France*	72	B7
Meppen	*Germany*	64	C4
Merano/Meran	*Italy*	72	G4
Mercury Islands	*New Zealand*	118	E3
Mergui Archipelago	*Myanmar (Burma)*	106	B4
Merida	*Venezuela*	50	C2
Mérida	*Mexico*	46	G4
Mérida	*Spain*	70	D6
Meridian	*United States*	34	J5
Merlitopol	*Ukraine*	60	H5
Merrick	*United Kingdom*	67	J6
Mersa Fatma	*Eritrea*	91	H5
Merseburg	*Germany*	65	G5
Mersin	*Turkey*	80	F5
Mértola	*Portugal*	70	C7
Merzedes	*Uruguay*	53	K5
Mesa de Yambi	*Colombia*	50	C3
Mesa Verde National Park	*United States*	32	E4
Meschede	*Germany*	64	D5
Messina	*Sicily (Italy)*	75	K10
Messiniakós Kólpos	*Greece*	78	E8
Mesuji	*Indonesia*	112	D3
Meta	*South America*	50	D2
Metauro	*Italy*	73	H7
Metz	*France*	68	M4
Meuse	*France / Belgium*	68	L3
Meuzenti	*Chad*	89	J5
Mexicali	*Mexico*	46	A2
Mexican Hat	*United States*	32	E4
Mexico	*Central America*	46	C4
Mexico	*United States*	36	H4
Mexico City (Ciudad de Mexico)	*Mexico*	46	D5
Mezen	*Russia*	60	J1
Mezenskaya Guba	*Russia*	60	J1
Mi-Shima	*Japan*	110	F6
Miami (FL)	*United States*	35	K6
Miami (OK)	*United States*	34	H4
Miass	*Russia*	61	M3
Michalovce	*Slovakia*	63	L9
Michigan	*United States*	36	J3
Michipicoten	*Canada*	43	P7
Micronesia	*Oceania*	114	F4
Mid-Alantic Ridge	*Atlantic Ocean*	48	G2
Middelburg	*Netherlands*	56	G3
Middle Andaman Islands	*India*	105	F6
Middlesbrough	*United Kingdom*	67	M7
Midland	*Canada*	37	L3
Midland	*United States*	33	F5
Midyan	*Saudi Arabia*	91	G2
Mielec	*Poland*	63	L7
Mieres	*Spain*	70	E2
Mihaylovgrad	*Bulgaria*	77	L6
Mijares	*Spain*	71	K4
Mikkeli	*Finland*	58	P6
Mikonos	*Greece*	78	H7
Mikun	*Russia*	61	L2
Mikuni-Sammyaku	*Japan*	111	K5
Mikura-Jima	*Japan*	111	K7
Miladunmadulu Atoll	*Maldives*	105	B7
Milan (Milano)	*Italy*	74	D3
Milano (Milan)	*Italy*	74	D3
Mileh Tharthar	*Iraq*	82	D3
Miles City	*United States*	30	E2
Milford Sound	*New Zealand*	119	B7
Mill Island	*Canada*	42	R4
Millau	*France*	69	J9
Mille Lac Lakes	*United States*	31	H2
Millerova	*Russia*	60	J5
Milos	*Greece*	78	G8
Milwaukee	*United States*	36	J3
Min Jiang	*China*	108	F5
Min Shan	*China*	108	C4
Minami-Tori-Shima (Marcus)	*Japan*	114	F3
Mindanao	*Philippines*	107	H5
Minden	*Germany*	64	D4
Mindoro	*Philippines*	107	G4
Mindoro Strait	*Philippines*	107	G4
Mineral Wells	*United States*	34	G5
Mingechaurskoye Vdkhr.	*Azerbaijan*	81	M3
Minicoy	*Laccadive Islands (India)*	105	B7
Minna	*Nigeria*	93	F3
Minneapolis	*United States*	36	H2
Minnesota	*United States*	31	G2
Minnesota River	*United States*	31	G2, H3
Miño	*Spain / Portugal*	70	C2
Minot	*United States*	31	F2
Minsk	*Belarus*	60	F4
Miranda de Ebro	*Spain*	70	H2
Mirtóon Pélagos	*Greece*	78	F7
Mirzapur	*India*	104	D3
Miskolc	*Hungary*	76	H1
Misratah	*Libya*	90	C1
Missinipe	*Canada*	43	L5
Mississippi	*United States*	34	H5
Mississippi Delta	*United States*	34	H6
Missoula	*United States*	30	D2
Missouri	*United States*	34	H4
Missouri River	*United States*	31	F2 - H4
Mitchell	*United States*	31	G3
Mitchell River	*Australia*	117	H3
Mito	*Japan*	111	L5
Mittellandkanal	*Germany*	64	F4
Miyake-Jima	*Japan*	111	K6
Miyakonojo	*Japan*	110	F8
Miyazaki	*Japan*	110	F8
Mjsa	*Norway*	59	F6
Mladá Boleslav	*Czech Republic*	63	D7
Mljet	*Croatia*	76	E7
Mn	*Denmark*	59	G9
Mns Klint	*Denmark*	64	H2
Mo i Rana	*Norway*	58	H3
Moa	*West Africa*	92	B3
Moa (Banks Island)	*Australia*	117	H2
Moab	*United States*	30	E4
Mobile	*United States*	34	J5
Moctezuma	*Mexico*	32	D6
Modane	*France*	72	B5
Modena	*Italy*	74	E4
Moers	*Germany*	64	B5
Mogadouro	*Portugal*	70	D4
Mohawk	*United States*	37	M3
Mohéli	*Comoros*	95	G6
Möhne	*Germany*	57	M3
Mojave Desert	*United States*	29	C4
Mokp'o	*South Korea*	110	C6
Molat	*Croatia*	76	B5
Molatón	*Spain*	71	J5
Moldau (Vltava)	*Czech Republic*	63	D8
Molde	*Norway*	58	D5
Moldova	*Europe*	60	F5
Molfetta	*Italy*	76	D8
Moline	*United States*	36	H3
Mölln	*Germany*	64	F3
Molokai	*Hawaii (U.S.)*	29	(2)E2
Molopo	*South Africa*	96	C5
Molucca Sea	*Indonesia*	113	C3
Moma	*Russia*	103	Q3
Mombasa	*Kenya*	95	F4
Momskiy Khrebet	*Russia*	103	Q3
Monaco	*Europe*	69	N10
Monadhliath Mountains	*United Kingdom*	66	J4
Moncayo	*Spain*	71	J3
Mönh Hayrhan Uul	*Mongolia*	101	S8
Monchegorsk	*Russia*	60	G1
Mönchengladbach	*Germany*	65	B5
Monclova	*Mexico*	46	D3
Moncton	*Canada*	45	U7
Mondego	*Portugal*	70	C4
Monfalcone	*Italy*	73	J5
Monforte	*Spain*	70	C2
Mongo	*Chad*	90	C5
Mongol Altain Nuruu	*Mongolia*	108	A1
Mongolia	*Asia*	102	H7
Mongu	*Zambia*	96	C3
Mono Lake	*United States*	29	C4
Monopoli	*Italy*	76	E9
Monroe	*United States*	34	H5
Monrovia	*Liberia*	92	B3
Mons	*Belgium*	57	G4
Mont Blanc	*France / Italy*	72	B5
Mont Cameroun	*Cameroon*	93	F4
Mont du Guéra	*Chad*	93	H2
Mont Forel	*Greenland*	120	(1)U3
Mont Tremblant	*Canada*	37	M2
Mont-de-Marsan	*France*	69	E10
Montana	*United States*	30	D2
Montauban	*France*	69	G9
Montbéliard	*France*	72	B3
Monte Bello Islands	*Australia*	116	B4
Monte Carlo	*Monaco*	74	B5
Monte Cinto	*Corsica (France)*	74	C6
Monte del Papa	*Italy*	75	K8
Monte Ferru	*Sardinia (Italy)*	75	C8
Monte Perdido	*Spain*	71	L2
Monte Rosa	*Italy / Switzerland*	72	C5
Monte Rotondo	*Corsica (France)*	74	D6
Monte Viso	*France / Italy*	72	C6
Montecristo	*Italy*	74	E6
Monterey	*United States*	29	B3
Monterey Bay	*United States*	29	B3
Monteria	*Colombia*	50	B2
Monterrey	*Mexico*	46	E3
Montes Claros	*Brazil*	51	J7
Montes de León	*Spain*	70	D2
Montes de Toledo	*Spain*	70	F5
Montes Universales	*Spain*	71	J4
Montevideo	*Uruguay*	53	K5
Montgomery (AL)	*United States*	35	J5
Montgomery (GA)	*United States*	35	K5
Montgomery Center	*United States*	37	M3
Montluçon	*France*	69	H7
Montmagny	*Canada*	37	M2
Montpelier	*United States*	37	M3
Montpellier	*France*	69	J10
Montréal	*Canada*	37	M2
Monts Bagzane	*Niger*	89	G5
Monts Bambouto	*Cameroon*	93	F3
Monts d'Arrée	*France*	68	B5
Monts de la Margeride	*France*	69	J8
Monts de la Medjerda	*Tunisia / Algeria*	75	C12
Monts de Tabursuq	*Tunisia / Algeria*	75	C12
Monts des Ksour	*Algeria / Morocco*	89	E2
Monts du Forez	*France*	69	J8
Monts du Velay	*France*	69	J8
Monts Kundelungu	*Democratic Republic Of Congo*	94	D6
Monts Malimba	*Democratic Republic Of Congo*	94	D5
Monts Mandara	*Nigeria*	94	A1
Monts Mandara	*Cameroon*	90	B5
Monts Mandingues	*Mali*	88	C6
Monts Marungu	*Democratic Republic Of Congo / Zambia*	94	D5
Monts Mitumba	*Democratic Republic Of Congo*	94	D5
Monts Mugila	*Democratic Republic Of Congo*	94	D5
Monts Nimba	*Guinea*	92	C3
Monts Notre-Dame	*Canada*	45	T7
Montserrat	*Caribbean*	47	M5
Monza	*Italy*	74	D3
Monzón	*Spain*	71	L2
Moorhead	*United States*	31	G2
Moose Jaw	*Canada*	43	K6
Moosehead Lake	*United States*	37	N2
Moosonee	*Canada*	43	Q6
Mopti	*Mali*	92	D2
Mora	*Sweden*	59	H6
Mora	*Spain*	70	G5
Mora	*Portugal*	70	B6
Morane	*French Polynesia*	115	N8
Moratuwa	*Sri Lanka*	105	C7
Moray Firth	*United Kingdom*	66	K4
More Laptevykh (Laptev Sea)	*Russia*	102	L2
Morecambe Bay	*United Kingdom*	67	K8
Morehead	*Papua New Guinea*	113	F4
Morella	*Spain*	71	K4
Moresby Island	*Canada*	29	(1)L5
Moreton Bay	*Australia*	117	K5
Moreton Island	*Australia*	117	K5
Morgan City	*United States*	34	H6
Morgantown	*United States*	37	L4
Morhange	*France*	57	K6
Morioka	*Japan*	111	L4
Morlaix	*France*	68	B5
Mornington Island	*Australia*	117	G3
Morocco	*North Africa*	88	D2
Morogoro	*Tanzania*	95	F5
Mörön	*Mongolia*	102	G7
Morón de la Frontera	*Spain*	70	E7
Moroni	*Comoros*	95	G6
Morozovst	*Russia*	60	J5
Morriston	*United States*	35	K4
Morvan	*France*	68	K6
Moscow	*United States*	28	C1
Moselle	*France*	57	K6
Moskenesya	*Norway*	58	G3
Moskow (Moskva)	*Russia*	60	H3
Moskva (Moskow)	*Russia*	60	H3
Moss	*Norway*	59	F7
Mossoró	*Brazil*	51	K5
Most	*Czech Republic*	65	J6
Mostaganem	*Algeria*	89	F1
Mosty	*Belarus*	63	P4
Mosul (Al Mawsil)	*Iraq*	82	D2
Motala	*Sweden*	59	H7
Motril	*Spain*	70	G8

SATELLITE ATLAS OF THE WORLD

Motu One	*French Polynesia*	**115**	**L7**
Mouhoun (Black Volta)	*West Africa*	**92**	**E3**
Moulins	*France*	**69**	**J7**
Moulmein	*Myanmar (Burma)*	**106**	**B3**
Moundou	*Chad*	**94**	**B2**
Mount Afo	*Philippines*	**113**	**C1**
Mount Apo	*Philippines*	**107**	**H5**
Mount Ararat (Büyük Agr Daç)	*Turkey*	**81**	**L4**
Mount Aspiring	*New Zealand*	**119**	**C7**
Mount Augustus	*Australia*	**116**	**C4**
Mount Blackburn	*United States*	**40**	**C4**
Mount Columbia	*Canada*	**41**	**H6**
Mount Cook	*New Zealand*	**119**	**D6**
Mount Desert Island	*United States*	**37**	**N3**
Mount Egmont	*New Zealand*	**118**	**E4**
Mount Elbert	*United States*	**30**	**E4**
Mount Essendon	*Australia*	**116**	**D4**
Mount Everest	*Nepal / China*	**104**	**E3**
Mount Graham	*United States*	**32**	**E5**
Mount Halcon	*Philippines*	**107**	**G4**
Mount Hayes	*United States*	**40**	**B4**
Mount Hermon	*Lebanon*	**84**	**C3**
Mount Hood	*United States*	**28**	**B1**
Mount Huxley	*New Zealand*	**119**	**C7**
Mount Islo	*United States*	**120**	**(1)FF3**
Mount Jackson	*Antarctica*	**120**	**(2)LL2**
Mount Kenya / Kirinyaga	*Kenya*	**95**	**F4**
Mount Kiangarow	*Australia*	**117**	**K5**
Mount Kirkpatrick	*Antarctica*	**120**	**(2)X1**
Mount Kosciusko	*Australia*	**117**	**J7**
Mount Liebig	*Australia*	**116**	**F4**
Mount Logan	*United States*	**29**	**(1)J3**
Mount McKinley	*Alaska (U.S.)*	**29**	**(1)G3**
Mount Meharry	*Australia*	**116**	**C4**
Mount Menzies	*Antarctica*	**120**	**(2)M2**
Mount Minto	*Antarctica*	**120**	**(2)X2**
Mount Murchison	*New Zealand*	**119**	**D6**
Mount Ossa	*Australia*	**117**	**J8**
Mount Owen	*New Zealand*	**119**	**E5**
Mount Pinatubo	*Philippines*	**107**	**G3**
Mount Pulog	*Philippines*	**107**	**G3**
Mount Rainier	*United States*	**28**	**B1**
Mount Richmond	*New Zealand*	**119**	**E5**
Mount Roberts	*Australia*	**117**	**K5**
Mount Robson	*Canada*	**41**	**H6**
Mount Rushmore	*United States*	**31**	**F3**
Mount Shasta	*United States*	**29**	**B2**
Mount Sneffels	*United States*	**32**	**E4**
Mount St. Helens	*United States*	**28**	**B1**
Mount Stanley	*Uganda*	**94**	**E3**
Mount Suckling	*Papua New Guinea*	**117**	**J1**
Mount Travers	*New Zealand*	**119**	**E6**
Mount Troodos (Olympus)	*Cyprus*	**79**	**Q10**
Mount Vernon	*United States*	**36**	**J4**
Mount Victoria	*Myanmar (Burma)*	**106**	**A2**
Mount Waddington	*Canada*	**41**	**F6**
Mount Whitney	*United States*	**29**	**C3**
Mount Woodroffe	*Australia*	**116**	**F5**
Mount Ziel	*Australia*	**116**	**F4**
Mountain Home	*United States*	**30**	**C3**
Mountains of Connemara	*Ireland*	**67**	**D8**
Mounts Bay	*United Kingdom*	**67**	**H12**
Mourne Mountains	*United Kingdom*	**67**	**G7**
Mouth of the Shannon	*Ireland*	**67**	**C9**
Mouths of the Niger	*Atlantic Ocean*	**93**	**F4**
Mouydir	*Algeria*	**89**	**F4**
Moyale	*Ethiopia / Kenya*	**95**	**F3**
Mozambique	*Southern Africa*	**97**	**E3**
Mozambique Channel	*Mozambique*	**87**	**G8**
Mrtú	*Colombia*	**50**	**C3**
Mt. Pleasant	*United States*	**36**	**K3**
Mt. Ward	*New Zealand*	**119**	**C6**
Mtwara	*Tanzania*	**97**	**G2**
Muchinga Mountains	*Zambia*	**94**	**E6**
Mudan Jiang	*China*	**109**	**H2**
Mudanjiang	*China*	**109**	**H2**
Mudurnu	*Turkey*	**79**	**N4**
Mufulira	*Zambia*	**94**	**D6**
Mugodzhary	*Kazakhstan*	**101**	**K8**
Muhu	*Estonia*	**59**	**M7**
Mukachevo	*Ukraine*	**77**	**K1**
Mukawwar	*Sudan*	**91**	**G3**
Mulaku Atoll	*Maldives*	**105**	**B8**
Mulanje Mountains	*South Africa*	**97**	**F3**
Mulde	*Germany*	**64**	**H5**
Mulegé	*Mexico*	**32**	**D6**
Mulgrave Island	*Australia*	**117**	**H2**
Mulhacén	*Spain*	**70**	**G7**
Mülheim	*Germany*	**65**	**C5**
Mulhouse	*France*	**68**	**M6**
Mull	*United Kingdom*	**66**	**G5**
Multan	*Pakistan*	**83**	**K3**
Mumbai (Bombay)	*India*	**105**	**B5**
Muna	*Russia*	**102**	**L3**
München (Munich)	*Germany*	**65**	**G8**
Münden	*Germany*	**65**	**E5**
Munifah	*Saudi Arabia*	**85**	**C3**
Münster	*Germany*	**64**	**C5**
Muntii Apuseni	*Romania*	**77**	**K3**
Muntii Harghita	*Romania*	**77**	**P3**
Munzur Silselesi	*Turkey*	**81**	**H4**
Muonio	*Finland*	**58**	**M3**
Muonio älv	*Sweden*	**58**	**M2**
Muoniojoki	*Finland*	**58**	**M2**
Muqayshit	*United Arab Emirates*	**85**	**E4**
Muqdisho (Mogadishu)	*Somalia*	**95**	**H3**
Mur	*Austria / Slovakia*	**73**	**L4**
Mura	*Austria / Slovakia*	**73**	**M4**
Murashi	*Russia*	**61**	**K3**
Murat	*Turkey*	**81**	**J4**
Murat Dag	*Turkey*	**79**	**M6**
Murcia	*Spain*	**71**	**K6**
Mures	*Romania*	**63**	**L11**
Murgab	*Turkmenistan / Afghanistan*	**83**	**H2**
Müritz	*Germany*	**64**	**H3**
Murmansk	*Russia*	**100**	**E4**
Muroran	*Japan*	**111**	**L2**

Muros	*Spain*	**70**	**B2**
Muroto-Zaki	*Japan*	**110**	**H7**
Murray River	*Australia*	**117**	**G6**
Mururoa	*French Polynesia*	**115**	**M8**
Mus-Haja	*Russia*	**103**	**Q4**
Musala	*Bulgaria*	**77**	**L7**
Muscatine	*United States*	**36**	**H3**
Musgrave Ranges	*Australia*	**116**	**F5**
Muskegon	*United States*	**36**	**J3**
Muskogee	*United States*	**34**	**G4**
Musoma	*Tanzania*	**95**	**E4**
Musu-Dan	*North Korea*	**110**	**E3**
Mutsu-Wan	*Japan*	**111**	**L3**
Muyezerskiy	*Russia*	**58**	**S5**
Muzaffarnagar	*India*	**104**	**C3**
Muzaffarpur	*India*	**104**	**E3**
Muztag	*China*	**104**	**E1**
Muztagata	*China*	**101**	**P10**
Mwali (Mohéli)	*Comoros*	**97**	**G2**
Mwanza	*Tanzania*	**95**	**E4**
Mweelrea	*Ireland*	**67**	**D8**
Mwene-Ditu	*Democratic Republic Of Congo*	**94**	**C5**
My Tho	*Vietnam*	**106**	**D4**
Myanmar (Burma)	*Southern Asia*	**104**	**F4**
Mymensingh	*Bangladesh*	**104**	**F4**
Myrdalsjökull	*Iceland*	**58**	**(1)D3**
Myrtle Beach	*United States*	**35**	**L5**
Mys Aniva	*Russia*	**103**	**Q7**
Mys Chaplino	*Russia*	**103**	**Z4**
Mys Chelyuskin	*Russia*	**100**	**V2**
Mys Govena	*Russia*	**103**	**V5**
Mys Kanin Nos	*Russia*	**100**	**G4**
Mys Lopatka	*Russia*	**103**	**T6**
Mys Meganom	*Ukraine*	**60**	**H6**
Mys Navarin	*Russia*	**103**	**X4**
Mys Olyutorskiy	*Russia*	**103**	**W5**
Mys Sarych	*Ukraine*	**80**	**E1**
Mys Shelogskiy	*Russia*	**103**	**V2**
Mys Svatoy Nos	*Russia*	**103**	**P2**
Mys Svyatoy Nos	*Russia*	**60**	**J1**
Mys Tarkhankut	*Ukraine*	**60**	**G5**
Mys Taygonos	*Russia*	**103**	**T4**
Mys Terpeniya	*Russia*	**103**	**Q7**
Mys Tolstoy	*Russia*	**103**	**T5**
Mys Yelizavety	*Russia*	**103**	**Q6**
Mysore	*India*	**105**	**C6**
Myvatn	*Iceland*	**58**	**(1)E2**
Mzuzu	*Malawi*	**95**	**E6**
Mzuzu	*Zambia*	**97**	**E2**

N

N.W.Christmas Island Ridge	*Oceania*	**115**	**K4**
N´ Djamena	*Chad*	**93**	**H2**
Naberezhnyye Chelny	*Russia*	**61**	**L3**
Nabeul	*Tunisia*	**75**	**E12**
Nabire	*Indonesia*	**113**	**E3**
Nabulus	*Israel*	**84**	**C4**
Nacala	*Mozambique*	**97**	**G2**
Nacogdoches	*United States*	**33**	**H5**
Nadiad	*India*	**104**	**B4**
Nadym	*Russia*	**61**	**Q1**
Nagano	*Japan*	**111**	**K5**
Nagaoka	*Japan*	**111**	**K5**
Nagasaki	*Japan*	**110**	**E7**
Nagercoil	*India*	**105**	**C7**
Nagoya	*Japan*	**111**	**J6**
Nagpur	*India*	**104**	**C4**
Nagykanizsa	*Hungary*	**76**	**E3**
Nagykörös	*Hungary*	**63**	**J10**
Naha	*Japan*	**109**	**H5**
Nahr Al´ Asi	*Turkey / Syria / Lebanon*	**80**	**G6**
Nahr an Nil (Nile)	*Africa*	**91**	**F2**
Nairobi	*Kenya*	**95**	**F4**
Najd	*Saudi Arabia*	**82**	**D4**
Nakambé (White Volta)	*West Africa*	**92**	**D2**
Nakano-Shima	*Japan*	**110**	**G6**
Nakhodka	*Russia*	**102**	**N8**
Nakuru	*Kenya*	**95**	**F4**
Nalchik	*Russia*	**81**	**K2**
Nam Co	*China*	**104**	**F2**
Namakzar-e Shahdad	*Iran*	**85**	**H1**
Namangan	*Uzbekistan*	**101**	**N9**
Namib Desert	*Namibia*	**96**	**A3**
Namibe	*Angola*	**96**	**A3**
Namibia	*Southern Africa*	**96**	**B4**
Namous	*Algeria*	**89**	**E2**
Nampula	*Mozambique*	**97**	**F3**
Namsos	*Norway*	**58**	**F4**
Namur	*Belgium*	**68**	**K3**
Nan Hai (South China Sea)	*China*	**108**	**F6**
Nan Ling	*China*	**108**	**E5**
Nanaimo	*Canada*	**41**	**G7**
Nanatsu-Jima	*Japan*	**111**	**J5**
Nanchang	*China*	**108**	**F5**
Nancowry	*India*	**105**	**F7**
Nancy	*France*	**68**	**M5**
Nanded	*India*	**105**	**C5**
Nanga Parbat	*Pakistan*	**104**	**B1**
Nangnim-Sanmaek	*North Korea*	**110**	**D3**
Nanjing	*China*	**109**	**F4**
Nanning	*China*	**108**	**D6**
Nanpan Jiang	*China*	**106**	**C2**
Nantes	*France*	**68**	**D6**
Nantucket Island	*United States*	**37**	**M3, N3**
Nanumea	*Tuvalu*	**114**	**H6**
Nanuque	*Brazil*	**51**	**J7**
Nanyang	*China*	**108**	**E4**
Napier	*New Zealand*	**118**	**F4**
Naples (FL)	*United States*	**35**	**K6**
Naples (Napoli)	*Italy*	**75**	**J8**
Naples (UT)	*United States*	**30**	**E3**
Napoli (Naples)	*Italy*	**75**	**J8**
Narbonne	*France*	**69**	**J10**
Nardo	*Italy*	**75**	**N8**

Nares Strait	*United States*	**120**	**(1)Y1**
Narew	*Poland*	**62**	**L4**
Narmada	*India*	**104**	**B4**
Narsarsuaq	*Greenland*	**44**	**X4**
Narva	*Estonia*	**59**	**M8**
Narvik	*Norway*	**58**	**J2**
Naryan-Mar	*Russia*	**61**	**L1**
Naryn	*Kyrgyzstan*	**101**	**P9**
Nashville	*United States*	**35**	**J4**
Nasik	*India*	**104**	**B4**
Naskov	*Denmark*	**64**	**G2**
Nassau	*Cook Islands*	**115**	**K7**
Nassau	*Bahamas*	**35**	**L5**
Nassau	*Bahamas*	**35**	**L6**
Natal	*Brazil*	**51**	**K5**
Natchez	*United States*	**34**	**H5**
Natchitoches	*United States*	**34**	**H5**
Natitingou	*Benin*	**93**	**E2**
Nauru	*Nauru*	**114**	**G5**
Nauru	*Oceania*	**114**	**G6**
Navajo Lake	*United States*	**32**	**E4**
Navoi	*Uzbekistan*	**101**	**M9**
Navojoa	*Mexico*	**32**	**D6**
Nazca	*Peru*	**50**	**C6**
Nazca Ridge	*Pacific Ocean*	**49**	**C6**
Nazilli	*Turkey*	**79**	**L7**
Náxos	*Greece*	**78**	**H7**
Ndola	*Zambia*	**94**	**D6**
ndros	*Greece*	**78**	**G7**
Nebit Dag	*Turkmenistan*	**83**	**F2**
Neblina	*Venezuela / Brazil*	**50**	**D3**
Nebraska	*United States*	**31**	**F3**
Nebrodi	*Sicily (Italy)*	**75**	**J11**
Neckar	*Germany*	**65**	**E7**
Neder-Rijn	*Netherlands*	**57**	**J3**
Neftekamsk	*Russia*	**61**	**L3**
Negev	*Israel*	**84**	**B6**
Negro	*South America*	**53**	**K5**
Negros	*Philippines*	**107**	**G5**
Neiße	*Poland / Germany*	**63**	**D7**
Neiva	*Colombia*	**50**	**B3**
Nellore	*India*	**105**	**D6**
Nelson	*New Zealand*	**119**	**E5**
Nelson River	*Canada*	**38**	**N5**
Neman	*Lithuania / Belarus*	**59**	**N10**
Nëmërckë	*Albania*	**78**	**C4**
Nemunas	*Russia / Lithuania / Belarus*	**59**	**M9**
Nen Jiang	*China*	**109**	**G1**
Nene	*United Kingdom*	**67**	**P9**
Nepal	*Southern Asia*	**104**	**D3**
Nequén	*Argentina*	**52**	**H6**
Neretva	*Bosnia-Herzegovina*	**74**	**M5**
Nerva	*Spain*	**70**	**D7**
Neskaupstadur	*Iceland*	**58**	**G2**
Netanya	*Israel*	**84**	**B4**
Netherlands	*Europe*	**57**	**H2**
Netherlands Antilles	*Caribbean*	**47**	**L6**
Nettiling Lake	*Canada*	**44**	**T3**
Nettuno	*Italy*	**75**	**G7**
Neu-Ulm	*Germany*	**65**	**F8**
Neubrandenburg	*Germany*	**64**	**J3**
Neuchâtel	*Switzerland*	**68**	**M6**
Neufchâteu	*France*	**72**	**A2**
Neumünster	*Germany*	**64**	**E2**
Neusiedler See	*Austria*	**73**	**M2**
Neuss	*Germany*	**65**	**B5**
Neustrelitz	*Germany*	**64**	**J3**
Neuwerk	*Germany*	**64**	**D3**
Neuwied	*Germany*	**65**	**C6**
Nevada	*United States*	**29**	**C3**
Nevado de Ampato	*Peru*	**50**	**C7**
Nevado de Illampu	*Bolivia*	**50**	**D7**
Nevado de Sajama	*Bolivia*	**50**	**D7**
Nevado Palomani	*Bolivia / Peru*	**50**	**D6**
Nevers	*France*	**69**	**J7**
New Albany	*United States*	**36**	**J4**
New Bern	*United States*	**35**	**L4**
New Britain	*Papua New Guinea*	**114**	**E6**
New Brunswick	*Canada*	**39**	**T7**
New Brunswick	*United States*	**37**	**M3**
New Caledonia	*France*	**114**	**G7**
New Delhi	*India*	**104**	**C3**
New Elm	*United States*	**31**	**H3**
New Georgia	*Solomon Islands*	**114**	**F6**
New Glasgow	*Canada*	**45**	**U7**
New Guinea	*South East Asia*	**113**	**E4**
New Hampshire	*United States*	**37**	**M3**
New Hanover	*Papua New Guinea*	**114**	**F6**
New Haven	*United States*	**37**	**M3**
New Iberia	*United States*	**34**	**H5**
New Ireland	*Papua New Guinea*	**114**	**F6**
New Jersey	*United States*	**37**	**M4**
New London	*United States*	**37**	**M3**
New Mexico	*United States*	**32**	**E5**
New Orleans	*United States*	**34**	**H6**
New Plymouth	*New Zealand*	**118**	**E4**
New Siberian Islands	*Russia*	**103**	**P1**
New South Wales	*Australia*	**117**	**H6**
New York	*United States*	**37**	**L3**
New York	*United States*	**37**	**M3**
New Zealand	*New Zealand*	**118**	**B4**
Newark	*United States*	**37**	**M3**
Newburyport	*United States*	**37**	**M3**
Newcastle	*Australia*	**117**	**K6**
Newcastle Creek	*Australia*	**116**	**F3**
Newcastle upon Tyne	*United Kingdom*	**67**	**M6**
Newfoundland	*Canada*	**39**	**V7**
Newfoundland and Labrador	*Canada*	**39**	**U5**
Newport	*United Kingdom*	**67**	**L10**
Newport	*United States*	**37**	**N3**
Newton (IO)	*United States*	**31**	**H3**
Newton (KS)	*United States*	**34**	**G4**
Neyriz	*Iran*	**85**	**F2**
Ngangla Ringco	*China*	**104**	**D2**
Nganglong Kangri	*China*	**104**	**D2**
Ngangze Co	*China*	**104**	**E2**
Ngaoundéré	*Cameroon*	**93**	**G3**

Ostend (Oostende)	*Belgium*	56	F3
Östersund	*Sweden*	58	H5
Ostfriesische-Inseln	*Germany*	64	B3
Ostrava	*Czech Republic*	63	H8
Ostreleka	*Poland*	59	L10
Ostróda	*Poland*	62	J4
Ostroleka	*Poland*	62	L4
Ostrov Anzhu	*Russia*	103	P1
Ostrov Arkticheskogo Instituta	*Russia*	100	P2
Ostrov Ayon	*Russia*	103	V3
Ostrov Belyy	*Russia*	100	M3
Ostrov Beringa	*Russia*	103	V6
Ostrov Bollyakhovsky	*Russia*	103	Q2
Ostrov Bolshoy Begichev	*Russia*	100	W3
Ostrov Chechen	*Russia*	81	M2
Ostrov Faddeyevskiy	*Russia*	103	Q1
Ostrov Iturup / Etorofu-To	*Russia*	103	R8
Ostrov Karaginskiy	*Russia*	103	U5
Ostrov Kolguyev	*Russia*	100	H4
Ostrov Kotelnyy	*Russia*	103	P1
Ostrov Kunashir / Kunashiri-To	*Russia*	103	Q8
Ostrov Maly Lyakhovskiy	*Russia*	103	Q2
Ostrov Mednyy	*Russia*	103	V6
Ostrov Novaya Sibir	*Russia*	103	R1
Ostrov Oleniy	*Russia*	100	P3
Ostrov Onekotan	*Russia*	103	S6
Ostrov Paramushir	*Russia*	103	S6
Ostrov Peschanyy	*Russia*	102	K2
Ostrov Shumshu	*Russia*	103	T6
Ostrov Sibiryakova	*Russia*	100	P3
Ostrov Stolbovoy	*Russia*	102	N2
Ostrov Urup	*Russia*	103	R7
Ostrov Vaygach	*Russia*	100	K3
Ostrov Vrangelya (Wrangel)	*Russia*	103	Y2
Ostrova Izvestiy	*Russia*	100	P2
Ostrova Medvezhi	*Russia*	103	U2
Ostrova Sakhalin	*Russia*	103	Q6
Ostrova Shantarskiye	*Russia*	103	P6
Ostrów Wielkopolski	*Poland*	62	G6
Osumi-Shoto	*Japan*	110	E8
Otaru	*Japan*	111	L2
Otnes	*Norway*	59	F6
Otok	*Croatia*	76	B6
Otsu	*Japan*	111	J6
Otta	*Norway*	59	E6
Ottawa	*Canada*	45	R7
Ottawa (IL)	*United States*	36	J3
Ottawa (KS)	*United States*	31	G4
Otwock	*Poland*	62	L5
Ötztaler Alpen	*Austria*	72	F4
Ou-Sammyaku	*Japan*	111	L4
Ouachita Mountains	*United States*	34	H5
Ouaddai	*Chad*	90	C5
Ouagadougou	*Burkina Faso*	92	D2
Ouargla	*Algeria*	89	G2
Ouarzazate	*Morocco*	88	D2
Oued Djedi	*Algeria*	89	F2
Oued el Ma	*Mauritania*	88	D4
Oued Moulouya	*Morocco*	88	E2
Oued Rheris	*Morocco*	88	E2
Oued Sous	*Morocco*	88	D2
Ouésso	*Congo*	94	B3
Oujda	*Morocco*	89	E2
Oulu	*Finland*	58	N4
Oulujärvi	*Finland*	58	P4
Oulujoki	*Finland*	58	P4
Ouse	*United Kingdom*	67	P9
Outer Hebrides	*United Kingdom*	66	F4
Oviedo	*Spain*	70	E1
Owando	*Congo*	94	B4
Owatonna	*United States*	31	H3
Owen Sound	*Canada*	36	K3
Owensboro	*United States*	36	J4
Oxford	*United Kingdom*	67	M10
Özarfjöraar	*Iceland*	58	(1)E1
Ozark	*United States*	35	J5
Ozark Plateau	*United States*	33	H4
Ozero Baykal (Lake Baikal)	*Russia*	102	H6
Ozero Beloye	*Russia*	60	H2
Ozero Ilmen	*Russia*	60	G3
Ozero Imandra	*Russia*	60	G1
Ozero Issyk Kul	*Kyrgyzstan*	101	P9
Ozero Khanka (Lake Khanka)	*China / Russia*	109	J1
Ozero Kitay	*Ukraine*	77	S4
Ozero Onezhskoye (Lake Onega)	*Russia*	60	H2
Ozero Sevan	*Armenia*	81	L3
Ozero Taymyr	*Russia*	100	U3
Ozero Tengiz	*Kazakhstan*	101	M7
Ozero Umbozero	*Russia*	58	T3
Ozero Verhni Kujto	*Russia*	58	R4
Ozero Yalpug	*Ukraine*	77	R4
Ozero Zaysan	*Kazakhstan*	101	Q8

P

P'yongyang	*North Korea*	110	C4
Paarl	*South Africa*	96	B6
Pabianice	*Poland*	62	J6
Pacific City	*United States*	28	B1
Pacific Ocean	*Pacific Ocean*	99	U9
Padang	*Indonesia*	112	C3
Paderborn	*Germany*	64	D5
Padova	*Italy*	74	F3
Padre	*United States*	33	G6
Paducah	*United States*	34	J4
Paektu-San	*North Korea*	110	E3
Paengnyong-Do	*South Korea*	110	C5
Pag	*Croatia*	76	B5
Pagai Selatan	*Indonesia*	112	B3
Pagai Utara	*Indonesia*	112	B3
Pagan	*Northern Mariana Islands (U.S.)*	114	E4
Pagasitikós Kólpos	*Greece*	78	E5
Pagatan	*Indonesia*	113	A3
Pahang	*Malaysia*	106	C6
Páhnes	*Greece*	78	F9
Päijänne	*Finland*	59	N6
Paikü Co	*China*	104	E3
Pajala	*Sweden*	58	M3
Pakistan	*Southern Asia*	83	J4
Paks	*Hungary*	63	H11
Palagruza	*Croatia*	76	D7
Palana	*Russia*	103	T5
Palau	*Oceania*	114	D5
Palau	*Palau*	114	D5
Palau Breueh	*Indonesia*	112	A1
Palawan	*Philippines*	107	F5
Palembang	*Indonesia*	112	C3
Palencia	*Spain*	70	F2
Palermo	*Sicily (Italy)*	75	H10
Paljavaam	*Russia*	103	W3
Palk Strait	*India / Sri Lanka*	105	C7
Pallasovka	*Russia*	61	K4
Palm Beach	*United States*	35	K6
Palm Springs	*United States*	29	C4
Palma	*Spain*	71	N5
Palmerston	*Cook Islands*	115	K7
Palmerston North	*New Zealand*	118	E5
Palmira	*Colombia*	50	B3
Palmyra Atoll	*United States*	115	K5
Palu	*Indonesia*	113	A3
Pamir	*Tajikistan*	101	N10
Pamlico Sound	*United States*	35	L4
Pampa	*United States*	33	F4
Pampa del Tamarugal	*Chile*	52	H2
Pampas	*Argentina*	52	H6
Pamplona	*Spain*	71	J2
Panama City	*Panama*	50	B2
Panama City	*United States*	35	J5
Panama-Canal (Canal de Panamá)	*Panama*	47	J7
Panamá	*Central America*	47	H7
Panay	*Philippines*	107	G4
Panevézys	*Lithuania*	59	N9
Pangutaran	*Philippines*	113	A1
Pantanal	*Brazil*	51	F7
Pantelleria	*Italy*	75	G12
Pantoja	*Peru*	50	B4
Pápa	*Hungary*	76	E2
Papakura	*New Zealand*	118	E3
Papenburg	*Germany*	64	C3
Papua New Guinea	*Oceania*	114	E6
Papuk	*Croatia*	76	E4
Paragould	*United States*	34	H4
Paraguay	*South America*	52	J3
Paraguay	*South America*	53	K3
Parakou	*Benin*	93	E2
Paramaribo	*Surinam*	51	F2
Paramo Frontino	*Colombia*	50	B2
Paraná	*Argentina*	52	J5
Paraná	*South America*	53	L3
Parc National de la Salonga	*Democratic Republic Of Congo*	94	C4
Parchim	*Germany*	64	G3
Parczew	*Poland*	62	M6
Pardubice	*Czech Republic*	63	E7
Paris	*France*	68	H5
Paris (TN)	*United States*	34	J4
Paris (TX)	*United States*	34	G5
Park City	*United States*	30	D3
Parkersburg	*United States*	36	K4
Parma	*Italy*	74	E4
Parnaíba	*Brazil*	51	J4
Parnassos (Liákoura)	*Greece*	78	E6
Párnon ros	*Greece*	78	E7
Parnu	*Estonia*	59	N7
Páros	*Greece*	78	G7
Parpaillon	*France*	72	B6
Pascagoula	*United States*	34	J5
Pasman	*Croatia*	76	C6
Passau	*Germany*	65	J8
Pasto	*Colombia*	50	B3
Pastora Peak	*United States*	32	E4
Patagonia	*Argentina*	52	G7
Pátmos	*Greece*	78	J7
Patna	*India*	104	E3
Patomskoye Nagorye	*Russia*	102	K5
Pátrai	*Greece*	78	D6
Patuca	*Honduras*	47	G5
Pau	*France*	69	E10
Paulatuk	*Canada*	40	G3
Pavia	*Italy*	72	E5
Pavlodar	*Kazakhstan*	101	P7
Paxoi	*Greece*	78	B5
Pazardzhik	*Bulgaria*	77	M7
Pazartas Burun	*Turkey*	80	D3
Peace River	*Canada*	42	J5
Pec	*Yugoslavia*	76	H7
Pechora	*Russia*	61	M1
Pechorskoye More	*Russia*	100	J4
Pecos	*United States*	33	F5
Pecos River	*United States*	33	F5
Pécs	*Hungary*	63	H11
Pedreiras	*Brazil*	51	J4
Pedro Juan Caballero	*Paraguay*	51	F8
Peene	*Germany*	64	J3
Peer	*Belgium*	57	J3
Peera Peera Poolanna Lake	*Australia*	117	G5
Peever	*United States*	31	G2
Pegasus Bay	*New Zealand*	119	E6
Pegu	*Myanmar (Burma)*	106	B3
Pegu Yoma	*Myanmar (Burma)*	106	B2
Pegunungan Iran	*Malaysia / Indonesia*	107	E6
Pegunungan Jayawijaya	*South East Asia*	113	E3
Pegunungan Maoke	*South East Asia*	113	E3
Pegunungan Sudirman	*South East Asia*	113	E3
Pegunungan van Rees	*South East Asia*	113	E3
Pekalongan	*Indonesia*	112	D4
Pélagos	*Greece*	78	F5
Pekanbaru	*Indonesia*	112	C2
Pelinaion	*Greece*	78	J6
Peljesac	*Croatia*	76	E7
Pellg i Drinit	*Albania*	78	B3
Pellworm	*Germany*	64	D2
Pelly Mountains	*Canada*	40	E4
Pelotas	*Brazil*	53	L5
Pematangsiantar	*Indonesia*	112	B2
Pemba	*Mozambique*	97	G2
Pemba	*Tanzania*	95	G5
Pembina	*United States*	31	G2
Pembroke	*Canada*	37	L2
Peña Trevinca	*Spain*	70	D2
Peña Ubiña	*Spain*	70	E1
Pend Oreille Lake	*United States*	28	C1
Pend Orielle	*United States*	28	C1
Pendik	*Turkey*	79	M4
Pendleton City	*United States*	28	C1
Peng Hu Lieh-Tao	*Taiwan*	107	F2
Peniche	*Portugal*	70	A5
Peninsular Malaysia	*Malaysia*	106	C6
Penner	*India*	105	C6
Pennines	*United Kingdom*	67	L7
Pennsylvania	*United States*	37	L3
Penny Highlands	*Canada*	44	T3
Penrhyn	*Cook Islands*	115	L6
Pensacola	*United States*	35	J5
Pentenwell Lake	*United States*	36	J3
Penticton	*Canada*	41	H7
Pentland Firth	*United Kingdom*	66	K3
Penza	*Russia*	60	J4
Penzhinskaya Guba	*Russia*	103	U4
Peoria	*United States*	36	J3
Pergunungan Natuna	*Malaysia*	112	F2
Périgueux	*France*	69	8
Peristéri	*Greece*	78	D5
Perm	*Russia*	61	M3
Pernik	*Bulgaria*	77	L7
Perpignan	*France*	69	J11
Perth	*Australia*	116	C6
Pertuis Breton	*France*	69	D7
Pertuis dAntioche	*France*	69	D7
Peru	*South America*	50	B5
Peru-Chile Trench	*Pacific Ocean*	48	D5
Perugia	*Italy*	74	G5
Pesaro	*Italy*	73	H7
Pescara	*Italy*	74	J6
Peshawar	*Pakistan*	83	K3
Peshkopia	*Albania*	76	H8
Petaluma	*United States*	29	B3
Peter I. Island	*Antarctica*	120	(2)JJ3
Peterborough	*United Kingdom*	56	C2
Peterborough	*Canada*	45	R8
Petermann Ranges	*Australia*	116	E4
Petermanns Bjerg	*Greenland*	120	(1)T2
Petersburg	*United States*	35	L4
Petites Pyrénées	*France*	71	M1
Petre Bay	*New Zealand*	119	(1)B1
Petrified Forest National Park	*United States*	32	E4
Petrila	*Romania*	77	L4
Petrolina	*Brazil*	51	J5
Petropavlovsk	*Kazakhstan*	61	P4
Petropavlovsk-Kamchatskiy	*Russia*	103	T6
Petrozavodsk	*Russia*	60	G2
Pevek	*Russia*	103	W3
Pfälzer Wald	*Germany*	65	C7
Pforzheim	*Germany*	65	D8
Phanom Dang Raek	*South East Asia*	106	C4
Philadelphia	*United States*	37	M3
Philippines	*South East Asia*	107	G5
Phnom Penh	*Cambodia*	106	D4
Phoenix	*United States*	32	D5
Phoenix Island	*Kiribati (Pacific Ocean)*	115	J6
Phou Bia	*Laos*	106	C3
Piacenza	*Italy*	74	D3
Pianosa	*Italy*	74	K6
Piatra Neamt	*Romania*	77	P3
Piave	*Italy*	74	G3
Pic Boby	*Madagascar*	97	H4
Pic d nie	*France*	71	K2
Pic Tousside	*Chad*	90	C3
Picacho del Centinela	*Mexico*	32	E6
Picayune	*United States*	34	J5
Pico	*Azores (Portugal)*	88	(1)B2
Pico Bolivar	*Venezuela*	50	C2
Pico de Almanzor	*Spain*	70	E4
Pico de Teide	*Canary Islands (Spain)*	88	B3
Picos de Europa	*Spain*	70	E1
Pidurutalagala	*Sri Lanka*	105	D7
Piedras Negras	*Mexico*	32	E6
Pielinen	*Finland*	58	Q5
Pierre	*United States*	31	F3
Pietermaritzburg	*South Africa*	96	E5
Pietersburg	*South Africa*	96	D4
Pik Abrigen	*Russia*	103	R4
Pik Kommunizma	*Tajikistan*	83	K2
Pik Pobedy	*China*	101	P9
Pila	*Poland*	62	F4
Pilica	*Poland*	62	K6
Pinang	*Malaysia*	112	C1
Pinar	*Spain*	70	E8
Pinar del Rio	*Cuba*	47	H4
Píndos Oros	*Greece*	78	D5
Pine Bluff	*United States*	34	H5
Pine Bluffs	*United States*	31	F3
Pine Island Bay	*Antarctica*	120	(2)GG2
Pinerolo	*Italy*	72	C6
Pingvallavatn	*Iceland*	58	(1)C2
Pingxiang	*China*	108	E5
Pinneberg	*Germany*	64	E3
Pinta	*Ecuador*	50	(1)A1
Piombino	*Italy*	74	E6
Pireás	*Greece*	78	F6
Pirin	*Bulgaria*	78	F3
Pirineos (Pyrenées)	*France / Spain*	71	K2
Pirmasens	*Germany*	65	C7
Pirna	*Germany*	65	J6
Pirot	*Yugoslavia*	77	K6
Pisa	*Italy*	74	E5
Pisek	*Czech Republic*	63	D8

Pistilfjördur	Iceland	58	(1)F1
Pistol River	United States	28	B2
Pitcairn Islands	Pacific Ocean	115	P8
Pite älv	Sweden	58	L4
Piteå	Sweden	58	L4
Pitesti	Romania	77	M5
Pitkjaranta	Russia	60	G2
Pitt Island	New Zealand	119	(1)B2
Pitt Strait	New Zealand	119	(1)B2
Pittsburg	United States	33	H4
Pittsburgh	United States	37	L3
Piura	Peru	50	A5
Pjórsá	Iceland	58	(1)D2
Placentia Bay	Canada	45	W7
Plackovica	Macedonia	78	E3
Plainview	United States	33	F5
Planalto de Mato Grosso	Brazil	48	F5
Planalto do Bié	Angola	96	B2
Planalto do Brasil (Brazilian Highlands)	Brazil	51	J7
Plasencia	Spain	70	D4
Plateau du Bemaraha	Madagascar	97	G3
Plateau du Djado	Niger	90	B3
Plateau du Tademaït	Algeria	89	F3
Plateaux Batéké	Congo	94	A4
Plateaux Batéké	Congo	93	G5
Platte	Seychelles	97	(2) C2
Platte River	United States	31	G3
Plattsburgh	United States	37	M3
Plauer See	Germany	64	H3
Plaven	Germany	65	G6
Plesetsk	Russia	60	J2
Pleven	Bulgaria	77	M6
Plituice	Croatia	74	K4
Pljesevica	Bosnia-Herzegovina/Croatia	76	C5
Pljevlja	Yugoslavia	76	G6
Plock	Poland	62	J5
Plöckenstein / Plechy	Germany / Austria / Czech Republic	65	J8
Ploiesti	Romania	77	P5
Plöner See	Germany	64	F2
Plovdiv	Bulgaria	77	M7
Plymouth	United Kingdom	67	J11
Plymouth	United States	37	M3
Plymouth Sound	United Kingdom	67	A3
Plzen	Czech Republic	63	C8
Po	Italy	74	E4
Pobeda	Russia	120	(1)A3
Pocatello	United States	30	D3
Podgorica	Yugoslavia	78	B2
Podkamennaya Tunguska	Russia	102	E4
Poel	Germany	64	G2
Poggibonsi	Italy	72	G7
Pogórze Karpackie	Poland	63	J8
Pohnpei	Micronesia	114	F5
Pohorje	Slovakia	76	C3
Point Arena	United States	29	B3
Point Conception	United States	29	B5
Point Culver	Australia	116	E6
Point dEntrecasteaux	Australia	116	B7
Point Lay	Alaska (U.S.)	29	(1)E2
Point Reyes	United States	29	B3
Pointe de Barfleur	France	56	B5
Pointe de Grave	France	69	D8
Pointe de la Coubre	France	69	D8
Pointe de lEst	Canada	45	U7
Pointe de Penmarch	France	68	A6
Pointe du Raz	France	68	A5
Pointe Noire	Congo	93	G5
Poitiers	France	69	F7
Pojezierze Wielkopolsko-Kujawskie	Poland	62	F5
Pokhvistnevo	Russia	61	L4
Pola de Siero	Spain	70	E1
Poland	Europe	62	F5
Polatli	Turkey	79	Q5
Polillo Islands	Philippines	107	G4
Poluostrov Rybachiy	Russia	58	S1
Polyarny Ural	Russia	61	N1
Polynesia	Oceania	115	J6
Pommersche Bucht	Germany / Poland	64	K2
Pomorskiy Proliv	Russia	61	K1
Ponca City	United States	34	G4
Ponferrada	Spain	70	D2
Ponoy	Russia	60	J1
Pont-Audemer	France	56	D5
Ponta Albina	Angola	96	A3
Ponta da Baleia	Brazil	51	K7
Ponta da Barra	Mozambique	97	F4
Ponta da Barra Falsa	Mozambique	97	F4
Pontevedra	Spain	70	B2
Pontianak	Indonesia	112	D3
Pontivy	France	68	C5
Ponza	Italy	75	H8
Pool-Plateau	Antarctica	120	(2)LL1
Poole	United Kingdom	67	L11
Poona (Pune)	India	105	B5
Poplar Bluff	United States	34	H4
Poprad	Slovakia	63	K8
Porcupine River	United States / Canada	40	C3
Pordenono	Italy	73	H5
Pori	Finland	59	L6
Porpoise Bay	Antarctica	120	(2)T3
Porsangen	Norway	58	N1
Porsuk Baraj	Turkey	79	N5
Port Angeles	United States	28	B1
Port Arthur	United States	34	H6
Port Charlotte	United States	35	K6
Port Elizabeth	South Africa	96	D6
Port Gentil	Gabon	93	F5
Port Harcourt	Nigeria	93	F4
Port Huron	United States	36	K3
Port Lavaca	United States	33	G6
Port Moresby	Papua New Guinea	114	E6
Port of Spain	Trinidad and Tobago	47	M6
Port Phillip Bay	Australia	117	H7
Port Said (Br Sa'îd)	Egypt	91	F1
Port St. Lucie	United States	35	K6
Port Sudan (Bur Sudan)	Sudan	91	G4
Port-au-Prince	Haiti	47	K5
Port-Louis	Mauritius	97	(1) B2
Portage La Prairie	Canada	43	M7
Portalegre	Portugal	70	C5
Portales	United States	33	F5
Porthill	United States	28	C1
Porthmós Kafiréos	Greece	78	G7
Portimão	Portugal	70	B7
Portland (ME)	United States	37	M3
Portland (OR)	United States	28	B1
Portland Bill	United Kingdom	67	L11
Porto	Portugal	70	B3
Pôrto Alegre	Brazil	53	L5
Porto Santo (Madeira)	Portugal	88	B2
Pôrto Velho	Brazil	50	E5
Porto-Novo	Benin	93	E3
Portsmouth	United Kingdom	67	N11
Portsmouth (NH)	United States	37	M3
Portsmouth (OH)	United States	36	K4
Porttipahdan Tekojärvi	Finland	58	N2
Portugal	Europe	70	B6
Posadas	Argentina	53	K4
Potenza	Italy	75	K8
Potes	Spain	70	F1
Potosí	Bolivia	50	D7
Potsdam	Germany	64	H4
Poughkeepsie	United States	37	M3
Poverty Bay	New Zealand	118	G4
Powell River	Canada	41	G7
Poyang Hu	China	108	F5
Poza Rica de Hidalgo	Mexico	46	E4
Pozarevac	Yugoslavia	76	J5
Poznan	Poland	62	F5
Pozoblanco	Spain	70	F6
Pra	West Africa	92	D3
Prague (Praha)	Czech Republic	63	D7
Praha (Prague)	Czech Republic	63	D7
Praia	Cape Verde	92	A5
Praslin	Seychelles	97	(2) C1
Prato	Italy	74	F5
Pratomagno	Italy	73	G7
Pregel	Russia	62	K3
Premuda	Croatia	76	B5
Prenj	Bosnia-Herzegovina	76	E6
Preparis North Channel	South East Asia	106	A3
Presa V. Carranza	Mexico	32	E6
Prescott	United States	32	D5
Presidio	United States	33	F6
Presov	Slovakia	63	L8
Presque Ilse	United States	37	N2
Prestány	Slovakia	63	G9
Preston	United Kingdom	67	K8
Pretoria	South Africa	96	D5
Pretov	Czech Republic	63	G8
Pribilov Islands	Alaska (U.S.)	29	(1)C4
Pribram	Czech Republic	63	C8
Priego	Spain	71	H4
Prijedor	Bosnia-Herzegovina	76	D5
Prikaspiyskaya Nizmennost	Kazakhstan	101	H8
Prilep	Macedonia	78	D3
Primorsko-Akhtarsk	Russia	60	H5
Prince Albert	Canada	38	K6
Prince Albert Sound	Canada	42	H2
Prince Charles Island	Canada	42	R3
Prince Edward Island	Canada	39	U7
Prince Edward Island (P.E.I)	Canada	39	U7
Prince George	Canada	41	G6
Prince of Wales Island	Alaska (U.S.)	29	(1)L4
Prince of Wales Island	Australia	117	H2
Prince of Wales Island	Canada	42	L2
Prince Rupert	Canada	41	E6
Princess Charlotte Bay	Australia	117	H2
Príncipe	São Tomé and Príncipe	93	F4
Pripyat	Belarus	60	F4
Pristina	Yugoslavia	78	D2
Privas	France	69	K9
Prizren	Yugoslavia	78	C2
Professor van Blommesteen Meer	Surinam	51	F3
Profitis Ilias	Greece	78	E8
Prokopyevsk	Russia	101	Q7
Proliv Dmitriya Lapteva	Russia	103	P2
Proliv Karskiye Vorota	Russia	100	K3
Proliv Longa	Russia	103	X3
Proliv Sannikova	Russia	103	P2
Proliv Vilkitskogo	Russia	100	U2
Providence	Seychelles	97	(2) B2
Providence	United States	37	M3
Providencia	Caribbean	47	H6
Provins	France	68	J5
Provo	United States	30	D3
Prudhoe Bay	United States	29	(1)H1
Prüm	Germany	65	B6
Prusków	Poland	62	K5
Prut	Europe	77	R3
Prydz Bay	Antarctica	120	(2)N3
Psará	Greece	78	H6
Pskov	Russia	60	F3
Pskovskoye Ozero (Lake Peipus)	Russia	60	F3
Pucallpa	Peru	50	C5
Pudasjärvi	Finland	58	P4
Puebla de Zaragoza	Mexico	46	E5
Pueblo	United States	31	F4
Puente-Genil	Spain	70	F7
Puerto Montt	Chile	52	G7
Puerto Penasco	Mexico	32	D5
Puerto Rico	Caribbean	47	L5
Puertollano	Spain	70	F6
Puig Mayor	Spain	71	N5
Pukapuka	French Polynesia	115	N7
Pula	Croatia	73	J6
Pulau Adi	Indonesia	113	D3
Pulau Ambon	Indonesia	113	C3
Pulau Bacan	Indonesia	113	C3
Pulau Bali	Indonesia	112	F4
Pulau Banggi	Malaysia	107	F5
Pulau Bangka	Indonesia	112	D3
Pulau Belitung	Indonesia	112	D3
Pulau Biak	Indonesia	113	E3
Pulau Bintan	Indonesia	112	C2
Pulau Breueh	Indonesia	106	A5
Pulau Buru	Indonesia	113	C3
Pulau Buton	Indonesia	113	B4
Pulau Damar	Indonesia	113	C4
Pulau Dolak	Indonesia	113	E4
Pulau Enggano	Indonesia	112	C4
Pulau Flores	Indonesia	113	B4
Pulau Kabaena	Indonesia	113	B4
Pulau Karakelong	Indonesia	113	C2
Pulau Kobroor	Indonesia	113	D4
Pulau Komoran	Indonesia	113	E4
Pulau Langkawi	Indonesia	112	B1
Pulau Laut	Indonesia	112	F3
Pulau Lingga	Indonesia	112	C3
Pulau Lombok	Indonesia	112	F4
Pulau Madura	Indonesia	112	E4
Pulau Mangole	Indonesia	113	C3
Pulau Maya	Indonesia	112	D3
Pulau Misool	Indonesia	113	D3
Pulau Morotai	Indonesia	113	C2
Pulau Muna	Indonesia	113	B3
Pulau Natuna Besar	Indonesia	112	D2
Pulau Nias	Indonesia	112	B2
Pulau Obi	Indonesia	113	C3
Pulau Padangtikar	Indonesia	112	D3
Pulau Panaitan	Indonesia	112	C4
Pulau Peleng	Indonesia	113	B3
Pulau Pini	Indonesia	112	B2
Pulau Roma	Indonesia	113	C4
Pulau Salawati	Indonesia	113	D3
Pulau Salayar	Indonesia	113	A4
Pulau Samosir	Indonesia	112	B2
Pulau Sanana	Indonesia	113	C3
Pulau Sangihe	Indonesia	107	G6
Pulau Sangir	Indonesia	113	B2
Pulau Selaru	Indonesia	113	D4
Pulau Selayar	Indonesia	112	G4
Pulau Siberut	Indonesia	112	B3
Pulau Simeuluë	Indonesia	112	B2
Pulau Singkep	Indonesia	112	C3
Pulau Sipura	Indonesia	112	B3
Pulau Sumba	Indonesia	113	B4
Pulau Sumbawa	Indonesia	112	F4
Pulau Supiori	Indonesia	113	E3
Pulau Taliabu	Indonesia	113	B3
Pulau Tanahbala	Indonesia	112	B3
Pulau Tanahmasa	Indonesia	112	B2
Pulau Tarakan	Indonesia	113	A2
Pulau Timor	Indonesia	113	B4
Pulau Trangan	Indonesia	113	D4
Pulau Waigeo	Indonesia	113	D2
Pulau We	Indonesia	112	B1
Pulau Wetar	Indonesia	113	C4
Pulau Wokam	Indonesia	113	D4
Pulau Wowoni	Indonesia	113	B3
Pulau Yamdeno	Indonesia	113	D4
Pulau Yapen	Indonesia	113	E3
Pulawy	Poland	62	M6
Pulkkila	Finland	58	N4
Pullman	United States	30	C2
Puma Yumco	China	104	F3
Puncak Jaya	Indonesia	113	E3
Puncak Mandala	Indonesia	113	F3
Puncak Trikora	Indonesia	113	E3
Pune (Poona)	India	105	B5
Puno	Peru	50	C7
Punta Almina	Spain	70	E9
Punta Angamos	Chile	52	G3
Punta Arenas	Chile	52	G9
Punta Carreta	Peru	50	B6
Punta da Narca	Angola	93	G6
Punta del Faro	Sicily (Italy)	75	K10
Punta Eugenia	Mexico	46	A3
Punta Falcone	Sardinia (Italy)	75	B8
Punta Gallinas	Colombia	50	C1
Punta Gorda	United States	29	B2
Punta Lavapié	Chile	52	F6
Punta Lengua de Vaca	Chile	52	G5
Punta Licosa	Italy	75	J8
Punta Mala	Panama	47	J7
Punta Mariato	Panama	47	H7
Punta Negra	Peru	50	A5
Punta Sarga	Western Sahara	83	B4
Purcell Mountains	United States / Canada	38	H6
Pórisvatn	Iceland	58	(1)D2
Puruvesi	Finland	58	Q6
Pusala Dag	Turkey	79	Q7
Pusan	South Korea	110	E6
Puslahta	Russia	60	H2
Puulavesi	Finland	58	P6
Puy de Sancy	France	69	H8
Puysegur Point	New Zealand	119	B8
Pyaozero	Russia	58	R3
Pyasina	Russia	100	S3
Pyasinskiy Zaliv	Russia	100	Q3
Pyatigorsk	Russia	81	K1
Pyé	Myanmar (Burma)	106	B3
Pyhäjärvi	Finland	59	M6
Pyhäjoki	Finland	58	N4
Pyramid Lake	United States	29	C3
Pyrenées (Pirineos)	France / Spain	71	K2

Q

Qaal Jafr	Jordan	84	D6
Qarqan He	China	101	R10
Qatar	Middle East	85	D4
Qazvin	Iran	82	E2
Qena	Egypt	91	F2
Qeshm	Iran	85	F3
Qian Shan	China	109	G2

Qilian Shan	*China*	108	B3
Qin Ling	*China*	108	D4
Qingdao	*China*	109	G3
Qinghai Hu (Koko Nor)	*China*	108	C3
Qinhuangdao	*China*	109	F2
Qiqihar	*China*	109	G1
Qogir Feng / K2	*Pakistan / India*	104	C1
Qom	*Iran*	82	F3
Qornet es Saouda	*Lebanon*	84	D2
Quakenbrück	*Germany*	64	C4
Quanzhou	*China*	108	F5
Quardho	*Somalia*	95	H2
Quartzsite	*United States*	32	D5
Québec	*Canada*	39	S6
Québec	*Canada*	45	S7
Quedlinburg	*Germany*	64	G5
Queen Alexandra Range	*Antarctica*	120	(2)W1
Queen Charlotte Islands	*Canada*	41	E6
Queen Charlotte Sound	*Canada*	41	E6
Queen Charlotte Strait	*Canada*	41	F6
Queen Elizabeth Islands	*Canada*	42	J2
Queen Maud Gulf	*Canada*	42	L3
Queen Maud Mountains	*Antarctica*	120	(2)EE1
Queensland	*Australia*	117	H4
Queenstown	*New Zealand*	119	C7
Quelimane	*Mozambique*	97	F3
Quelpart I. (Cheju Do)	*South Korea*	110	D7
Quemoy	*Taiwan*	107	F2
Quesada	*Spain*	70	G5
Quesnel Lake	*Canada*	41	G6
Quetta	*Pakistan*	83	J3
Quezon City	*Philippines*	107	G4
Qui Nhon	*Vietnam*	106	D4
Quillan	*France*	69	H11
Quilon	*India*	105	C7
Quimper	*France*	68	A5
Quincy	*United States*	36	H4
Quito	*Ecuador*	50	B3

R

Raalte	*Netherlands*	57	K2
Raas Caseyr	*Somalia*	95	J1
Raas Xaafun	*Somalia*	95	J1
Rab	*Croatia*	76	B5
Rába	*Hungary*	73	M3
Rabat	*Morocco*	88	D2
Rach Gia	*Vietnam*	106	C5
Racine	*United States*	36	J3
Radan	*Yugoslavia*	76	J6
Radez	*France*	69	H9
Radford	*United States*	35	K4
Radom	*Poland*	62	L6
Raevavae	*French Polynesia*	115	M8
Rafsanjan	*Iran*	85	G1
Ragusa	*Italy*	75	J12
Raippaluoto	*Finland*	58	L5
Raipur	*India*	104	D4
Rajahmundry	*India*	105	D5
Rajkot	*India*	104	B4
Rajshahi	*Bangladesh*	104	E4
Raleigh	*United States*	35	L4
Ralik Chain	*Marshall Islands*	114	G5
Ramapo Deep	*Pacific Ocean*	111	M8
Ramlat Dahm	*Saudi Arabia*	82	E6
Rampur	*India*	104	C3
Ramree	*Myanmar*	106	A3
Ranchi	*India*	104	D4
Randers	*Denmark*	59	F8
Rangoon (Yangon)	*Myanmar (Burma)*	106	B3
Rapa	*French Polynesia*	115	M8
Rapallo	*Italy*	72	E6
Rapid City	*United States*	31	F3
Raroia	*French Polynesia*	115	M7
Rarotonga	*Cook Islands*	115	K8
Ras al Hadd	*Oman*	83	H5
Ras al Hazrah	*United Arab Emirates*	85	D4
Ras al Kuh	*Iran*	85	G4
Ras al Milh	*Libya*	90	E1
Ras al Mutaf	*Iran*	82	F4
Râs Banâs	*Egypt*	91	G3
Ras Beddouza	*Morocco*	88	C2
Ras Burun	*Egypt*	84	A5
Ras Dashen	*Ethiopia*	91	G5
Ras Dubayah	*United Arab Emirates*	85	E4
Ras Hadarba	*Sudan*	82	C5
Ras Isa	*Yemen*	82	D6
Ras Jaddi	*Pakistan*	83	H4
Ras Jwani	*Pakistan*	83	H5
Ras Kasar	*Sudan / Eritrea*	91	G4
Ras Madrakah	*Oman*	83	G6
Ras Mushayrib	*United Arab Emirates*	85	D4
Râs Nouâdhibou	*Mauritania*	88	B4
Ras Shagara	*Sudan*	91	G3
Ras Shartah	*Oman*	85	G3
Ras-e Barkan	*Iran*	85	C2
Ras-e Nay Band	*Iran*	85	D3
Rasht	*Iran*	82	E2
Rason Lake	*Australia*	116	D5
Rastalt	*Germany*	65	D8
Rasul	*Iran*	85	F3
Rat Islands	*Alaska (U.S.)*	29	(3)B1
Ratak Chain	*Marshall Islands*	114	H4
Rathenow	*Germany*	64	H4
Rathlin Island	*United Kingdom*	66	G6
Ratlam	*India*	104	C4
Raukumara Range	*New Zealand*	118	F4
Rauma	*Finland*	59	L6
Raurkela	*India*	104	E4
Ravenna	*Italy*	74	G4
Rawaki	*Kiribati (Pacific ocean)*	115	J6
Rawalpindi	*Pakistan*	83	K3
Rawlins	*United States*	30	E3
Rayakosti	*Russia*	58	Q2
Razgrad	*Bulgaria*	77	P6
Reading	*United Kingdom*	67	N10
Rebun-To	*Japan*	111	L1
Recife	*Brazil*	51	L5
Recklinghausen	*Germany*	64	C5
Recknitz	*Germany*	64	H2
Reconquista	*Argentina*	52	K4
Red Deer	*Canada*	41	J6
Red Lakes	*United States*	31	H2
Red River	*United States*	34	H5
Red Sea	*Middle East*	91	G2
Redditch	*United Kingdom*	56	B2
Redwood National Park	*United States*	28	B2
Regensburg	*Germany*	65	H7
Reggane	*Algeria*	89	F3
Reggio di Calabria	*Italy*	75	K10
Reggio nell Emilia	*Italy*	74	E4
Reghin	*Romania*	77	M3
Regina	*Canada*	43	L6
Reims	*France*	68	K4
Reindeer Lake	*Canada*	43	L5
Reliance	*Canada*	42	K4
Relizane	*Algeria*	71	L9
Remscheid	*Germany*	65	C5
Rendsburg	*Germany*	64	E2
Rennes	*France*	68	D5
Reno	*Italy*	74	F4
Reno	*United States*	29	C3
Reprêsa de Itaipu	*Brazil*	53	L3
Reprêsa de Tucuruí	*Brazil*	51	H4
Repulse Bay	*Australia*	117	J4
Repvåg	*Norway*	58	N1
Requena	*Spain*	71	J5
Réservoir Gouin	*Canada*	45	R7
Réservoir Pipmoacan	*Canada*	45	S6
Resh Teh-ye Kuh Ha-ye Alborz	*Iran*	82	F2
Resistencia	*Argentina*	52	K4
Resolution Island	*New Zealand*	119	A7
Resolution Island	*Canada*	44	U4
Rethel	*France*	57	H5
Réunion (France)	*South Africa*	97	(1) B2
Reus	*Spain*	71	M3
Reutlingen	*Germany*	65	E8
Reykjavik	*Iceland*	58	(1)B2
Reynosa	*Mexico*	34	G6
Rezekne	*Latvia*	59	P8
Rezvaya	*Turkey / Bulgaria*	79	K2
Rhein (Rhine)	*Central Europe*	64	B5
Rheine	*Germany*	64	C4
Rheinisches Schiefergebirge	*Germany*	57	K4
Rhin (Rhine)	*France / Germany*	65	C8
Rhine (Rhein)	*Central Europe*	64	B5
Rho	*Italy*	72	E5
Rhode Island	*United States*	37	M3
Rhodes (Ródhos)	*Greece*	79	L8
Rhondda	*United Kingdom*	67	K10
Rhum	*United Kingdom*	66	G4
Rhône	*France / Switzerland*	72	C4
Rhön	*Germany*	65	E6
ri Váltou	*Greece*	78	D5
Ria de Arosa	*Spain*	70	A2
Ría de Muros y Noya	*Spain*	70	A2
Ria de Pontevedra	*Spain*	70	A2
Ria de Santa Marta	*Spain*	70	C1
Ria de Vigo	*Spain*	70	B2
Ribble	*United Kingdom*	67	L8
Ribnica	*Slovenia*	75	J3
Riccione	*Italy*	73	H7
Richardson Mountains	*Canada*	40	D3
Richland	*United States*	28	B1
Richmond	*United States*	35	L4
Richmond (KY)	*United States*	36	K4
Riesa	*Germany*	65	J5
Rif	*Morocco*	88	D1
Rifstangi	*Iceland*	58	(1)F1
Riga	*Latvia*	59	N8
Rigolet	*Canada*	39	V6
Rijeka	*Croatia*	76	B4
Rila	*Bulgaria*	77	L7
Rimini	*Italy*	74	G4
Rîmnicu Sarat	*Romania*	77	Q4
Rîmnicu Vîlcea	*Romania*	77	M4
Rimouski	*Canada*	37	N2
Ringvassy	*Norway*	58	J1
Rinia	*Greece*	78	H7
Rio Bavispe	*Mexico*	32	E6
Rio Branco	*Brazil*	50	D5
Rio Bravo	*Mexico*	34	G6
Rio Bravo del Norte	*Mexico*	46	D3
Rio Cuarto	*Argentina*	52	J5
Rio de Janeiro	*Brazil*	53	N3
Rio de la Plata	*South America*	53	K5
Rio Gallegos	*Argentina*	52	H9
Rio Grande	*Brazil*	53	M3
Rio Grande	*Brazil*	53	L5
Rio Grande	*United States*	33	F6
Rio Negro	*South America*	50	E4
Ripoll	*Spain*	71	N2
Rishiri-To	*Japan*	111	L1
Ritchies Archipelago	*India*	105	F6
River Cess	*Liberia*	92	C3
River Gorge	*United States*	36	K4
River Inlet	*Canada*	41	F6
Rivera	*Uruguay*	53	K5
Riverton	*United States*	30	E3
Rivière aux Feuilles	*Canada*	39	S5
Rivière-du-Loup	*Canada*	37	N2
Rivoli	*Italy*	72	C5
Riyadh (Ar Riyad)	*Saudi Arabia*	82	E5
Rm	*Denmark*	59	E9
rmos Vistonias	*Greece*	78	G4
Rnne	*Denmark*	62	D2
Roanoke	*United States*	35	L4
Roanoke Rapids	*United States*	35	L4
Robertsport	*Liberia*	92	B3
Rochefort	*France*	69	E8
Rochefort	*Belgium*	57	J4
Rochegda	*Russia*	60	J2
Rochester	*United States*	37	L3
Rock Falls	*United States*	36	J3
Rock Hill	*United States*	35	K4
Rock Springs	*United States*	30	E3
Rockall Bank	*United Kingdom*	66	C4
Rockefeller Plateau	*Antarctica*	120	(2)CC1
Rockford	*United States*	36	J3
Rockglen	*Canada*	30	E2
Rockport	*United States*	29	B3
Rocky Mount	*United States*	35	L4
Rocky Mountains	*United States / Canada*	38	E5
Rodopi	*Bulgaria / Greece*	78	F3
Ródhos (Rhodes)	*Greece*	79	L8
Roes Welcome Sound	*Canada*	42	P4
Roeselare	*Belgium*	56	G4
Rogers	*United States*	33	H4
Rohtak	*India*	104	C3
Roja	*Latvia*	59	M8
Rolla	*United States*	34	H4
Roman	*Romania*	77	P3
Roman-Kos	*Ukraine*	80	F1
Romania	*Europe*	77	L4
Rome (GA)	*United States*	35	J5
Rome (NY)	*United States*	37	L3
Rome (Roma)	*Italy*	74	G7
Rona	*United Kingdom*	66	H2
Roncagua	*Chile*	52	G5
Ronco	*Italy*	73	H6
Ronne Ice Shelf	*Antarctica*	120	(2)LL2
Ronneby	*Sweden*	62	E1
Roraima	*Venezuela/Brazil*	50	E2
Rosario	*Argentina*	52	J5
Rose	*American Samoa*	115	K7
Rosemary Bank	*United Kingdom*	66	C2
Rosenheim	*Germany*	65	H9
Rosiori de Vede	*Romania*	77	M5
Roskilde	*Denmark*	62	B2
Ross Ice Shelf	*Antarctica*	120	(2)Z2
Ross River	*Canada*	40	E4
Ross Sea	*Antarctica*	120	(2)Z2
Rossan Point	*Ireland*	67	D7
Rossano	*Italy*	75	L9
Rossnava	*Slovakia*	63	K9
Rossosh	*Russia*	60	H4
Rostock	*Germany*	64	H2
Rostov-na-Donu	*Russia*	60	H5
Roswell	*United States*	32	F5
Rota	*Northern Mariana Islands (U.S.)*	114	E4
Rotenburg	*Germany*	64	E3
Rothaargebirge	*Germany*	65	D5
Roti	*Indonesia*	116	D2
Rottenburg	*Germany*	65	D8
Rotterdam	*Netherlands*	57	H3
Rottumerplaat	*Netherlands*	64	B3
Rotuma	*Fiji*	114	H7
Roturua	*New Zealand*	118	F4
Roubaix	*France*	68	J3
Rouen	*France*	68	G4
Rousay	*United Kingdom*	66	K2
Rouses Point	*United States*	37	M2
Rouyan-Noranda	*Canada*	43	R7
Rovaniemi	*Finland*	60	F2
Rovaniemi	*Finland*	58	P3
Rovereto	*Italy*	72	G5
Rovigo	*Italy*	73	G5
Rovno	*Ukraine*	60	F4
Rowley Island	*Canada*	42	Q3
Royal Canal	*Ireland*	67	G8
Royal Tunbridge Wells	*United Kingdom*	56	D3
Royan	*France*	69	D8
Roztocze	*Poland*	63	M7
Rsita	*Romania*	76	K5
Rt Kamenjak	*Croatia*	73	J6
Rt Savudrija	*Croatia*	73	J5
Ruacana Falls	*Namibia / Angola*	96	A3
Ruapehu	*New Zealand*	118	E4
Ruapuke Island	*New Zealand*	119	C8
Rub al Khali	*Saudi Arabia*	82	E6
Rubtsovsk	*Russia*	101	Q7
Rudnyy	*Kazakhstan*	61	N4
Rugby	*United Kingdom*	56	B2
Rügen	*Germany*	64	J2
Rugles	*France*	56	D6
Ruhnu	*Estonia*	59	M8
Ruhr	*Germany*	57	L3
Rumbek	*Sudan*	94	D2
Rundu	*Namibia*	96	B3
Ruo Shui	*China*	108	C2
Rur	*Germany*	65	B5
Rurutu	*French Polynesia*	115	L8
Ruse	*Bulgaria*	77	N6
Russellville	*United States*	33	H4
Russia	*Russia*	62	K3
Russia	*Asia*	60	J3
Rustavi	*Georgia*	81	L3
Ruston	*United States*	34	H5
Rutland	*India*	105	F6
Rutland	*United States*	37	M3
Ruvuma (Rovuma)	*Tanzania*	97	F2
Ruvuma/Rovuma	*Central Africa*	95	F6
Ruzomberok	*Slovakia*	63	J8
Rwanda	*Central Africa*	94	D4
Ryazan	*Russia*	60	H4
Rybinskoye Vdkhr.	*Russia*	60	H3
Rybnik	*Poland*	63	H7
Rybnitsa	*Moldova*	77	R2
Rypin	*Poland*	62	J4
Ryukyu Islands (Ryukyu-Shoto)	*Japan*	109	G6
Ryukyu-Shoto (Ryukyu Islands)	*Japan*	109	G6
Rzeszów	*Poland*	63	M7
Rzhev	*Russia*	60	G

SATELLITE ATLAS OF THE WORLD

S

s Hertogenbosch/Den Bosch	Netherlands	57	J3
s-Gravenhage (Den Haag) (The Hague)	Netherlands	68	J1
S. Sandwich Islands	South Atlantic Ocean	120	(2)C4
Saale	Germany	65	G6
Saalfeld	Germany	65	G6
Saarbrücken	Germany	65	C7
Saaremaa	Estonia	59	M7
Sabac	Yugoslavia	76	G5
Sabadell	Spain	71	N3
Sabah	Malaysia	107	F5
Sabha	Libya	89	H3
Sabi	South Africa	97	E4
Sabinas Hidalgo	Mexico	33	F6
Sabkhat al Bardawil	Egypt	84	A5
Sabkhat Ghuzayyil	Libya	90	C2
Sabkhat Shunayn	Libya	90	D1
Sabkhat Tawurgha	Libya	90	B1
Sable Island	Canada	45	V8
Sabzevar	Iran	101	K11
Sachs Harbour	Canada	40	G2
Sack	Ukraine	63	N6
Sacramento	United States	29	B3
Sadd el Aali	Egypt	82	B4
Sado	Portugal	70	B6
Sado-Shima	Japan	111	K4
Safi	Morocco	88	D2
Safid Kuh	Afghanistan	83	H3
Safonovo	Russia	61	K1
Saga	Japan	110	E7
Sagami-Nada	Japan	111	K6
Sagar	India	104	C4
Sagiz	Kazakhstan	61	L5
Sagres	Portugal	70	B7
Saguia el-Hamra	Western Sahara	88	C3
Sagunto	Spain	71	K5
Sahagún	Spain	70	E2
Sahara	Africa	88	D4
Sahara-Atlas	Algeria	89	F2
Saharanpur	India	104	C2
Sahel	West Africa	92	C1
Sahiwal	Pakistan	83	K3
Sahra at Tih	Egypt	84	A6
Sahra Marzuq	Libya	90	B3
Sahra´ Bayyudah	Sudan	91	F4
Sahra´ Rabyanah	Libya	90	C2
Sahyadri / Western Ghats	India	105	B5
Saidabad	Iran	85	F2
Saigon (Ho Chi Minh)	Vietnam	106	D4
Saimaa	Finland	60	F2
Saint Jérôme	Canada	37	M2
Saint Lawrence River	Canada	37	M2
Saint Lô	France	56	B5
Saint Pierre	Seychelles	97	(2) A2
Saint-Brieuc	France	68	C5
Saint-Denis	South Africa	97	(1) B2
Saint-Denis	France	68	H4
Saint-Étienne	France	69	K8
Saint-Dié	France	68	M5
Saint-Dizier	France	68	K5
Saint-Gaudens	France	69	F10
Saint John	Canada	45	T7
Saint-Nazaire	France	68	C6
Saint-Omer	France	56	F4
Saintes	France	69	E8
Saipan	Northern Mariana Islands (U.S.)	114	E4
Sajó	Hungary	63	K9
Sakai	Japan	110	H6
Sakar	Bulgaria	78	J3
Sakarya	Turkey	80	E4
Sakata	Japan	111	K4
Saki	Nigeria	93	E3
Sakishima-Gunto	Japan	109	G5
Sal	Cape Verde	92	(1)B1
Salé	Morocco	88	D2
Salamanca	Spain	70	E3
Salar de Atacama	Chile	52	H3
Salar de Uyuni	Bolivia	52	H3
Salas de los Infantes	Spain	70	G2
Salavat	Russia	61	M4
Salda Gölü	Turkey	79	M7
Saldanha	South Africa	96	B6
Saldus	Latvia	59	M8
Salekhard	Russia	61	P1
Salem	India	105	C6
Salem	United States	28	B2
Salerno	Italy	75	J8
Salina	Italy	75	J10
Salinas	United States	29	B3
Salinta	Romania	63	L11
Salisbury	United Kingdom	56	B3
Salisbury	United States	37	L4
Salisbury Island	Canada	42	R4
Salisbury Plain	United Kingdom	67	L10
Salla	Finland	58	Q3
Salmon	United States	30	D2
Salon-de-Provence	France	69	L10
Saloniki (Thessaloniki)	Greece	78	E4
Salor	Spain	70	D5
Salsk	Russia	60	J5
Salt Lake City	United States	30	D3
Salta	Argentina	52	H3
Saltillo	Mexico	33	F6
Salton Sea	United States	29	C4
Salvador	Brazil	51	K6
Salween (Nu Jiang)	South East Asia	108	B6
Salyótarján	Hungary	63	J9
Salzach	Germany / Austria	65	H9
Salzburg	Austria	73	J3
Salzgitter	Germany	64	F4
Salzwedel	Germany	64	G4
Samar	Philippines	107	H4
Samara	Russia	61	L4

Samarinda	Indonesia	112	F3
Samarkand	Uzbekistan	101	M10
Sambor	Ukraine	63	N8
Samburg	Russia	61	R1
Samokov	Bulgaria	78	F2
Sámos	Greece	79	J7
Samothráki	Greece	78	H4
Samsun	Turkey	80	G3
San Andrés	Caribbean	47	H6
San Andros	Bahamas	35	L6
San Angelo	United States	33	F5
San Antonio	United States	33	G6
San Carlos de Bariloche	Argentina	52	G7
San Clemente	United States	29	C4
San Cristóbal	Ecuador	50	(1)B2
San Cristóbal	Solomon Islands	114	G7
San Cristóbal	Venezuela	50	C2
San Diego	United States	29	C4
San Doná di Piave	Italy	73	H5
San Felipe	Mexico	32	D5
San Francisco	United States	29	B3
San Francisco del Oro	Mexico	32	E6
San Joaquin Valley	United States	29	B3
San José	Costa Rica	50	A2
San José	Mexico	46	B3
San Jose	United States	29	B3
San Juan	Puerto Rico	47	L5
San Juan	Argentina	52	H5
San Juan Basin	United States	32	E4
San Julián	Argentina	52	H8
San Luis Obispo	United States	29	B3
San Luis Potosi	Mexico	33	F7
San Luis Valley	United States	32	E4
San Marino	Europe	74	G5
San Miguel de Tucuman	Argentina	52	H4
San Pablo	Philippines	107	G4
San Pedro Sula	Honduras	46	G5
San Pietro	Sardinia (Italy)	75	C9
San Rafael	Argentina	52	H5
San Remo	Italy	72	C7
San Salvador	Bahamas	47	K4
San Salvador	Ecuador	50	(1)A2
San Salvador	El Salvador	46	F6
San Sebastián	Spain	71	H1
San Severo	Italy	76	C8
San-Pédro	Côte dIvoire	92	C3
San´a´	Yemen	82	D6
Sanaga	West Africa	93	G4
Sanandaj	Iran	82	E2
Sand	Norway	59	D7
Sandakan	Malaysia	112	F1
Sandanski	Bulgaria	77	L8
Sanday	United Kingdom	66	L2
Sandefjord	Norway	59	E7
Sanderson	United States	33	F5
Sandy Cape	Australia	117	K4
Sangerhausen	Germany	65	G5
Sangli	India	105	B5
Sanhago del Estrero	Argentina	52	J4
Sankt Pölten	Austria	73	L2
Sankt Wendel	Germany	65	C7
Sankt-Peterburg (St. Petersburg)	Russia	60	G2
Sankuru	Democratic Republic Of Congo	94	C4
Sanlúcar de Barrameda	Spain	70	D8
Sanok	Poland	63	M8
Santa Ana	United States	46	A2
Santa Barbara	United States	29	C4
Santa Catalina	United States	29	C4
Santa Cruz	Bolivia	50	E7
Santa Cruz	Ecuador	50	(1)A2
Santa Cruz	Canary Islands (Spain)	88	B3
Santa Cruz Islands	Solomon Islands	114	G7
Santa Fé	Argentina	52	J5
Santa Fe	United States	32	E4
Santa Isabel	Solomon Islands	114	F6
Santa Luzia	Cape Verde	92	(1)B1
Santa Maria	Brazil	53	L4
Santa Maria	Ecuador	50	(1)A2
Santa Maria	Azores (Portugal)	88	(1)B2
Santa Maria	United States	29	B4
Santa Marta	Colombia	50	C1
Santa Rosa	Argentina	52	J6
Santa Rosa	United States	29	B3
Santander	Spain	70	F1
Santarém	Brazil	51	G4
Santarém	Portugal	70	B5
Santiago	Chile	52	G5
Santiago de Compostela	Spain	70	B2
Santiago de Cuba	Cuba	47	J4
Santo Antão	Cape Verde	92	(1)A1
Santos	Brazil	53	M3
São Jorge	Azores (Portugal)	88	(1)B2
São José do Rio Prêto	Brazil	51	H8
São Luís	Brazil	51	J4
São Miguel	Azores (Portugal)	88	(1)B2
São Nicolau	Cape Verde	92	(1)B1
São Paulo	Brazil	53	M3
São Tiago	Cape Verde	92	(1)B2
São Tomé	São Tomé and Principe	93	F4
São Tomé and Príncipe	West Africa	93	F4
São Vicente	Cape Verde	92	(1)A1
Saône	France	69	K7
Saoura	Algeria	89	E3
Sapiéntza	Greece	78	D8
Sapporo	Japan	111	L2
Sarajevo	Bosnia-Herzegovina	76	F6
Saramati	Myanmar (Burma)	106	B1
Sarangani Islands	Philippines	113	B1
Saransk	Russia	60	K4
Sarasota	United States	35	K6
Sarasota	United States	35	K6
Saratoga Springs	United States	37	M3
Saratov	Russia	60	K4
Sarawak	Malaysia	107	E6
Sardegna (Sardinia)	Italy	54	E3
Sardinia (Sardegna)	Italy	75	C9

Sarektjåkkå	Sweden	58	J3
Sargasso Sea	Central America	47	L3
Sargodha	Pakistan	83	K3
Sarh	Chad	90	C6
Sarigan	Northern Mariana Islands (U.S.)	114	E4
Sarine	Switzerland	72	C4
Sarinena	Spain	71	K3
Sarir Kalanshiyu	Libya	90	D2
Sariyer	Turkey	77	R8
Sark	United Kingdom	67	L12
Sarnia	Canada	45	Q8
Saronikós Kólpos	Greece	78	F7
Saros Körfezi	Turkey	80	B3
Sarr Tibesti	Libya	90	C3
Sarrebourg	France	68	N5
Sarreguemines	France	57	L5
Saryer	Turkey	79	L3
Sarykamys	Kazakhstan	61	L5
Sarykamyshkoye Ozero	Turkmenistan / Uzbekistan	101	K9
Sasebo	Japan	110	E7
Saskatchewan	Canada	38	K6
Saskatoon	Canada	43	K6
Sassandra	West Africa	92	C3
Sassari	Sardinia (Italy)	75	C8
Saßnitz	Germany	64	J2
Sassuolo	Italy	72	F6
Sata-Misaki	Japan	110	F8
Satu Mare	Romania	77	K2
Saudi Arabia	Middle East	82	D4
Saül	French Guyana	51	G3
Sault Saint Marie	Canada	36	K2
Saumur	France	68	E6
Saurimo	Angola	94	C5
Sausalito	United States	29	B3
Sava	Europe	73	K4
Sava	Croatia	76	C4
Savaii	Western Samoa	115	J7
Savannah	United States	35	K5
Savannah River	United States	35	K5
Save	South Africa	97	E4
Savoie	France	69	M8
Savolinna	Finland	58	Q6
Savona	Italy	72	D6
Sawu	Indonesia	116	D2
Sawu Sea	Indonesia	113	B4
Sayn-Sand	Mongolia	102	J8
Sázava	Czech Republic	63	E8
Scafell Pike	United Kingdom	67	K7
Scapa Flow	United Kingdom	66	K3
Schaalsee	Germany	64	F3
Schaffhausen	Switzerland	72	D3
Scharhörn	Germany	64	D3
Schawäbisch Hau	Germany	65	E7
Schefferville	Canada	44	T5
Scheibbs	Austria	73	L2
Schelde	Belgium	57	H3
Schiermonnikoog	Netherlands	57	J1
Schio	Italy	72	G5
Schladming	Austria	73	J3
Schleiden	Germany	65	B6
Schleswig	Germany	64	E2
Schruns	Austria	72	E3
Schwabach	Germany	65	G7
Schwandorf	Germany	65	H7
Schwäbische Alb	Germany	65	D8
Schwarzwald	Germany	65	D9
Schwedt	Germany	64	K3
Schweinfurt	Germany	65	F6
Schwerin	Germany	64	G3
Schweriner See	Germany	64	G3
Sciassa	Italy	75	K11
Scotia Ridge	Atlantic Ocean	49	F9
Scotland	United Kingdom	66	H5
Scott Island	Antarctica	120	(2)Z3
Scottsbluff	United States	31	F3
Scranton	United States	37	L3
Sea of Azov	Ukraine	60	H5
Sea of Japan	East Asia	110	H4
Sea of Japan (Tong-Hae / Nippon-Kai)	South East Asia	109	J2
Sea of Marmara (Marmara Denizi)	Turkey	80	B3
Sea of Ochotsk (Hok-Kai)	East Asia	111	M1
Sea of the Hebrides	United Kingdom	66	F5
Seal Point	South Africa	96	C6
Searcy	United States	34	H4
Seaside	United States	28	B1
Seattle	United States	28	B1
Seaward Kaikoura Range	New Zealand	119	E6
Sebkha Azzel Matti	Algeria	89	F3
Sebkha de Timimoun	Algeria	89	F3
Sebkha de Tindouf	Algeria	88	D3
Sebkha Mekherrhane	Algeria	89	F3
Sebkhet Oumm ed Dros Guebli	Mauritania	88	C4
Sebkhet Oumm ed Dros Telli	Mauritania	88	C4
Sebkra du Ndaghamcha	Mauritania	88	B5
Secretary Island	New Zealand	119	B7
Sedan	France	57	H5
Sedano	Spain	70	G2
Segezha	Russia	60	G2
Ségou	Mali	88	D6
Segovia	Spain	70	F4
Segre	Spain	71	L3
Seguam Island	Alaska (U.S.)	29	(3)D1
Séguéla	Côte dIvoire	92	C3
Segura	Spain	71	J6
Seiland	Norway	58	M1
Seine	France	68	J5
Sekondi-Takoradi	Ghana	92	D4
Selat Balabac	Malaysia / Philippines	107	F5
Selat Mentawai	Asia	112	B3
Selecka Planina	Macedonia	78	D3
Selenter See	Germany	64	F2
Selfoss	Iceland	58	C3
Selkirk Mountains	United States / Canada	41	H7
Selsey Bill	United Kingdom	68	E3

Selwyn Lake	*Canada*	42	L4
Selwyn Mountains	*Canada*	40	E4
Semarang	*Indonesia*	112	E4
Semipalatinsk	*Kazakhstan*	101	P7
Sendai	*Japan*	111	L4
Sendai-Wan	*Japan*	111	L4
Senegal	*Mauritania*	88	C5
Senigallia	*Italy*	72	J7
Senj	*Croatia*	76	B5
Senja	*Norway*	58	J2
Senkaku-Gunto	*Japan*	109	G5
Sens	*France*	68	H5
Senta	*Yugoslavia*	76	H4
Seoul (Soul)	*South Korea*	110	D5
Sepúlveda	*Spain*	70	G3
Sept-Iles	*Canada*	45	T6
Sequoia National Park	*United States*	29	C3
Seram (Ceram)	*Indonesia*	113	C3
Sérifos	*Greece*	78	G7
Serov	*Russia*	61	N3
Serowe	*Botswana*	96	D4
Serra do Mogadouro	*Portugal*	70	D3
Serra da Estrela	*Portugal*	70	C4
Serra da Mantiqueira	*Brazil*	53	M3
Serra da Neve	*Angola*	96	A2
Serra da Nogueira	*Portugal*	70	D3
Serra de Maracaju	*Brazil*	53	K3
Serra de Monchique	*Portugal*	70	B7
Serra do Espanhaço	*Brazil*	48	G5
Serra do Gerês	*Spain*	70	C3
Serra do Mar	*Brazil*	53	L4
Serra do Marão	*Portugal*	70	C3
Serra dos Parecis	*Brazil*	50	E5
Serra Geral	*Brazil*	53	L4
Serra Geral do Paraná	*Brazil*	51	H6
Serra Namuli	*Mozambique*	97	F3
Sérrai	*Greece*	78	F3
Serranía de Cuenca	*Spain*	71	H4
Sète	*France*	69	J10
Sétif	*Algeria*	89	G1
Setit	*North East Africa*	91	G5
Seto Naikai	*Japan*	110	G6
Sétubal	*Portugal*	70	B6
Sevastopol	*Ukraine*	60	G6
Severn	*United Kingdom*	67	L10
Severnaya Dvina	*Russia*	60	J2
Severnaya Zemlya	*Russia*	100	S1
Severnyy Ural	*Russia*	61	M2
Severo-Sibirskaya Nizmennost (North Siberian Plain)	*Russia*	100	S3
Severodvinsk	*Russia*	60	H2
Sevier Lake	*United States*	30	D4
Sevilla	*Spain*	70	E7
Sèvre	*France*	69	E7
Seychelles	*Indian Ocean*	97	(2)A2
Seymour	*United States*	36	J4
Sfax	*Tunisia*	89	H2
Sfîntu Gheorghe	*Romania*	77	N4
Shaib Nisah	*Saudi Arabia*	85	B4
Shakhty	*Russia*	60	J5
Shakotan-Misaki	*Japan*	111	K2
Shaluli Shan	*China*	108	B4
Shanghai	*China*	109	G4
Shanghang	*China*	107	F1
Shannon	*Ireland*	67	E9
Shantou	*China*	108	F6
Shaoguan	*China*	108	E5
Shaoxing	*China*	109	G4
Shaoyang	*China*	108	E5
Shaqra	*Saudi Arabia*	85	A4
Shark Bay	*Australia*	116	B5
Shark Reef	*Australia*	117	J2
Sharya	*Russia*	60	J3
Shashe	*South Africa*	96	D4
Shashi	*China*	108	E4
Shasta Lake	*United States*	29	B2
Shatt al Arab	*Middle East*	85	B1
Shawinigan	*FallsCanada*	37	M2
Shawinigan Falls	*Canada*	45	S7
Sheboygan	*United States*	36	J3
Sheffield	*United Kingdom*	67	M8
Sheffield	*United States*	34	J5
Shelby (MT)	*United States*	30	D2
Shelby (NC)	*United States*	35	K4
Shelbyville	*United States*	35	J4
Shelikof Strait	*Alaska (U.S.)*	29	(1)F4
Shelter Point	*New Zealand*	119	C8
Shenyang	*China*	109	G2
Sherbro Island	*Sierra Leone*	92	B3
Sherbrooke	*Canada*	45	S7
Sheridan	*United States*	30	E3
Shetland Islands	*United Kingdom*	66	N1
Sheykh Shoeyb	*Iran*	85	E2
Shib Kuh	*Iran*	85	D2
Shibushi-Wan	*Japan*	110	F8
Shijiazhuang	*China*	108	E3
Shikoku	*Japan*	110	G7
Shikoku-Sanchi	*Japan*	110	G7
Shikotan-To	*Russia*	103	R8
Shikotsu-Ko	*Japan*	111	L2
Shilega	*Russia*	60	J2
Shiliguri	*India*	104	E3
Shilla	*India*	104	C2
Shillong	*India*	106	A1
Shimoga	*India*	105	C6
Shimonoseki	*Japan*	110	F6
Shinyanga	*Tanzania*	95	E4
Shiono-Misaki	*Japan*	110	H7
Shirane-San	*Japan*	109	K3
Shiretoko-Misaki	*Japan*	111	N1
Shiriya-Zaki	*Japan*	111	L3
Shizuoka	*Japan*	111	K6
Shkodër	*Albania*	78	B2
Shoshoni	*United States*	30	E3
Shraz	*Iran*	82	F4
Shreveport	*United States*	34	H5
Shubar-Kuduk	*Kazakhstan*	61	M5

Shul	*Middle East*	85	D1
Shule He	*China*	108	B2
Shumen	*Bulgaria*	77	P6
Shur	*Iran*	85	E2
Sialkot	*Pakistan*	83	K3
Siargao	*Philippines*	107	H5
Siauliai	*Lithuania*	59	M9
Sibenik	*Croatia*	76	C6
Siberia	*Russia*	100	Q4
Sibiu	*Romania*	77	M4
Sibut	*Central African Republic*	93	H3
Sibuyan	*Philippines*	107	G4
Sibuyan Sea	*Philippines*	107	G4
Sicilia (Sicily)	*Italy*	75	H11
Sicilian Channel	*Italy*	75	F11
Sicily (Sicilia)	*Italy*	75	H11
Sidi Aissa	*Algeria*	71	P9
Sidney (MT)	*United States*	31	F2
Sidney (OH)	*United States*	36	K3
Sidorovosk	*Russia*	61	S1
Siedlce	*Poland*	62	M5
Siegen	*Germany*	65	D6
Siena	*Italy*	74	F5
Sierra de Alcaraz	*Spain*	71	H6
Sierra de Almijara	*Spain*	70	F8
Sierra de Aracena	*Spain*	70	C7
Sierra de Gúdar	*Spain*	71	K4
Sierra de Gata	*Spain*	70	D4
Sierra de Gredos	*Spain*	70	E4
Sierra de Guadarrama	*Spain*	70	F4
Sierra de la Peña	*Spain*	71	J2
Sierra de Taibilla	*Spain*	71	H7
Sierra Leone	*West Africa*	92	B3
Sierra Madre	*Mexico*	46	F5
Sierra Madre Occidental	*Mexico*	46	C3
Sierra Madre Oriental	*Mexico*	46	D4
Sierra Mojada	*Mexico*	33	F6
Sierra Morena	*Spain*	70	E6
Sierra Nevada	*Spain*	70	G8
Sierra Nevada	*United States*	29	B3
Sierra Vista	*United States*	32	D5
Sierras de Córdoba	*Argentina*	52	H5
Sifnos	*Greece*	78	G8
Sig	*Algeria*	71	K9
Sighetu Marmatiei	*Romania*	77	L2
Sighisoara	*Romania*	77	M3
Signy Island	*South Atlantic Ocean*	120	(2)A3
Sikeston	*United States*	34	J4
Sikhote-Alin	*Russia*	102	N8
Sikinos	*Greece*	78	G8
Silhouette	*Seychelles*	97	(2) B1
Siling Co	*China*	104	E2
Silistra	*Bulgaria*	77	Q5
Siljan	*Sweden*	59	H6
Silka	*Russia*	102	K6
Silvretta Gruppe	*Austria / Switzerland*	72	F4
Simbirsk	*Russia*	61	K4
Simferopol	*Ukraine*	60	G6
Simi	*Greece*	79	K8
Simmern	*Germany*	65	C7
Simpson Desert	*Australia*	117	G5
Simrishamn	*Sweden*	59	H9
Sinai	*Egypt*	84	A6
Sindelfingen Böblingen	*Germany*	65	E8
Sines	*Portugal*	70	B7
Singapore	*Asia*	112	C2
Singen	*Germany*	65	D9
Singkawang	*Indonesia*	112	D2
Sinj	*Croatia*	76	D6
Sinjavina	*Yugoslavia*	76	G7
Sinop Burun	*Turkey*	80	F3
Sinsheim	*Germany*	65	D7
Sintana	*Romania*	63	C11
Sinuiju	*North Korea*	110	C3
Sion	*Switzerland*	69	N7
Sioux City	*United States*	31	G3
Sioux Falls	*United States*	31	G3
Sir Bani Yas	*United Arab Emirates*	85	E4
Sir Edward Pellew Group	*Australia*	117	G3
Siracusa (Syracuse)	*Sicily (Italy)*	75	K11
Siros	*Greece*	78	G7
Sisak	*Croatia*	76	D4
Sistema Central	*Spain*	70	D4
Sistema Penibético	*Spain*	70	E8
Sistemas Béticos	*Spain*	70	E8
Sittwe	*Myanmar (Burma)*	106	A2
Siwalik Range	*Nepal / India*	104	D3
Sjasstroj	*Russia*	60	G2
Sjlland	*Denmark*	59	F9
Skadarsko Jezero	*Yugoslavia*	76	G7
Skiathos	*Greece*	78	F5
Skagen	*Denmark*	59	F8
Skagerrak	*Norway / Denmark*	59	D8
Skaidi	*Norway*	58	Ni
Skarsvåg	*Norway*	58	N1
Skeena Mountains	*Canada*	40	E5
Skegness	*United Kingdom*	56	D1
Skellefte älv	*Sweden*	58	K4
Skellefteå	*Sweden*	58	L4
Skhiza	*Greece*	78	D8
Skien	*Norway*	59	E7
Skierniewic	*Poland*	62	K6
Skiftet Kihti	*Finland*	59	L7
Skikda	*Algeria*	89	G1
Skiros	*Greece*	78	G6
Skjálfandafljöt	*Iceland*	58	(1)E2
Skjálfandi	*Iceland*	58	(1)E1
Skopje	*Macedonia*	78	D2
Skópelos	*Greece*	78	F5
Skye	*United Kingdom*	66	G4
Slagelse	*Denmark*	64	G1
Slantsy	*Russia*	60	F3
Slatina	*Romania*	77	M5
Slavkoje	*Ukraine*	63	N9
Slavonski Brod	*Croatia*	76	F4
Slavskoje	*Ukraine*	77	L1
Slavyansk	*Ukraine*	60	H5

Slievefelim Mountains	*Ireland*	67	E9
Sligo	*Ireland*	67	E7
Sliven	*Bulgaria*	77	P7
Slobozia	*Romania*	77	Q6
Slomim	*Belarus*	59	N10
Slovakia	*Europe*	63	H9
Slovenia	*Europe*	73	K5
Slyne Head	*Ireland*	67	C8
Smallingerland	*Netherlands*	57	K1
Smallwood Réservoir	*Canada*	45	U6
Smederevo	*Yugoslavia*	76	H5
Smålandsfarvandet	*Denmark*	64	G1
Smith Falls	*Canada*	37	L3
Smla	*Norway*	58	D5
Smoky Hills	*United States*	31	G4
Smolensk	*Russia*	60	G4
Smolikas	*Greece*	78	C4
Smolyan	*Bulgaria*	77	M8
Smyrna (Izmir)	*Turkey*	80	B4
Snake River	*United States*	28	C2
Snåsavatn	*Norway*	58	F4
Snderborg	*Denmark*	59	E9
Sneek	*Netherlands*	57	J1
Snezka	*Czech Republic / Poland*	63	E7
Snowdon	*United Kingdom*	67	J9
Snowdonia	*United Kingdom*	67	J9
Sobaek-Sanmaek	*South Korea*	110	D6
Sobat	*Central Africa*	91	F6
Sochi (Soci)	*Russia*	81	H2
Soci (Sochi)	*Russia*	81	H2
Society Islands	*French Polynesia*	115	L7
Socorro	*United States*	32	E5
Socotra	*Yemen*	83	F7
Sodankylä	*Finland*	58	P3
Södehamn	*Sweden*	59	J6
Södra Kvarken	*Sweden / Finland*	59	K6
Sofia (Sofiya)	*Bulgaria*	77	L7
Sofiya (Sofia)	*Bulgaria*	77	L7
Sofporog	*Russia*	58	R4
Sogamoso	*Colombia*	50	C2
Sognefjorden	*Norway*	59	C6
Sohâg	*Egypt*	91	F2
Sohuksan	*South Korea*	110	C6
Soissons	*France*	56	G5
Sojoson-Man	*North Korea / China*	110	C4
Söke	*Turkey*	79	K7
Sokolov	*Czech Republic*	63	B7
Sokolov Podlaski	*Poland*	59	M10
Sokoto	*Nigeria*	93	F2
Sokoto	*West Africa*	93	E2
Solapur	*India*	105	C5
Solihull	*United Kingdom*	56	B2
Solimões	*South America*	50	D4
Solingen	*Germany*	65	C5
Sollefteå	*Sweden*	58	J5
Solomon Islands	*Oceania*	114	G6
Solta	*Croatia*	76	D6
Soltau	*Germany*	64	E4
Solunska	*Macedonia*	78	D3
Solway Firth	*United Kingdom*	67	K7
Solwezi	*Zambia*	94	D6
Somalia	*Central Africa*	95	H3
Sombar	*Yugoslavia*	76	G4
Somerset	*United States*	35	K4
Somerset Island	*Canada*	42	M2
Somes	*Hungary / Romania*	77	L2
Somme	*France*	68	H3
Son	*India*	104	D4
Söndre Strmfjord	*Greenland*	39	V3
Sondrio	*Italy*	72	E4
Songea	*Tanzania*	95	F6
Songera	*Tanzania*	106	F2
Songhua Hu	*China*	109	H2
Songhua Jiang	*China*	109	H1
Songkhla	*Thailand*	106	C5
Sonneberg	*Germany*	65	G6
Sonsorol Islands	*Palau*	113	D1
Sont	*Denmark / Sweden*	59	G9
Sopka Shiveluch	*Russia*	103	U5
Sopron	*Hungary*	76	D2
Sora	*Italy*	74	H7
Sorel	*Canada*	37	M2
Soria	*Spain*	71	H3
Soroki	*Moldova*	77	R1
Sorraia	*Portugal*	70	B5
Sorsele	*Sweden*	58	J4
Sort	*Spain*	71	M2
Sortavala	*Russia*	58	R6
Sosnow	*Poland*	63	J7
Sotra	*Norway*	59	C6
Souix Lookout	*Canada*	43	N7
Souk Ahras	*Tunisia*	75	B12
Soul (Seoul)	*South Korea*	110	D5
Soumussalmi	*Finland*	58	Q4
Sound of Jura	*United Kingdom*	66	H6
Sound of Raasay	*United Kingdom*	66	G4
Sound of Sleat	*United Kingdom*	66	G5
Sousse	*Tunisia*	89	H1
South Africa	*South Africa*	96	C6
South Andaman	*India*	105	F6
South Aulatsivik Island	*Canada*	44	U5
South Australia	*Australia*	116	F5
South Bend	*United States*	36	J3
South Carolina	*United States*	35	K5
South China Sea (Nan Hai)	*China*	108	F6
South Dakota	*United States*	31	F3
South Downs	*United Kingdom*	67	N11
South East Cape	*Australia*	117	J8
South Georgia	*South Atlantic Ocean*	53	P9
South Island	*New Zealand*	119	C7
South Korea	*South East Asia*	109	H3
South Orkney Islands	*South Atlantic Ocean*	120	(2)A4
South Platte River	*United States*	31	F3
South Portland	*United States*	37	M3
South Ronaldsay	*United Kingdom*	66	L3
South Taranaki Bight	*New Zealand*	118	D4
South Uist	*United Kingdom*	66	F4

Tanafjord	Norway	58	Q1
Tanami Desert	Australia	116	F3
Tanca	Peru	50	C7
Tanega-Shima	Japan	110	F8
Tanezrouft	Algeria	89	E4
Tanezrouft-Tan-Ahenet	Algeria	89	F4
Tanga	Tanzania	95	F5
Tanggula (Dangla) Shan	China	104	E2
Tanggula Shan	China	104	F2
Tangier	Morocco	88	D1
Tangra Yumco	China	104	E2
Tanimbar Islands	Indonesia	114	D6
Tanjung Cina	Indonesia	112	C4
Tanjung Deyong	Indonesia	113	E4
Tanjung Guhakolak	Indonesia	112	C4
Tanjung Libobo	Indonesia	113	C3
Tanjung Mengkalihat	Indonesia	113	A2
Tanjung Pangkalsiang	Indonesia	113	B3
Tanjung Perkam	Indonesia	113	E3
Tanjung Selatan	Indonesia	112	E3
Tanjung Sopi	Indonesia	113	C2
Tanjung Vals	Indonesia	113	E4
Tannu Ola	Mongolia / Russia	101	S7
Tanta	Egypt	91	F1
Tanzania	Central Africa	95	E5
Taos	United States	32	E4
Taoudenni	Mali	88	E4
Taïyetos	Greece	78	E7
Tapa	Estonia	59	N7
Tapajós	South America	51	F4
Tappi-Zaki	Japan	111	K3
Tapul	Philippines	113	B1
Tara	Yugoslavia	76	G6
Tara	Yugoslavia	76	G6
Tara	Russia	61	Q3
Taranto	Italy	75	M8
Tararua Range	New Zealand	118	E5
Tarasa	India	105	F7
Tarawa	Kiribati (Pacific Ocean)	114	H5
Tarbagataj	Kazakhstan	101	Q8
Tarbes	France	71	L1
Tarábulus (Tripoli)	Libya	90	B1
Tarija	Bolivia	51	E8
Tarim Basin	China	101	Q10
Tarim He	China	101	Q9
Tarko-Sale	Russia	61	R2
Tarn	France	69	G10
Tärnaby	Sweden	58	H4
Tarnobrzeg	Poland	63	L7
Tarnow	Poland	63	L7
Taroudannt	Morocco	88	D2
Tarragona	Spain	71	M3
Tarrasa	Spain	71	M3
Tarso Emisu	Chad	90	C3
Tarsus	Turkey	80	F5
Tartagul	Argentina	51	E8
Tartu	Estonia	59	P7
Tartus	Syrius	84	C2
Tarut	Saudi Arabia	85	D3
Tashauz	Turkmenistan	101	K9
Tashkent	Uzbekistan	101	M9
Tasikmalaya	Indonesia	112	D4
Tåsinge	Denmark	64	F2
Tasman Bay	New Zealand	118	D5
Tasman Sea	Australia	117	K7
Tasmania	Australia	117	J8
Tassili-Najjer	Algeria	89	G3
Tassili-Oua-n-Ahaggar	Algeria	89	F4
Tata Mailau	Indonesia	113	C4
Tatabánya	Hungary	76	F2
Tatarbunary	Ukraine	77	S4
Tatarskiy Proliv	Russia	103	Q7
Tathlina Lake	Canada	38	H4
Tatry	Poland / Slovakia	63	J8
Taunus	Germany	65	D6
Taurage	Lithuania	62	M2
Tauranga	New Zealand	118	F3
Tauroa Point	New Zealand	118	D2
Tauyskaya Guba	Russia	103	R5
Tavda	Russia	61	P3
Tavda	Russia	61	N3
Tavoy	Myanmar (Burma)	106	B4
Tawau	Malaysia	107	F6
Tawitawi	Philippines	113	A2
Tay	United Kingdom	66	K5
Taza	Morocco	88	E2
Tbilisi (Tiflis)	Georgia	81	L3
Tczew	Poland	62	H3
Tecer Daglari	Turkey	80	G4
Tecuci	Romania	77	Q4
Tedzhen	Turkmenistan / Afghanistan	83	H2
Tees	United Kingdom	67	L7
Tegucigalpa	Honduras	47	G6
Teheran (Tehran)	Iran	82	E2
Tehi-n-Isser	Algeria	89	G3
Tehran (Teheran)	Iran	82	E2
Tejo	Spain / Portugal	70	B5
Teke Burun	Turkey	78	J6
Tekirdag	Turkey	79	K3
Tekke Burun	Turkey	78	H4
Tel Aviv-Yafo (Jaffa)	Israel	84	B4
Telukan Darvel	Malaysia	107	F6
Telukan Labuk	Malaysia	107	F5
Telukbetung	Indonesia	112	D4
Temirtau	Kazakhstan	61	Q4
Temple	United States	33	G5
Temuco	Chile	52	G6
Ten Degree Channel	Andaman Islands and Nicobar	105	F7
Tenali	India	105	C5
Ténéré	Niger	89	G5
Ténéré du Tafassasset	Niger	89	G4
Tenerife	Canary Islands (Spain)	88	B3
Ténès	Algeria	71	M8
Tennessee	United States	35	J4
Tennessee River	United States	35	J5
Tepic	Mexico	26	F7
Tepic	Mexico	46	D4
Teplice	Czech Republic	65	J6
Teramo	Italy	74	H6
Terceira	Azores (Portugal)	88	(1)B2
Teresina	Brazil	51	J5
Terminillo	Italy	74	H6
Terneuzen	Netherlands	57	G3
Terni	Italy	74	G6
Ternopol	Ukraine	60	F5
Terre Haut	United States	36	J4
Tersakan Gölü	Turkey	79	Q6
Terschelling	Netherlands	57	J1
Teruel	Spain	71	J4
Teseney	Eritrea	91	G4
Tessiner Alps	Switzerland / Italy	74	C2
Testa del Gargano	Croatia	76	D8
Teton Village	United States	30	D3
Tétouan	Morocco	88	D1
Tetovo	Macedonia	78	D2
Teutoburger Wald	Germany	64	D4
Tevriz	Russia	61	Q3
Texarkana	United States	34	H5
Texas	United States	33	G5
Texel	Netherlands	57	H1
Thabana Ntlenyana	Lesotho	96	D5
Thailand	South East Asia	106	C3
Thames	United Kingdom	67	P10
Thanjavur	India	105	C6
Thásos	Greece	78	G4
The Black Sugarloaf	Australia	117	K6
The Cheviot	United Kingdom	66	L6
The Dalles	United States	28	B1
The Everglades	United States	35	K6
The Gulf	Middle East	85	C2
The Hague (s-Gravenhage) (Den Haag)	Netherlands	68	J1
The Needles	United Kingdom	56	B4
The Round Mountain	Australia	117	K6
The Solent	United Kingdom	67	M11
The Wash	United Kingdom	67	P8
The Weald	United Kingdom	67	N10
Themiet el Had	Algeria	71	N9
Thermaikós Kólpos	Greece	78	E4
Thessaloniki (Saloniki)	Greece	78	E4
Thetford mines	Canada	37	M2
Thiés	Senegal	88	B6
Thiladunmathi Atoll	Maldives	105	B7
Thionville	France	57	K5
Thira (Santorini)	Greece	78	G8
Thomasville	United States	35	K5
Thompson	Canada	43	M5
Thomson River	Australia	117	H4
Thonon-les-Bains	France	72	B4
Thousand Islands	Canada	37	L3
Thrakikó Pélagos	Greece	78	G4
Three Kings Islands	New Zealand	118	C2
Thun	Switzerland	69	N7
Thunder Bay	Canada	43	P7
Thuner See	Switzerland	72	C4
Thüringer Wald	Germany	65	F6
Ti-n-Toumma	Niger	89	H5
Tianjin	China	108	F3
Tiber Reservoir	United States	30	D2
Tibesti	Chad	90	C3
Tibet	China	104	D2
Tiburón	Mexico	46	B3
Tidjika	Mauritania	88	C5
Tiel	Netherlands	57	J3
Tien Shan	China	101	Q9
Tienen	Belgium	57	H4
Tietê	Brazil	53	L3
Tiflis (Tbilisi)	Georgia	81	L3
Tifton	United States	35	K5
Tighina	Moldova	77	S3
Tigris (Dicle)	Middle East	85	B1
Tihamat Ash Sham	Saudi Arabia	82	D5
Tijuana	Mexico	46	A2
Tikhoreck	Russia	60	J5
Tikhvin	Russia	61	G3
Tiksi	Russia	102	M2
Tilburg	Netherlands	57	J3
Tillamook	United States	28	B1
Tillanchang	India	105	F7
Tilos	Greece	79	K8
Timanskiy Kryazh	Russia	100	H5
Timaru	New Zealand	119	D7
Timimoun	Algeria	89	F3
Timisoara	Romania	76	J4
Timmins	Canada	43	Q7
Timor	Indonesia	114	C6
Timor Sea	South East Asia	113	C5
Tinaca Point	Philippines	107	G5
Tindouf	Algeria	88	D3
Tinée	France	72	C6
Tingsryd	Sweden	62	D1
Tinos	Greece	78	H7
Tirana (Tiranë)	Albania	78	B3
Tiranë (Tirana)	Albania	78	B3
Tiraspol	Moldova	77	S3
Tiraz Mountains	Namibia	96	B5
Tiree	United Kingdom	66	F5
Tirgoviste	Romania	77	N5
Tîrgu Jiu	Romania	77	L4
Tîrgu Mures	Romania	77	M3
Tirunelveli	India	105	C7
Tisza	Europe	76	H2
Titov Veles	Macedonia	78	D3
Titov vrh	Macedonia	78	C3
Titovo Uzice	Yugoslavia	76	G6
Tizi Ouzou	Algeria	89	F1
Tjeukemeer	Netherlands	57	J2
Tjörn	Sweden	59	F8
Toamasina	Madagascar	97	J3
Toba & Kakar Ranges	Pakistan	83	J3
Tobago	Central America	50	E1
Tobi	Palau	113	D2
Tobolsk	Russia	61	P3
Tobseda	Russia	61	L1
Todoga-Saki	Japan	111	M4
Togo	West Africa	92	E3
Toi-Misaki	Japan	110	F8
Toïl	Algeria	89	F1
Tok-To (Take-Shima)	South Korea / Japan	110	G5
Tokara-Retto	Japan	114	D2
Tokelau	New Zealand	115	J6
Tokuno-Shima	Japan	109	H5
Tokushima	Japan	110	H7
Tokyo	Japan	111	K6
Tokyo-Wan	Japan	111	K6
Tôlanaro	Madagascar	97	H4
Toledo	Spain	70	G5
Toledo	United States	36	K3
Toledo Bend Reservoir	United States	34	H5
Toliara	Madagascar	97	G4
Tolmezzo	Italy	73	J4
Toluca de Lerdo	Mexico	46	D5
Tolyatti	Russia	101	H7
Tomaszów Mazowiecki	Poland	62	K6
Tombouctou	Mali	88	E5
Tomelloso	Spain	70	G5
Tomkinson Ranges	Australia	116	E6
Tomsk	Russia	101	R6
Tong-Hae / Nippon-Kai (Sea of Japan)	South East Asia	109	J2
Tonga	Oceania	115	J7
Tonga Islands	Tonga	115	J8
Tonga Trench	Oceania	115	J8
Tongatapu Group	Tonga	115	J8
Tonghua	China	110	C3
Tongjoson-Man	North Korea	110	D4
Tonle Sap	Cambodia	106	C4
Tonopah	United States	29	C3
Tooele	United States	30	D3
Topeka	United States	31	G4
Topozero	Russia	58	R4
Tori-Shima (Japan)	Japan	114	E3
Torino (Turin)	Italy	74	B3
Törmänen	Finland	58	P2
Tormes	Spain	70	E3
Tirnaveni	Romania	77	M3
Torne älv	Sweden	58	L3
Torne träsk	Sweden	58	K2
Tornio	Finland	58	N4
Tornionjoki	Finland	58	N3
Toronto	Canada	45	R8
Toros Daglari	Turkey	80	E5
Torquay	United Kingdom	67	K11
Torrelavega	Spain	70	F1
Torres Strait	Australia	117	H2
Torreón	Mexico	46	D3
Torrington	United States	31	F3
Tortona	Italy	72	D6
Tortosa	Spain	71	L4
Torun	Poland	62	H4
Torysa	Slovakia	76	J1
Torzhok	Russia	60	G3
Totma	Russia	60	J3
Tottori	Japan	110	H6
Tougan	Burkina Faso	92	D2
Toul	France	72	A2
Toulon	France	69	M10
Toulouse	France	69	G10
Tourcoing	France	68	H3
Tournai	Belgium	56	G4
Tours	France	68	F6
Townsville	Australia	117	J3
Toyama	Japan	111	J5
Toyama-Wan	Japan	111	J5
Toyohashi	Japan	111	J6
Tozeur	Tunisia	89	G2
Trablous (Tripoli)	Lebanon	84	C2
Trabzon	Turkey	81	H3
Trail	Canada	41	H7
Trapani	Italy	75	G11
Traunsee	Austria	73	J3
Traunstein	Germany	63	B10
Travers City	United States	36	J3
Traverse City	United States	36	J3
Treasure Cay	Bahamas	35	L6
Trebic	Czech Republic	63	E8
Tregosse Islets	Australia	117	K3
Trelew	Argentina	52	H7
Trelleborg	Sweden	62	C2
Tremiti	Italy	76	C7
Trencin	Slovakia	63	H9
Trent	United Kingdom	67	M9
Trento	Italy	74	F2
Trenton	United States	37	M3
Treviso	Italy	73	H5
Trier	Germany	65	B7
Trieste	Italy	74	H3
Triglav	Slovakia	76	A3
Trikkala	Greece	78	D5
Trinec	Czech Republic	63	H8
Trinidad	Central America	50	E1
Trinidad	Bolivia	51	F2
Trinidad and Tobago	Caribbean	47	N6
Trinity Bay	Canada	45	W7
Tripoli (Tarábulus)	Libya	89	H2
Tripoli (Trablous)	Lebanon	84	C2
Tristan Da Cunha	Atlantic Ocean	87	B9
Trivandrum	India	105	C7
Trnava	Slovakia	73	N2
Trofors	Norway	58	G4
Trois Rivières	Canada	45	S7
Troitsko-Pechorsk	Russia	61	M2
Tromso	Norway	58	K2
Trondheim	Norway	58	F5
Trondheimsfjorden	Norway	58	F5
Trout Lake	Canada	40	G4
Troy	United States	35	J5
Troyan	Bulgaria	77	M7
Troyes	France	68	K5
Trujillo	Peru	50	B5

Trung Phan	South East Asia	106	D3
Truro	Canada	45	U7
Trutnov	Czech Republic	63	E7
Trysilelva	Norway	59	G6
Tsaris Mountains	Namibia	96	B4
Tshuapa	Central Africa	94	C4
Tsiafajavona	Madagascar	97	H3
Tsimlyanskoye Vdkhr.	Russia	60	J5
Tsu	Japan	111	J6
Tsuchiura	Japan	111	L5
Tsugaru-Kaikyo	Japan	111	L3
Tsumeb	Namibia	96	B3
Tsuruoka	Japan	111	K4
Tsushima	Japan	110	E6
Tsushima-Kaikyo (Korea Strait)	South Korea / Japan	110	D7
Tuamotu Archipelago	French Polynesia	115	M7
Tubruq	Libya	90	D1
Tubuai	French Polynesia	115	M8
Tubuai Islands	French Polynesia	115	L8
Tucson	United States	32	D5
Tucuruí	Brazil	51	H4
Tudela	Spain	71	J2
Tuktayuktuk	Canada	40	E3
Tula	Russia	60	H4
Tulcea	Romania	77	R4
Tuloma	Russia	58	R2
Tulsa	United States	33	G4
Tumaco	Colombia	50	B3
Tundzha	Bulgaria	77	P7
Tunis	Tunisia	89	H1
Tunisia	North Africa	89	G2
Tununak	Alaska (U.S.)	29	(1)D3
Tuostakh	Russia	103	P3
Tupelo	United States	34	J5
Tura	Russia	102	G4
Turda	Romania	77	L3
Turgay	Kazakhstan	61	N5
Turgayskaya Stolovaya Strana	Kazakhstan	61	N4
Turgovishte	Bulgaria	77	P6
Turia	Spain	71	K5
Turimiquire	Venezuela	50	E2
Turin (Torino)	Italy	74	B3
Turkey	Europe	80	F4
Turkmenistan	Asia	83	G2
Turks and Caicos Islands	Caribbean	47	K4
Turku / Åbo	Finland	59	L6
Turnhout	Belgium	57	H3
Turnu Magurele	Romania	77	M6
Turquino	Cuba	47	J4
Turtle Island	Australia	117	K3
Tuscaloosa	United States	34	J5
Tuskagee	United States	35	J5
Tuticorin	India	105	C7
Tuttlingen	Germany	65	D9
Tutuila	American Samoa	115	K7
Tuul Gol	Mongolia	102	H7
Tuvalu	Oceania	114	H6
Tuxtla Gutiérrez	Mexico	46	F5
Tuz Gölü	Turkey	80	E4
Tuzla	Bosnia Herzegovina	76	F5
Tver	Russia	60	H3
Tweed	United Kingdom	66	L6
Twilight Cove	Australia	116	E6
Twin Falls	United States	30	D3
Twin Islands	Canada	43	Q6
Two Thumb Range	New Zealand	119	D6
Tyan Shan	China	101	Q9
Tychy	Poland	63	J7
Tyler	United States	33	G5
Tyne	United Kingdom	67	M7
Tyrifjorden	Norway	59	E6
Tyrrhenian Sea (Mare Tirreno)	Italy	75	G9
Tyumen	Russia	61	P3

U

Uaupés	Brazil	50	D4
Ubangi	Central Africa	94	B2
Ubangi Chari	Central African Republic	94	B2
Ube	Japan	110	F7
Uberaba	Brazil	53	M2
Uberlândia	Brazil	51	H7
Uchiura-Wan	Japan	111	L2
Udachny	Russia	102	G4
Udaipur	India	104	B4
Uddevalla	Sweden	59	F7
Uddjaur	Sweden	58	K3
Udine	Italy	74	H2
Udskaya Guba	Russia	103	P5
Uecker	Germany	64	K3
Ueda	Japan	111	K5
Ufa	Russia	61	M4
Uganda	Central Africa	95	E3
Ugljan	Croatia	76	C5
Uherské Hradiste	Czech Republic	63	G8
Uíge	Angola	93	H6
Uji-Gunto	Japan	110	E8
Ujjain	India	104	C4
Ujung Pandang	Indonesia	113	A4
Ukhta	Russia	61	L2
Ukiah	United States	29	B3
Ukmerge	Lithuania	62	P2
Ukraine	Europe	60	G5
Ulaanbaatar	Mongolia	102	H7
Ulan Ul Hu	China	104	F1
Ulan-Ude	Russia	102	H6
Ulhasnagar	India	104	B5
Ullung Do	South Korea	109	J3
Ulm	Germany	65	F8
Ulsan	South Korea	110	E6
Ulubat Gölü	Turkey	80	C3
Uludag	Turkey	80	C3
Uluguru Mountains	Tanzania	95	F5
Ulutau	Kazakhstan	61	P5
Ulya	Russia	103	Q5
Umba	Russia	58	T3
Ume älv	Sweden	58	K4
Umeå	Sweden	58	K5
Umm As Samim	Oman	83	G5
Umm Durman (Omdurman)	Sudan	91	F4
Umnak Island	Alaska (U.S.)	29	(1)D5
Umtata	South Africa	96	D6
Una	Croatia	74	L3
Unalaska Island	Alaska (U.S.)	29	(1)D5
Ungava Bay	Canada	44	T5
Ungava Peninsula	Canada	44	S5
Unije	Croatia	76	B5
Unimak Island	Alaska (U.S.)	29	(1)E5
Union City	United States	34	J4
United Arab Emirates	Middle East	85	E5
United Kingdom	Europe	66	M5
United States	North America	26	E4
Unst	United Kingdom	66	N1
Unza	Russia	60	J3
Upington	South Africa	96	C5
Upolu	Western Samoa	115	J7
Upper Klamath Lake	United States	28	B2
Upper Lough Erne	United Kingdom	67	F7
Upper Red Lake	United States	31	H2
Uppsala	Sweden	59	K7
Ural	Kazakhstan	61	L4
Ural Mountains (Uralsskiy Khrebet)	Russia	101	K7
Uralsk	Kazakhstan	61	L4
Uralskiy Khrebet (Ural Mountains)	Russia	101	K7
Uranium City	Canada	43	K5
Uray	Russia	61	N2
Urbino	Italy	73	H7
Urfa	Turkey	81	H5
Urfa Yaylâsi	Turkey	81	H5
Urgench	Uzbekistan	101	L9
Uritskiy	Kazakhstan	61	P4
Uruapan del Progreso	Mexico	46	D5
Uruguaiana	Brazil	53	L3
Uruguay	Uruguay	53	K5
Uruguay	South America	53	K5
Ürümqi	China	101	R9
Uryupinsk	Russia	60	J4
Usak	Turkey	79	M6
Usambara Mountains	Tanzania	95	F4
Usedom	Germany / Poland	64	J3
Usetín	Czech Republic	63	G8
Ushuaia	Argentina	52	H9
Usinsk	Russia	61	M1
Ussel	France	69	H8
Ussuri	Russia	102	N7
Ussuriysk	Russia	110	G1
Ust-Ilimsk	Russia	102	G5
Ust-Isilma	Russia	61	L1
Ust-kamchatsk	Russia	103	U5
Ust-Nera	Russia	103	Q4
Usti nad Labem	Czech Republic	65	K6
Ustica	Italy	75	H10
Usumacinta	Guatemala	46	F5
Utah	United States	30	D4
Utah Lake	United States	30	D3
Utena	Lithuania	59	N9
Utica	United States	37	M3
Utrecht	Netherlands	57	J2
Utrera	Spain	70	E7
Utsjoki	Finland	58	P2
Utsunomiya	Japan	111	K5
Uvéa	Wallis and Futuna	115	J7
Uvalde	United States	33	G6
Uvira	Democratic Republic Of Congo	94	D4
Uvs Nuur	Mongolia	101	S7
Uyo	Nigeria	93	F3
Uzbekistan	Asia	101	L9
Uzgorod	Poland	63	M9
Uzhgorod	Ukraine	77	K1
Uzungwa Range	Tanzania	95	F5
Uzunköprü	Turkey	77	P8

V

Vaal	South Africa	96	D5
Vaasa	Finland	58	L5
Vác	Hungary	76	G2
Vadehavet	Denmark	64	D1
Vadodara	India	83	K5
Vads	Norway	58	Q1
Vågsfjorden	Norway	58	J2
Váh (Vág)	Slovakia	63	H10
Val-dOr	Canada	37	L2
Valdagno	Italy	72	G5
Valdepenas	Spain	70	G6
Valdivia	Chile	52	G6
Valdosta	United States	35	K5
Valence	France	69	K9
Valencia	Spain	71	K5
Valenciennes	France	56	G4
Valentine	United States	31	F3
Valga	Estonia	59	P8
Valjevo	Yugoslavia	76	G5
Vall de Uxó	Spain	71	K5
Valladolid	Spain	70	F3
Vallée de lAzaouak	Mali / Niger	89	F5
Vallée du Tilemsi	Mali	89	F5
Valle	Norway	59	D7
Valletta	Malta	75	J13
Valleyfield	Canada	37	M2
Valli di Comacchio	Italy	73	H6
Valmiera	Latvia	59	N8
Valparaíso	Chile	52	G5
Valuyki	Russia	60	H4
Van	Turkey	81	K4
Van Diemen Gulf	Australia	116	F2
Van Gölu	Turkey	81	K4
Vanceboro	United States	37	N2
Vancouver	Canada	41	G7
Vancouver Island	Canada	41	F7
Vänern	Sweden	59	G7
Vänersborg	Sweden	59	G7
Vanna	Norway	58	K1
Vannes	France	68	C6
Vansittart Island	Canada	42	Q3
Vanua Levu	Fiji	114	H7
Vanuatu	Oceania	114	G7
Var	France	72	B6
Varanasi	India	104	D3
Varangerfjord	Norway	58	Q1
Varazdin	Croatia	76	D3
Varberg	Sweden	59	G8
Vardar	Macedonia	78	D3
Varese	Italy	72	D5
Varkous	Finland	58	Q5
Varna	Bulgaria	77	R6
Värnamo	Sweden	59	G8
Varniai	Lithuania	62	M2
Vasa Barris	Brazil	51	K6
Vaskaganish	Canada	45	R6
Västerås	Sweden	59	J7
Västervik	Sweden	59	J8
Vasto	Italy	74	J6
Vatican City	Europe	74	G7
Vatnajökull	Iceland	58	(1)E2
Vättern	Sweden	59	H7
Vaubecourt	France	57	J6
Vaucouleurs	France	72	A2
Växjö	Sweden	59	H8
Vega	Norway	58	F4
Vejle	Denmark	59	E9
Velebit	Croatia	76	C5
Velez	Bosnia-Herzegovina	76	F6
Vélez-Málaga	Spain	70	F8
Velika Kapela	Croatia	76	B4
Velikaya	Russia	103	W4
Velikiye-Luki	Russia	60	G3
Veliko Turnovo	Bulgaria	77	N6
Velingrad	Bulgaria	77	M7
Velino	Italy	74	H6
Vellore	India	105	C6
Velsk	Russia	60	J2
Veluwemeer	Netherlands	57	J2
Velzen	Germany	64	F4
Venezia (Venice)	Italy	74	G3
Venezuela	South America	50	D2
Venice (Venezia)	Italy	74	G3
Venraij	Netherlands	57	J3
Ventimiglia	Italy	69	N10
Ventotene	Italy	75	H8
Ventspils	Latvia	59	L8
Venus Bay	Australia	117	H7
Veracruz Llave	Mexico	46	E5
Verbania	Italy	72	D5
Vercelli	Italy	72	D5
Verdon	France	72	B7
Verdun	France	57	J5
Vereeniging	South Africa	96	D5
Verhovina	Ukraine	77	M1
Verhoyanskiy Khrebet	Russia	102	M3
Vermont	United States	37	M3
Vernon	France	56	E5
Vernon	United States	33	G5
Véroia	Greece	78	E4
Verona	Italy	74	E3
Versailles	France	68	G5
Verviers	Belgium	57	J4
Vesoul	France	68	L6
Vestbygd	Norway	59	D7
Vesterålen	Norway	58	H2
Vestfjorden	Norway	58	H2
Vestvågy	Norway	58	G2
Vesuvio	Italy	75	J8
Veszprém	Hungary	76	E2
Vetlanda	Sweden	59	G8
Vézère	France	69	G8
Viana de Castelo	Portugal	70	B3
Viangchan (Vientiane)	Laos	106	C3
Viareggio	Italy	72	F7
Viborg	Denmark	59	E8
Vic	Spain	71	N3
Vicenza	Italy	74	F3
Vichy	France	69	J7
Vicksburg	United States	34	H5
Victoria	Australia	117	H7
Victoria	China	107	E2
Victoria	Papua New Guinea	114	E6
Victoria	United States	33	G6
Victoria	Canada	41	G7
Victoria de Durango	Mexico	46	D4
Victoria Falls	South Africa	96	D3
Victoria Island	Canada	42	K2
Victoria Nile	Uganda	95	E3
Victoria Strait	Canada	42	L3
Vidal	United States	32	D5
Vidin	Bulgaria	77	K6
Viedma	Argentina	52	J7
Vienna (Wien)	Austria	73	M2
Vienne	France	68	F6
Vientiane (Viangchan)	Laos	106	C3
Vierwaldstätter See	Switzerland	72	D3
Vierzon	France	68	H6
Vietnam	South East Asia	106	C2
Vigevano	Italy	72	D5
Vigo	Spain	70	B2
Vihena	Brazil	50	E6
Viitasaari	Finland	58	N5
Vijayawada	India	105	C5
Vik	Iceland	58	D3
Vikhren	Bulgaria	77	L8
Vikna	Norway	58	F4
Vila Real	Portugal	70	C3
Vilaine	France	68	D6
Vilanova i la Geltrú	Spain	71	M3
Viliya	Northern Europe	62	P3
Viljandi	Estonia	59	N7

Villablino	Spain	70	D2
Villach	Austria	73	J4
Villagarcia de Arosa	Spain	70	B2
Villahermosa	Mexico	46	F5
Villalba	Spain	70	C1
Villefranche-sur-Saône	France	69	K7
Villena	Spain	71	K6
Vilnius	Lithuania	59	N9
Vilyuy	Russia	102	K4
Vilyuyskoye Vdkhr.	Russia	102	J4
Vinaroz	Spain	71	L4
Vincennes	United States	36	J4
Vindelälven	Sweden	58	K4
Vindhya Range	India	104	C4
Vinkovci	Croatia	76	F4
Vinnitsa	Ukraine	60	F5
Vinson Massif	Antarctica	120	(2)JJ2
Vir	Croatia	76	C5
Vire	France	56	C6
Virful Moldoveanu	Romania	77	M4
Virful Pietrosul	Romania	60	E5
Virgin Islands	U.K. (Caribbean)	47	L5,M5
Virginia	United States	35	L4
Virginia Beach	United States	35	L4
Virovitica	Croatia	76	E4
Virrat	Finland	58	M5
Virton	Belgium	57	J5
Virtul Peleaga	Romania	77	K4
Vis	Croatia	76	D6
Visayan Sea	Philippines	107	G4
Visby	Sweden	59	K8
Viscount Melville Sound	Canada	42	J2
Viseu	Portugal	70	C4
Vishakhapatnam	India	105	D5
Vistula (Wisla)	Poland	62	L6
Vitebsk	Belarus	60	G3
Viterbo	Italy	74	G6
Viti Levu	Fiji	114	H7
Vitön	Northern Europe	120	(1)N2
Vitoria	Spain	70	H2
Vitória	Brazil	53	N3
Vitorog	Bosnia-Herzegovina	76	D5
Vittel	France	72	A2
Vittorio Veneto	Italy	73	H5
Vivero	Spain	70	C1
Vjazma	Russia	60	G3
Vladikavkaz	Russia	81	L2
Vladimir	Russia	60	J3
Vladivostok	Russia	110	F2
Vlasic	Yugoslavia	76	G5
Vlasic	Bosnia-Herzegovina	76	E5
Vlieland	Netherlands	57	H1
Vlorë	Albania	78	B4
Vltava (Moldau)	Czech Republic	63	D8
Vltave	Czech Republic	65	K6
Vogelsberg	Germany	65	E6
Voghera	Italy	72	E5
Volcan Corcovado	Chile	52	G7
Volcan Cotopaxi	Ecuador	50	B4
Volcan Domuyo	Argentina	52	G6
Volcan Lanin	Chile / Argentina	52	G6
Volcán Baru	Panama / Costa Rica	50	A2
Volcán Irazu	Costa Rica	47	H6
Volcán Tajumulco	Guatemala	46	F6
Volga	Russia	61	K4
Volgodonst	Russia	60	J5
Volgograd	Russia	60	J5
Vologda	Russia	60	H3
Volzhskiy	Russia	60	J5
Vorderrhein	Switzerland	72	D4
Vories Sporádes (Sporades)	Greece	78	F6
Vorkuta	Russia	100	L4
Vormsi	Estonia	59	M7
Voronezh	Russia	60	H4
Voru	Estonia	59	P8
Vosges	France	68	M6
Vostochnyy Sayan	Russia	102	F6
Vostocno-Sibirskoye More (East Siberian Sea)	Russia	103	T2
Vostok	Kiribati (Pacific Ocean)	115	L7
Vranica	Bosnia-Herzegovina	76	E5
Vranje	Yugoslavia	78	D2
Vratsa	Bulgaria	77	L6
Vrbas	Bosnia-Herzegovina	76	N6
Vrbovsko	Croatia	76	C4
Vrsac	Yugoslavia	76	J4
Vukovar	Croatia	76	F4
Vuktyl	Russia	61	M2
Vulcano	Italy	75	K10
Vólos	Greece	78	F5
Vyatka	Russia	120	L4
Vyborg	Russia	60	F2
Vyshniy-Volochek	Russia	60	G3
Vytegra	Russia	60	H2
Vyvenka	Russia	103	V4

W

Wa	Ghana	92	D3
Waal	Netherlands	57	J3
Wabash	United States	36	J4
Wabe Shebele	Ethiopia / Somalia	95	G2
Waco	United States	33	G5
Wad al Batin	Middle East	85	B2
Wad ash Shati	Libya	90	B2
Wad Medani	Sudan	91	F5
Waddeneilanden	Netherlands	57	H1
Waddenzee	Netherlands	57	J1
Wadi al Arish	Egypt	84	A6
Wadi al Inab	Saudi Arabia / Jordan	84	D6
Wadi Bair	Saudi Arabia / Jordan	84	E5
Wadi Halfa	Sudan	91	F3
Wadi Jabjabah	Sudan	91	F3
Wadi Srhan	Saudi Arabia / Jordan	84	E5
Wadi Watir	Egypt	84	B7
Wahat Jalu	Libya	90	D2
Waigeo	Indonesia	113	D2
Waitaki River	New Zealand	119	D7
Wakasa-Wan	Japan	110	H6
Wakayama	Japan	110	H6
Wake	United States	114	G3
Waku-Kungo	Angola	94	B5
Walbrzych	Poland	63	F7
Waldport	United States	28	B2
Wales	United Kingdom	67	J9
Wales	Alaska (U.S.)	29	(1)D2
Wales Island	Canada	42	P3
Walla Walla	United States	28	C1
Wallis and Futuna	France (Pacific Ocean)	115	J7
Walliser Alps	Switzerland	72	C4
Walsall	United Kingdom	56	B2
Walt Disney World	United States	35	K6
Walvis Bay	Namibia	96	A4
Wanganui	New Zealand	118	E4
Wanganui	New Zealand	118	E4
Wangerooge	Germany	64	C3
Wangpan Yang	China	109	G4
Wanxian	China	108	D4
Warangal	India	105	C5
Warburton Range	Australia	116	E5
Warnow	Germany	64	G3
Warren	United States	37	L3
Warrensburg	United States	31	H4
Warsaw (Warszawa)	Poland	62	L5
Warszawa (Warsaw)	Poland	62	L5
Warta	Poland	62	F5
Wasatch Range	United States	30	D3
Washburn	United States	31	F2
Washington	United States	36	J4
Washington	United States	28	B1
Washington D.C.	United States	37	L4
Wasserkuppe	Germany	65	E6
Waterberg Plateau	Namibia	96	B3
Waterbury	United States	37	M3
Waterloo	United States	36	H3
Watertown (NY)	United States	37	L3
Watertown (SD)	United States	31	G3
Watson Lake	Canada	40	F4
Watton	United Kingdom	56	D2
Wausau	United States	36	J3
Wawa	Canada	43	Q7
Waycross	United States	35	K5
Wear	United Kingdom	67	L7
Webi Shabelle	Ethiopia / Somalia	95	H3
Weddell Sea	Antarctica	120	(2)A2
Weert	Netherlands	57	J3
Wei He	China	108	D4
Weiden	Germany	65	H7
Weima	Germany	65	G5
Weinheim	Germany	65	D7
Weisse Elster	Germany / Czech Republic	65	H5
Weissenfels	Germany	65	G5
Weitra	Austria	73	K2
Weldona	United States	31	F3
Welkom	South Africa	96	D5
Welland	Canada	37	L3
Welland	United Kingdom	67	N9
Wellesley Islands	Australia	117	G3
Wellington	New Zealand	119	F5
Wells	United States	30	D3
Wels	Austria	73	K2
Wendover	United States	30	D3
Wenman	Ecuador	50	(1)A1
Wenzhou	China	109	G5
Werra	Germany	65	E5
Wertheim	Germany	65	E7
Wesel	Germany	57	K3
Weser	Germany	64	E3
Weserbergland	Germany	64	E5
Wessel Islands	Australia	117	G2
West Alps	France	72	B6
West Cape	New Zealand	114	G10
West End	Bahamas	35	L6
West Falkland	South Atlantic Ocean	53	J9
West Palm Beach	United States	35	K6
West Siberian Plain	Russia	100	N5
West Virginia	United States	35	K4
Westerly	United States	37	M3
Western Australia	Australia	116	D5
Western Sahara (Morocco)	West Africa	88	C4
Western Samoa	Oceania	115	J7
Westerschelde	Netherlands	68	J2
Westerwald	Germany	65	C6
Westport	United States	29	B3
Westport	New Zealand	119	D5
Westray	United Kingdom	66	K2
Westree	Canada	36	K2
Wewela	United States	31	G3
Wexford	Ireland	67	G9
Weyburn	Canada	31	F2
Weymouth	United Kingdom	68	C3
Whakatane	New Zealand	118	F3
Whangarei	New Zealand	118	E2
Wheeler	United States	28	B1
Wheeler Peak	United States	32	E4
Wheeling	United States	36	K4
Whistler	Canada	41	G7
White Bay	Canada	39	V6
White Horse Hills	United Kingdom	67	L10
White Island	Canada	42	Q3
White Mountain Peak	United States	29	C4
White Mountains	United States	40	B3
White Nile	Central Africa	91	F6
White Nile (Bahr al Jabal)	Central Africa	94	E2
White River	United States	37	M3
White Sea (Beloye More)	Russia	60	H1
White Volta (Nakambé)	West Africa	92	D2
Whiteface Mountain, 1483	United States	37	M3
Whitehorse	Canada	40	E4
Whitsunday Island	Australia	117	J4
Wichita	United States	33	G4
Wichita Falls	United States	33	G5
Wicklow Mountains	Ireland	67	G9
Wielun	Poland	63	H6
Wien (Vienna)	Austria	73	M2
Wiener Neustadt	Austria	73	M3
Wiesbaden	Germany	65	C6
Wigtown Bay	United Kingdom	67	J7
Wildspitze	Austria	72	F4
Wilhelmshaven	Germany	64	C3
Wilkes-Barre	United States	37	L3
Williamsport	United States	37	L3
Willis Group	Australia	117	K3
Williston	United States	31	F2
Williston Lake	Canada	41	G5
Willmar	United States	31	G3
Wilmington (DL)	United States	37	L4
Wilmington (NC)	United States	35	L5
Wilsons Promontory	Australia	117	J7
Winchester	United Kingdom	56	B3
Windhoek	Namibia	96	B4
Windsor	Canada	36	K3
Windsor Locks	United States	37	M3
Windward Islands	Caribbean	47	M6
Windward Passage	Central America	47	K5
Winfield	United States	33	G4
Winnemucca	United States	29	C2
Winnipeg	Canada	43	M7
Winona	United States	31	H3
Winsen	Germany	64	F3
Winslow Atoll	Kiribati (Pacific Ocean)	115	J6
Winston-Salem	United States	35	K4
Winter haven	United States	35	K6
Winterthur	Switzerland	72	D3
Wisconsin	United States	36	H3
Wisla (Vistula)	Poland	62	L6
Wismar	Germany	64	G3
Witham	United Kingdom	67	N8
Witten	Germany	65	C5
Wittenberg	Germany	64	H5
Wittenberge	Germany	64	G3
Wittlich	Germany	68	M3
Wittstock	Germany	64	H3
Wloclawek	Poland	62	J5
Wolf Creek	United States	30	E2
Wolf Point	United States	30	E2
Wolfenbüttel	Germany	64	F4
Wolfsberg	Austria	73	K4
Wolfsburg	Germany	64	F4
Wolin	Poland	62	D4
Wollaston Lake	Canada	43	L5
Wollongong	Australia	117	K6
Wologisi Mountains	Liberia / Guinea	92	B3
Wolverhampton	United Kingdom	67	L9
Wonju	South Korea	109	H3
Wonsan	North Korea	110	D4
Wood River	United States	36	H4
Woonsocket	United States	37	M3
Wooramel River	Australia	116	B5
Worchester	United States	37	M3
Worms	Germany	65	D7
Wörther See	Austria	73	K4
Worthing	United Kingdom	56	C4
Wroclaw	Poland	63	G6
Wu Jiang	China	108	D5
Wuhan	China	108	E4
Wuhu	China	108	F4
Wuliang Shan	China	108	C6
Wunstorf	Germany	64	E4
Wuppertal	Germany	65	C5
Würzburg	Germany	65	F7
Wurzen	Germany	65	H5
Wusuli Jiang	China / Russia	102	N7
Wutai Shan	China	108	E3
Wuxi	China	109	G4
Wuyi Shan	China	108	F5
Wuzhou	China	108	E6
Wye	United Kingdom	67	L10
Wyoming	United States	30	E3
Wyzyna Krakowsko-Czestochowska	Poland	63	H6
Wyzyna Lubelska	Poland	63	M6

X

Xanthí	Greece	78	G3
Xi Jiang	China	108	E6
Xi'an	China	108	D4
Xiamen	China	108	F6
Xiangfan	China	108	E4
Xiangtan	China	108	E5
Xijir Ulan Hu	China	104	E1
Xingu	South America	51	G4
Xining	China	108	C3
Xinyang	China	108	E4
Xisha Qundao	China	107	E3
Xuefeng Shan	China	108	D5
Xuzhou	China	108	F4

Y

Yablonovyy Khrebet	Russia	102	J6
Yaku-Shima	Japan	110	F8
Yakutat Bay	United States	40	C5
Yakutsk	Russia	102	M4
Yalinga	Central African Republic	94	C2
Yalova	Turkey	77	S9
Yalu	East Asia	110	C3
Yalutorovsk	Russia	61	P3
Yam Ha Melah (Dead Sea)	Israel	84	C5
Yam Kinneret (L.Tiberias)	Israel	84	C4
Yamagata	Japan	111	K4
Yamaguchi	Japan	110	F6
Yambol	Bulgaria	77	P7
Yamoussoukro	Côte dIvoire	92	C3
Yamzho Yumco	China	104	F3
Yana	Russia	102	N3
Yangon (Rangoon)	Myanmar (Burma)	106	B3

Name	Country	Page	Grid
Yanji	China	110	E2
Yankton	United States	31	G3
Yanskiy Zaliv	Russia	103	P2
Yantai	China	109	G3
Yaoundé	Cameroon	93	G4
Yap	Micronesia	114	D5
Yar-Sale	Russia	61	Q1
Yardimci Burun	Turkey	80	D5
Yare	United Kingdom	56	E2
Yariga	Japan	111	J5
Yarmouth	Canada	45	T8
Yaroslavl	Russia	60	H3
Yatsushiro	Japan	110	F7
Yatta Plateau	Kenya	95	F4
Yazd	Iran	83	F3
Yazoo City	United States	34	H5
Yazovir Iskur	Bulgaria	77	L7
Yedi Burun	Turkey	79	L8
Yekaterinburg	Russia	61	N3
Yell	United Kingdom	66	M1
Yellow Sea (Huang Hai / Hwang-Hae)	South East Asia	109	G3
Yellowknife	Canada	42	J4
Yellowstone Lake	United States	30	D3
Yellowstone National Park	United States	30	D3
Yellowstone River	United States	30	E2
Yemen	Middle East	82	E7
Yenisey	Russia	100	R4
Yenisey Skiy Kryazh	Russia	100	T6
Yeniseyskiy Zaliv	Russia	100	P3
Yeo Lake	Australia	116	D5
Yeovil	United Kingdom	68	C3
Yerbogacen	Russia	102	H4
Yeres	France	56	F6
Yerevan	Armenia	81	L3
Yesil	Kazakhstan	61	P4
Yichang	China	108	E4
Yildiz Daglari	Turkey	80	B3
Yinchuan	China	108	D3
Yingkou	China	110	B3
Yioúra	Greece	78	G7
yios Evstrátios	Greece	78	H5
Ylikitka	Finland	60	F1
Ylivieska	Finland	58	N4
Yogyakarta	Malaysia	112	E4
Yokohama	Japan	111	K6
Yokosuka	Japan	111	K6
Yola	Nigeria	93	G3
Yonago	Japan	110	G6
Yonne	France	68	J5
York	United Kingdom	67	M7
Yorkshire Wolds	United Kingdom	67	M7
Yosemite National Park	United States	29	C3
Yoshkar Ola	Russia	61	K3
Yosu	South Korea	110	D6
Youngstown	United States	36	K3
Yu Shan	Taiwan	107	G2
Yuan Jiang	China / Vietnam	108	C6
Yuba City	United States	29	B3
Yucatan Channel	Mexico	47	G4
Yuerdon	Switzerland	69	M6
Yugoslavia	Europe	76	G6
Yukon	Alaska (U.S.)	29	(1)E3
Yukon Territory	Canada	38	D4
Yulin	China	108	E6
Yulongxue Shan	China	108	C5
Yuma	United States	32	D5
Yun-Gui Gaoyuan	China	106	C1
Yunkai Dashan	China	106	D2
Yurimaguas	Peru	50	B5
Yuzhno Sakhalinsk	Russia	103	Q7
Yvetot	France	56	D5

Z

Name	Country	Page	Grid
Zaandam	Netherlands	57	H2
Zacatecas	Mexico	32	E7
Zadar	Croatia	73	L6
Zadar	Croatia	76	C5
Zadetkyi Kyun	Myanmar (Burma)	106	B5
Zafra	Spain	70	D6
Zagreb	Croatia	76	D4
Zagros Mountains (Kuhha-ye Zagros)	Iran	82	F3
Zahedan	Iran	83	G4
Zajecar	Yugoslavia	77	K6
Zákinthos	Greece	78	C7
Zala	Hungary	73	N4
Zalaegerszeg	Hungary	76	D3
Zalau	Romania	77	L2
Zaliv Aniva	Russia	103	Q7
Zaliv Faddeya	Russia	100	V2
Zaliv Kresta	Russia	29	(1)B2
Zaliv Ozernoy	Russia	103	U5
Zaliv Petra Velikogo	Russia	110	F2
Zaliv Shelikhova	Russia	103	T4
Zaliv Terpeniya	Russia	103	Q7
Zaliv Wislany	Russia / Poland	59	K9
Zambezi	South Africa	96	C3
Zambia	South Africa	96	D2
Zamboanga	Philippines	107	G5
Zamora	Spain	70	E3
Zamósé	Poland	63	N7
Zamzam	Libya	90	B1
Zanjan	Iran	82	E2
Zanzibar	Tanzania	95	F5
Zanzibar	Tanzania	95	F5
Západné Karpaty (Carpathians)	Poland / Slovakia	63	H8
Zapadno-Sibirskaya Ravnina	Russia	100	N5
Zapadny Sayan	Mongolia	101	R7
Zaragoza	Spain	71	K3
Zaria	Nigeria	93	F2
Zary	Poland	62	E6
Zarzaïtine	Algeria	90	A2
Zatoka Pomorska	Poland / Germany	62	D3
Zawierzie	Poland	63	J7

Name	Country	Page	Grid
Zd	Hungary	76	H1
Zehdenick	Germany	64	J3
Zeimena	Lithuania	59	N9
Zeitz	Germany	65	H5
Zelenoborski	Russia	58	S3
Zenica	Bosnia-Herzegovina	76	E5
Zeya	Russia	102	M6
Zeyskoye Vdkhr.	Russia	102	M6
Zgierz	Poland	62	J6
Zgorzelec	Poland	63	D6
Zhangjiakou	China	108	F2
Zhangzhou	China	108	F6
Zhanjiang	China	108	E6
Zhaxi Co	China	104	D2
Zhengzhou	China	108	E3
Zhigansk	Russia	102	L3
Zhoushan Qundao	China	109	G4
Zibo	China	108	F3
Zielona Góta	Poland	62	E6
Zigong	China	108	C5
Zilina	Slovakia	63	H8
Zillertaler Alpen	Austria	73	G3
Zimbabwe	South Africa	96	D3
Zinder	Niger	89	G6
Zion National Park	United States	32	D4
Zirje	Croatia	76	C6
Zittau	Germany	65	K5
Zlatroust	Russia	61	M3
Zlín	Czech Republic	63	G8
Znojmo	Czech Republic	63	F9
Znojmo	Slovakia	73	M2
Zohreh	Middle East	85	C1
Zouérat	Mauritania	88	C4
Zonguldak	Turkey	79	P3
Zrenjanin	Yugoslavia	76	H4
Zrinska Gora	Bosnia-Herzegovina / Croatia	76	D4
Zug	Switzerland	72	D3
Zuger See	Switzerland	72	D3
Zugspitze	Austria /Germany	72	F3
Zunyi	China	108	D5
Zürich	Switzerland	72	D3
Zürichsee	Switzerland	72	D3
Zut	Croatia	76	C6
Zuwarah	Libya	90	B1
Zvaduz	Liechtenstein	72	E3
Zvolen	Slovakia	63	J9
Zwickau	Germany	65	H6
Zwickauer Mulde	Germany	65	H6
Zwolle	Netherlands	57	K2
Zyrardów	Poland	62	K5
Zyrjanka	Russia	103	S3
Zywiec	Poland	62	J8

The World, Pacific Projection

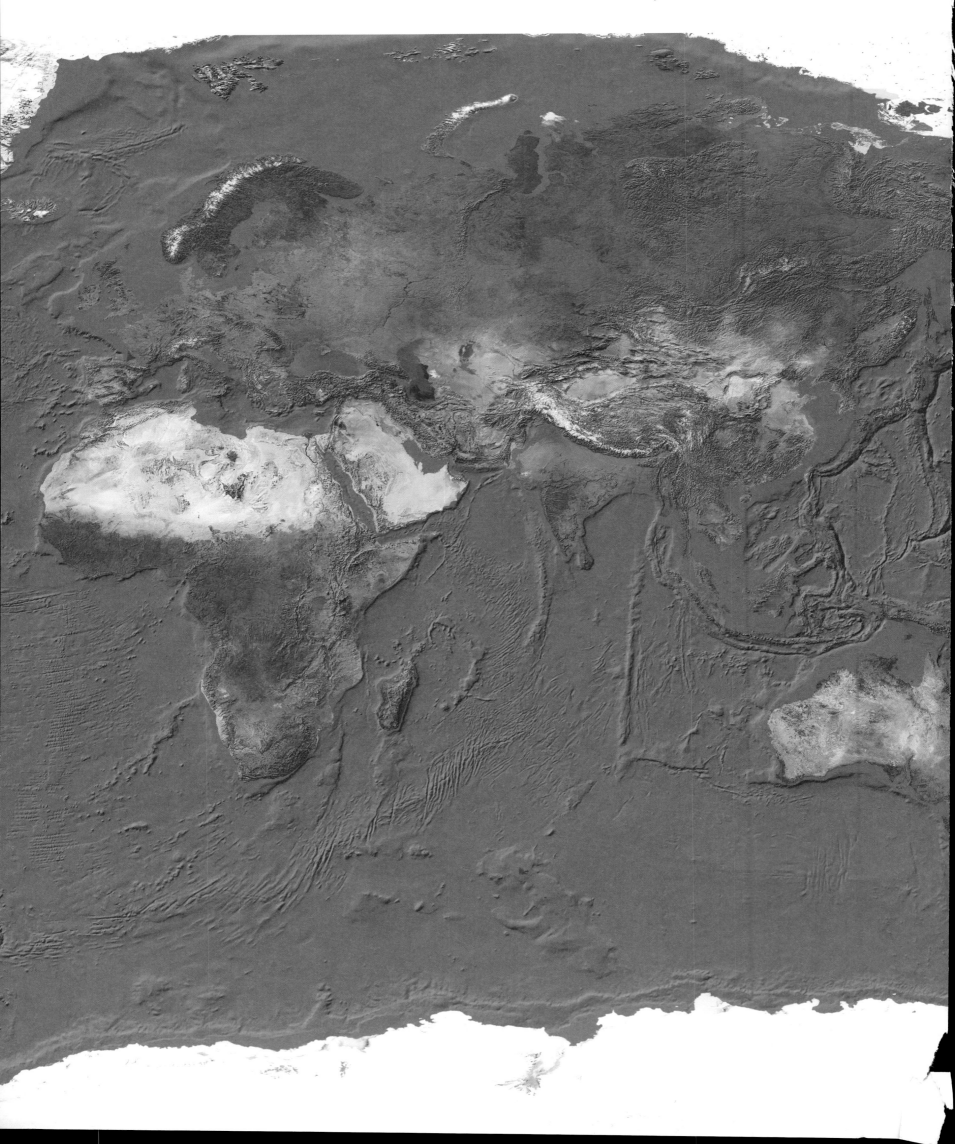